MW01154258

CREATING THE "NEW MAN"

Perspectives on the Global Past

Jerry H. Bentley and Anand A. Yang
SERIES EDITORS

Interactions: Transregional Perspectives on World History
Edited by Jerry H. Bentley, Renate Bridenthal, and Anand A. Yang

Contact and Exchange in the Ancient World
Edited by Victor H. Mair

Seascapes: Maritime Histories, Littoral Cultures, and Transoceanic Exchanges
Jerry H. Bentley, Renate Bridenthal, and Kären Wigen

Anthropology's Global Histories: The Ethnographic Frontier in German New Guinea, 1870–1935
By Rainer F. Buschmann

Creating the "New Man": From Enlightenment Ideals to Socialist Realities
By Yinghong Cheng

Creating the "New Man"

From Enlightenment Ideals to Socialist Realities

Yinghong Cheng

University of Hawai'i Press
Honolulu

Printed in the United States of America
14 13 12 11 10 09   6 5 4 3 2 1

Library of Congress Cataloging-in-Publication Data
Cheng, Yinghong.
   Creating the new man : from enlightenment ideals to
socialist realities / Yinghong Cheng.
       p. cm. —
(Perspectives on the global past)
   Includes bibliographical references and index.
   ISBN 978-0-8248-3074-8 (hard cover : alk. paper)
  1. Communism and society.   2. Human behavior.
3. Political psychology.   I. Title.
   HX542.C4683 2009
   306.3'45—dc22
                                    2008030193

University of Hawaiʻi Press books are printed on acid-free
paper and meet the guidelines for permanence and durability
of the Council on Library Resources.

Designed by Elsa Carl, Clarence Lee Design

Printed by The Maple-Vail Book Manufacturing Group

For my generation

Contents

Acknowledgments

I owe warmest thanks to many individuals whose support was indispensable for this project. The support and advice of Patrick Manning, my main dissertation adviser, have overarched the entire process, from conceptualization through development of the project. His major contribution was helping me understand how a work in communist studies fits into the framework of world history and how that framework signifies its importance. From the beginning, he encouraged me with the idea that, as a global movement, world communism had not received adequate attention from world historians and that a study of the "new man" would be a worthwhile effort in this emerging field. I also owe him very much in terms of the development and improvement of my English writing and editing skills, an equally crucial element in my academic progress. Paul Hollander, professor emeritus of sociology at the University of Massachusetts, has been another intellectual inspiration for me. His work on the attractiveness of world communism to various groups of Western intellectuals—especially in its self-proclaimed mission to uplift human nature—gave me a valuable perspective from which to examine the global impact of world communism. William Ratliff, an expert on Cuba and Sino-Cuban relations at the Hoover Institution, has been always supportive and, with his broad knowledge and insights in the field, increased my understanding of the two countries' revolutions. Christina Gilmartin, a historian on China at Northeastern University, helped me consolidate the chapter on China, which is the most detailed section of the book. Adam McKeown of Columbia University read many parts of the dissertation when he taught at Northeastern University and I was a PhD candidate there. As a world historian with a particular interest in China, Adam also helped me figure out how to integrate the two fields in a book-length project.

I want to thank Bin Yang, Eric Martin, Pam Brooks, Jeffery Sommers, and David Kalivas, among many others of my fellow PhD students at Northeastern University, whose conversations with me over time have supplemented those of advisers and professors. Ana Serra generously shared with me some of her research results regarding the "new man" in Cuba, which was a timely aid in my revision of that chapter.

Jerry Bentley and Anand Yang, the editors of the series Perspectives on the Global Past, deserve my appreciation for encouraging me to keep working on the revision when I was not quite certain whether I would be able to accomplish the task while carrying a heavy teaching load. Pamela Kelley of the University of Hawai'i Press has been always with me, an efficient editor whose experience and knowledge have guided me through the entire process.

Finally, I thank Ying, my wife, for being with me throughout the time of my research and writing.

CREATING THE "NEW MAN"

Introduction

> All human history is nothing but a continuous transformation of
> human nature.
> —Karl Marx

The communist movement of the last century was remarkably successful worldwide in establishing the party-state and carrying out
projects aimed at a total social transformation. But behind the ideological, political, and social changes was a more ambitious and comprehensive goal: to remold the mind, psychology, and even character of individuals
by means of various party and state policies designed for a "new man" and,
through this "new man," to make history and perpetuate the revolution.[1]
The "Soviet Man," "Mao's good soldiers," and "Let them all become Che"
are only a few examples of the regimes' aspirations for the creation of such
a new person. Even in the early 1980s, when socioeconomic stagnation
plagued the Soviet Union and omens of decline began to loom larger,
Mikhail Suslov, the Soviet ideology and propaganda chief, was still declaring
that "the formation of the New Man is the most important component" of
the endeavors of the Soviet state.[2]

As a global movement, world communism has not received adequate
attention from historians adopting "global perspectives" in recent years, and,
more generally speaking, political history of the twentieth century seems to
be a less favorable topic for many world historians. Colonialism, empires,
comparative economic development, migration, trade, cultural exchange,
race and ethnicity, gender, family, and diseases are some of the most popular
world historical themes. This trend in global historical discussions is perfectly justifiable in the sense that global history focuses on long-term socioeconomic and cultural development, whereas political history often deals
with sociopolitical changes that, at least in most specific cases, take place
in a relatively short time span and often are driven by domestic dynamics.
Another reason for inadequate attention paid to world communism in today's
global historical discussions is perhaps a scholarly fatigue caused by too
much attention paid to the issue from the mid- to the late twentieth century,

with enormous scholarship involving invaluable data collection and regime analysis. Quite understandably, produced in such a historical context and often with a sense of urgency to meet very immediate political and ideological needs, a great many of these works today read to some extent like the diagnosis, prognosis, and autopsy of a particular regime.

More than a decade into the postcommunist era and with the increasing effectiveness of a global perspective in interpreting worldwide developments, the time has come for scholarly discussion of world communism in parameters appropriate to its magnitude. In this book I treat world communism as a global historical phenomenon and focus on a more humanistic dimension: the interaction between revolutionary change and human nature. This global perspective is mainly reflected in a three-case study examining the Soviet Union, China, and Cuba, buttressed by tracing the intellectual and ideological roots of the communist concept of human malleability and perfectibility back to the Western intellectual and political tradition since the Enlightenment, as well as the historical traditions in those countries themselves. The global perspective also extends to include the responses from contemporary social movements outside the communist world to its aspiration for changing human nature.

The communist revolution's impact on the human mind in various forms is anything but new in communist studies. For example, political education and ideological development are hardly topics to be found missing in any survey works on the communist regime, let alone in studies focused on its political and ideological dimensions. A more specific subject, and the one perhaps closest to the issue of the new man, is thought reform, or brainwashing. The term "thought reform" was coined by the Chinese communists in the early 1940s when they were engaged in the "Yan'an Rectification" to make party members identify completely with the organization, whereas the term "brainwashing," with a negative connotation, was created by Western observers in the early 1950s as the Chinese communists came to be known for applying the techniques invented in Yan'an to control people's minds nationwide.[3] As Hu Ping, a Chinese political and intellectual author, well known since the late 1970s, once noted, the techniques used by a government to influence or even shape people's thoughts and attitudes could be traced back to the very beginning of political history, but communist thought reform/brainwashing distinguished itself from those traditional techniques in a number of ways. One is that thought reform/brainwashing is meant to replace people's old ideas with new ones, whereas in most other techniques the intention is to more firmly implant ideas that already exist and are endorsed by tradition and culture. The sort of replacement of ideas found in thought reform/brainwashing is therefore bound to create tension and conflict in the human mind. The other distinguishing feature is that thought reform/brainwashing is by definition exclusive and therefore becomes possible only in a closed system that rejects any ideological alternatives, whereas in most other techniques a ruling ideology or mainstream value system does not necessarily monopolize all ideological or moral discourses. In addition, although thought reform/brainwashing is imposed on the individual in a closed system, in theory it must take effect through the individual's cooperation; therefore incarceration or a similar situation in which the individual is completely deprived of freedom could not be taken as a typical example of the thought reform/brainwashing process.[4]

The above discussion is important in understanding how the communist revolution's subjection of the human mind to political power constitutes an important part in the concept of the new man. But the issue of a new man itself is much more sweeping: it includes a calculated and systematic cultivation of ideas and perceptions, consciousness and subconsciousness, personal character, psychology, and even physical constitution. The new man was created not just to ensure that new ideas would replace old ones and that the party's tasks would be carried out, thus avoiding becoming merely a topic in political history, but also to stand up as an alternative human model that dwarfed all prior or contemporary types of human being. In this sense the new man obtained a significance in world history or even beyond, as a new stage in human evolution. Communist leaders and their propagandists explicitly and repeatedly articulated this aspiration, clearly indicating their awareness of the significance of their revolution in human evolution. In the early stages of the Russian Revolution, Leon Trotsky believed that the ultimate purpose of communist revolution was to "harmonize" man as an animate being and to "master first the semiconscious and then the subconscious process in his own organism." He went on to say that "even purely physiological life will become subject to collective experiments."[5] More than sixty years later, a Soviet propaganda pamphlet entitled *The Soviet People* proudly pronounced that the country had become the "motherland of a new and higher type of *Homo sapiens: Homo sovieticus.*" It went on to give the reader a balance sheet of the progress; as a critic summarized it, "millions of years had been needed for the cell to advance to the stage of *Homo sapiens,* to reach the level of man endowed with reason, but it took only sixty for him to be cleansed of all impurities," thus giving birth to "a new biological specimen."[6] Driven by the same aspiration, during the heyday of the Cuban revolution, Fidel Castro announced that human evolution had stopped for two to three thousand years, but his revolution would bring mankind out of this "prehistoric" stage by creating a new type of Cuban.[7]

The fundamental concern of the present book, therefore, is how communist revolution strove to create a new model of human being, morally and psychologically superior to all other types hitherto known in world civilization, and how this task paralleled its efforts in creating a new society, which was also believed to be superior to all known human societies. In examining these topics, the book addresses a number of questions, such as these: What are the intellectual and ideological roots of the idea of the new man? How was this idealistic and utopian goal linked with specific political and economic programs? How much were national and cultural traditions reflected in the respective regimes' policies for the new man, a concept based on a universal communist ideology? In what ways did the developments of the new man in the Soviet Union, China, and Cuba affect each other? How did communist efforts in search of an alternative human model attract people beyond the communist world in a time of social crisis (in the West) and nation building (in the newly independent countries)? Given that this is a subject regarding the relationship between political power and human development, a moral concern is perhaps inevitable: Was the communist experiment with human nature a new moral and spiritual crusade—a Sisyphean labor doomed to failure, nevertheless arousing admiration? Or was it just another case of terrible abuse of ideology and state power in manipulating people's psychology and shaping their lives, something that is not unique in world history?

In the first chapter, I discuss some origins of the idea of remaking people during the Enlightenment, the French Revolution, and other European intellectual and political movements. The major part of the chapter, however, is devoted to the creation of the Soviet Man, the first such communist new man in world history. I start with a discussion of the Russian intelligentsia's expectation, which influenced the Bolsheviks, for a revolutionary new man in the mid-nineteenth century. The chapter details ideological and political developments related to the Soviet new man and analyzes how the profile of the Soviet Man gradually softened as the country experienced industrialization and modernization. These developments inevitably led to the revival of old-fashioned social stratification and occupational division, which compromised the revolutionary traits entailed by the communist new man.

Chapter 2, on China, begins with its expectation of a new character for the nation's revival at the turn of the twentieth century. The communist experiment with human nature in China can be divided into three stages: the Yan'an period (the late 1930s and the first half of the 1940s); the 1950s to the early 1960s; and the Cultural Revolution (1966–1976). The chapter details how the idea of the new man was developed and put into practice through various vehicles, such as thought reform, model emulation, and large-scale resettlement from cities to the countryside, along with productive campaigns. It also describes how the Chinese efforts were stimulated by China's perception of the "Soviet lesson"—that the goal of the new man was compromised by economic efficiency.

Chapter 3, on the Cuban experience, starts with the nationalistic discourse on the new Cuban, who was expected to accomplish the task of national independence and development; it then focuses on the revolutionary effort toward creating the new man in the 1960s. The chapter details the Cuban perception of the new man and his role in pushing the revolution through stages, from nationalist to socialist and even communist, in a relatively short time, culminating in the Revolutionary Offensive (1968–1970). It also examines how the issue of the new man was associated with Cuba's relations with China and the Soviet Union.

The fourth chapter surveys the global influence of the Russian, Chinese, and Cuban new men. It first introduces how theory and practice in these three countries were emulated or echoed in many other socialist countries or revolutionary movements, and then examines how Western intellectuals, discontent with their own societies in the 1930s and the 1960s, were drawn to the communist "new man" in hopes of finding an alternative human model. The chapter also looks at how, to a certain extent, some Third World leaders were inspired by the communist new man to seek moral and political resources for the sake of their own nation building and national character formation.

The literature on the communist new man is scattered in numerous scholarly works, but focused narratives and analyses are fewer than what the importance of the topic merits. Among those focused works, Mikhail Heller's *Cogs in the Soviet Wheel* (1988) is an excellent sociological and historical analysis of the mechanism and process through which *Homo sovieticus* was planned and fashioned. The main value of Heller's work is in its insightful analysis of the innate drive behind the professed sociopolitical goals of the Soviet leaders (especially the founding figures of the regime) to reshape human nature, and in its systematic description of the way the regime managed to destroy traditional and institutional boundaries protecting people from state power and "atomize" them into defenseless individuals subject to remolding. One particularly interesting point in Heller's book is his conceptualization of "nationalization of time." Heller argues that, by manipulating the concept of time, the Soviet authorities established a new temporal horizon on which people's lives were confined to a "past-present-future" framework; thus a person who so understood history and accordingly positioned himself on this temporal/spatial coordinate axis, as a result was willing to accept his party-assigned task in his life span with an outlook to the future. Such an argument helps identify the communist revolution's significance in the history of human civilization in terms of the correlation between the human perception of time/space and a life goal confined by a ruling ideology.

Many authors have also highlighted the importance of the new man in understanding the ultimate goal and fundamental dynamics of communist revolution in their works on particular communist regimes. For example, Richard Pipes, in his *Russian Revolution* (1990), highlights the issue and traces the origin of the idea back to Enlightenment thinkers such as Claude-Adrien Helvétius. Andrei Sinyavsky's *Soviet Communism: A Cultural History* (1990) includes a chapter focusing on the image of the Soviet new man, especially in official propaganda of the 1920s and 1930s. Gao Hua's book *That Is How the Red Sun Rose: The Origin and Development of the Yan'an Rectification* (published in Chinese, 2000) examines how Maoist theory and practice of remolding human mind and character started in Yan'an as early as the late 1930s. In the studies of Cuban communism, attention to the new man has been reflected in some American scholars' works. Among them, Michael Lowy's *The Marxism of Che Guevara: Philosophy, Economics, and Revolutionary Warfare* (1973) and Sheldon B. Liss' *Fidel! Castro's Political and Social Thoughts* (1994) recognize the essential role of the new man in the vision of the revolution and future society held by both Cuban leaders. Monographic efforts devoted to the issue, however, have been insufficient.[8] John Kosa's *Two Generations of Soviet Man: A Study in the Psychology of Communism* (1962) is a rare exception. The book discusses how the Soviet model of the new man was introduced to Eastern European peoples after World War II and how the character of the Soviet Man was modified in other lands to suit national traditions. Anita Chan's *Children of Mao: Personal Development and Political Activism in the Red Guard Generation* (1985) studies the "political socialization" of Chinese youth under Mao and their "political desocialization" after Mao, thus delineating the trajectory of the regressive evolution of the new man.

In the following chapters, in which the above literature is referenced and discussed, the descriptions and analyses of the development and global influence of the communist new man attempt to identify the significance of the communist revolution in world history. Within the field of communism studies, the evolution of the new man not only reflects the fundamental goals and the rise and fall of the three most influential communist regimes but also demonstrates their interactions regarding one of the most critical issues. When extended to a broader world-historical vision, the examination of the new man vertically connects communist revolution with a more profound and enduring tradition of human society throughout history, instead of treating it as merely a twentieth-century political phenomenon. Horizontally, it shows the connections between communist revolution and contemporary noncommunist social movements worldwide, instead of limiting our understanding of communist revolution to a narrowly defined ideological and political framework. Overall, I think that the communist experiment of creating the new man serves as an example of an overarching theme throughout world history: whenever significant social transformation proceeds, a much deeper and more anxious concern about human development amid the changing circumstances may lie beneath the various political and economic goals people claim at the time. This concern consists of two parts: one is to what extent and for what purpose the new circumstances can shape or reform human nature, and the other is to what extent and for what purpose this "remade" creature can serve political power and make history.

One

From the Enlightenment to the Soviet New Man

The idea of remaking people sprang directly from the Enlightenment. The main emphasis of the Enlightenment was the science of man—that is, finding what human nature is, how it is formed, and the mutual influences between it and society. Most Enlightenment thinkers held a materialistic world outlook and viewed the human mind as a mechanism determined by and responding to the environment. Beginning with epistemological theory, which relates human physical sensation to the generation of knowledge and ideas, such Enlightenment thinkers as Helvétius, d'Alembert, Condorcet, and Hume tended to view all mental activities as initiated by external stimuli. As John Locke's famous metaphor expresses it, the human mind is just a "blank tablet," and therefore "man's mind (including his thoughts, desires, and motivations), the part of man which is of most interest to the social reformer, was viewed as a mechanism."[1] This explanation served as the basis for the assumption that people could be refashioned or reformed through appropriate manipulation of circumstances. Locke's idea—and others similar to his—regarding the relationship between education, environment, and human development were very influential in Europe at the time. The notion that an Englishman could be made was well received even by many British colonizers settled in India. It was customary for them to send their children, many of whom were of mixed race, back to the British Isles to be whipped into the desirable shape.[2] This practice continued in later centuries as colonial authorities encouraged elite native youths to go to Europe for education, in the hope that the European environment would result in a favorable attitude toward their colonial masters. In some other cases, colonizers created communities in a more Europeanized environment within the colony and would grant natives who were born and lived in these communities citizenship of the European country. The French "Four Communes" *(quatre vieilles)* in West Africa in the mid-nineteenth century exemplified such a practice and the idea behind it: that human nature was shaped and changed by its environment.

But, as Nicholas Capaldi concluded, not only were "all thinkers of the enlightenment . . . agreed on the overwhelming importance of environment in shaping human nature," but they also "unanimously recognized that social reform involved the manipulation of and accommodation to environmental factors."[3] In this regard, Claude-Adrien Helvétius, a member of the French Encyclopedists and one of the theorists of modern education, deserves some further discussion. His "environmental behaviorism" theory not only attributed all intellectual and moral capabilities to external education—that is, the total cumulative environment from the moment of one's birth—but also had far-reaching social and political implications. He believed that people acted upon the principle of seeking pleasure and avoiding pain, and therefore individual conduct always automatically led to satisfying self-interest. It was futile to establish virtues by exalting altruism and condemning selfishness; rather, he emphasized "the necessity of law," stating that "the only method to form virtuous citizens, is to unite the interest of the individual with that of the public." Among the methods used to bring up a "virtuous citizen," he believed, "the most efficacious is to habituate him from his most tender age" by placing himself under the most educationally desirable circumstances.[4]

Helvétius' environmental behaviorism represented the radical wing of Enlightenment thinking concerning human nature and it influenced the history of education as a means of political socialization. The main problem, however, was the absence of the understanding of the metaphysical dimension of the human mind. Even some Marxists expressed their reservations about his perception of the mind, although in general they respected him as a forerunner of materialism, which was a "politically correct" philosophy from their point of view. For example, Plekhanov, the founder of Russian Marxism whose interpretation of Marxism was more sophisticated than Lenin's, once said, "The question as to whether there exists in man an immaterial substance to which he owes his psychic life does not enter into the sphere of Helvetius' investigations."[5] Another problem was that Helvétius oversimplified the process of human cognition and equalized—or, more exactly, reduced—all individual minds to the same physiopsychological level. Such simplification and reduction would pave the way for educators to apply the same methods to disciplining students indiscriminately, regardless of personal talents, inclinations, and temperaments. The absence of a respect for nonmaterialistic aspects of the human mind and the neglect of individual peculiarities, under certain circumstances, would inevitably lead to an attitude that treated humans as material for social experimentation.

Helvétius' belief in the role of political education in making "virtuous citizens," expressed by the sanguine dictum "l'éducation peut tout," thus implied a justification for a totalitarian state. It was for these reasons that Isaiah Berlin, the prominent philosopher against totalitarian and absolute power in the twentieth century, listed Helvétius as one of the six "enemies of human liberty." Berlin pointed out that while other Enlightenment thinkers believed a number of environmental factors, such as weather, climate, and even geography, were involved in shaping human nature, Helvétius believed that education, in its broad sense, was the only one. For Helvétius, as Berlin put it, human nature was "infinitely flexible and pliable; a kind of natural stuff which nature and circumstances, but above all education, shape as they will," and that a person was "a piece of clay in the hands of the potter to mould as he pleases."[6]

Jean-Jacques Rousseau, another Enlightenment thinker, is valuable to this discussion as well. His role in the development of radical ideologies and revolutionary regimes in modern history is undeniable, as is his perception of creating a new man.

Rousseau is known for his argument that human beings are born good but become corrupted by civilization. This idea clearly shows his affinity with environmental behaviorism. Like Helvétius, Rousseau advocates changing human nature through political education, especially at an early age, and displays an overt contempt for ordinary people's pathetically limited capability of enduring such a reformation. In *The Social Contract*, for instance, he wrote, "People, [like] men, are easy to handle only in their youth. They become incorrigible as they grow older. . . . People cannot even tolerate talk of making them happy, like those stupid and cowardly patients who tremble at the sight of a doctor," and "In general, peoples that are worn out by a long enslavement and the resulting vices lose both the love of country and the sentiment of happiness. They console themselves for their misfortune by imagining it is impossible to be better off."[7] Such an attitude of resignation toward people's acceptance of their lot can lead to a conviction of the necessity of imposing social change on their behalf by political power. It is also an attitude commonly found in the literature of radical and communist movements in the later centuries.

But Rousseau's major contribution to the making of the new man is his much stronger statement regarding transforming individuals into collectives and the responsibilities of the enlightened elite in such a process:

> One who dares to undertake the founding of the people should feel that he is capable of changing human nature, so to speak; of transforming each individual, who by himself is a perfect and solitary whole, into a part of a larger whole from which this individual receives, in a sense, his life and his being; of altering man's constitution in order to strengthen it; of substituting a social and moral existence for the independent and physical existence we have all received from nature. He must, in short, take away man's own forces

in order to give him force that is foreign to him and that he cannot make use of without the help of others.[8]

Therefore, although "Man is born free," the more important thing to Rousseau is that "he will be forced to be free."[9] "Making citizens" has been considered to be the main thesis of Rousseau's political theory by some authors.[10]

THE JACOBIN REGIME: THE FIRST STATE EXPERIMENT IN REMAKING PEOPLE

The first regime attempting to materialize ideas espoused by Helvétius and Rousseau regarding changing human nature was Robespierre's Jacobin dictatorship, which divided people into "good" and "evil" and strove to make people "virtuous" by law and education.

"I know but two parties," Robespierre declared, "that of the good citizens, and that of the bad."[11] Many works on the French Revolution and Robespierre have come to the conclusion that Robespierre was above all a revolutionary educator of the nation, rather than a statesman. As one author states, "he [Robespierre] saw himself as a messianic schoolmaster, wielding a very big stick to inculcate virtue," and "he came to conceive the Revolution itself as a school, but one in which knowledge would always be augmented by morality."[12] Even more than that, as another author believes, Robespierre's self-appointed mission was "not instruction of the mind only, but education of the character."[13] His numerous speeches in the Jacobin Club and at public festivals and gatherings were thus full of moral preaching.

Robespierre was fully aware of the enormous difficulty of educating people. As he put it, "We must have a civil code, and we must have a system of education. . . . The latter task is perhaps more difficult than one imagines, and the second travail will possibly be no less painful than the first."[14] The "reign of terror," in this sense, may well be interpreted as an effective way to inculcate moral codes into citizens' minds and make them virtuous, by exploiting fear of punishment. Considering that both Helvétius and Rousseau had suggested that people would be easier to shape when they were young, note that in July 1793 Robespierre proposed a uniform physical, mental, and moral training for all girls from five to eleven and all boys from five to twelve. This training would have been put into practice within a few years if the Jacobin regime had managed to survive. As a revolutionary leader assuming a pedagogical mission, Robespierre exhibited enthusiasm and meticulous concerns for early education that would reappear in Maoist and Castroist efforts in shaping young generations in China and Cuba.

Michel Lepeletier, one of Robespierre's associates, proposed another educational program. Called the "houses of national education," it was designed for elementary schooling and would come to include not only children but parents as well. "Its essence was to bring together those two pillars of the moralized republic: the school and the family," as Simon Schama observes.[15] These proposals were seriously discussed in the National Convention, the major organ of the revolutionary power, but failed to be implemented due to the regime's short time in power. However, they still showed a fundamental goal of revolutionary education: eliminating the difference between family and society as one way to change the social environment. This idea would also be adopted by the communists in their educational reforms.

The French Revolution created a tradition of political symbolism, which ritualized ideologies and political agenda through public displays of revolutionary sentiments, such as festivals, parades, rallies, speeches, songs, music, collective recitation of the "Declaration of the Rights of Man," and the burning of evil symbols while venerating good ones. This political symbolism had a clear purpose of creating a new social and cultural environment to influence people's political and ideological stand. As Mona Ozouf argues:

> This presupposes trust in men's ability to be educated: like the pedagogy of the Enlightenment, the organizers of the festivals inherited a fervent belief in the ability to train minds, and their projects, even more clearly than their pedagogical treaties, reveal the poisonous consequences of their faith in human plasticity. . . . "Since it is a good thing to know how to use men as they are, it is even better to make them in the way one needs them to be." This forceful formula comes from Rousseau's *Discours d'économie politique* which was repeated, if with less verbal felicity.[16]

The same author concludes that "without festivals, there was no hope of 'throwing the nation into the mold.'"[17] Such a practice of "molding" people by "throwing" them into mass rallies or other magnificent public events would be seen again in the twentieth-century revolutionary movements, creating a festival euphoria and giving people a feeling of "being reborn." As Lenin once pointed out, revolution was a joyful festival for the masses.

Although the Jacobin regime lasted only for a few months, it was in miniature the twentieth-century experiment of remaking people on a national scale. Not surprisingly, the French Revolution greatly inspired communist regimes. But the communists were more confident as they conducted their social experiments. The Jacobins used social justice and revolutionary virtue to justify their social experiment, but for the communists, it was a matter of the mandate of history based on scientific law they claimed they had discovered. As Che Guevara once said, although the men of the French Revolution "gave so many beautiful things to mankind," they were still the "instruments of history." Only after the October Revolution, he argued, were people able to consciously direct and construct history.[18]

MARX'S VISIONS OF THE NEW MAN

After Enlightenment thinkers and the Jacobins, Karl Marx contributed some philosophical premises regarding the issue of the new man. Marx held a materialist and environmental-determinist view of human nature. As he put it: "The mode of production determines the general character of the social, political and spiritual process of life. It is not the consciousness of man that determines their existence, but on the contrary, their social existence determines their consciousness."[19] More specifically, he said, "the human essence is no abstraction inherent in each single individual. In its reality it is the ensemble of social relations." In Marxist terms, "social relations" mainly refers to people's class status in a binary structure, such as freeman and slave, patrician and plebeian, lord and serf, and guild master and journeyman. In this way Marxism inherited environmental determinism from the Enlightenment but limited it to social class structure and attributed sociopolitical ideas and concepts to such a structure.

Since human nature, in Marx's view, was determined by social class relations, and these relations changed along with the mode of production (the infrastructure of social structure), it was logical that human nature was not a static substance but a result of continuous social change. "All history is nothing but a continuous transformation of human nature," argued Marx.[20] For example, human nature had been seen as a "selfish pleasure calculator" by some philosophers, but Marx believed that such a feature was just a part of bourgeois routine, which prevailed only in capitalist societies but had been misinterpreted as universal and innate in human nature.[21]

As some scholars have argued, Marxist rejection of the idea that human nature is essentially unchangeable not only provided a philosophical basis for attacking the concept of man as inherently self-regarding in Western liberal-democratic thinking but also laid the foundation for state-run social engineering to reshape human nature in line with the ruling ideology and government goals by systematically designing and manipulating the social and cultural environment. "Furthermore," Donald Munro observes, "besides eliminating the self-regarding portrait of man, the Marxist critique of enduring essences also suggests that there are no immutable attributes that place theoretical limits on man's reducibility."[22]

But as often happens among philosophers, Marxian rejection of the concept of an abstract and unchangeable human nature was inconsistent with another of his concepts regarding human nature: alienation. Marx, especially the so-called "young Marx," argued that in societies with private ownership of the means of production, in which people who possessed nothing were forced to work, human nature had been "alienated" by such compelled labor. Only when people worked for themselves could this "alienation" be overcome and could they become "human" again. Thus Marx seemed to suggest the existence of an original human nature, which had been lost under capitalism, but would regain itself in communist society when people believed that they worked for themselves and work was no longer a burden but a pleasure. This theoretical inconsistency was not acknowledged by most communist regimes, and they tended to refer to the theory of alienation as an "early" or "young" Marxian concept, implying a certain degree of reservation. In China, during the beginning of the post-Mao era, reform-minded intellectuals exploited the concept of alienation to justify their quest for loosening party and state control over social and individual lives. They claimed that there was an abstract human nature that was distorted not only by economic exploitation but also, or even more so, by overextended political power. Such an argument—"alienation under socialism"—was soon determined by the party to be harmful and was subsequently suppressed.[23]

Like his Enlightenment forerunners, Marx also took great interest in education as a means of reshaping human nature, to replace "alienated man" with "well-developed man." For this he advocated the integration of education with productive labor as the major vehicle, especially at tender ages. The British Factory Reform Act (1833) allowed a half-day education, half-day labor program for working-class boys. Marx noticed that these boys seemed fresher and performed much better in their study than bourgeois children who never were enrolled in full-day school. In one of his letters to the Central Committee of the First International, Marx proposed that, in the future, children should become productive laborers from the age of nine years. He went on to detail that they should be divided into three age groups: ages nine to thirteen should work two hours per day; ages fourteen and fifteen years, four hours; and ages sixteen to seventeen, six hours. In the resolutions of the First Congress of the First International, Marx further developed his future educational outline, stating that "by education we understand three things," and those were "mental, bodily and technological training, which imparts the general principles of all process of production, and simultaneously initiates the child and young person in the practical use and handling of the elementary instruments of all trades." The cost of such technological education would be covered by selling the products manufactured by those children. He firmly believed that such an integration of education with labor would "raise the working class far above the level of the higher and middle class."[24] Marx's educational concepts consequently became the goals for socialist education pursued in the Soviet Union during the 1920s, and even more so in China from the late 1950s to the early 1970s and Cuba during the 1960s. When the experiments of creating the new man were conducted in these countries, the integration of labor with education was taken as a fundamental step.

THE NEW MAN OF THE NINETEENTH-CENTURY RUSSIAN INTELLIGENTSIA

As a specific term, "new man" first entered European and world political language in the 1860s and was associated with a particular political group: the Russian intelligentsia who emerged as a revolutionary force and claimed to change Russian society.

Influenced by western European revolutionary ideologies and political changes, the advocacy for political and social reforms in feudal and absolute-monarchist tsarist Russia had created and intensified political tension in the first half of the nineteenth century. The failed Decembrist Rebellion of 1825—led by a group of Russian nobles under the influence of European liberalism, which challenged absolute monarchy—revealed the extent of political division within the ruling class. Many Decembrists were exiled to Siberia after their failed coup, often accompanied by their faithful wives, setting a moral example for Russia's future revolutionaries. Their successors were Russian intelligentsia, an estranged intellectual elite expelled from politics by the tsarist regime and frustrated by its rejection of reforms. With a nonnobility social class background and under the influence of radical Enlightenment ideas (a materialistic view of the world, and of human nature in particular), their political dissent—associated with the idea of "socialism"—was more uncompromising than that of their forerunners. This political stratum came of age in the 1860s, when Russia's defeat in the Crimean War (1853–1856) forced the tsarist regime to engage in some social reforms (emancipating the serfs, for example), thus creating an atmosphere conducive to airing political dissent.

Members of the Russian intelligentsia were known for their deep-seated animosity to the status quo and their fanatical craving for an ideal society, so much so that they saw no meaning in their lives if they could not completely commit themselves to their cause. As Vladimir C. Nahirny has pointed out, their "attachment to and orientation toward these ideas" were great: "like a lover with his beloved, they did not hesitate to play out their whole lives around them."[25] According to a Russian populist author, there was even an inner relationship between the personality and the ideology: "It is not enough for him [the intellectual] to have a political program, a social theory; he must find in this program and this theory a place for himself, his personality, his sentiments, and his conscience."[26] The representatives— Grigoryevich Belinsky, Gavrilovich Chernyshevsky, Nikolai Dobroliubov, Peter Lavrov, and Pyotr Tkachev, along with many less well known— exemplified this commitment with their own lives and personal characters. Belinsky, for instance, displayed an intense attachment to ideas and the ignorance of individuals. He expressed his idea of socialism, for example, in statements such as "Everything from it, for it, and toward it," "I explain in its terms my life, your life, and the life of all those whom I meet on the road of life," and "Person is nothing to me now—conviction is everything."[27]

It is in this context that the idea of the new man was conceptualized. In Nahirny's analysis, the Russian intelligentsia's vision of future society rarely included established and concrete institutions of a civil society, such as law, contract, family relations, social customs, individual interest, and social distinction. Rather, for Belinsky, as an example, the foundation for future society consisted of some abstract and collective ideas, such as "sociality" and "humanity." "Sociality" referred to an individual's commitment to ideals and convictions on behalf of the society, while "humanity" meant a socioeconomically homogenous community, because Belinsky thought that a society based on "heterogeneous elements" and different individual interests was "pitiable" and "inhuman." As Nahirny writes, "Implicit in this notion of sociality is the image of a 'new man.' Unlike a member of the civil society, an independent and egoistic individual, this new man is imbued with the spirit of sacrifice for [and] love of mankind, but a love cultivated by ideology and education."[28] Such a new man would create new social bonds before a new society was established.

It was against this background that a fictional image created by Chernyshevsky's novel *What Is to Be Done? The Story about the New Man* (1861) crystallized the idealized attributes of the much-expected new man.[29] The novel quickly drew the attention of the author's restless contemporaries and gained the term currency. Rakhmetov, the heroic antagonist of the novel, is identified as "belonging to a new breed" whose attributes represent a whole new generation of the revolutionary intelligentsia. As a self-appointed messianic figure aware of his mission to liberate the people, he develops a materialist worldview, a clear vision of the future, and the iron will required to apply whatever means necessary to overthrow the establishment. In order to make himself more familiar with the people and their suffering, he has measured the whole of Russia on foot and has worked at cutting timber, quarrying stone, and hauling riverboats with laborers. More than that, he disciplines himself and toughens his will through self-denial or even self-torture. For instance, he forces himself to stay up for days by drinking strong coffee, sleeps on a bed of nails, and takes cold-water baths.

One notable characteristic of Chernyshevsky's new man is his rejection of any human affection, especially between the sexes, if it is not associated with common political interest. As the protagonist puts it, "I must suppress any love in myself: to love means to bind my hands. . . . I must not love." The incompatibility between sexuality and political commitment is part of the novel's theme. As Elizabeth A. Wood points out, "Its male characters are obsessed with their relationships to their ideas of women: either they as men should devote themselves to anticipating women's every emotion and responding to the point of absenting themselves or they should reject all intimate contact with women as inherently distracting from the larger cause."[30] The novel in general treats women as equal to men, on the ground that they are both dedicated to the revolution. In this sense it establishes some fundamental principles for the new men in dealing with their sexual life and love affairs: they should be ascetic and practice self-denial if such human desire and relationship become an impediment to their cause and divert their attention and energy from their commitment. That explains why many Russian revolutionaries in the nineteenth century and most Bolsheviks in the twentieth century were husband and wife in comradeship, as were communists of many other countries. The novel also established a pattern for revolutionary literature in dealing with a sexual relationship: to minimize it or even not to mention it, as if it did not exist, and if mentioning it was unavoidable, then subjecting it to the comradeship context. The most extreme case of exclusion of sexual relationship from revolutionary literature and art was in China's Cultural Revolution, where virtually all heroic characters who were exalted in all kinds of artistic works seemed sexless, as they were all without companions of the opposite sex. In communist political terminology, "personal problems," a vague phrase to outsiders, was often used when sex-related matters of party members and cadres were referred to. The phrase was self-explanatory in suggesting that such issues were inherent in nature but undesirable in party politics.

Chernyshevsky thus fused ideology into personality, transforming an individual into a new man. By this he inspired Russian intelligentsia throughout the second half of the nineteenth century. When a revolutionary was arrested, often one of the first questions he or she was expected to answer was, "When and where did you read *What Is to Be Done?*" Furthermore, the novel's influence went beyond the nineteenth century. During the Soviet years the book was listed as the most recommended nineteenth-century Russian literary work and was translated into many languages in the socialist camp.

The Bolsheviks, especially Lenin himself, regarded Chernyshevsky as their forerunner. As a matter of fact, it was neither Marx nor Engels who influenced Lenin's formative years, but Chernyshevsky. Recalling his early intellectual experience, Lenin once acknowledged:

> I became acquainted with the works of Marx, Engels and Plekhanov, but it was only Chernyshevsky who had an overwhelming influence on me, beginning with his novel *What Is to Be Done?* Chernyshevsky's great service was not only that he showed that every right-thinking and really decent person must be a revolutionary, but something more important: what kind of revolutionary, what his principles ought to be, how he should aim for his goal, what means and methods he should employ to realize it.

Lenin also described the book as "a work which gives one a charge for a whole life."[31] In Lenin's collective works, Chernyshevsky is the author most quoted—more than three hundred times.

During the 1860s and 1870s, Chernyshevsky's new man was embodied by some young revolutionaries who dedicated or even sacrificed themselves to the revolution. One example was Peter Zaichnevskii, who wrote the manifesto "Young Russian," advocating a revolution that would turn society upside down and eliminate all the allies of the existing order. A more renowned example was Serge Nechaev, who was the founder of a militant revolutionary organization, the People's Revenge. A dedicated but autocratic revolutionary, Nechaev expressed his political ideas in his *Revolutionary Catechism*. It elaborates the rules and principles—many already sketched by Chernyshevsky—that a revolutionary's life must follow. The *Catechism* starts with the statement: "The revolutionary is a doomed man. He has no interests of his own, no affairs, no feelings, no attachments, no belongings, not even a name. Everything in him is absorbed by a single exclusive interest, a single thought, a single passion—the revolution."[32]

Although the Bolsheviks and communists in other countries never acknowledged any ideological connection between them and Nechaev—largely due to his reputation of being unscrupulous, using lies to convince his comrades, and even killing one of them who did not believe him—the portrayal of the revolutionary in the *Catechism* in essence shared the major characteristics of a "genuine" communist or a new man. For example, Che Guevara, an ardent advocate and himself an example of the communist new man, once described the attributes of revolutionaries, which sounded identical to those expressed in the *Catechism:* "The leaders of the revolution have children who do not learn to call their father with their first faltering words; they have wives who must be part of the general sacrifice of their lives to carry the revolution to its destination; their friends are strictly limited to their comrades in revolution. There is no life outside the revolution."[33]

But such "new men" among the Russian intelligentsia were only a small group of revolutionary elite—"the salt of the earth," as Chernyshevsky described them in his novel. It was quite clear that this handful of revolutionaries might perhaps start a revolution but certainly would not be able to overthrow the autocracy without the support of the masses.

During the 1870s the Russian new men were represented by the Populists, a variation of the intelligentsia. Desperately seeking revolutionary forces, they idolized Russian peasantry, the *muzhik*s, believing they were born socialists and morally superior by nature, by virtue of their preservation of village communal tradition and their simple and natural lifestyle. This idolization of the muzhiks in populist tradition "alleges that it has discerned virtues which are morally superior to those found in the educated and in the higher social class."[34] Their revolutionary potential would be released if they were approached by radical intelligentsia. Thus the Populists launched a "Going to the People" movement to educate and organize the Russian peasants. In doing so, many participants claimed to integrate themselves with the peasants, absorbing high morality from them while transferring revolutionary ideologies to them. In order to approach the peasants, many Populists put on country-style attire and lived the way of villagers. But the muzhiks responded with moral indifference and political inertia to this unrequited devotion. Alienated and isolated in the countryside, many of the intellectuals soon became disillusioned with the alleged "revolutionary potential" and moral quality of peasants and even suffered emotionally, so much so that some of them in their loneliness talked to ovens and imagined that they were speaking to their friends afar in their own language.[35] This ideological fantasy and subsequent disillusion about peasants and the moral purification of village life would reappear in the twentieth century, especially in China and Cuba, when some communist regimes sent intellectuals and students to "integrate" with peasants, disseminating culture and revolutionary ideology among them while "learning from" peasants politically and morally.

The Populist frustration with Russian peasants soon turned some revolutionaries to acts of terrorism, such as the assassinations of the tsar and his ministers, but the rest of the intelligentsia dismissed such methods. Instead of placing their hope on Russia's peasants, they began to seek a new social class associated with modern industry and the acquisition of political consciousness. When examining the ideological connections between the Russian intelligentsia and the later revolutionary movements, Maurice Meisner points out a key influence of the former upon the latter: "These 'new men' were the elite of young intellectuals who were capable of imposing their socialist consciousness on the historical reality and providing guidance for the masses. . . . The 'new men' of the intelligentsia were to be only catalytic agents in a revolutionary process in which all would become 'new men' in a new and just society."[36]

LENIN: THE CONQUEST OF CONSCIOUSNESS OVER SPONTANEITY

At the turn of the nineteenth century, the vexing question that had tormented the Russian intelligentsia since the 1870s—that the revolution had to be carried out by dedicated men—became increasingly keenly felt among its members. Having become disillusioned with Russian peasants, the intelligentsia shifted its hopes to the proletariat, as Russian Social Democrats—that is to say, Marxists—replaced Populists as the leading political opposition of the tsarist regime.

But in reality, as Lenin anxiously observed, the trade union movement, which was dominant in organizing workers at that time throughout Europe, was leading the workers only toward economic aims. Lenin called this tendency "economism" and came to the conclusion that the labor movement, if developed spontaneously and not guided by Marxist ideology, would inevitably become petit bourgeois and satisfy itself with economic gains. The only solution to this problem, according to Lenin, was to form a well-disciplined and strictly centralized party composed of full-time professional revolutionaries to inject revolutionary ideology into the working class, replacing their "spontaneity" with "consciousness." Cultivating class consciousness, or political awareness, among workers thus became the revolutionary elites' primary task. Lenin outlined his thesis in his famous pamphlet *What Is to Be Done?* (1902), whose title reflected Chernyshevsky's influence on him.

In 1907, when a revolutionary storm was gathering momentum, Maxim Gorky, a literary ally of the Russian Socialist Democrats, published his novel *Mother*. This novel describes how an old, illiterate, and downtrodden housewife of a working-class family is enlightened by revolutionary ideas and hardened by political struggle, thus transforming herself into an ardent and conscious fighter. The novel therefore addressed exactly the type of question Lenin and his comrades were concerned with at the time, and it offered an example—although fictional—of politically educating workers and their families. If the new man had originally been personified by elite intelligentsia and portrayed by Chernyshevsky in his *What Is To Be Done?* then Gorky, a half century later, had added a working-class figure to the new-man gallery.

On his way to London for the party's Fifth Congress, Lenin met Gorky in Germany and obtained the novel's manuscript. As he read it, Lenin immediately found the political implication of this literary work. He invited Gorky to London to appear at the congress as a special guest and praised his work as "a very timely book." The book established Gorky's fame as "proletarian writer," and the novel was introduced to the party's grassroots activists. After the October Revolution, *Mother* was honored as a classic piece of "socialist realism"—the official doctrine of socialist literature and arts, portraying the perfect image of the new man.

Ironically, however, Gorky, Lenin's ally during the first decade of the century, turned out to be his enemy in the years immediately before and after the October Revolution. When Lenin urged the Bolsheviks to be prepared for a socialist revolution right after the February Revolution of 1917, which had just introduced in Russia an incipient liberal democracy, his proposal was questioned and even criticized by most Bolshevik leaders. Gorky disagreed with him as well, on the grounds that the Russian people were far from ready for such radical social change and that the fictional revolutionary "Mother" did not typify the bulk of the masses in reality. Gorky argued that a stage of "bourgeois democracy" and a sound foundation of material wealth were indispensable for Marx's idea of socialism in Russia.

Having witnessed the disorder and atrocity brought about by the mobs instigated by the Bolsheviks after the October Revolution, Gorky discovered that his high spirits, which had inspired him to write *Mother* ten years earlier, had evaporated. He founded a newspaper, *Novaia zhizn'* (New Life), in which he started a column titled "Untimely Thoughts." In the articles, Gorky rejected any political plan for a radical social change. As he put it, "this nation must work a great deal in order to acquire an awareness of its identity, of its human dignity; this nation must be tempered and cleansed of its inbred slavery by the slow flame of culture."[37] Pessimistic and critical of the so-called Russian national character, he described it as "ignorant and uncultured," "brutalized by the old system," "animalistic," and "demagogically flattered." With this national character in action, Gorky believed that the revolution Lenin and Trotsky were imposing on Russia would become a senseless and brutal tragedy at worst and a reckless social experiment at best. As he tersely expressed it, "the working class is for a Lenin what ore is for a metalworker." He also made frequent comparisons between Lenin and the notorious Nechaev, implying that Lenin was sacrificing the whole nation for his revolutionary fantasy. By June 1918, Lenin's tolerance of his old friend was gone, and he ordered the closing of Gorky's newspaper.

THE "SOVIET MAN": THE FIRST
VARIANT OF THE COMMUNIST NEW MAN

The October Revolution and the subsequent establishment of the Soviet regime constituted the first time in human history that a government attempted to carry out social engineering to reshape a people on a large scale. All Soviet leaders were apparently aware of this. As Anatoly Lunacharski, the first Soviet commissioner of education, put it: "Little by little a new man is being born . . . [and] we must follow the exact process of his birth."[38]

Soviet Leaders' Vision of the New Man

As soon as he had the state power in hand and was facing everyday reality, Lenin began to develop a pessimistic sentiment regarding the stubbornness of people against policies designed on their behalf. According to Gorky, after listening to Beethoven's sonatas one day in Moscow, Lenin, still in the mood of the music, commented:

> But I can't listen to music very often, it affects my nerves. I want to say sweet, silly things and pat the heads of people who, living in a filthy hell, can create such beauty. One can't pat anyone on the head nowadays, they might bite your hand off. They ought to be beaten on the head, beaten mercilessly, although ideally we are against doing any violence to people. Hm—what a hellishly difficult job![39]

But other Bolshevik leaders, although most of them skeptical about the possibility of a victorious socialist revolution when Lenin first laid down his plan, demonstrated more fanaticism and confidence in their mandate of reshaping humans when power was in their hands.

Leon Trotsky, whose importance in the October Revolution was second only to Lenin's in the Bolshevik leadership, had an encounter with Darwinism when he was developing his own sociopolitical outlook. Many years later he recalled, "The idea of evolution and determinism—that is, the idea of a gradual development conditioned by the character of the material world—took possession of me completely."[40] With this early influence as the backdrop, his vision of the future "socialist man" ended up with fanciful characteristics:

Man will at last begin to harmonize himself in earnest. He will make it his business to achieve beauty by giving the movement of his own limbs the utmost precision, purposefulness and economy in his work, his walk and his play. He will try to master first the semiconscious and then the subconscious process in his own organism, such as breathing, the circulation of the blood, digestion, reproduction, and, within necessary limits, he will try to subordinate them to the control of reason and will. Even purely physiologic life will become subject to collective experiments.[41]

Here Trotsky not only developed Lenin's thesis of "consciousness" conquering "spontaneity" from a physiological perspective but added to it the viewpoint of a nineteenth-century machine-age optimist.

Stalin is known for his penchant to compare humans to raw material or mechanical parts. At Lenin's funeral, he delivered a eulogy that has become well known for its metaphorical assertion: "We communists are people of a special mold. We are made of special material."[42] On another occasion Stalin said that people could be remolded just as "a gardener cultivates his favorite fruit tree." "Engineers of the human soul" was Stalin's favorite metaphorical title for educators, propaganda workers, and writers. But perhaps the most typical Stalinist metaphor in this regard was made known at a celebration of victory in World War II, when Stalin implied that the Soviet "new man" had subdued the Nazi "Aryan race" as he proposed a famous toast: "I drink to the simple people, ordinary and modest, to the 'cogs,' who keep our great state machine in motion."[43] The cog metaphor was later borrowed by other communist regimes to vividly describe the collectively indispensable but individually replaceable role of ordinary people in the revolutionary machine, and in some instances—in Maoist China, for example—the screw, a smaller and humbler part of the machine, replaced the cog. (Stalin was not the first one to liken the individual human to a "cog in the machine." Kant made this comparison to highlight the awareness of individuals that they have a role to play as a particular segment in society, as Foucault interpreted, but had no "blind and foolish obedience."[44]) Bukharin once proposed that the goal of the revolution was to "alter people's actual psychology" and that "one of the priorities of scientific planning is the question of the systematic preparation of new man, the builders of socialism,"[45] although now more firsthand materials describe him as the one with some humaneness in the post Lenin Bolshevik leadership. It is in this sense that Frank S. Meyer, a former American communist in charge of cadre training in the 1930s who later broke from the party, made the following observation of the communist conceptualization of people: "'People' are conceived of, not as those who make up the association, those for whom the association exists, but rather as material to be developed, fertilized, watered—and pruned. . . . At any rate, the written material proves by the words interchangeable with 'people' that it has a very different connotation than in ordinary English. In place of it can be substituted 'forces,' 'elements,' 'material,' 'cadres.'"[46]

"Conditioned Reflection": A Misused Physiological Premise for Reshaping the Human Mind

In a very peculiar manner, a Russian physiologist's work inspired the social engineering by the Bolshevik regime of remaking the human mind. Ivan Petrovich Pavlov (1849–1936), a leading physiologist from the 1890s, set forth a theory of the "conditioned reflex" and won the Nobel Prize for medicine and physiology in 1904. Pavlov noticed that dogs salivated when they were hungry and spotted food. Every time Pavlov fed a dog in his study, he rang a bell. After many repetitions the dog salivated whenever it heard the bell ring, even without seeing food, because a link between the sound and food had been established in its physiological response mechanism. This experiment led Pavlov to develop a theory that not only animals but humans as well could respond to certain signals through the mechanism of the conditioned reflex. Pavlovian theory has been recognized as an important contribution to physiology and is found in American middle school textbooks today. But Bolsheviks quickly found in it scientific evidence to support their new-man project: by manipulating the environment—especially repeating signals with ideological and political messages—human consciousness could be reshaped or created. As Joost A. M. Meerloo pointed out: "Through a conditioned repetition of indoctrination, bell ringing and feeding, the Soviet man is expected to become a conditioned reflex machine, reacting according to a prearranged pattern, as did the laboratory dogs. At least, such a simplified concept is roaming around in the minds of some of the Soviet leaders and scientists."[47]

Lenin in general regarded the old intelligentsia, especially the well-established scholars, as hostile and potentially dangerous to the revolution. In 1919, when Cheka (the Soviet secret police) was making mass arrests among scientists and scholars, Gorky wrote a letter to Lenin in support of those ill-fated intellectuals and said the "mind of the people" was being destroyed. To this, Lenin retorted that the intelligentsia was the "shit" of the people, not the "mind."[48] But Lenin recognized the ideological implications of Pavlovian theory and treated Pavlov as a rare exception. He issued a decree on January 24, 1921, in honor of "the outstanding scientific services of academician I. P. Pavlov, which are of enormous significance to the working class of the whole world."[49] While thousands of Russian scientists not only were out of supplies for their research but also were struggling with hunger, cold, and diseases, Pavlov's laboratory was supported by the government with three golden rubles per month in the most difficult years of the civil war (1918–1920). During Stalin's years, the government showered Pavlov with honors and titles and maintained some institutions—such as the Pavlovian Front and the Scientific Council on Problems of Physiological Theory of the Academician I. P. Pavlov—as part of the Academy of Sciences, to study, develop and apply Pavlov's theory.

Although Pavlov's world fame may have contributed to the official recognition and treatment he received, what must have been in the minds of Bolshevik leaders was the political and ideological implication of his theory. One fact illustrating the connection between science and ideology in this regard is that from the 1920s to the 1950s, while Pavlovian theory dominated Soviet biological and physiological studies, genetics was condemned as "bourgeois pseudoscience." With its emphasis on human biological inheritance, genetics had implications for the limits of remolding individuals. For this reason the theory was condemned as "bourgeois," "idealistic," and "pseudoscientific" by the Soviet Union and later by most other communist countries.[50]

Despite all of the governmental endorsements, Pavlov was never ideologically in conformity with the Bolsheviks. For him, any efforts to apply his theory beyond the field of physiology and for political purpose had nothing to do with his intention. He challenged Marxian materialist doctrines and rejected their application in the guidance of scientific research, as was officially required. Politically, he thought Lenin's proposal of world revolution was not only unrealistic but also destructive to Russia's already shaky social infrastructure in the wake of the war and revolution. He expressed these thoughts openly in his lectures around 1920, and because he was so influential, Bukharin had to initiate a press campaign to discredit him. Pavlov afterward kept his silence, but he never let his private sphere, especially his laboratories, be touched by official propaganda. In 1933 British author H. G. Wells visited him and found that it was as if he were visiting a place outside the Soviet Union. Pavlov, in Wells' presence, ridiculed the official belief that "Marxian materialism" was the guideline for scientific research.[51]

Establishment of the Party School System

The Bolshevik government was the first government in world history to establish a special school system of ideological indoctrination and character cultivation to provide the regime with qualified cadres and functionaries, who would not only staff administrative and managerial positions but also personify the ideal of the new man. Higher education, as a major institution of the old culture and socio-ideological environment, bore the brunt of revolutionary changes from the very beginning: the autonomy of universities was abolished, and the faculties of philosophy, history, law, and theology in particular were practically purged. The study of Marxist historical-dialectical materialism was required in the curriculum, and all of those who rejected this change had to leave the institution and sometimes even the country.

In the meantime, Bolsheviks had decided that the conventional educational system, no matter how reformed, was still incapable of fulfilling the task of bringing up the new man. To remedy the situation, they established special colleges, or communist universities, free from any vestige of the old educational system. The Sverdlov University in Moscow—founded in 1919 in memory of Yakov Sverdlov (1885–1919), one of the party leaders who died shortly after the October Revolution—was one of the flagships in this effort. The bulk of the students at Sverdlov were chosen from among soldiers and workers or low-ranking party functionaries. According to one source, in 1919–1920, 45.7 percent of the students were listed as workers, 12 percent were former metalworkers, and most of them had only primary education.[52] The admission required letters of certification from their supervising party organizations. Its curriculum was predominated by Marxist texts and party documents, along with some courses in natural science and Russian and European politics. The students were also engaged in all kinds of political meetings, theatrical performances, and propaganda activities. In addition, the integration of work and study was also part of their curriculum. Graduates were assigned jobs across the country to act as functionaries to ensure that the party's lines were followed. Other institutions of a similar nature were established. Zinoviev College at Leningrad—named after Grigory Zinoviev (1883–1936), one of the party's leaders and the head of the Comintern (Communist International)—was particularly for non-Russian peoples. The University for Eastern Workers and Peasants in Moscow, founded in 1919, was a pedagogical tool for the Comintern. Its particular task was to "permit the backward Eastern nations [Chinese and Indian, for example] to share in communist enlightenment." And the Marx-Engels Institute, also founded in 1919, was the highest theoretical training center for cadres. In addition to these more formal educational institutions, many workers' faculties were established nationwide to provide workers and low-ranking cadres with part-time study programs, often directly linked to their work and schooling.

Political Socialization of Childhood and Adolescence

A more systematic effort involved in the creation of the new man was the complete and intensive political socialization of the new generations.

"Political socialization" in general refers to a process of identity formation by which "a junior member of a group or institution is taught its values, attitudes and other behaviors."[53] More specifically, it is "the learning process by which the political norms and behaviors acceptable to an ongoing political system are transmitted from generation to generation,"[54] and it "opens up a social world to the individual—the world of political allegiances and alliances, political rules and rituals, political personalities and policies, political symbols and behaviors."[55] As a result of political socialization, "The citizen acquires a complex of beliefs, feelings, and information which help him comprehend, evaluate, and relate to the political world around him."[56]

As so defined, political socialization is common to all societies for making citizens, especially of young people. However, political socialization under communist regimes distinguished itself from others in two aspects. The first was that it went far beyond what is necessary for instilling in junior members basic norms and values a society requires—for example, identifying oneself with and maintaining loyalty to the nation and observing behavioral patterns accepted by the society and the culture. Political socialization in many societies limits explicit political symbols associated with a particular regime, while ideological principles of the system may be emphasized. It also entails spontaneous and autonomous efforts from all segments of society (family and local and religious communities, for example). In contrast, political socialization under communist regimes was excessive in all aspects. It was conducted solely to achieve acceptance of the party's authority and identification of the party with the state and nation to the extent that the party and its leaders were deified, and the ideological doctrine of the party comprised the norms for everyday life. In other words, loyalty to a particular regime and even its leaders, instead of allegiance to a nation and observance of its cultural and moral norms, was the objective of political socialization under communist regimes. There was no spontaneous and autonomous involvement, and the whole process was highly centralized, well coordinated, and imposed on the individual through various organizations according to his or her age and occupation.

The second distinction of political socialization under communist regimes was the belief that ideological formation and accompanying personality development could not be completed only by education in which the individual was a passive recipient. Rather, it was a dynamic process in which individuals were mobilized and organized to involve or commit themselves in political action. They learned through practice, and ideology/politics was made a part of their life experience as early as childhood. The emphasis on direct and early participation of the to-be-made citizens in political, ideological, and even economic activities has been evident. These activities included

everything that could be associated with political and ideological implication, ranging from critiques of erroneous ideas to literacy campaigns and
cultivation of certain types of crops or raising livestock. An anatomy of the
Communist Youth League, the Young Pioneers, and the Little Octobrists—
the Soviet creation of an interconnected system for bringing juveniles
and young adolescents to ideological maturity through organization and
participation—illustrates the excessiveness of political socialization under
communist regimes.

Almost at the same time that Lenin proposed replacing "spontaneity"
with "consciousness" in Russian workers through political education at the
turn of the century, he raised the same question regarding developing the
youth to become the party's reserves. He pointed out that "spontaneously
developing a youth movement needed the assistance of proletarian revolutionaries, especially in acquiring an integral and consistent socialist world
outlook."[57] During the 1905–1908 revolution, at Lenin's request, the Bolsheviks "resolutely exposed attempts by the bourgeois and petit bourgeois
parties to distract the proletarian youth from revolutionary struggle." After
the October Revolution, he emphasized the need to establish a youth organization independent from but attached to the party. In October 1918 the
Russian Communist Youth League was established at the First All-Russian
Congress of Workers and Peasants; it was later shortened to Komsomol.
According to a later definition, the chief task of the Komsomol was

> to help the Party educate young men and women in the high ideals of
> Marxism-Leninism and in the heroic tradition of revolutionary struggle
> by the examples of self-scarifying labor set by the workers, kolkhozniki
> (members of the collectives), and intelligentsia. It is also its task to develop
> and strengthen in the youth a class approach to all aspects of social life and
> to train staunch and well-educated builders of communism who will be
> devoted to their work.[58]

In practice, the Komsomol functioned first of all as a "transmission
belt," as it was called, linking the party with the youth and the population in
general. The new man was created through struggle, not merely by attending lectures and engaging in reading and discussion. The Komsomol pioneered many campaigns to materialize the party's projects of social change,
through which its members were expected to transform themselves as well.
In the civil war, the Komsomol provided more than 75,000 of its members
to the Red Army from 1918 to 1920. In the 1920s it promoted a literacy
campaign and was engaged in eradicating all kinds of remnants of the old
social environment, such as religious ideas, cultural prejudices, and "bour-

geois philistinism, private property holders' psychology, and self-seeking attitude toward work."[59] The members of the Komsomol were highly distinguishable especially in the countryside, where they organized reading groups and clubs and distributed books, magazines, posters, and leaflets. They initiated socialist emulation in 1927, organized "light cavalry" against bureaucratism in 1928, and shock brigades of competition in the first Five-Year Plan (1929–1932, accomplished ahead of time). The Komsomol was attributed with the completion of a number of key industrial projects such as Dneproges Power Station, the Moscow and Gorky automobile plants, the Stalingrad Tractor Plant, the Magnitogorsk Metallurgical Combine, and the Turksib Railroad. In the forced collectivization campaign of the 1930s, millions of Komsomol members organized Red Plowman brigades and Agricultural Scout teams to carry out the task of smashing traditional Russian peasantry and village life and introducing the new, collective one, often ushered in by mechanized facilities in rural communities. The image of the Komsomol members in the village at this particular time was often associated with the tractor, a fetishized machine symbolizing the new life and new peasant, as a then-popular slogan demonstrated: "Komsomol members—to the tractor!"

The Komsomol also functioned as the patron of the Young Pioneers. The Young Pioneers, due to the age limits of its members, did not form any administrative hierarchy; therefore its practical direction was assigned by the party to the Komsomol. The Central Committee of the Komsomol was responsible for the operation of its younger-brother organization nationwide, and Komsomol members at all levels (city, district, town, village, and school) assumed the obligation of directing and supervising the Young Pioneers' activities within their administrative parameters.

The Young Pioneers came into being after the Komsomol, but Bolshevik attention paid to childhood and early adolescent ideological development emerged much earlier. Lenin and other Bolshevik leaders had been obsessed with the development of Russian Scouts, which was introduced from the West in 1909 under the patronage of Tsar Nicholas II (Tsarevitch Alexei was actually the first Scout) and became popular in many tsarist Russian cities. It was seen by the Bolsheviks as a major competitor in winning children, so they disbanded it in 1919. After the Komsomol was established, the party assigned it the task of creating a brother organization. The Komsomol organized a special commission to carry out the task, and senior Bolsheviks—especially N. K. Krupskaya, Lenin's wife and a national grandmother figure—were intensively involved in the commencement and instruction of the organization. It was officially established in May 1922, at the Second Congress of the Komsomol.

The principles of the Young Pioneers were "the ideological tempering of children and adolescents, bringing them into active participation in sociopolitical life, and teaching them organizational habits": "By facilitating the shaping of the children's civic awareness, the Pioneer organization gives their projects a political character and educates them in revolutionary ideas and fidelity to the traditions of older generations."[60] The routine activities of the Young Pioneers were organized in a ritualistic and especially militaristic manner, including the Ceremonial Pledge, the "Song of the Young Leninists," and a combination of military-style uniforms and a red scarf tied around the neck, in addition to parades, camp bonfires, excursions, group gymnastics, and so on.[61] In schools, normally a class formed a detachment, and the school a brigade. Military defense workers were developed in the form of circles of young marksmen, orderlies, and signalers. Military games were part of the collective extracurricular activities. A. S. Makarenko, a Soviet educator known for his educational camp for delinquent young adults, once said:

> Among traditions, I especially cherish the militarization games; . . . my collective was militarized to a degree. Our terminology, taken out of military life, included such words as "unit commander" and "guard." We also incorporated its rituals, such as banners, drills, uniforms, guard duty and roll calls. . . . I find it necessary to perpetuate this trend since it reinforces the life of the collective and adds beauty to it.[62]

Therefore, for Makarenko, militarization even had an aesthetic value. His methods were widely adopted by the normal education system during the 1930s.

The establishment of the Young Pioneers in schools created confusion in its early years among educators who were used to a more conventional and unified school system. They strove to restrict its influence by merging the organization with regular school activities and the curriculum. But these efforts were soon condemned by the watchful party in a special decree issued in April 1932. The decree demanded that the independent role of the Young Pioneers in political education must not be blurred with routine educational activities.

As with the Komsomol, but to a lesser degree, members of the Young Pioneers were actively involved in political activities such as literacy and cultural campaigns fighting remnants of the old Russia, especially in the countryside. They also participated in the propaganda for the forced collectivization during the 1930s. Official accounts praised their zeal, and the names of a number of Young Pioneers who were allegedly murdered by *kulak*s were entered in the Book of Honor of the All-Union Pioneer Organization. But to what extent their heroic deeds were the creation of Soviet propaganda has been a matter of debate. The true story of Pavlik Morozov is illuminative in this regard. Morozov was the most celebrated child-hero of the 1930s. The official account held that he was born to a peasant family and became a dedicated member of the Pioneers. During Stalin's collectivization campaign in the early 1930s, he reported his father's liaison with anti-Soviet bandits (forging documents for them) and was murdered by vicious family members after his father was sentenced. The thirteen-year-old boy instantly became a hero, and his name was entered in the Soviet shrine for the new man, and statues and images of him could be seen in numerous schools. His alleged murder caused great sensation, and the trial of the murderers made the headlines nationwide. But some recent investigations have suggested a much less ideologically mature and politically dedicated child and even a completely different scenario about his death. Whatever the truth, the Soviet government had succeeded in establishing a model of the juvenile new man who put revolutionary consciousness above family loyalty and even rebelled against his parents, a pattern that would be followed by children of other communist countries, especially in China's thought-reform campaigns and the Cultural Revolution.[63]

At the bottom of the organizational ladder were the Little Octobrists, for children seven to nine years old. The organization was created in 1924, and the name originally referred to children born in 1917, the year of the revolution, thus carrying the meaning of the new man in a literal sense. Little Octobrists was for elementary school students from the first to the third grade. Each grade formed a group divided into subgroups called Little Stars, with five children each. The emblem of the Little Octobrists was a little red flag, and its members wore a ruby-colored five-pointed star badge that bore a portrait of Lenin in his childhood. Just as the Young Pioneers were directed by the Komsomol, the Little Octobrists were under the supervision of the Young Pioneers, with each group of Little Octobrists led by one Young Pioneer. The ideological education for the Little Octobrists was less intensive, and the political task was much lighter. All of its members were expected to be qualified to join the Young Pioneers when they entered fourth grade.

Educational Revolution

The Bolsheviks put into practice Marx's idea of an early integration of work and education, the key concept in educating the new man. In 1918 Anatol Lunacharski, the first commissioner of Soviet education, issued the first report on education, in which seven basic principles were enunciated: first, labor as the basis of teaching and education; second, "early fusion of productive labor and academic institutions"; third, polytechnic education, meaning all-round development of the individual; fourth, the school as a productive commune; fifth, manual labor as a part of everyday school life; sixth, productive, creative, and artistic endeavors; and seventh, emphasis on the child as a "social creature."[64]

The 1920s witnessed a radical educational experiment aimed at creating a well-rounded person. Even Soviet educators themselves called this period "experimental." Several theoreticians drew the blueprints for this reform. In 1919 Paul Blonsky, one of the forerunners of Soviet pedagogy, published *The Unified Labor School,* proposing a single school system organized at three interrelated levels, with provision for the unimpeded progress of the child from the first grade to the ninth or tenth. In this school, manual labor, or "socially useful activities," formed the major part of the curriculum.[65] The Soviet educators proudly called this school "a school that does" rather than "a school that talks," because in this school the students learned by practice and participation rather than from listening and taking notes. Some educators argued that many traditional academic subjects should be either reduced or abolished. The most radical idea was the "withering away of the school," raised by V. N. Shul'gin, director of the Institute of School Methods in Moscow. His vision of Soviet education foresaw that children would grow up "not in a school, not in a kindergarten," but in "the factory, the mill, the agricultural economy, the class struggle."[66]

When the 1930s came, Stalin's industrialization and Five-Year Plans required Soviet schools to produce the type of new man that had sufficient technical, engineering, and managerial knowledge and skills. In reality, however, the party found that the educational reform represented by the experiments conducted in institutions such as the unified labor school system, with its unorganized curricula and freedom from discipline, had failed the Soviet state. The party came to the conclusion that the Soviet new man could not be created in a laissez-faire way. Starting from the early 1930s, the party and the government issued a series of decrees to restore traditional and formal education, with a slogan of "the mastery of knowledge." The party condemned the educational reforms of the 1920s as an "extreme Left tendency." In August 1932 the Central Committee of the party issued an order with meticulous prescriptions, such as the following: "The chief form of the organization of instruction in the primary and secondary school must be recitation with a given group of pupils following a strict schedule of studies."[67] Thereafter, Soviet education developed its distinct feature: a rigorous system of marks, examinations, disciplines, reports, promotions, awards, heavy emphasis on textbooks, strict distinctions between different subjects, great respect, and absolute obedience to the educators. The later Soviet hierarchy was founded in the echelons of bureaucrats and technocrats educated by this system. This system was introduced to many socialist countries during the 1950s and 1960s but came under attack in China and Cuba as they began to get rid of Soviet influences and tried to mold their own type of new man.

The Models of the Soviet New Man

Model emulation was a major vehicle for transforming human nature and creating the new man. The Soviet regime produced numerous models of the new man, ideological symbols in the flesh, represented by civil war heroes, model workers or labor heroes, exemplary cadres, and scientists who conscientiously worked for the new state.

During the 1920s Soviet newspapers intensively introduced and exalted models of the new man to promote the campaign of emulation. Jeffrey Brooks used obituaries and eulogies in *Pravda*, the party's daily, to demonstrate characteristics of Soviet heroes, which invariably emphasized selflessness and sacrifice, such as this example: "In 1921 a deceased Party member was recalled as a good comrade, 'who never considered himself.'" In the same year, a eulogy for M. P. Ivanitskaia, an official at the Central Executive Committee, read: "During the course of the winter, I tried to convince M.P. to get a reasonable room, since the room she occupied was cold and full of smoke, but she answered: 'The majority of workers live in these conditions; why should I have a good room and not they?'" When Mikhail Frunze, a famous civil war military leader, died in 1925, his fellow Bolshevik leaders wrote, "Comrade Frunze had no personal life but strove with all his force for common socialist ideas," and "his life was torture; he lived only because he believed in the final victory of the working class." The total devotion to the revolutionary cause and self-denial of any kind of personal comfort often led not only to asceticism but to rejection of ordinary family life, as one report of an exemplary woman indicated: "At home, her children and husband await her, but she continues to work. . . . All her strength, despite her weak health, she gives to social work, forgetting the needs of her own 'personal' life and finding her sole satisfaction in work among the family of workers."[68] All of these are reminiscent of Nechaev's description of a revolutionary. To indicate the difference between the new man in the context of the Soviet society and a common "good man" in any other society, the party's propaganda always emphasized that class awareness, political consciousness, and faith in the revolution, rather than a spontaneous impulse of beneficent acts of a good and moral human, were the motivations behind these morally superior acts.

The labor heroes were another type of "new man." The most celebrated one was Alexei Stakhanov, a Donbas miner who significantly exceeded his quota in the summer of 1935 (102 tons of coal, instead of the usual 7 tons, in a single shift, on August 30). Covered in *Pravda*'s sensational reports, Stakhanov's achievement came in the nick of time: Stalin's Five-Year Plans of industrialization were demanding extraordinary productivity. Sergo Ordzhonikidze, the commissar of heavy industry, seized the opportunity to initiate a campaign of emulation and competition, named after the labor hero. "Stakhanovites" later became the title of Soviet labor heroes and pace-setters. A Soviet writer attributed the emergence of such heroes, originally referring to Stakhanov himself, explicitly to the Soviet program for creating the new man: "Yesterday a peasant, a sullen poor peasant, today he is remade in the Bolshevik crucible into an advanced worker, the pride of his class and country—he has become before one's eyes a strong person of tomorrow."[69]

The most influential model of the "Soviet man," however, was Nikolai Ostrovsky, a civil war veteran, and Pavel Korchagin, the fictional hero he created in his autobiographical novel. Ostrovsky joined the Red Army in the civil war when he was a teenager and continued to serve the party in the 1920s and 1930s, mainly fighting antirevolutionaries and *kulak*s in Ukraine. His many wounds resulted in his becoming paralyzed and partially blind when he was still young. Bedridden in his thirties, he decided to write an autobiographical novel to educate the new generations with examples of his own and his comrades' revolutionary devotion. The course of writing the book was another battle in his life, and he sustained himself with the idea that the work would be his last service for communism.

The novel, *That Is How Steel Was Tempered*, was published in 1935, and Pavel Korchagin, its protagonist, became an instant symbol of the Soviet new man. The novel describes the formation and development of a young communist of working-class origins, his childhood, his participation in the civil war, and the subsequent socialist construction era. What makes the pro-tagonist a hero is not just his actions but his frequent contemplations on the actions. The most profoundly moving episodes in the novel are the moments when he ponders the meaning of life as he strives and sacrifices. The theme of the book is just what the title suggests: how to temper a young man from a tender teenager into a tough revolutionary in the crucible of war and revolu-tion. In fact, comparing the battle-hardened revolutionary to iron and steel had been a favorite metaphor in communist literature. For instance, Nikolai Tikhonov, a revolutionary poet during the early years of the civil war, once wrote: "Life taught me with rifle and oar / lashed with wild winds against / my back like knotted cords / Life made me calm and capable / simple—like nails of iron."[70] Many other authors also used the metaphor of iron in describing the new man. Aleksei Gastev, a proletarian poet, in his 1918 poem "We Grow out of Iron" proclaimed the creation of a titanic communist new man fashioned among "workbenches, furnaces, forges" as "fresh iron blood poured into my veins."[71] Vladimir Kirillov, another radical poet of the time, hailed the arrival of "the iron messiah" who was "the savior, the lord of the earth / the master of titanic forces / In the roar of countless steel machines / In the radiance of electric suns."[72] But no one surpassed Ostrovsky in popularizing the metaphor with a life story and exemplary devotion. After his book was published, it topped the lists of the most recommended revolutionary literary works, and the author became a celebrity; even his house became an educational institution for pilgrims.

But there was a behind-the-scenes story unknown at the time the author's fame was at its peak. When Lenin introduced the New Economic Policy in the early 1920s by utilizing some noncommunist methods—such as allowing small private businesses to reappear and peasants to sell their extra products in a free market and encouraging foreign investments to revive the economy—Ostrovsky felt disappointed and even disenchanted with the revolution, at least for a while. He joined sectarian groups in the party that opposed Lenin's compromise, but such activities were subsequently suppressed by the party. Ostrovsky, taking it as part of his historical account, put this experience in the draft of his book, but the censors dropped it to ensure that they had a perfect model of the new man who always toed the party line and drifted to neither right nor left. Later on, as the official historical account was changed to serve Stalin's and his successors' political needs, the novel underwent many revisions with new additions.

The book, known as one of those "red classics" for communists in many countries, had a significant impact on political education in the world communist movement by virtue of being published in multiple languages, with millions of copies in circulation. Fidel Castro included it on the reading list he established during his incarceration (he and his comrades were sentenced to jail briefly after their attack on the Moncada military barracks in 1953) to educate his junior fellow guerrilla soldiers. Chin Peng, the legendary leader of the Malayan communist movement who became the general secretary of the Communist Party of Malaya in his early twenties and led the party until 1989, read the book when he was a student in middle school in the late 1930s and once again in the late 1940s, when he was leading the guerrilla war in the jungles of Malaya. He admitted that his first encounter with the book helped him to establish a revolutionary faith and that revisiting the book deepened his understanding of the revolution.[73] In China some chapters of the book were first translated from its Japanese version in the late 1930s, and the complete Chinese version (translated from English) appeared in 1942. The book was a powerful inspiration for the radical youth who sought to fulfill their lives with political actions. The Chinese version of the book was circulated among overseas Chinese as well, and it was very likely that when Chin Peng (a Chinese) first encountered the book, he read the incomplete version, but the second time he read the complete one. The book's Chinese version, directly translated from Russian, appeared in the early 1950s, with an enormous circulation. Wu Yunduo, one of the most celebrated wartime heroes who was paralyzed by many wounds, wrote an autobiography as his last service to the party in the early 1950s, as Ostrovsky had done in the 1930s. He was subsequently awarded the accolade of "China's Pavel Korchagin" (Wu's story is discussed in chapter 2). Many people who were born in the 1950s and 1960s have claimed that the influence of the book was so deep-seated in their upbringing that its title and the name of the protagonist often arouse a youthful sentiment and nostalgia in them later in life, even though many of them do not think the book's political and ideological implications are still relevant to today's China.

An event related to *That Is How Steel Was Tempered* in China at the turn of the century may reveal the extent of the complicated influence of the Soviet novel. In 1999 a Chinese television group went to Ukraine to shoot a series based on the novel, with all actors and actresses recruited locally. The group was motivated by the rather bizarre combination of a sentiment of nostalgia for a bygone revolutionary era and a desire to achieve a market success by exploiting exotic foreign scenes. The series was shown in 2000 and caused a sensation: large numbers of a new edition of the book were sold even before the show started, and many Chinese newspapers ran special forums and invited readers to discuss the book's significance in history and its value in China's present-day political education.[74] Although the official ideological intent behind the show was apparent and the sensation was also a result of calculated promotion by the media, the response from the public was to a great extent spontaneous. But the discussion also reflected the much more diverse nature of postcommunist Chinese society, as some participants ventured to compare Pavel Korchagin with Bill Gates and asked which one was more admirable and should be regarded as a model for today's Chinese youth. In responding to this confusion, *Zhongguo qingnian bao* (Chinese Youth Daily) and *Beijing qingnian bao* (Beijing Youth Daily), two major official newspapers for Chinese youth, invited readers representing a wide range of occupations and age groups to discuss the comparability of the fictional Soviet man and the real American Microsoft giant. The discussion finally concluded with a compromising tone: "Who the real hero is—Pavel Korchagin or Bill Gates—is not important. What is really important is to deepen our youth's understanding of Pavel Korchagin's spirit and to make their pursuit in their lives nobler through this discussion."[75]

More discordant voices, however, were raised by iconoclastic historians in the wake of the dissolution of the USSR. They questioned the historical credibility of the book, since it was allegedly based on a true historical figure's life experience. They pointed out the numerous revisions at the Stalinist party's hand to create and re-create a fictional hero who always toed the ever-changing official line and whose image always fit the ever-modified official historical account. Jiang Changbin, an international-affairs expert who participated in the retranslation of the book in the 1970s, wrote a widespread online article to dampen the fever. Jiang confessed that when he was first drawn to the book in the early 1950s, "I was naive and ignorant." He said the media promotion of the book made him very apprehensive, and he felt the urge to alert readers about the book's negative implications. Moreover, Jiang argued that the "antirevolutionaries" whom Ostrovsky fought in real life and Korchagin fights in the novel were actually the Ukrainian nationalists. In today's Ukraine they are respected as national heroes and martyrs for the nation's independence from Soviet Russia. Jiang revealed complaints he had received from his Ukrainian friends about the Chinese disregard of their national sentiment associated with that type of history. He also pointed out that much of the "revolutionary dedication" praised in the book was actually a senseless effort to export revolution to Eastern Europe, which in fact undermined Soviet Russia's economy, and that many "*kulaks*" condemned or eliminated in the novel were nothing more than ordinary Russian peasants who were unhappy with Stalin's collectivization. Jiang's criticism of the novel and of the TV series sparked a fresh round of discussion that was more charged with ideological and political overtones.[76]

THE NEW SOVIET WOMAN AND THE SUBLIMATION OF SEXUALITY

While the moral and ideological characteristics of the Soviet new man could in general apply to both male and female, some specific references should be added to highlight the distinctive characteristics in the evolution of the Soviet "new woman." The image of a new Russian woman began to appear in some literary works back in the mid-nineteenth century, such as Chernyshevsky's *What Is To Be Done?* and Turgenev's *On the Eve* (1860). They portray women who are repulsed by the traditional gender roles and bourgeois philistines, while developing a burgeoning idea of freedom and social engagement. In real life, Sofia Perovskaya and her female comrades personified and radicalized this new woman by joining a revolutionary terrorist organization named People's Will, participating in the assassination of the tsar, and being caught and executed in the early 1880s.

Female Bolsheviks, such as Inessa Armand, Alexandra Kollontai, Nadezhda Krupskaia, Konkordiia Samoilova, and Klavdiia Nikolaeva, to name the most famous ones, were inspired by those revolutionary pioneers but emerged as supporters of revolutionary collectivism or class awareness rather than individual heroic impulse. They betrayed their middle- or upper-class backgrounds and devoted themselves to revolution, often with a record of longtime underground life or exile, being sentenced to Siberia and a damaged health. Most of them were Lenin's staunch supporters in the critical time when he was planning a socialist revolution in 1917, while the majority of Bolshevik leaders were doubtful about the chance for its success. After the October Revolution, these women formed a conspicuous female echelon in Bolshevik leadership and were the most aggressive agitators and propagandists for educating and recruiting women on behalf of the regime. At times their rhetoric demonstrated certain feminist tendencies, such as female independence and "free love," as opposed to "bourgeois" sexual relations and family structure based on either class status or money. Kollontai's long article "The New Woman" (1918) and her *Love of Worker Bees* (1923) and *Autobiography of a Sexually Emancipated Communist Woman* (1927) were advocacy or prophecy of a new socially, psychologically, and bodily liberated woman whose personal needs coincided with the "class interest" of working people, as she assumed that the "winged Eros" was "for the benefit of the collective." For her, the postrevolutionary Russia should be an Eden for men and women unfettered from bourgeois and feudal restraints, as she declared, "Live and love. Like bees among the lilac! Like birds deep in the garden! Like grasshoppers in the grass!"[77] She also acknowledged that this type of "new woman" had emerged beyond Soviet Russia, thus revealing her awareness of a broader feminist movement.[78]

The sexual emancipation Kollontai pioneered, both with her writings and her personal life (she married several times and had a number of affairs), was reinforced by the revolution's rejection of traditional mores and, as a result, led to an unleashing of sexual freedom among youth, justified by the "glass of water" theory, meaning that having a sexual affair was just as natural and casual as drinking a glass of water. But this burgeoning sexual revolution, far beyond the feminist development of the time, was denounced by Lenin himself, as he always stayed alert for any "spontaneous" tendency, not just in the political sense. He once complained to Klara Zetkin, a leading female figure in German and European communism of the time, that "because of this 'glass of water theory' our young people have gone out of their minds" and "the so-called 'new sexual life' practiced by the young people and often by adults as well seems to me quite often to be a variation on the good old bourgeois brothel."[79] Eventually the Soviet authority rejected Kollontai's style of indiscriminate selection in one's sexual life and launched antipromiscuity campaigns, especially among university students and young party members. The ideological line regarding sexuality was to replace the "old" bourgeois criterion with a new one, which took the issue not as a personal affair but as part of the class struggle. The revolutionary norms of sexual behavior demanded, "Sexual selection should be based on class, revolutionary-proletarian expediency."[80] As Barbara Evans Clements summarized, the new Soviet woman eventually emerged as "modest, firm, dedicated, sympathetic, courageous, bold, hard-working, energetic, and often young" and "gave no thought to her personal welfare," ready to endure any physical hardship, torture, and sacrifice.[81] For such an utterly devoted person, sexuality as part of individual needs was by and large deemed to be distractive and undesirable.

The official attitude toward promoting sexual sublimation or denial was well reflected in the portrait of the Soviet new woman and new man. As discussed earlier, in his *What Is To Be Done?* Chernyshevsky had rejected love and sexual relationship for the sake of utter devotion. Soviet literature in the 1920s and 1930s inherited this tradition and established a classical antithesis between work and love. In a popular drama, *Leather Man in a Leather Jacket,* for example, the antagonist's only aspiration is to improve efficiency in his work, so much so that he does not discuss love with his young bride. Instead what is discussed in their talks is their working relationship, and to the same extent the wife is a devoted science student who considers love a "mere banality." In another drama, named *Where the Pine Trees Rustle,* a girl is waiting to rendezvous with her boyfriend and wondering why he wants to date her at this time. Suddenly she realizes the only possible explanation: he must anxiously want to tell her about his new production process.

The Gradual Softening of the Soviet New Man

In the history of communism as a state power, a fundamental dilemma is the contradiction and balance between ideological goals and practical needs. In the late 1920s and early 1930s, as Stalin proposed his plan for a rapid industrialization for the survival of the only socialist country within a hostile capitalist world, economic efficiency began to demand more policy preference against ideological purity. One critical question was whether to adopt some approaches and methods appealing to individual incentives, which had proven effective in promoting productivity and creativity under capitalism.

In theory, the selfless new men and women would carry out economic tasks without thinking of material compensation, as that was what they had been created for, but in practice no sensible Soviet leader would blur the distinction between idealism and reality, between a handful of true pioneers and the masses, and between the moments of revolutionary fanaticism and the years of postrevolutionary drudgery. Even Lenin retreated from the earlier War Communism to the New Economic Policy in the early 1920s, allowing private businesses and foreign investments to return to Russia and thereby administering a heavy blow to those naive communists like Ostrovsky.

Therefore, in the entire 1930s, as the slogan "Tempos decide everything!" echoed throughout the Soviet Union, Stalin began to reintroduce the mechanism of social stratification (which had been destroyed by the revolution), mainly by differentiations in material compensation and social status. In a famous speech made in 1931 defending this policy, Stalin denounced "equality mongering" in the wage system and began to encourage differences in compensation—wages, salaries, bonuses, prizes, and other forms of reward, such as housing and vacations—to stimulate individual incentive for production. This policy set in motion a "rigid system of social stratification," as many Sovietologists observed during the cold war years.[82]

One telling example was the material rewards received by the Stakhanovites. One source indicates that the average worker's wage was 150 to 200 rubles a month, plus pension payments of 25 to 50 rubles, while the Stakhanovites earned from 700 to 2,000 rubles a month in 1935, and in 1936 the amount rose as high as 4,000.[83] In addition, Stakhanovites had various privileges. For example, the All-Union Central Trade Union Council granted them priority in the allocation of union-operated vacation homes and resort areas, as well as shopping in special stores where goods normally unseen or in shortage were offered primarily for party and government bureaucrats of certain ranks.

Evidence of growing social stratification was reflected even more in the restoration and institutionalization of ranks and titles to recognize different levels in education, experience, and administration. The state instituted hierarchical systems to identify the different ranks and distinguish the elite in all kinds of professions. For example, for workers there were several levels of wages and benefits based on skills and productivity; in the Red Army, new military titles such as "lieutenant," "captain," "major," "colonel," and "marshal" were introduced. Among the artists, the title "people's artist" not only denoted a political honor but also carried material benefits such as prizes, houses, vacations, or state-sponsored overseas travels. Such policies undoubtedly stimulated production and administrative efficiency and gained support for the regime from the elite. But in essence they were driven by material incentive—a fundamentally noncommunist stimulus—and in reality this led to negation of the egalitarianism the revolution had once promised. As soon as a class of vested interests formed, no matter what the original purpose of the policies that brought it up was, this class would preserve and promote its privileged status. As Trotsky observed in the 1930s after he was expelled from the Soviet Union by Stalin:

> Never has the Soviet Union known such inequality as now. . . . Wages of 100 rubles a month for some and of 800 to 1,000 for others. Some live in barracks and their shoes are worn out; others ride in luxurious cars and live in magnificent apartments. Some struggle to feed themselves and their families; others, besides their cars, have servants, a dacha near Moscow, a villa in the Caucasus, and so on.[84]

The development of social stratification apparently promoted, though rarely officially acknowledged, values contradictory to the morals of the new man. For example, the age-old preference for mental work and prejudice against physical labor were revived. Soviet parents were often caught in a contradiction between a desirable career for their children and a grim reality. As one parent complained, "Many of us are to blame for spoiling our children, asking them when they are still in rompers, 'What do you want to be when you grow up?' and falling into rapture at their answers—an academician, a ballerina, or something else of that sort. And now these same children are called upon to be steel smelters, rolling mill operators, forge hands—dirty, hot, and hard jobs."[85]

This trend continued to develop, especially during the post–World War II years, as Soviet society became more complex, resulting from a profound transformation toward a more modernized and urbanized society. Thus the pursuits and styles of individual life in Soviet society became more diverse and sophisticated, challenging the ideal of the new man, which was still officially promoted by the party but increasingly inconsistent with daily reality.

THE DISCUSSION ON INCENTIVES: A "SOCIALIST COLD WAR" AND ITS FAR-REACHING IMPACT

One conspicuous sign of the social and political changes was an economic discussion on incentives that started in the early 1960s. The debate emerged as an inevitable result of a contradiction in Soviet society: although the economy and technology had become more modernized, efficiency was lagging behind because of a lack of incentives at both enterprise and individual levels. The debate was initiated by E. Liberman, an economist, who published an article in *Pravda* on September 2, 1962, under the title "The Plan, Profits and Bonuses," recommending "the introduction of an incentive system for enterprises with incentive payments based on the degree to which production economies—measured by profitability—actually have been increased."[86] Libermanism, as it was called then and afterward, advocated economic reforms that would apply more market mechanisms, such as independent management and individual incentives, and would further loosen state control (decentralization) and diminish egalitarianism. The reformists who stood behind Liberman were those so-called "men of the sixties," consisting of intellectuals, technicians, and administrators. All economic mechanisms and incentives advocated by Liberman and his like-minded economists were definitely conducive to accelerating production but, in the eyes of orthodox Marxists, would undoubtedly foster and further promote a socioeconomic environment unfavorable to the spirit of the new man.

This discussion stirred sympathetic response from Eastern European countries, whose economic development was more advanced than their counterparts in Asia. Some discussants even raised the bold concept of "market socialism" or "socialist market economy," which the Chinese used in the 1990s to legitimate their economic reforms within socialism and even promoted to the Cubans.[87] The Eastern European reformist communists took advantage of this discussion and further developed it into a discourse that demanded more national independence within the Soviet bloc and more individual freedom within the socialist state. The summit of this reformist wave was the Prague Spring of 1968. In the document elaborating reformist ideology, the Central Committee of the Czechoslovakian Communist Party clarified its position in the debate as follows:

> When attempting today to do away with equalitarianism, to apply the principle of actual achievements in the appraisal of employees we have no intention of forming a new privileged stratum. . . . The principle of actual achievements raises the technical standard, profitability and productivity of labour, respect and authority of the managers responsible, the principle of material incentive, [and] it stresses the growing importance of qualification of all workers.[88]

The committee claimed that what was under attack was not moral incentive, the communist principle for the new man, but "equalitarianism," or egalitarianism:

The harmfulness of equalitarianism lies in the fact that it puts careless workers, idlers and irresponsible people to advantage as compared with the dedicated and diligent workers, the unqualified compared with the qualified, the technically and expertly backward people as compared with the talented and those with initiative.[89]

This reform was interpreted by China and Cuba as a regressive step from communism or even a sign of betrayal, which prompted them to engage in ideological criticism of Soviet-style reformist thinking. In China, Sun Yefang, the director of the Institute of Economics of the Chinese Academy of Sciences, for example, wrote a research report in 1963 emphasizing the importance of interest, cost, and efficiency in management, and criticizing the implications of the rigid Stalinist-Maoist centralized planning system. But he was immediately accused of being a "revisionist," dismissed from his post, and sent to the countryside to be "reeducated" through physical labor.[90] In Cuba the whole leadership was divided into two camps and engaged in a "great debate" on incentives. (This debate and its ideological implications are discussed in detail in chapter 3.)

The debate was also closely watched by people beyond socialist countries but concerned about the relationship between economic development and ideological purity. Peter Clecak, a contemporary Western Marxist sympathetic to the moral incentive stand, dubbed the debate "a socialist cold war."[91] Clecak wrote a lengthy article introducing and analyzing the debate in 1969, in the wake of the Prague Spring, while the Chinese and Cubans continued to respond to the Soviet discussion with their radical anti-material-incentive campaigns in the Cultural Revolution and the Revolutionary Offensive. With the goal of the new man in mind, Clecak instinctively sensed the dilemma the entire world of communism was facing at that moment: "by governing behaviour, incentives directly affect the rate of economic growth, and by governing consciousness, they indirectly accelerate or retard the emergence of socialist man."[92] In the next two chapters, especially the chapter on Cuba, the impact of this debate is further discussed.

The Awakening of the Individuality of the Soviet Youth in the 1960s

All of the above developments prepared the ideological ground for new generations in the Soviet Union to develop ideas and values based on their individuality. One form of evidence that showed the changing profile of the Soviet new generation was the self-portrait reflected in literary works. As Marc Slonim points out:

In the 1960s a surprisingly large number of plays, novels, and stories tried to catch the salient traits of a new generation. Some authors maintained that young Soviet men and women were morally and physically healthy, good workers, and loyal Communists (the best example of this literature was *The Young Leaves,* by Alexander Rekemchuk). Others found their young contemporaries amazingly similar in many ways to their opposite numbers in the capitalist countries (hence the enormous success in Russia of Salinger's *The Catcher in the Rye*). There was a stir, a feeling of discontent among youth, a critical attitude toward society, a growing interest in fresh ideas, an impatient rejection of boring formulas—all of which made them the natural allies of the liberals.[93]

One development that ironically connected Russian youth with the outside world was the annual World Youth Festival, which was sponsored by the Soviet bloc and took place in the capitals of the bloc on a rotating basis in the 1950s. The purpose of the festival was to promote Soviet values and recruit sympathizers among the youth of the noncommunist world, but the participants from all corners of the globe brought with them different and often more colorful lifestyles and a more open attitude toward the world, along with fancier attire and exotic music. The festival actually became an eye-opening experience for many urban young Russians, and they became familiar with or even fascinated by jazz and rock-and-roll music. René Fueloep-Miller, who observed Soviet culture and its new man in the 1920s, lived long enough to comment on the festival's impact on young Russians:

> Ever since the World Youth Festival brought fifteen thousand youths from five continents to the Soviet capital, young Russians have been comparing their regimented life with the less restricted routines of their Western contemporaries. Certain features of Western life caught their fancy immediately, especially jazz, rock 'n roll, and later even the twist. To counter the trend Moiseyer was officially commissioned to introduce a number of new Russian dances based on folk music, but although these dances are full of charm, the younger generation has gravitated toward wilder and jerkier rhythms.[94]

Growing up in this environment, Soviet youth became more restless, and their individuality was awakened, represented often by their preoccupation with sexuality, a subject forbidden or suppressed by the regime for decades. Descriptions of love and relationships between the two sexes became conspicuous in novels and poems, and a group of Leningrad paint-ers exhibited the first nude seen in forty years. The sexless heroes and hero-ines in the literature produced in the 1920s and 1930s were no longer appre-ciated by readers. The awakening individuality was substantially reflected among poets. For many of them, the laureate of "engineers of the human soul"—a Stalinist phrase for Soviet writers and educators—was too heavy to carry. They instead desired a more individually oriented career and therefore advocated "art for art's sake" in expressing themselves. Yevgeny Yevtushenko, the most popular avant-garde poet of the time, defined his supposedly sacred post in a rather frivolous tone: "I make my career by trying not to make one." He also approved of a personality more sophisticated and self-centered than the simple and determined image of the new man: "I am diverse, I am hardworking and idle / I am purposeful and unpurposeful." Another poet, V. Tysbin, proclaimed, "'I' is equivalent to 'we,' or one can even say that 'I' can be more than 'we.'" It would not be an exaggeration to say that by the mid-1960s the "spontaneity," condemned by Lenin at the beginning of the century and believed to have been replaced by "consciousness" with system-atic and tremendous efforts after the revolution, had returned with tenacity and resilience.

Seeming to illustrate the extent that the would-be "Soviet new man" had gone astray in reality was an event in the mid-1960s that stunned the world. Svetlana Alliluyeva, the daughter of Stalin, defected to the United States in March 1966. On a trip accompanying the ashes of her husband (a disillusioned Indian communist who spent many years in the Soviet Union) back to India, she sought asylum at the US embassy. Upon arriving in Amer-ica, she made speeches and published two books (*Twenty Letters to a Friend* and *Only One Year*) attacking the Soviet regime, her father, and others still in power, for crimes committed in the 1930s. Despite being born in 1924 and having been brought up by her family (most relatives on her mother's side were dedicated Bolsheviks as well), Alliluyeva had emerged not as a selfless and sexless new Soviet woman but as a self-centered young lady who had pursued her own happiness and for that had come to a collision course with her father long before her defection. Instead of being tempered into a piece of steel, she came out as a piece of slag, and her betrayal was a heavy blow to the myth of the new man that had become part of the Soviet image. Although her books revealed that her father's tyrannical behavior on private occasions had contributed to her rebellious spirit, her more general observation of the Soviet system and the people supposedly personifying the heralded values of such a system played a more important role in her decision to defect.

Notwithstanding all of the above trends that had undermined the ground on which the Soviet man stood, the official propaganda never changed or toned down its "new man" rhetoric. At exactly the same time as the awakening of the sense of individuality among Soviet youth, the official "new man" rhetoric was suddenly articulated in a high pitch in the Soviet media. On April 12, 1961, the Soviet Union astonished the world by sending a spacecraft into orbit around the earth. This scientific marvel provided *the regime with a new drive for its new man propaganda.* Yurii Gagarin, the astronaut, was celebrated as a model of the Soviet man, conquering outer space. As Soviet media quickly pointed out, "the Soviet cosmonaut is not merely a victor of outer space, not merely a hero of science and technology, but first and foremost he is a real, living, flesh-and-blood *new man,* who demonstrates in action all the invaluable qualities of the Soviet character, which Lenin's Party has been cultivating for decades."[95] According to Slava Gerovitch, the "political project of creating the public image of the aviator as a new Soviet man" began as early as the 1930s and was promoted by Stalin himself, when the Soviet popular culture was filled with "man-machine" metaphors. On the surface, the "man" controlled the "machine," to show the power, strength, and intelligence of the new Soviet man. But in reality the Soviet system often made the operation as automatic as possible, so much so that the human factor was in general regarded as a backup and pilots jokingly summarized the content of the spacecraft manual in four words: "Do not touch anything!" Some cosmonauts labeled this tendency "the domination of automata" and attributed it to the "general ideological attitude toward the individual as an insignificant cog in the wheel."[96]

POSTSCRIPT

The concept of the new man, or the idea of remaking people, together with a belief in human malleability facilitated by environmental determinism, originated in the Enlightenment and was first tested in the French Revolution. During the nineteenth century, Marxism and especially the Russian radical intelligentsia further developed this idea with more specific ideological and moral attributes. At the turn of the twentieth century, Lenin conceptualized the idea and shifted its emphasis from creating revolutionary vanguards to educating the masses; he also stressed the necessity of using "consciousness" to replace "spontaneity." The Russian Revolution allowed the first nationwide experiment of remolding people; the institutions and methods introduced for that purpose were inherited by socialist countries established later. But as the Soviet Union was modernized and urbanized, the development of state bureaucracy and technocracy became the backbone of Soviet society. Along with this social change was a gradual replacement of moral incentive, collective interest, and revolutionary consciousness by material incentive, individual interest, and awareness of individuality. This change occurred as one example of a modern society compromising its ideological goal for economic and social development, but it was criticized by some fellow socialist societies as a betrayal. History thus paved the way for the new man to reemerge in China and Cuba.

Two

"Be Mao's Good Soldiers"
Creating the New Man in China

As the second most influential communist revolution in the twentieth century, the Chinese Revolution promoted its own type of new man. The Chinese new man had some features in common with the Soviet man, the prototype of the communist new man, but it also had distinctive traits, derived from China's cultural tradition but more so from its unique revolutionary experience. The notion of an ideal human arose as early as the 1910s in China, when some intellectuals advocated a fundamental change in the "national character" entailed by modernization. The nationalistic nature of this new man was overshadowed by a communist one as the communist movement rose to dominate China's political life. The Yan'an Rectification (in the first half of the 1940s) was the first attempt to reshape people's minds and character on a large scale through intensive and often forceful thought reform. After the communist victory on the mainland, the Chinese embarked on nationwide social engineering in the hope of remolding the whole country, especially during the Great Leap Forward (the late 1950s) and the Cultural Revolution (the mid-1960s to the mid-1970s). Since Mao's ideas and personal preferences dominated China's political culture, and Mao himself was the most important figure behind this social engineering, the image of the Chinese new man, to a great extent, reflected Mao's perception of the ideal human.

THE CONFUCIAN PERSPECTIVE ON HUMAN NATURE AND ITS INFLUENCE

Chinese communism's ideas and practices regarding the new man were influenced by Marxism and the Soviet Union. But immersed in a civilization known for its philosophical and humanistic tradition, the Chinese communists also drew inspiration from their cultural heritage.

The traditional Chinese political philosophy placed virtue above wisdom as the most important trait for good rulers and believed in the power of moral emulation. Behind such a cultural tradition was an assumption of the malleability of human nature. The legends about Yao, Shun, and Yu—

48

the three most respected sage-kings (around the twenty-third and twenty-second centuries BCE), who ruled with benevolence and diligence—are examples. The Confucian ideas of *ren* (benevolence), *li* (sense of propriety), and *xiao* (filial piety) were all exalted moral qualities embodied by *jun zi*, an ideal moral person. Political ideology, government, and moral education all come together for Confucius: if *jun zi* with *ren*, *li*, and *xiao* were cultivated through education and incorporated in government, then the ordinary people would follow their examples. Therefore, moral education and emulation were essential in establishing a good society. As he put it: "When those who are in high positions perform well all their duties to their relations, the people are aroused to virtue."[1] *Great Learning,* one of the Four Classics of Confucianism, states: "When the ruler, as a father, a son, and a brother, is a good model, then the people imitate him." Throughout Chinese history, becoming a *jun zi* was expected of intellectuals and administrators. In addition, there were numerous moral models not as perfect as *jun zi* but prominent in specific areas associated with their respective social duties or family obligations, such as incorruptible officials, filial sons, widows remaining faithful to their deceased husbands while looking after their heirs, and so on. The methods for promoting such a model emulation varied from the building of temples, monuments, and archways to calligraphic inscriptions written by emperors or high-ranking officials in honor of the models.

Some Confucian theorists even raised the question of reshaping human nature with enforced measures. Xunzi, one of the prominent Confucians who was also under legalist influence and lived in the era of the Warring States (403–201 BCE), likened human nature to warped lumber. In order to straighten out such lumber for appropriate use, it was necessary for carpenters to apply heat, steam, hammering, bending, and other methods. Xunzi believed that human nature, self-centered and recalcitrant, was just like such crooked lumber, and that rulers should use harsh measures to straighten out these human materials.[2]

Another cultural element that influenced the practice of making the communist new man in China was the belief that intensive study of classical texts could internalize Confucian values and thus could have enormous effects on people's moral and spiritual transformation. Neo-Confucianism, a Confucian response to the increased influence of Daoism and especially Buddhism in the Song dynasty (960–1279 CE), is an example. It identified Confucianism with "moral principles of the universe" and claimed that intensive study of Confucian texts and profound meditation, accompanied by comparing the sage's words with one's own thoughts and conduct, would bring about self-purification. For neo-Confucians, life was an endless journey of self-reform in which the individual moved toward the goal of being a *sheng ren,* a saint morally superior to a *jun zi.* In a way this process resembled the Zen Buddhist approach toward "enlightenment." Wang Yangming, a prominent neo-Confucian of the Song dynasty, was an example of such self-perfection. Before he died, he felt that, after a lifelong struggle against all undesirable thoughts, his mind and soul were so pure that, "There is nothing left in my mind but a holy emptiness." Many centuries later, in the Yan'an Rectification, Xie Juezai, a senior communist leader with a sound Confucian education, recounted this story in association with his experience of constant self-reform.[3] The communists used this story to illustrate the necessity of constantly reforming themselves even until the last moment of their lives.

All of these traditional elements—the belief in human malleability, the practice of model emulation, and the belief in the effects of study of texts—can be clearly seen in Chinese communist efforts to reshape human nature in identical or modified manifestations.

THE EARLY EXPECTATION FOR THE NEW MAN

As had been true in Russia, in China the expectation and conceptualization of the new man emerged with the formation of a politically alienated intelligentsia. But in China the intelligentsia was especially frustrated by the nation's failures in modernization and protection of itself in the face of foreign powers. Therefore the original profile of the new man in the Chinese context was more associated with nationalism, rather than socialism or Enlightenment ideas.

From 1840 to the early 1900s, China was humiliated in wars with the West and Japan, and was forced to make concessions and accept imperialist spheres of influence and Western cultural and religious penetration resulting from numerous unequal treaties. The sense of a crisis of national disintegration naturally questioned Confucianism's relevance in modern times. The experimentation with Western economic and political systems in the Self-Strengthening Movement (1860s–1890s) and the One-Hundred-Day Reform (1899) did not bring China any efficient and endurable result in modernization into the early twentieth century. Many Chinese intellectuals thus turned to Japan and Germany, seeking experience of backward nations catching up with world powers. For them, the German and Japanese successes in achieving "rich nation, strong army" were admirable, not only because those countries had transformed their economic and political systems but also because they had embarked on reforms to change citizens' attitudes and psychology. Some Chinese intellectuals were also influenced by social Darwinism and saw their own civilization as outdated and "moribund" in the world of "the survival of the fittest." From this perspective, they began to blame China's "national character" for the failure of modernization. In general, the "national character" included but was not limited to characteristics such as political indifference, succumbing to fate with resignation, a slavish attitude toward authority, lack of individual initiative, and resistance to social change. As a result, the intellectuals shifted their attention from political and economic reforms to cultural regeneration or moral redemption, aiming at remolding people's minds as the premise for national revival. With that change began the conception of the new man.

Liang Qichao, a leading intellectual at the turn of the twentieth century, was probably the first to raise the question of creating a new national character. Liang was an admirer of Meiji Japan's enlightened intellectuals such as Fukuzawa, who thought the key to Japan's modernization was to "elevate the moral standards of men and women of my land to make them truly worthy of a civilized nation."[4] As Philip Huang points out, Liang drew the same conclusions for his own country: "China must develop a new kind of individual Chinese in order to modernize."[5] In 1902 and 1903 Liang coined the term *xin min,* literally meaning "new people" (as Joseph Levenson translated it) or "new citizens" (as Philip Huang translated it), to refer to the type of Chinese who would carry out the task of national redemption. Liang founded a periodical called *Xin min cong bao* (Journal of New People) and published "Xin min shuo" (On the New People) and "Xin min yi" (Essence of the New People). He not only coined and popularized the term but also put together some characteristics for such a *xin min,* including a strong sense of nationalism and patriotism, a spirit of adventure, awareness of personal rights and freedom, a sense of autonomy, self-esteem, the ability to form a cohesive community, persistence, a sense of responsibility, a militaristic mentality, a public ethic, and a private morality.

All of these incipient ideas about the new man were further developed in the New Culture Movement, founded in the mid-1910s when the slogan "Down with Confucianism" echoed among intellectuals and urban youth and the term "new man" began to enter Chinese social and political discussions. In 1915 Chen Duxiu, a leading intellectual and founder of the Chinese Communist Party, inaugurated a periodical entitled *Xin qing nian* (New Youth). Along with the influential *New Youth,* other reputable periodicals in the New Culture Movement also bore names clearly indicating their expectation of a moral and spiritual transformation of the Chinese people, such as *Xin fu nu* (New Woman) and *Shao nian zhong guo* (Juvenile China).

In an article entitled "New Youth" (September 1916), Chen advocated a "spiritual revolution" for Chinese youth. He profiled "old" Chinese youth as physically weakened by the burden of Confucian studies and spiritually bound by outdated traditions.[6] Li Dazhao, Chen's contemporary and also a leading figure in the New Culture Movement and a cofounder of the Chinese Communist Party, called for a campaign to create a "young China." According to Li, the ideal "young China" would be a country accomplishing both physical and spiritual renovation and achieving a real harmony between people's souls and flesh.[7] The New Culture Movement intelligentsia also appreciated Nietzsche's idea of "superman"—disregarding the implications of the promotion of this ideal person in the German-European social and cultural context, the intelligentsia believed that an assertive, ambitious Chinese character aware of the mission to revive the nation was preferable to the old-fashioned, submissive, and humble character soaked with Confucian ideas. Li Dazhao, for example, introduced Nietzsche and maintained that his "superman" was an ideal model for the new Chinese youth's self-remolding.

As a young man obsessed with national and social crisis, Mao was deeply influenced by all of these ideas and had his own vision of the new Chinese. As early as 1917, Mao had come to the conclusion that a spiritual revolution was the most urgent task for reconstructing society. In his words, this task consisted of "reforming philosophy, reforming ethics, and fundamentally changing people's thought."[8] He attributed German success in becoming a world power to Hegelian and Kantian philosophies—"the highest" spirit for a nation. Had China such new philosophy to remold people's thought, it would become a strong nation as well. Mao developed a vague notion of "cosmic truth"—a spiritual entity from which the universe had originated and that dominated the natural world and human society—as the core concept of the new philosophy for the new Chinese.[9] He combined his "cosmic truth" with Nietzsche's "superman" and divided people into three categories, according to their understanding of the "cosmic truth": saints, sages, and unwashed (or petty men). As he put it: "The saints have completely mastered the cosmic truth, and sages have learnt a great deal of that truth, while the unwashed are totally unaware of that truth."[10] "The unwashed" not only included all physical workers but also applied to people engaged in religious, legal, and political occupations, as long as they were not aware of Mao's "universal truth" and thus had no meaning in their lives. For Mao, although they were as busy as ants, their labor did nothing to uplift them or society. Therefore the mission of saints and sages was to lead, educate, and transform the unwashed.

The years immediately before and after the May Fourth Movement witnessed a phenomenon similar to what had happened in Russia decades earlier: the emergence of numerous organizations (societies, study groups, and clubs) of intellectuals and students who intentionally disciplined themselves with revolutionary ideologies and attempted to reach ordinary people for their enlightenment. As with the periodicals founded in the New Culture Movement, the names of many such organizations—Xin min xue hui (New People's Study Society), Shao nian zhong guo (Juvenile China), Shao nian zhong guo xue hui (Young China Society), Xin fu ne (New Woman), Xin ren xue she (New Man Society)—explicitly indicated their purpose: creating a new type of Chinese.

Among these organizations, the New People's Study Society—founded in April 1918 by Mao Zedong and Cai Hesen in Changsha, Hunan Province—is the most famous. With most members being students inspired by the ideas of the New Culture Movement, its main characteristics were collective study, strict discipline, and a sense of historical mission. As Jane L. Price points out, "The society's concern with collective discussion and criticism, group discipline, and character development foreshadowed later Chinese Communist organizational trends."[11] In the society, Mao and his friends intentionally hardened themselves through Spartan methods such as "living in the mountains on a minimum of food, sleeping in the open, bathing in cold streams in November, [and] going shirtless and shoeless." They also took long excursions to see the country.[12] All of this was reminiscent of the heroes in Chernyshevsky's *What Is To Be Done?* who imposed strict discipline and toughened themselves under harsh circumstances to prepare for their historical mission.

These young intellectuals were also inspired to educate the masses and launched a movement called Going to the People (or Going to the Villages). Li Dazhao introduced the 1870s–1880s Russian movement of the same name as an example of young, educated people going to the countryside and enlightening the peasants while tempering themselves. For example, in March 1919 a group of radical students at Beijing University organized the Mass Education Speech Corps, aiming "to enrich their knowledge about the working people and awaken their consciousness." The corps first established its lecture halls in working-class districts in Beijing and then extended its activities to the villages in the city's vicinity. After the May Fourth Movement, its example was emulated in other parts of China. This campaign set a precedent for political movements that decades later would dominate communist China's educational project for urban youth, especially during the Cultural Revolution. The integration of urban youth with peasants and workers through working together was taken as the most important and effective way to reshape educated youth ideologically and morally.

All of the above ideas, organizations, and activities clearly show that in the first two decades of the twentieth century, as a response to a social and national crisis, many Chinese intellectuals believed that the old "national character" was impeding China's modernization and that a transformation of the people was more critical than changes in economic or political systems. This was the very bud of the development of a Chinese new man.

But the profile of the new man was not well defined in political terms at that stage. In general, the individual's responsibility to society and obligation to the nation were the foundations for the sense of historical mission, enmeshed with the quest for individual freedom and development. Most publications, organizations, and activities promoting the idea of the new man were spontaneous responses to the national crisis by individuals and groups who were loosely connected to each other under that peculiar circumstance, without a cogent ideological proposition or an effective organizational network. These circumstances began to change in the mid-1920s. As the Communist Party emerged as one of the two most influential political parties (along with the Nationalist Party), communist ideology began to prevail among young radicals. With the development of the Chinese communist movement, the question of creating a new man gradually changed from a vaguely defined task of reshaping the national character by voluntary commitment—as intellectuals such as Liang Qichao, Chen Duxiu, Li Dazhao, and the young Mao had proposed from a philosophical perspective and as many students exercised in small groups—to training communist cadres and fighters under the well-defined ideological guideline imposed by a Leninist party.

But unlike that in Russia, Chinese society did not have a developed and organized working class in which the communists could inculcate revolutionary ideology. In addition, Chinese workers in urban centers were subject to influences reflecting a diverse society: secret organizations, gangs, pledged or sworn brotherhoods or sisterhoods, associations based on common provincial or prefecture origins, and a variety of religious beliefs. In such a society, during the first years after its establishment in 1921, the party—holding to Marxist ideology and insisting on political consciousness as the only criteria for recruiting members—was able to recruit members and establish cells only among the radical intellectuals. It could not approach the masses, nor could it exert influence on national politics. For Lenin the answer to the question "What is to be done?" was to train and organize the revolutionary vanguard, to inculcate Marxism into the working class by members of a revolutionary elite, and to replace "spontaneity" with political consciousness. In China, however, the issue was whether the party should modify its recruitment criteria to accommodate a more diverse society and thereby enhance its competitiveness.

Therefore, as Hans J. van de Ven stressed in his study of the development of the Chinese Communist Party in the 1920s, many party leaders were keenly aware of their weakness in competing with other political forces and demanded a change in the party's line. As one participant in the party's Third Congress (1923) put it:

> We cannot have any illusions about the idea that we can locate many ready-made party members in Chinese society. . . . At this point, the great majority of local party functionaries are the victims of an erroneous concept. They believe that each party member must understand Marxism, that he must have a high level of capability, and that not developing the quality of the membership but developing only its numbers is not only without benefit but also causes the party organization to become even more loose. . . . This erroneous concept is a hindrance to the transformation of the party into a mass party.[13]

As a result of its demand, the party decided to adopt a policy of uniting with the Nationalists to take advantage of its mass foundation in order to recruit members beyond the intellectuals. It is possible that these new recruits were largely appreciated for their political activism rather than their ideological maturity. The change brought about a significant growth in numbers of the party's membership: from less than 1,000 before 1924 to 10,000 in the beginning of 1926. In the next one and a half years, as the party joined the Northern Expedition (aimed at uniting China, eliminating the warlords, and abolishing unequal treaties with foreign powers) with Nationalists, its membership rose to 57,967 by April 1927.[14]

In the course of transforming the party from an intellectual clique into a mass party, the ideological prerequisites for communists undoubtedly had to be compromised to some extent, in light of the party's recruitment and influence. In the following decade (1927–1937), the historical situation completely changed. The communists broke with the Nationalists and fought a civil war for ten years. Although the party established many academies and short-term educational programs to train cadres and functionaries, long-term ideological education quite often had to be subordinated to immediate political and military needs. Thus, as in the earlier years, the communists were unable to establish a systematic and comprehensive training program to educate and discipline party members. Such development had to await the coming of the Yan'an period.

MAO ZEDONG AND LIU SHAOQI'S CONCEPTS OF HUMAN NATURE

Just as the perceptions of human nature as defined by Lenin, Stalin, and other Bolshevik leaders guided the new man project in the Soviet Union, so did the ideas of Mao and other Chinese communist leaders guide the creation of the Chinese new man.

Throughout his political career, Mao never limited his role to leader of the party and state; he aspired to be a moral mentor of the whole nation as well. As his personal cult culminated in the Cultural Revolution, he dismissed such titles as "great leader," "great helmsman," and "great supreme commander." Rather, as he told Edgar Snow in the early 1960s, "only the word 'teacher' would be retained—that is, simply school teacher."[15] Superficially it sounded like a modest self-description, in contrast to those grandiose titles. But in the Chinese traditional cultural context, the teacher embodied Confucian values and enjoyed high respect as the purveyor and distributor of norms.

As a self-appointed national teacher, Mao's concept of human nature was typified by his statement derived from Marxism: "Is there such a thing as human nature? Of course there is. But there is only human nature in the concrete, no human nature in the abstract. In a class society there is only human nature that bears the stamp of a class; human nature that transcends classes does not exist."[16]

Liu Shaoqi, who ascended to the CCP's leadership to become second only to Mao in the early 1940s, had great influence on the party's ideological education and organizational development from the 1940s until the mid-1960s. Liu's views on human nature and accordingly his thoughts about the necessity of thought reform were also part of the theoretical foundation of the new man project in China, especially before the Cultural Revolution.

In an article entitled "On People's Class Nature," published in 1942, Liu divided human nature into two parts: social and natural, a dichotomy that shows the influence of Confucianism, which separated the social from the animal dimension in human nature. Social nature included "psychology, thought, consciousness, opinion, habits and so forth." In societies with class distinctions, all people were divided into different classes, and accordingly their social nature was determined by their class status.[17] Liu illustrated the correlation between people's class status and social nature in a rather mechanical manner. For example, peasants relied upon their small piece of privately owned land and lived in traditional villages; therefore they were politically conservative, and their visions were parochial, always looking backward and lacking in cooperative spirit. But on the other hand they were also able to stand up against exploitation and to demand political equality, if they faced excessive exploitation and abuse. Proletarians, in contrast, possessed nothing and had to work together; they were more radical, understanding the importance of cooperation and discipline by virtue of modern industry. The communist consciousness, according to Liu and derived from Marx, was the understanding of and belief in the historical mission of the proletariat. The same sociopolitical analysis, based on a mechanically understood historical materialism, led Liu to attribute all negative moral features to exploitative classes. Because they possessed everything but did not have to work, Liu argued, luxuriousness, laziness, brutality, a sense of hierarchy, competition (in order to gain maximum profits and eliminate rivals, not for the sake of productivity), and monopoly thus typified the behaviors and mentality of feudal landlords and the bourgeoisie.

The emphasis on class labels, however, constituted only one side of the Chinese communist leader's view of human nature. If everything in human nature was so mechanically determined by class status and therefore unchangeable, then the question of education and reeducation would not exist at all. On the contrary, Mao, Liu, and other leaders believed in human malleability and held that human nature—or human thought, more specifically—was at the mercy of the social environment. It was possible that people of working-class origin could be contaminated by bourgeois ideas and habits, and conversely, people with a bourgeois or petit bourgeois background could be rehabilitated through education, often combined with heavy physical labor. Physical labor, which was regarded as characteristic of a lifestyle belonging solely to workers and peasants, would have a mystical quality in redeeming people of nonproletarian origin. For the communists, therefore, class origin was just a reference for constant education and reeducation, either for cleaning up all deep-rooted bourgeois ideology or for further uplifting oneself.

Liu's best-known pamphlet, entitled *How to Be a Good Communist*, written in the early 1940s, emphasized the importance of never-ending self-reform, an issue often neglected by many communists who had thought they were already "communists." Liu examined a number of ideological and political problems existing among Chinese communists, signs that the revolutionaries were not pure. Even if some communists did not have these problems, they would still be faced with new problems emerging in new situations as the revolution progressed. He concluded: "Therefore people should realize the necessity of self-reform and see themselves as reformable. They should not assume themselves as unchangeable, perfect, saintlike, and thus needing no more reform. This is not meant to insult them but to recognize the inevitability of the progress of nature and society. Otherwise, people could not achieve progress."[18]

It is noticeable that in this pamphlet Liu reinforces his argument about the necessity of self-reform by referring to Confucius' and Mencius' experiences in purposeful and constant self-cultivation. Liu points out that, as great as Confucius and Mencius were, they still keenly felt it necessary to self-reform.[19] Liu's argument clearly shows the cultural connection between Confucianism and Chinese communist ideology regarding ideological education and personality cultivation.

In the final analysis, for Liu, history was a course of shaping and reshaping people's class character and, accordingly, their social natures. Proletariats and communists were no exception. He envisaged the ultimate stage of human reshaping: "In the period of reform in future socialist society, a period from socialism to communism, proletariats constantly reconstruct the society and constantly reshape human nature. In the meantime they constantly reshape their own nature and character. When communist society comes, the class distinctions among people will be eliminated, and so will their class character. This is the entire course of reforming human nature."[20]

Mao discussed the issue of self-reform often with a more anti-intellectual and populist tone, instead of emphasizing abstract notions such as "class nature" or "class consciousness." In 1942, he addressed a group of men of letters and artists from urban areas with largely a petit bourgeois background who had come to Yan'an (the main revolutionary base from 1936 to 1947) in search of a revolutionary career. In speaking to them, Mao used his own experience of changing his attitude toward working people as an example of self-education and asked them to wholeheartedly embrace reeducation through integration with peasants and workers:

> Here I might mention the experience of how my own feelings changed. I began life as a student, and at school I acquired the ways of being a student; I then used to feel undignified to do even a little manual labor. . . . At that time I felt that intellectuals were the only clean people in the world, while in comparison workers and peasants were dirty. I did not mind wearing the clothes of other intellectuals, believing them to be clean, but I would not put on clothes belonging to a worker or peasant, because they were dirty. But after I became a revolutionary and lived with workers and peasants and with soldiers of the revolutionary army, I gradually came to know them well, and they gradually came to know me well too. It was then, and only then, that I fundamentally changed the bourgeois and petit bourgeois feelings embedded in me since the bourgeois-school years. I came to understand that, in comparison with the workers and peasants, the intellectuals were unclean. In the last analysis, the workers and peasants are the cleanest people, and even though their hands are soiled and their feet smeared with cow dung, they are really cleaner than the bourgeois and petit bourgeois intellectuals. That is what is meant by a change in feelings, a change from one class to another.[21]

For Mao, Liu, and their associates, it was not only that people who had already joined the revolution could be made purer by self-reform but also that those who had once opposed the revolution could possibly be rehabilitated through remolding. One example of such human malleability was the rehabilitation of some captured Nationalist generals and of Pu Yi, the last emperor of the Qing dynasty and later the emperor of Manchukuo (Japan's puppet state in northeastern China from 1933 to 1945). They were incarcerated as war criminals after 1949. Although people like them might have been considered incorrigible criminals and sent to the firing squad in other socialist countries, in China they were treated differently. While hundreds and thousands of their low-ranking subordinates were indeed sent to a firing squad, these underwent a long course of thought reform, consisting of intensive ideological study, confession, self-criticism, and physical labor (growing vegetables and raising poultry for themselves, for example). Many of them, the last emperor included, were considered rehabilitated and set free in early 1960s. They were subsequently granted various official titles—representative of the Chinese People's Political Consultative Conference, for example—and became the showcase of the miraculous power of "reeducation" and change of human nature by Mao and the Communist Party.

Many authors of studies on Chinese communism have pointed out this unbounded belief in human malleability. For example, R. F. Price wrote many years ago, "Mao regards man as a product of his social class, with his ideas and habits strongly determined by his origin. But at the same time he appears to have an almost infinite belief in man's ability to rise above these limitations."[22] Recently another author pointed out: "The utopian character of Marxism-Leninism–Mao Zedong Thought implies that the ideology has an 'unconstrained vision' of human nature and human potential. Men and women are believed to be perfectible, particularly in regards to their moral perfectibility. In contrast, for example, to classical liberalism's conviction that human beings are inherently both good and bad, the Chinese Communists believe instead that moral improvement has no fixed limit."[23]

THE YAN'AN PERIOD: BEGINNING THE SYSTEMATIC REMOLDING OF HUMAN MINDS

In the mid-1930s, the communists survived their "Long March" and established some solid bases in northwestern China, centered in Yan'an, a remote and isolated mountainous area. It was in Yan'an that Mao established and consolidated his absolute authority over the party and "Mao Zedong's thought," which was said to be the integration of Marxism and the concrete reality of the Chinese revolution, was accepted as the party's ideology. Meanwhile, the war against Japanese invasion forced the Nationalists to form a united front with the communists. Therefore, ironically, in the second half of the 1930s and first half of 1940s, despite the country's being at war with the Japanese, the communists had a relatively safe and stable political and military position that enabled them to focus on their internal affairs.

Thus the Yan'an period was important in the development of Chinese communism, especially in terms of discipline, education, and organization. Having lost many veterans before and during the Long March, the communists found new sources for recruitment among urban youth, students, and intellectuals. These people felt alienated from the Nationalist government, doubting its resolve in resistance against Japan's invasion and its sincerity in the commitment to democracy. In reality, many of them were drawn in by the communists' propaganda that portrayed them as the saviors of the nation and promised democratic and liberal reforms. As a result, hundreds of thousands of students, teachers, artists, writers, and journalists poured into Yan'an, seeking a revolutionary career. In Marxist classification these new recruits were of petit bourgeois origin. Their enthusiasm and various sorts of expertise were useful for the revolution, but only after they had undergone a thorough political reeducation and ideological reform. Even when it came to those cadres who had survived the Long March and proven their revolutionary credibility, the party and Mao still felt the urge to reeducate them with the newly established "Mao Zedong's thought" and make sure they would be highly compliant with the new leadership and the new party ideology. In terms of party politics, Mao was worried about his newly established authority. Before he ascended to the top of the CCP leadership, the party had had a number of leaders who rose and fell; and he knew that Moscow, as the big brother of world communism, was more in favor of those who had stayed in Russia and was suspicious of those who had never made a pilgrimage to Moscow. To secure his power, Mao sought help in the traditional Chinese political and cultural context: a political authority buttressed by ethical and moral discourse.

For all of these reasons, from the early 1940s, Yan'an was turned into a closed "community of discourse," as David E. Apter points out, where political discussion and ideological education, guided by Mao's thought, bombarded everyone, day in and day out.[24] The result was a thoroughgoing thought reform and character-rebuilding campaign, which ultimately reshaped the party and prepared for victory in the civil war following the war against the Japanese.

Educational Institutions

The communists established numerous schools, formulating a new type of educational system. Among them were the Anti-Japanese Military and Political University, the Lu Xun Academy of the Arts, the Northwest Public School, the Central Party School, the Academy of Marxism-Leninism, the Women's University, Yan'an University, and the Academy of the Nationality, plus many special training programs and some vocational schools such as the School of New Characters. All veterans and new recruits had to be enrolled and educated in one of these institutions in accordance with their previous training or their expertise, before they could be trusted with assignment to party and government positions. The party circulated twenty-four documents as core curriculum in all of these schools, including Mao's "Reform Our Study," Liu's *How to Be a Good Communist,* and Chen Yun's *How to Be a Communist Party Member.* In addition to these educational institutions, the party established study groups in every party and government unit, so that those not enrolled in those schools could study these documents. The participants were asked to study them with religious piety. As a participant recalled:

> The documents and materials of the Rectification are plain in words but profound in implications. At first when you read them you thought you understood them all, but actually you did not. Once you read them again, you would find questions. These questions would lead you to read more and think more. The more you read and thought, the more you acquired the profound meaning. Reading one more time would give you a new feeling; thinking one more time would lead you to a new harvest.[25]

The densely concentrated educational institutions, the intensive ideological studies, the lectures and discussions, criticisms and self-criticisms—all of these created an overwhelmingly pedagogical and redemptive atmosphere that made Yan'an a "discourse community . . . like the ancient Greek Agora."[26] Virtually every practical matter could be dealt with through theoretical explanations and instructions, from the nature of Chinese society—past and present—to how to improve the use of the hoe in farming. In other words, Mao's thought provided guidelines for every abstract and practical matter.

Mao's Discourse of Model Emulation

In a speech made for the founding of a party academy, Mao envisaged the kind of people the party needed:

> We must educate a lot of people—the kind of people who are the vanguard of the revolution, who have political farsightedness, who are prepared for

battle and sacrifice, who are frank, loyal, positive and upright; the kind of people who seek no self-interest, but only national and social emancipation and forwardness in the face of hardships; the kind of people who are neither undisciplined nor fond of limelight, but practical, with their feet firmly on the ground. If China possesses many men like this, the tasks of the Chinese revolution can easily be fulfilled.[27]

Mao wrote three short essays to elaborate desirable revolutionary virtues, and each essay exalted an individual who embodied these virtues. The first article was entitled "In Memory of Norman Bethune" (1939). Bethune, a member of the Canadian Communist Party and a doctor, had come to China in 1938 in response to the call for supporting the Chinese against the Japanese invasion. He served the communist army with his medical expertise and died from infection while operating on wounded soldiers. The essay was a eulogy for him, in which Mao said:

> Comrade Bethune's spirit, his utter devotion to others without any thought of self, was shown in his great sense of responsibility in his work and his warm-heartedness towards all comrades and the people. Every communist must learn from him. . . . A man's ability may be great or small, but if he has this spirit, he is already noble and pure, a man of moral integrity and above vulgar interests, a man who is of value to the people.[28]

The second essay, "Serve the People," was a eulogy for Zhang Side, a member of the Guards Regiment of the Central Committee who was killed in 1944 by the collapse of a charcoal kiln in which he was working. In this essay Mao put more emphasis on sacrifice: "A man must die, but death can vary in its significance. The ancient Chinese writer Sima Qian said: 'Though death befalls all men alike, it may be weightier than Mount Tai or lighter than a feather.' To die for the people is weightier than Mount Tai."[29] The phrase "Serve the people" later became the most popular epithet characteristic of communist ethics in China. During the Cultural Revolution, in which Mao's moral teachings became everyday sermons for people, even Zhou Enlai, the premier of the People's Republic of China, pinned a little red badge on his chest inscribed with "Serving the People" to show his adherence to Mao's preaching.

The third essay, entitled "The Foolish Old Man Who Removed the Mountains," recounted a Chinese fable about how Yu Gong (meaning "foolish old man") was determined to remove two huge mountains blocking the access from his home to the outside. It was an impossible task, but Yu Gong and his sons undertook it, shovel by shovel. When a man named Zhi Shou (satirically meaning "wise old man," in contrast to "foolish old man") questioned and ridiculed Yu Gong's efforts, Yu Gong replied: "When I die, my sons will carry on; when they die, there will be my grandsons; and so on to infinity."[30] Eventually Yu Gong's resolve and spirit moved God, and the two mountains were removed from his doorstep. Mao interpreted this old fable with an exaltation of revolutionary faith and unyielding efforts, while "God" was to be understood as the Chinese people's sympathy for the revolutionaries and their role in the triumph of the revolution.

Mao was a master of vernacular Chinese, which began to replace traditional and more refined Chinese in the New Culture Movement and was thought to be more effective in disseminating revolutionary ideologies. Written in plain but lively language and averaging one thousand Chinese characters each, Mao's three articles were lucid narratives concisely portraying the moral qualities of model revolutionaries. In Chinese history, only Confucian masters had enlightened their disciples in this manner. As John Starr points out: "The pedagogical method employed in these articles is of particular interest, since it follows the principle commonly employed by Confucian predecessors of teaching moral lessons through the use of model figures."[31] The pedagogical relevance of these essays, though written in the late 1930s and mid-1940s, became even more conspicuous during the Cultural Revolution, when they were collectively called "the three old essays" (with "old" meaning "classical") and were printed in pamphlet form by the millions and even included in elementary Chinese textbooks. Studying and reciting them were often the first lesson in the morning, not only in schools but in various work units as well, when people gathered to start their days with Mao's moral preaching, to some extent resembling a religious community's morning prayer.

In addition to writing essays celebrating model revolutionaries, Mao also used other traditional methods to promote his role as a moral mentor for the party. For instance, hearing that Liu Hulan, a sixteen-year-old peasant girl who had joined the revolution, was executed by the Nationalists in 1947, Mao wrote a widely popularized epitaph, "Lived Great, Died Glorious," to be inscribed on her monument.

There were also some people, though few in number, who had the honor of becoming such models while still alive. For instance, in 1937 Mao wrote a well-publicized letter to Xu Teli, a veteran revolutionary, in which he lauded Xu as follows:

> You know a great deal but always feel a deficiency in your knowledge, whereas many "half-buckets of water" make a lot of noise. What you think is what you say or what you do, whereas other people hide filthy things

in a corner of their minds. You enjoy being with masses all the time, whereas some others enjoy being without the masses. You are always a model of obedience to the party and its revolutionary discipline, whereas some others regard the discipline as a restraint for others, but not for themselves. For you, it is "revolution first," "work first," and "other people first," whereas for some others it is "limelight first," "rest first," and "oneself first." You always pick the most difficult things to do, never escaping from your responsibilities, whereas some others choose easy work to do, always shunning responsibilities.[32]

While exemplary cadres and soldiers formed the majority of the model revolutionaries, the party also felt the urge to find or create models for peasants in Yan'an. Since taxes and food supply from peasants were the major revenue for the party, and peasant recruits were the major source of the communist army, cultivating political consciousness among peasants became a major ideological task. "Labor hero" was thus the title for the new peasant who had been transformed from a self-centered private farmer to a conscious contributor to the revolution by delivering more food to the government. One example was Wu Manyou. According to the official account, before communists came to Yan'an, Wu was so poor and produced so little that he had to sell his daughter in exchange for food. After the revolution and educated by the party, however, the grain Wu produced in a single year, after tax, was enough for his family to consume for three years. He not only satisfied his own needs but also became a vanguard in leading the peasants in his village to produce more grain and deliver more tax to the communist government. His village therefore also became a model village. Wu was said to be "a new man in the new society," and the party even launched a propaganda campaign, using newspapers and stages, to publicize his story. When the party created its first studio for newsreels, Wu's story was among the first set of films. But later developments showed that the party's promotion and exaltation of Wu was an illusion. Despite all of his extra food delivery to the revolution, Wu, the first peasant model in the Chinese communist revolution, was only a "petty peasant" who might be able to work hard and pay more tax out of gratitude to the party but had no intention of dying for any political commitment. In 1947, when Yan'an was occupied by the Nationalists, Wu was taken prisoner and betrayed the party. The Nationalists used his conversion and confession as propaganda and even let him make speeches broadcast by the Nationalist central radio. In the end, Wu proved he was not a new man yet.

In addition to Wu Manyou, there were other models representing the reformed peasants. Liu Shenghai was such an example. Before the revolution, he was an idler, spending time gambling and smoking opium (not uncommon among poor peasants and lower-class urban dwellers), so much so that his wife divorced him. But after the revolution, in the new society and under the government's education, Liu was rehabilitated and even became a labor hero. With government funding, he was able to help other peasants of his village to accomplish production quotas assigned by the government. Therefore the party proved that even gamblers and opium smokers could be redeemed and made into contributors to the new society. The old society, or the old social environment, had corrupted people, but the new one saved and transformed them.

The Rectification Campaign

The didactical methods of moral preaching and model emulation were based on voluntary acceptance, and therefore they were not forceful enough. More importantly, they promoted desirable qualities but were not designed to remove undesirable ones. A more effective means for remolding people, therefore, was needed. It was called thought reform, a distinctive Chinese invention in human remolding, and first appeared in the Yan'an Rectification and Rescue campaigns, both starting in 1942. The Rectification Campaign targeted "undesirable tendencies," such as "dogmatism, sectarianism, and bureaucratism," while the Rescue Campaign was staged to "rescue" the cadres and intellectuals who were considered to be under the Nationalist influence or even to have worked for the Nationalists as spies. Both campaigns were part of so-called cadre screening, which turned out to be a witch hunt, victimizing thousands of party members. It was prescripted for everyone to be actively involved in these campaigns, and the party evaluated each individual's performance, issuing a verification for every participant that either reconfirmed or revoked the individual's party membership.

The core of these campaigns was self-reform, consisting of self-exposure, self-criticism, and self-condemnation, under tremendous pressures. The campaign began with all participants "exposing" themselves to the party without reservation. They had to recount their personal history in a very detailed manner, such as naming all of their relatives and acquaintances, along with their political stands and occupations, and describing all of their activities prior to joining the revolution. The participants were particularly forced to expose their ideas and opinions, including those never spoken, and even their innermost and transitory thoughts that might reflect the influences of individualism, liberalism, and all kinds of petit bourgeois sentiments and nonproletarian ideologies. The party even asked participants to fill out a form called "little broadcast," on which the participants had to list any privately spread information and gossip among themselves about the party's leaders, supervisors, and other political and organizational matters.

When the Rectification started, *Jiefang ribao* (Liberation Daily), the party's major daily newspaper, published an editorial on March 9, 1942, entitled "Taking Off Pants and Cutting Off Tails." This was a metaphor for the humiliating and painful but necessary process of such confessions. Because many participants were reluctant to expose their thoughts, opinions, and any experience that might cause suspicion and interrogation, the self-exposure was likened to being ordered to take off one's pants in public. After such exposure, participants had to make harsh self-criticism and even renounce themselves; this was compared to forcefully cutting off part of one's body—with the "tail" metaphorically referring to the past that still dragged and hindered the person's progress. One specific method for "taking off pants and cutting off tails" was requiring all participants to keep a journal of daily words and deeds and be prepared at any time to submit it to the party. Mao himself demanded that all party members write and submit their journals and said it was the party's "iron discipline."[33]

Some participants later wrote vivid descriptions of their experiences in these campaigns. Zhang Xianling, a high-ranking official in the 1950s, recalled:

> Rectification was a thought revolution. In other words it was meant to eliminate all nonproletarian thoughts and to let proletarian thought strike roots in one's own brain and guide all personal actions. At that time there was a slogan called "from half-heart to whole-heart." "Whole-heart" meant that all of your thoughts were proletarian, while "half-heart" meant that there were still some nonproletarian vestiges. This was especially applicable to people like me who were born in petit bourgeois families. I had not undergone a thorough thought reform before I went to Yan'an (even today I am still not completely reformed). I had lots of petit bourgeois thoughts and ideas influenced by individualism. When I worked for the party, I quite often calculated my own gains and losses; therefore I of course was half-hearted. Thought revolution was to eliminate that petit bourgeois half-heart and convert it into a complete proletarian heart. It was of course not easy, because that half-heart was not like an armed enemy soldier and you could just fire a shot to kill him; neither was it like a pile of trash in a room that you could just clean with a broom. This petit bourgeois individualism took deep root in your innermost thought, and to clean it you had to fight yourself vehemently. Although this struggle took place inside everyone, it had an impact on our outside. I remember in the most intense days of that

thought struggle, many of us suffered from insomnia, and the cooks in the public dining hall kept complaining that there was too much food left. It was so because although petit bourgeois thought was bad, it had been in your mind for more than twenty years and you were somehow fond of it and could not be so determined to completely cut it off.[34]

Such painful personal confession, self-exposure, and self-renunciation came about, from the very beginning, under tremendous external pressure and organizational supervision. The participants had to expose their thoughts and confess any words or deeds unfavorable to the party in front of mass meetings, group gatherings, and the party's special committees. While a person was making a confession, other participants listened attentively. They asked all kinds of questions or expressed their suspicions that the speaker might not be telling the whole story and tried to debunk him or her by carping. The party's representatives took notes and evaluated everyone's "performance." This process could be repeated many times before the participant was deemed to be sincere and hiding nothing from the party. During this process, anyone who showed even the slightest signs of impatience and grievance would be deluged with ferocious mass criticism and would suffer special handling such as being confined in a small cell or even subjected to torture.[35]

As a matter of fact, self-reform is not unique in history. As John Kosa points out in his comparative study of the Soviet man and his duplicate in Eastern Europe, it was called catharsis in Western cultural and religious contexts, a process in which one becomes purified by self-scrutinizing daily behavior and thinking. Kosa notes that it is a "complex process," ending in a strengthened identification with the superego and strengthened confidence in oneself: "In our Western culture this self-criticism is carried out in loneliness or among a small circle of intimates. It is a private affair, undertaken at one's own discretion, carried on without publicity." He adds that communism, on the other hand, "made a public ritual out of self-criticism" and used it to strengthen the self-criticized one's identification with the party but also to deprive him or her of self-confidence.[36] It was in the Soviet Union that such private affairs became public for the first time. As Kosa observes, "This aspect of self-criticism had a special meaning for the peoples of Russia. Among them . . . public self-abasement and the acceptance of guilt and guilt feelings were rather common inclinations that were displayed before intimates and strangers alike and approved by the culture of the society." As in Yan'an, self-criticism was a public humiliation to many. Kosa conducted interviews with many Eastern Europeans who had immigrated to the United States after their countries became part of the Soviet bloc, and one of them recalled, "I felt as if I were standing stark naked in the center of a crowd and everybody was poking fun at me." The questions he had to answer were not necessarily political but included topics such as "sex life, drinking habits, financial affairs, or the social deportment of spouse and children."[37] It was very likely that such a Russian-originated practice spilled over to China through the members of the CCP who had studied and trained in Moscow in the late 1920s and during the 1930s.

The political and psychological impact brought about by these processes on individuals was so intense and traumatic that symptoms of obsession, nervousness, anxiety, and mental and physical disorder were very common. Many people not only suffered from insomnia and lost their desire for food, as Zhang Xianling described, but also had constant headaches and recurrences of old diseases, or even involuntary ejaculation among some male participants. More than that, there were numerous cases of suicide. According to one source, during the second half of 1943, in a single city (Yan'an) there were about fifty to sixty suicide cases.[38] Under tremendous pressure and in order to put an end to the torturous experience, many people chose to confess things they never did, often by acknowledging whatever the party asked them to admit, or they entered a mental state of confusion and disorder that often brought about the same result. The most absurd case was when many teenage girls were forced to "admit" in public that they were Nationalist sex spies.[39]

When the final stage of Rectification came, the party would write an evaluation for everyone. If the participants were considered to have passed all examinations and been reeducated, they would be accepted by the party. Gao Hua describes a feeling of rebirth or salvation among the participants who reached that point:

> Having gone through all of these processes, the new man was finally born. With the political evaluation of every individual made by their respective party units, the individuals found their new identity and ultimate meaning of life—they would belong to the party not only in terms of ideology but also in body and life, without reservation. From then on, an individualist or petit bourgeois (a "half heart") disappeared and a proletarian revolutionary fighter (a "whole heart") emerged.[40]

Once the individuals were acknowledged and accepted by the organization, it was as if they had "crossed the line dividing yin and yang [meaning hell and heaven], and they felt as if they were reborn, with all grievances and distresses gone overnight." Some people described this feeling as "going from the darkest night to the brightest dawn," and "seeing fresh red sunlight."[41]

Xie Juezai, the living model revolutionary who had been promoted by Mao and was one of the "Four Elders" among communists known for their Confucian education, published articles and poems in the *Liberation Daily* to illustrate the importance of thought reform by his own example. With his Confucian background, Xie described thought reform as excruciating during the process but exhilarating by the end. As Xie put it, thought reform was "totally changing oneself," as if one were "slowly boiling raw meat until it was well-done." He likened some methods and pressures used in the reform to "high fire" or "boiling" and others to "low fire" or "steaming," noting that the participants had to endure both.[42] He used Wang Yangming's famous deathbed saying—"There is nothing left in my mind but a holy emptiness"—as the title for one of his newspaper articles. The implication of this neo-Confucian quotation was that, to become a revolutionary moral saint, a person had to root out all undesirable thoughts from his or her mind.

In the final analysis, the Yan'an period created thought reform, a distinctive Chinese method, as one of the most powerful tools in remolding people and laid the foundation for the later social engineering of creating the new man in China. Carried out in a closed political environment and enforced by intensive study, confession, self-criticism, and group pressure, it was far more effective than ideological indoctrination and political education designed for a general audience under ordinary circumstances, because in thought reform all participants, or "educated" ones, were individually targeted and had to respond to all kinds of reform efforts in their own way and with their own answers, rather than coming up with a unanimous response. Like interrogation techniques, thought reform was designed to break human psychological barriers and to crush mental resistance. All of these methods would continue to be developed, reaching a high point in the 1960s.

In understanding the Yan'an Rectification and the subsequent thought reform used in China and some other communist regimes, modern anthropological theory about rituals may offer some interpretational thoughts. A three-stage theory developed by Arnold van Gennep and Victor Witter Turner—about rituals in which the participants transform their identities—is helpful in interpreting the Yan'an Rectification. The first stage is preliminary, in which participants are separated from their usual social setting and gather together. The second stage is liminal, in which the participants are "betwixt and between," "neither here nor there." It is a transitional period. The third is postliminary, a period in which the participant's new identity is obtained and confirmed. Psychologically the first stage comes with a feeling of isolation and expectation; the second is accompanied by uncertainty, confusion, helplessness, or even humiliation; the third establishes a new identity for the participant, whose admission to a new community creates a sense of relief, a feeling of being born again, and great excitement. The Yan'an Rectification took place in a closed space and was to a great extent ritualistic. Although individuals went to Yan'an voluntarily, they were soon put in isolation and under tremendous pressure to transform themselves and were finally admitted to the party as tested revolutionaries—new men or women. This identity transformation process often had a significant impact on the psychology of these individuals and engraved a permanent reminder in their minds to remain ideologically and politically loyal to the party.

THE EARLY 1950S: THOUGHT REFORM AMONG INTELLECTUALS AND STUDENTS

Their victory in 1949 gave the Chinese Communists the opportunity to remold people at the national level along with their task of social transformation. As Maria Hsia Chang put it, "With the acquisition of total power, this self-appointed vanguard [undertook] a program of comprehensive social engineering in order to remold human nature and transform society."[43]

The first project in reshaping people was a campaign (1950–1952) to expand thought reform as created during the Yan'an Rectification to the whole nation. The communists proclaimed that thought reform would be everyone's long-term ideological undertaking, but intellectuals and students were more obliged to it, because of their bourgeois or petit bourgeois origins and their role in cultural and social development. If in the Yan'an context thought reform was used to purify and toughen the party members' revolutionary will and make them obedient to the organization and to Mao unconditionally, then thought reform in the early 1950s was a political resocialization designed to erase ideological and cultural imprints of the traditional China and replace them with new ones in people who had no choice but to live under the new regime. This political resocialization was deemed to be indispensable for the regime to control and mobilize one of the most important parts of the population in implementing the major policies in social transformation. As Mao announced at the meeting of the Chinese People's Political Consultative Conference (October 1951), "Thought reform is first of all the thought reform of all kinds of intellectuals, and it is one of the most important conditions for a thoroughgoing democratic reform and gradual industrialization of our country."[44]

The intellectuals who were concentrated in educational institutions bore the brunt of the campaign. In August 1951 the central government passed a resolution on the reform of the educational system. This new system established an educational hierarchy: kindergarten, elementary schools, middle schools, colleges, and political schools or training programs. The purpose of integrating political schools or training programs into the public education system was "to reeducate young and old intellectuals with revolutionary ideology."[45] Under this system, all intellectuals and students who had completed their education prior to 1949 had to be enrolled in one of those political schools or training programs in order to be reeducated and to graduate with a certificate of political credibility. The communists applied the methods of Yan'an Rectification in this thought reform process: most of the political schools and programs were full-time (five days a week or even extending into the weekend), with many boarding schools to create a closed environment that included constant pressure on the participants, intensive ideological study, mass meetings and study sessions, exposure of personal and family histories, self-criticism, and finally an evaluation made by the party. All of these created a liminal situation for transforming the intellectuals' and students' ideological stand by applying tremendous political and psychological pressures. To show the effectiveness of the thought reform campaign and to apply more pressure on recalcitrant intellectuals and students, the communists publicized cases of "reformed" people in newspapers, especially prominent scholars, many of whom had been educated in the United States or elsewhere in the West. The content of their publicized confessions was mainly renunciation of their past and gratitude to the party for redemption.

Ge Tingshui, a professor of physics at Qinghua University, was educated in the United States during World War II and participated in research related to nuclear devices and radar systems. In recalling these experiences, he said, "I used to think this research was to help the Allies in the war against the fascists. I therefore not only emphasized the achievements of American science and technology but also was proud of my participation in it." But now, he said, he realized that it was senseless to talk about scientific achievements without mentioning whom these technologies served. After the war, Ge went to the University of Chicago, engaging in research on the strength of metals. In the late 1940s he returned to China and was forced to participate in the thought reform campaign. In the beginning of the campaign he admitted that his service for the US military was wrong, but he insisted that his work in Chicago was all right because it was for civilian use. But as the thought reform campaign deepened, especially after he repeatedly studied articles in the *People's Daily*, he came to understand that as long as scientists lived in a class-based society, their research would be supported by the government and their activities would inevitably benefit the ruling class.[46] Therefore, even his work for the University of Chicago was politically wrong, because it had been done in a capitalist society and had been funded in part by the US government.

Zhou Peiyuan, a noted physicist and later the dean of the Chinese Academy of Sciences, was also in America during World War II and participated in research on airplane-launched torpedoes. He recalled that experience as "a shameful page of my personal history" and said, "I want to condemn myself, condemn this would-be scientist who betrayed his people and was willing to help American butchers."[47]

The case of the confession and self-criticism of Qian Weichang is even more illustrative. Qian was one of the most well-known Chinese physicists and had been an important figure in communist China's weapons designs, especially in the 1960s and 1970s. The party used him as an example of "reeducated" bourgeois intellectuals, a patriotic and pro-communist scientist, showering him with various official titles. In the thought reform campaign of 1950–1952, Qian wrote a long, biographical article, narrating his life prior to 1949 with startling details that often involved his scientific friends. Recalling his youthful dream of study in the West and becoming a "distinguished professor," he said he stayed away from communist-led student movements in the 1930s with excuses such as "the revolution needs division of labor" and "the revolution needs scientists." When his dream of study abroad came true, he went to Canada and then America, participating in the development of rockets and jet engines for the US Army, but now this experience was associated with "a grave sense of guilt." In 1944, when Qinghua University offered him a position as associate professor, Qian was in the United States and thought he was worth much more, so he did not accept it. Later, in 1945, when the same university promised him a full professorship, he accepted and returned to Beijing. Like many intellectuals of the late 1940s, Qian was dissatisfied with the Nationalist government for its alleged corruption and incompetence and began to support anti-Nationalist and anti-American activities on campus that were led by the communists. But he confessed that, rather than being spurred by political consciousness, his participation was actually motivated by a selfish desire. If the communists defeated the Nationalists, he reasoned, his research would benefit from the restoration of order and peace under a competent government and he would fulfill his personal ambitions. Such a political attitude was based on the calculation of personal gain or loss and thus "was not able to hold up to the test," Qian told his readers. Then he revealed another dirty secret about himself. One year before the Liberation (as the communist victory in 1949 came to be known), Qian Xuesen, one of his friends who was conducting research at the California Institute of Technology, came back to China and advised him to return to America to continue his research in aeronautical engineering. Qian Xuesen argued that political chaos and lack of financial support would only make his time in China fruitless. Qian Weichang said, "I betrayed my country and shamefully agreed with his opinion." However, he did not go to the United States but stayed in Beijing. Why? "The reason that I did not go to America," he wrote, "was not because I had returned to side with the Chinese people, but because of a condition imposed by the American consulate when I was applying for a visa. They told me that I must pledge to join the military service should a war break out. I was afraid of death, and more than that, I was not willing to die for America. I decided to stay, thus escaping from falling into the evil abyss of American imperialists."[48]

It was very likely that Qian, like many intellectuals and cadres before and after him, exaggerated the dark side of his personal history by making up some details or thoughts hard to prove or disprove, to cater to the party's political needs. In any case, such self-degradation and self-humiliation of the old-generation intellectuals were indeed taken by the party as signs of submission to the new regime—if not necessarily signs of a new man—and would earn them the right to go back to their regular work. In addition, the "confessions" of these reputed and widely respected intellectuals served as models for the party to reinforce the thought reform targeted at younger generations. If those "big shots" had so willingly and completely "taken off their pants and cut off their tails," then why would others hesitate?

Young students and intellectuals were another main target of the campaign, and for them the first major task was to draw a line of ideological demarcation between themselves and their families, especially for those of nonworking-class origin. Although thought reform adopted certain Confucian and especially neo-Confucian techniques in ideologically transforming the individual, the revolution itself in general had significantly eroded the Confucian tradition of obligation and cohesiveness of the younger generation to elder generations. "Filial piety" had been denounced as a virtue of feudalism that was incompatible with loyalty to the party, so much so that betraying or even denouncing their bourgeois or feudal parents was proudly announced by many youths when they joined the revolution. For many the family ties were simply cut off for many years, and they even assumed different names. When the communists took over the whole country, they expanded this practice to the whole young generation and encouraged them to betray their politically backward or reactionary parents. One specific act associated with such a betrayal was to denounce one's family's class origin and even one's parents publicly. Many youths reported their parents' opinions on communists and their activities that were suspicious or politically incorrect. The act of tearing youths from their families was touted as a sign of ideological and spiritual "rebirth."

A typical example was Hu Sidu, a son of Dr. Hu Shi. Educated at Cornell University, Hu Shi was one of the most influential intellectuals in the May Fourth Movement and a champion of the New Culture Movement. He was the leading figure among Chinese liberal intellectuals in the 1930s and 1940s, and also, at the request of the Nationalist government, had served as China's ambassador to the United States during World War II, due to his connection and familiarity with America. Before the communists gained power, he left Mainland China, but one of his sons, Hu Sidu, was under communist influence and decided to stay. As soon as the communists came to power, a propaganda campaign was launched to denigrate Hu Shi and the liberalism he personified. Because of Hu's enormous influence among Chinese intellectuals, the party asked intellectuals who had personal connections with him to denounce him publicly. On September 22, 1950, *Dagong bao*, a communist-controlled daily newspaper published in Hong Kong, printed Hu Sidu's denunciation of his father. The son called his father "a public enemy of the people, and an enemy of myself" and vowed that he "must establish close relations with the working and farming class." Hu Sidu's denunciation was sensational among intellectuals, and the party exploited the case as an example of the power of thought reform. But they never really thought Hu Sidu was a reliable new man. In 1957 Hu Sidu, like numerous Chinese intellectuals of the time, responded to the party's call, soliciting criticism to help the party improve its work. When Mao launched an anti-rightist campaign that summer, secretly planning to catch those "hidden enemies" who took the bait and came out to criticize the party, Hu Sidu was labeled a "rightist" and committed suicide under unbearable pressures.

After a line was drawn between their own past and present, and between themselves and their families, the next stage in thought reform for intellectuals and students was to root out individualism and to implant collectivism as a moral principle and guideline for personal life. Collectivism versus individualism, the classical theme in creating the communist new man, and in principle applicable to people of all occupations and ages, was especially important for the youth in communist China, not only ideologically but even more so practically. From the very beginning, the communists faced the problem of employment in the cities. Because the state-controlled economy reduced and then eliminated private enterprise and the free labor market, the government was responsible for everyone's employment, especially that of the youth, and thus created a massive problem for itself. On the other hand, many employment opportunities created and needed by the government would attract very few people under normal circumstances, if based on voluntary choice. This employment problem appeared at different times with slightly different specific causes. One of the most important practices to solve or to reduce the employment problem was to use education in collectivism or communism to subdue individual preference in seeking a career, even choosing a residence, subjecting people to the economic needs of the party and the government.

In the early 1950s another problem was created by the war-torn economy and the government's engagement in a number of political and economic developments. In addition to the labor demand related to the Korean War, the government also embarked on large-scale industrial construction projects and planned to move millions of young people from coastal areas and urban centers to the newly pacified and scarcely populated border areas in the north and west (such as Inner Mongolia, Xinjiang, and Manchuria), in order to establish complexes of garrisons and farming units with other services, a traditional practice used by numerous dynasties in history to secure borders. In addition, as a long-term project, the party and the government also needed millions of educated youth to provide technological and literate services to China's vast countryside. These developments, however, often asked the participants to leave relatively comfortable urban settings and familiar environments in which they could live with ease. To overcome the unwillingness and resistance among targeted youth, therefore, the party launched campaigns promoting collectivist and socialist values as opposed to individualism, meaning to place the government's needs above individual preference.

The campaign of anti-individualism was ushered in by thought reform, in which the party had succeeded in forcing everyone to yield to its ideological and moral authority. The particular target in the campaign against individualism was the college graduate; most of them wished to stay in the cities and close to their families. The relationship among thought reform, the campaign against individualism, and the individual's obligations as a member of the new society was perfectly demonstrated in a speech delivered by Jiang Nanxiang, the minister of higher education, on July 2, 1952, at a rally of all college graduates in Beijing. Jiang contrasted the old and new societies by saying that in the former the graduates would seek jobs according to their own interests, while in the latter the government assigned jobs to everyone in the interest of the country. He pointed out that after thought reform, most graduates' political awareness had been significantly raised and they were prepared to accept work anywhere assigned by the government. But there were still "a small number" of graduates who accepted the assignment with resignation rather than with willingness and a cheerful mood. These graduates, according to Jiang, were reminiscent of the pre-1949 employment that put individuals' interests above the people's. Jiang told the graduates, "In order to better serve the people, every student must further clean up and completely abandon his or her individualist stand and view, in order to establish a collectivist revolutionary attitude toward life."[49]

Because of its long history of armed struggle and underground activities (from 1927 to 1949), Chinese communism had produced more martyrs than the Bolsheviks, and those martyrs became an important factor in China's political education for creating the new man. During the 1950s the wartime martyrs still dominated the shrine of heroes. In the meantime, however, economic development demanded that the party find and promote the type of new man who personified revolutionary virtues in peacetime.

Wu Yunduo, for example, was an outstanding individual case, not only symbolizing a transition from wartime to peacetime but also representing the influence of the Soviet new man in China. Wu was a laborer-turned-technician, working in the communist ammunition industry during the war against Japan, as well as the civil war. His job was to dismantle shells and explosives, with almost no protective equipment for himself. He was wounded three times, with one eye blinded and more than a hundred scars on his body. Like Nikolai Ostrovsky, who was a very popular figure in China during the 1950s, Wu also had spent his latter years in bed and had written a book as his last contribution to communism. For this he was called China's Pavel Korchagin.[50] His book, *Dedicating Everything to the Party*, was first published in 1952, followed by many reprints, and was described as "the textbook for life." In it he wrote, "The individual is merely a drop of water in the sea. Only when numerous drops come together can we form a great torrent. The moment it is separated from the sea, the drop dries out immediately."[51] He likened the individual to screws: fixed at junctures and indispensable for the whole machine, they were unassuming but dutiful. This metaphor sounded identical to the Soviet metaphor of the "iron nail" and later became a favorite maxim for the party. Thus a "revolutionary screw" became the synonym for the new man in China.

The highest form of revolutionary virtues in peacetime still demanded that the new men and women sacrifice their lives for the revolution, not in the battleground but often during events when the state or collective property was in danger. Xiang Xiuli, a female textile worker in Guangzhou, was such an example in the 1950s. She sacrificed her life to save the machine and textiles at her factory during a fire. After she died, central and provincial party leaders contributed to her epitaphic honors to promote a propaganda campaign publicizing her heroic deeds. From then on, to protect public property at the risk of one's life became another specifically emphasized quality of the new man. Some extreme examples of sacrifice of personal life for public property actually had nothing to do with a rational sense of property. For example, in the late 1950s, a well-publicized heroic tale described how a thirteen-year-old boy named Liu Wenxue gave his life for a couple of peppers. In this scenario, when Liu found a former landlord stealing peppers from a field belonging to the production team, he fought that landlord and was killed. Liu thus was posthumously promoted as an example for all Chinese children, and his picture was seen in every elementary and middle school. During the Cultural Revolution, some sent-down youths (urban-educated youths who were sent down to the countryside by the party to be reeducated by laboring and living with the peasants) sacrificed their lives to save timber from a flood and some sheep from a fire, according to official accounts. The exaltation and publicity of these models reflected one of the fundamental values of the new man: collective property, even as insignificant as a couple of peppers or a telephone pole, was symbolically much more valuable than an individual's life.

But not all new models of the 1950s and later had the chance to be tested in such dramatic life-or-death situations. Many of them gained prominence through their exceptional professional performance, motivated by their political consciousness rather than traditional professionalism. For example, in Shanghai, a bus driver named Min Suofu became a municipal celebrity. Min drove his bus for seven years with no record of any violation, accident, or delinquency and was always punctual. He became a labor hero and was selected to meet Mao—an honor granted to very few models. The official account attributed Min's achievement to his study of Mao's teaching of "serving the people," instead of mere professionalism.[52] Another example was Ma Xueli, a lathe worker in the Wuhan Heavy Machine Factory, who constantly improved and polished his expertise and made a number of technical innovations, thus becoming a labor hero of Hubei Province.

To be a model meant not only fulfilling one's own duty well but also helping others by example, especially those who were considered ideologically backward. This exemplary influence was one of the essential characteristics of the new man. Xiang Xiuli, for instance, helped such a backward worker on many occasions. It was difficult to approach this worker at first, because he was always sarcastic to the politically advanced model workers if they seemed to want to help him. Xiang Xiuli, however, watched him closely and found that he was fond of dancing. Then she deliberately approached him at dancing parties organized by the union of factory workers. In this way she disarmed his aloofness and succeeded in her ideological education plan.[53] Ma Xueli also helped a worker named Hu Xueling in his factory. Hu originally was an example of a backward worker, devoting his time only to paid work and believing the maxim, "Everyone for himself and let the devil take the hindmost."[54] But under Ma's influence, Hu gradually changed his attitude toward work and also became a model worker.

COLLECTIVIZATION AND THE PEOPLE'S COMMUNES: TRANSFORMING PEASANTS INTO NEW MEN

China was a predominantly agrarian country, and this remained unchanged after the communist takeover. As an essential part of remolding the whole nation, during the 1950s the regime launched a set of campaigns to transform the traditional individual farmer into a collective and socialist peasant. This endeavor was a daunting challenge in the history of world communism. Classical Marxism identified an independent peasantry with the preindustrial and precapitalist order, doomed to lose independence and to be thrown into the ranks of the proletariat by the expansion of capitalism. Politically, peasants were regarded as conservative or even reactionary because they clung to the social order associated with small and independent ownership of estates and the mode of individual production, rejecting any radical political changes targeting private property. They sometimes even served as the social basis for monarchist dictatorship; for example, French peasants had supported the monarchist restoration of Napoleon III, according to Marx's analysis in his *Eighteenth Brumaire of Louis Bonaparte*. In general, small and independent peasants were believed to have nothing in common with the proletarian socialist revolution of classical Marxism.

Lenin saw the peasantry as the most "spontaneous" social class, with little chance of being inculcated with revolutionary ideology. Even worse, according to his social analysis, the peasantry lived off "petty mercantile production" and constituted the breeding ground for capitalism due to its inclination toward class polarization. After the Bolshevik Revolution, Lenin once made the following comment on the peasantry: "Petty mercantile production engenders capitalism and a bourgeois ideology daily and spontaneously." As a matter of fact, the Russian civil war (1918–1920) was essentially a fight between Bolsheviks (supported by the army and city workers) and peasants, and in the early 1930s there was yet another campaign of collectivization against the peasants.

The context of the peasant question in the Chinese Revolution, however, was different from that in Marxian discourse and in the Russian Revolution. Supported by peasants and based in rural areas, the Chinese Revolution was defined as antifeudal rather than anticapitalist, and one of its basic tasks was to redistribute land in exchange for peasants' support for the revolution. For this reason some party leaders exalted the peasants' role in the Chinese Revolution as early as the late 1920s, as shown in Mao's famous "Report on an Investigation of the Peasant Movement in Hunan," for example. In time this high opinion of the peasants' revolutionary role developed into the party's guideline for "democratic and nationalist revolution," as Mao secured his leading position in the party. For this reason the Chinese Revolution has quite often been viewed as a "peasant revolution." Within this historical context, as some historians have pointed out, Mao himself displayed a strong populist view of the peasants, similar to that of the Russian populists. Mao's view not only acknowledged the political activism of the peasants but also celebrated their moral superiority over urban people, and intellectuals in particular.

This populist tendency continued to play a role, intermittently from the 1950s to the 1970s, in Maoist views on the relationship between peasants in the countryside setting and intellectuals, students, and cadres in the urban environment—the latter were thought to be obliged to receive reeducation from the former. But populism constituted only one dimension in the Maoist view regarding the peasants' role in the revolution. The communists had won peasants' support during the civil war, but the land reform also engendered a massive class of small and independent peasants, which, according to Marxist-Leninist theory, was economically backward and politically conservative. The task of socialist transformation in the countryside was to eliminate this class and transform the private and capitalist-oriented peasants into collective and socialist farmers by collectivizing their lands and major production tools and organizing them into collective farms. Economically, this socialist transformation was meant to maximize the state control over peasants in terms of acquisition of agricultural products for the sake of government projects—in particular, a quick industrialization. With this prospect in mind, as soon as the communists took over the country, the peasant problem began to loom as the next major undertaking in the revolution. The key issue the Chinese communists had to tackle was exactly what the Bolsheviks had faced in the late 1920s and early 1930s when Stalin launched his forced collectivization campaign: how to transform millions of traditional farmers into socialist agricultural producers by injecting communist ideology and forcing them to adapt to the socialist collective mode of production. Being aware of the peasants' traditional and entrenched self-centered mentality and their lack of collectivist spirit, Mao said in 1949, as land reform was still unfolding in China, "The serious problem is the education of the peasantry. The peasant economy is scattered, and the socialization of agriculture, judging by the Soviet Union's experience, will require a long time and painstaking work. Without socialization of agriculture, there can be no complete, consolidated socialism."[55]

Unlike the Soviet Union's forced collectivization in the 1930s, in which the party often sent armed cadres and workers to the countryside to implement the policy and then exiled recalcitrant peasants to Siberia, in China the collectivization proceeded in a relatively peaceful and gradual manner. Starting in the early 1950s, the party planned a three-phase process to transform Chinese peasants. The first was mutual-aid teams and required only mutual assistance in labor service, often seasonal and on a small scale (within the neighborhood). The second phase involved low-level agricultural producers' cooperatives in which the peasants "pooled their land and equipment together but [received] a return in proportion to them in harvest."[56] Draft animals were also included in the pool. The last phase was high-level agricultural producers' cooperatives in which rewards were determined by each member's labor and performance rather than by their collectivized property. It was a gradual course designed to diminish and finally eliminate the peasants' ideas and mentality associated with private property. As the collectivization of property and work was completed, the peasants also experienced a transformation in identity: from individual farmer to collective producer. For Mao, the transformation in the peasants' state of mind and lifestyle was much more fundamental and exciting than any of the previous political achievements, because it showed to what extent entrenched human nature could be changed by political campaign, even in those who had been regarded as the most conservative. As he once put it in a rather jubilant tone, "The victory in 1949 did not make me happy at all. But in 1955, when I saw so many peasants joining the cooperative, followed by the nationalization of private industry and commerce, I began to be really happy."[57]

While many Chinese peasants were still adjusting to life in the cooperatives, Mao initiated an even more radical and sweeping campaign aimed at creating communist new peasants from socialist farmers. Starting from the summer of 1958, the Great Leap Forward engulfed China. With an economic goal of quick industrialization, and particularly of surpassing some Western countries in the output of iron and steel, the Great Leap Forward was also an effort to accelerate the transformation from socialism to communism by skipping developmental stages viewed as necessary by classical Marxism. In the countryside, a new organization was introduced to replace the traditional way of rural life based on the individual family. With the wide publicity of Mao's verdict, "The people's commune is good," some 500 million Chinese peasants were mobilized in the campaign to establish people's communes. Mao declared in that year that the CCP's goal was to gradually and systematically organize industry, agriculture, commerce, culture, education, and the military into a "great commune, making it the basic unit of our society."[58] The dream of such a commune had its utopian tradition—for example, among the Russian populists and some Western utopian socialists such as Charles Fourier—but it had never been put into practice as a state experiment. One of the most frequently chanted slogans then was "Organize like an army, act like you're in combat, and live in a collective way."

"Organize like an army, act like you're in combat," according to Wu Zifu, the first secretary of the Party Committee of Henan Province, was "to organize peasants into the military units of platoons, companies, and battalions" and assign them productive and constructive tasks in a way that military tasks were assigned.[59] For example, in 1958, Xiyang County (in Shanxi Province) organized a "cooperative productive army." This "army" was divided into two parts: one was a crack corps, consisting of retired soldiers and regular militias organized into eleven regiments who would undertake tough work, such as building reservoirs and railway systems; the other was a common corps, staffed with common peasants and women performing regular agricultural and domestic work. The former was put on the "front line," maneuvered directly by the county's Party Committee, while the latter stayed in the "rear front," in their own villages.[60] As a matter of fact, most irrigation or transportation projects in the countryside during Mao's time were completed in such a military manner. As the *People's Daily* pronounced in 1958, in the countryside each day almost 100 million people were organized into a labor army for irrigation projects.[61]

"Live in a collective way" meant that many aspects of private life such as cooking and eating, rearing children, bathing, tailoring, and looking after the elderly were now collectivized and became a public matter. The most conspicuous form of such collective life was the free meal in the public dining halls set up in every village. By the end of 1959 there were about 3,919,000 public dining halls in which the peasants either had their free meals or shared their food. Many of these dining halls in just a couple of weeks consumed food that could normally have lasted for three months, and they became one cause for the famine from 1959 to 1961.[62]

Such an intrusion into private life not only illustrated the fanaticism of the Great Leap Forward but was also meant to root out the mentality and attitude of individual peasants on a daily basis. As Wu Zifu pointed out, the people's commune would "eliminate the ideas of private ownership and cultivate socialist and communist thought":

> Everyone who has visited the Shuiping Satellite Commune [one of the model communes in his province] or other communes established quite earlier found the difference in people's thought. They are charged with socialist enthusiasm and communist morality, because the residues of the

old modes of production and private property were decreasing every day. According to the principle of social consciousness determined by social existence, the socialist and communist consciousness will certainly expand.[63]

As the new generation of socialist peasants, children were particularly targeted in the people's commune campaign, and a specific measure was to integrate families with the commune and separate children from parents as much as possible. Like his utopian, Marxist, and Jacobin predecessors, Mao dreamed of a new society based on the "new village" (a notion directly inspired by utopian socialists and Russian populists) in which raising children, along with many other family functions, would be operated by the community.[64] One of Mao's young friends recalled that around 1920 Mao told him, "In the future ideal society, children should be separated from the parents and nurtured by the state."[65] Tao Zhu, the party's first secretary of Guangdong Province, was one of those who so aggressively substantialized Mao's ideas by establishing public kindergartens in the communes that he had to defend such projects in face of criticism from abroad. On December 12, 1958, when he answered questions posed by journalists from Hong Kong and Macao, he repudiated accusations that the people's communes were depriving peasants of freedom and undermining family structure. As for public kindergartens, he said that the institution not only freed women from carrying babies and young children when they went to work but also resolved an educational problem. As he put it, "Living in a collective, the children would naturally receive a social and collectivist upbringing and education. If they cultivate good collectivist and socialist conduct, in the future they will become a socialist new man. The integration of family education and social education is certainly much better than no education or only family education."[66]

Although launched with a great deal of fanfare, propaganda, and initial euphoria—and indeed the sincere embrace of many peasants in the beginning, in the hope of an immediate communist heaven on earth—the campaign for people's communes, together with the Great Leap Forward, proved to be detrimental to motivating the peasants. Mismanagement, disorder, and inefficiency increasingly characterized the campaign, with enormous amounts of food (including seeds) being consumed within a rather short period. Starting in 1959, Chinese society began to suffer a backlash from the Great Leap Forward and the people's communes, with millions starving to death. The party's bureaucrats had to beat a retreat, dissolving public dining halls, kindergartens, and other services and letting the peasants restore their family life. Many local cadres even went further, allowing the peasants to work on their private plots and sell their products at local markets in exchange for daily necessities. The experiment of creating communist new peasants had failed, but a few years later it would come back with new dynamics.

EDUCATIONAL REFORM OF 1958–1959

As in the Soviet Union, education was one of the major tools for transforming human nature in China. In the 1950s, China's educational system experienced a transformation, from imitating the Soviet model to exploring its own road.[67]

The early and mid-1950s was a time in which China's education followed the Soviet model. As Wei Chengsi has pointed out, Soviet educational theories were treated in China almost as a constitution:

> With the slogan that education "must completely and systematically learn from the advanced experiences of the Soviet Union," it was very logical to imitate or even duplicate the Soviet model. At that time, we massively introduced Soviet syllabi and textbooks. For example, we translated 1391 Soviet college textbooks; we also invited Soviet experts to give lectures, participate in school management, and guide our education according to Soviet pedagogy.[68]

But in 1957, as Mao accelerated the course to communism, an ideological divergence between China and the Soviet Union emerged. Education was one of the first areas in which the Chinese critique of the Soviet model appeared. The Soviet educational system was criticized for its emphasis on institutionalized education, strict discipline, classroom- and textbook-centered pedagogy, authority of teachers and administrators, and academic meritocracy. The Chinese were especially critical of achievement-based social distinctions that had been established and encouraged by the Soviet system. It was quite well known among Chinese intellectuals of the time that in the Soviet Union the salary gap between mental and manual labors was astonishingly deep. For example, in 1956 the salaries for a housekeeper (working in academic institutions), graduate, associate doctor, and doctor were respectively 30, 90, 240, and 480 rubles.[69] The Chinese argued that these policies had enlarged and deepened the gap between intellectuals—they used the term "spiritual nobles"—and workers and peasants. As a result the people educated in such a system could hardly be expected to be new men, but rather members of the new elite.

A crucial event in determining the course of the change was Mao's speech at the meeting of the State Council in February 1957. Later it was published under the title "On the Correct Handling of the Contradictions among the People." In the speech, Mao proposed, "Our educational policy must enable everyone who gets an education to develop morally, intellectually, and physically and become a cultured, socialist-minded laborer."[70] Previously, the sequence of moral (meaning "ideological" in this context), intellectual, and physical goals in primary and middle education had not been set, with the priority always given to the moral (ideological) one. For example, in 1952 the minister of education issued a document regulating the curriculum in elementary and middle schools, and the sequence was "intellect, morality, physical education, and aesthetics."[71] Many governmental documents referred to educational goals with an implication of academic emphasis, such as "red experts" (persons who were both politically and professionally qualified). Considering this context, Mao's priority of "socialist consciousness" and "laborer" was not untargeted.

In September 1958, as the Great Leap Forward and the campaign for people's communes were unfolding, the Central Committee of the party and the State Council jointly issued "The Directive on Education." It stressed the need to intensify ideological indoctrination and to integrate labor into the curriculum and pointed out the direction for education in the future: schools should run factories and farms, and vice versa. As a matter of fact, this idea came directly from Mao himself. That summer, he had demanded, "From now on, schools should run factories, and factories should run schools."

Under these guidelines, China's education made a sharp turn away from the Soviet track. One specific example was the abandonment of the proposed rank of "associate doctorate."[72] In June 1956, as a concrete step of learning from the Soviet Union and "marching toward sciences" (a slogan popular then, with an implication of following the Soviet model), the Ministry of Higher Education proposed to recruit graduate students for the degree of associate doctorate, with a four-year study program. But after Mao made his famous speech that February, the ministry issued an order the next month to call off the project, which had already enrolled 490 graduate students.

"The central question of this educational revolution," as Yang Xiufeng—the minister of higher education—pointed out, was "an integration of education with labor" and the cultivation of "a new man with both political consciousness and cultural knowledge, able to perform both mental and physical labor": "The reason for schools to run factories and farms is that schools not only educate new men but also manufacture new products, while the reason for factories and farms to run schools is that they not only manufacture new products but also new men." He especially noted that the labor in such factories and farms was voluntary and would "greatly promote a communist attitude toward labor."[73] Factories run by schools boomed overnight. According to one source, in 1958 there were 397 colleges and universities running 7,240 factories, and 13,000 middle schools running 144,000 factories.[74] Faculty and students were particularly involved in the iron-and-steel campaign, the major industrial goal of the Great Leap Forward, by setting up furnaces on campuses. By September 1958, students in most educational institutions above middle schools and, in some cases, senior grades in the elementary schools, had suspended their studies and plunged themselves into the campaign. According to the statistics from twenty provinces, 22,100 schools had established 86,000 furnaces.[75] The metaphorical connotation of the communist new man, tempered in the revolutionary fire and turning out as tough as iron and steel, was for the first time taken literally.

This educational revolution was also meant to continue the undertaking of eliminating individualism, which had been significantly weakened by the thought reform campaign in the early 1950s and by many other subsequent political and ideological campaigns. Within education, a breeding ground for individualism was found in the areas that encouraged the development of and rewarded excellence in intellectual and scholarly accomplishments, especially in advanced and highly specialized academic research and studies. The *People's Daily* published an editorial on April 13, 1958, entitled "Drag Bourgeois Individualism through the Mire." The editorial condemned various manifestations of "bourgeois individualism" in academia, including "art for art's sake," "science for science's sake," "becoming a world-class scientist," or "one-book-ism" (establishing an enduring authority on the basis of publishing a single successful book). The editorial even went so far as to attack academic work: "Guided by bourgeois individualism, academic research is based on individual proposals, without plan or emphasis. It is like a man without a backbone, with a possibility of having a perfect finger while the whole body is unable to stand up. We cannot rely upon such people to develop socialist economy and culture."[76]

This argument clearly indicated that it was the very nature of academic research—personal motivation and individual work—that was incompatible with socialist society and the type of people this society aspired to create. In accordance with this denunciation, numerous universities initiated "discussions" among students, many of whom were enticed to express their true thoughts and thus fell victim to the campaign. For example, when a history student at Xibei University naively insisted that the notion of "specialization of labor" and the distinction between intellectuals and common laborers were still necessary, he was inundated with criticism from his peers and accused of "selling bourgeois stuff" and trying to "pit the intellectuals against working people."[77]

In addition to generating individualism that was corrupting the new man, a highly specialized education also produced sophisticated but useless knowledge, thus misleading the new man or wasting his time. For example, biology students at Beijing University felt ashamed when they could not tell rice from wheat, and physics students were no use at all when they were asked to help peasants by designing hydraulic power stations. The faculty were even worse: a professor authoritative in botany could do nothing to save fruit trees from insect pests, and some zoology professors accidentally killed peasants' rabbits by overdosing them with medicine, based on their knowledge learned from foreign textbooks. In contrast, many peasants could do much better in dealing with these problems, and as a matter of fact it was these "uneducated" people who were teaching the "intellectuals." For example, peasants cured sick rabbits simply by using onions and pumping their stomachs instead of applying complicated Western veterinary methods. The students said disappointedly, "We can get a grade 5 when taking written exams, but if tested with real problems we can only get a 2."[78] In other words, the knowledge necessary for the new man could be acquired only through working with peasants and workers, rather than reading textbooks and taking notes at classroom lectures. One article published in 1958 even proposed that "the word 'study' should be eliminated in our society and replaced by the word 'work,' because 'work' implies any form of production and learning." The same article also suggested that the word "school" might be changed to the "garden for labor and production of the new generation."[79]

The educational experiment and debate were launched directly under Mao's personal guidance. As early as the New Culture Movement of the 1910s, when the "new youth" was the central topic of discussion among intellectuals, Mao had proposed the "work and study" school for future education, in which students would spend four hours per day engaged in agricultural work.[80] In later years his philosophical and epistemological assumptions facilitated this concept. In his "On Practice" and many other works, Mao claimed that the only reliable source for true knowledge was "practice" in social and productive activities. The term "practice" in the Maoist context often means "direct participation," and "knowledge" often refers to firsthand experience. Over the years Mao's suspicion of the value of book learning and institutionalized education grew stronger and was reinforced by his populist and anti-intellectual tendencies. In March 1958 he conversed with some members of the party's Central Committee, and the talk was later publicized under the title "Against Blind Faith in Learning." Mao said that academic training and institutional education had been proven to be unnecessary for intellectual or technological achievements in many cases. As he put it, "Ever since ancient times the people who founded new schools of thought were all young people without too much learning. They had the ability to recognize new things at a glance, and having grasped them, they opened fire on the old fogies." Mao listed Confucius, Jesus, Sakyamuni, Sun Yat-sen, and Marx as such people. His favorite examples of those who did not have a formal educational background but achieved great success were "Franklin of America," who had discovered electricity and "began as a boy," later becoming a biographer, politician, and scientist, and "Gorky of Russia," who "had only two years of elementary schooling." Mao also said: "Of course something can be learned at school; I don't propose to close all the schools. What I mean is that it is not absolutely necessary to attend school."[81]

Mao's distrust of formal education and China's educational experiment—integrating labor with study in 1958, guided by Mao's thoughts—were by no means a new invention. In Europe, during the course of the Industrial Revolution, some self-taught craftsmen and technicians who worked independently had accomplished important breakthroughs without formal training or assistance from thriving universities. Samuel Crompton (1753–1827), the inventor of the "spinning mule" that sparked a revolution in textile industry, was an outstanding example. Compared with James Watt, who worked many years for the University of Glasgow and whom Mao mentioned in one of his talks on education in the 1960s (see the section "Revolution in Education in the 1960s" later in this chapter) as another example of inventors without a university diploma, Crompton was even more independent from higher education and therefore would have been a more telling example for Mao's argument, had Mao read more on the subject. It is against this background that a Western variant of anti-intellectualism began to emerge, to exalt untutored talents and firsthand experience while questioning the value and use of university-based theoretical training.[82] This anti-intellectual ideology was more obviously reflected in the traditions of utopian socialism and Russian populism. For example, the French utopian socialist Fourier proposed that in his ideal phalanstery, in order to create well-rounded individuals, members would switch their jobs between intellectual and manual and between various types of manual work every two hours. With the same anticipation, Mao in 1958 suggested running a factory in his guard regiment: "How about taking four hours from your eight-hour study every day to participate in industrial work? In that way you will be able to be a worker as well as a soldier, and in the future you will be a 'red expert.'"[83] Also in Fourier's ideal society, education was to be based on the integration of working and living. The separation between mental and manual labor would disappear, along with intellectuals and experts. For Fourier, this was what a "harmonic education" really meant. The Russian populist Peter Kropotkin specifically proposed "school-work-shops" to replace institutions of higher education. As he put it, "We do not need these workers' schools. . . . We must close all universities, colleges, and other forms of higher education and use social financial resources to run school-workshops."[84] He even proposed that professors should do some heavy and dirty jobs, such as cleaning up buildings, to shorten the social distance between them and physical laborers. In practice, such anti-intellec-tualism was experimented with—to differing degrees—in the Soviet Union during the 1920s and in Cuba in the 1960s.

But when the Great Leap Forward and the people's commune cam-paign brought about disastrous economic consequences, forcing the party to retreat, the educational revolution was also reassessed. At the end of 1960 the Cultural and Educational Group of the party's Central Committee con-vened a meeting to review the previous two years' educational reform and criticized the erroneous tendencies as being "premature communist" and "commanding without the least investigation." As a result of this retreat, the Ministry of Education issued "Sixty Articles for Universities," "Fifty Articles for Middle Schools," and "Forty Articles for Elementary Schools," to restore order and normalcy in schools and to make it clear that the central task of school was education—meaning regular and institutionalized teach-ing and learning.

China's hasty educational transformation to communism from 1958 to 1959 and its retreat in the early 1960s resembled the Soviet experience in the 1920s and its turnaround in the early 1930s. This Soviet-Chi-nese parallel was reflected not only in the nearly identical rhetoric, pol-icies, and processes but even more so by the evidence of a critical Chi-nese interpretation of the Soviet experiment. Gong Yuzhi, a high-ranking party intellectual serving the department of propaganda of the CCP's Cen-tral Committee, published his memoir in 2008, in which he revealed a direct link of this Soviet-Chinese connection. Gong said that sometime in 1961 Mao came across some Soviet literature mentioning Stalin's critique and termination of the radical educational innovations in the early 1930s, and that Nadezhda Krupskaia, Lenin's widow, remained vocal—by virtue of her relationship with Lenin—in supporting some of the experimental policies emphasizing the importance of integrating work and study. Mao took a serious interest in this history and asked the department to conduct a study on the topic and give him a detailed report. Gong, who read Russian, took on the task, spent several months on it, and came up with a lengthy document titled "Some Materials about the Historical Development of the Soviet Educational Guideline," a meticulous introduction to the Soviet educational experiment of the 1920s and the Stalinist rectification in the early 1930s, with largely critical comments on the experiment. The document even pointed out the influence of some "Western bourgeois educational thoughts"—such as John Dewey's pragmatism, which advocated nontraditional pedagogical methods and "learning by doing"—upon Soviet educators such as Paul Blonsky and V. N. Shul'gin (introduced in chapter 1). In fact, John Dewey and many other Western educators did develop a profound interest in educational reforms in the Soviet Union. Dewey visited the country in 1928 but quickly abandoned his fondness for Stalin's Russia when the Great Purge came in the early 1930s.

Gong's document was internally circulated and was only made public in the form of an appendix in Gong's memoir some forty-five years later. Gong's reflection on the history of communist educational reforms clearly indicates the significance of such a Russian-Chinese parallel, given that the Chinese were unaware of the Russian experiment but came up with almost the same ideas, proposals, and the same process from bold advance to enforced retreat:

> Based on a revolutionary ideal of reforming education by integrating it with work, [the Russians] had developed a number of policies and practices, especially the "withering away of the school," which in reality destroyed education. I had known almost nothing about this history [before I conducted that research], and neither did most of comrades then engaged in education. Revolution seems doomed to have many twists and turns. In China our party first proposed the guideline of integrating education with productive labor in 1958, then was engaged in educational revolution during the Great Leap Forward, but finally in 1962 it set forth "Sixty Articles for Universities," "Fifty Articles for Middle Schools," and "Forty Articles for Elementary Schools," designed to rectify erroneous tendencies brought about by the [1958] guideline, which required too many social and political activities as well as physical work, resulting in disrupting schooling and lowering educational quality.[85]

It is unclear how Mao responded to this research report or to the historical lesson; perhaps the "twists and turns" in Russia had only reinforced his determination to carry out the educational revolution more thoroughly.

That was exactly what happened. After a temporary setback in the early 1960s, Mao initiated a new round of educational reform on a much larger scale and with more vigor, which served as one of the most important policies of the Cultural Revolution.

THE 1960S: NEW DYNAMICS

The first half of the 1960s started with a relatively mild political atmosphere but ended with an unprecedented upheaval—the Cultural Revolution. As part of this change, the social engineering of the new man accelerated and developed some new characteristics, especially the fervent personality cult of Mao and an unusual emphasis on the power of revolutionary faith and on self-sacrifice. Several internal and external elements converged to make this period special in the history of creating the Chinese new man.

The most important internal element was that the failure of the Great Leap Forward and the campaign of people's communes seriously harmed the party's, and especially Mao's, credibility among the people. To mend the damaged authority of the party and of Mao, the regime intensified ideological education, with the younger generations as a particular target. In this regard the party's strategy was to defend itself in an offensive way. Perceived as the most effective vehicle of ideological education for the new man, the exaltation and emulation of models were used to an unprecedented extent. In order to make model emulation more accessible to the younger generations, the party created and promoted a number of new models who had grown up after 1949 and were therefore identical to their contemporaries in their upbringing.

The external factor was, first of all, the Sino-Soviet split. The ideological debate between China and Russia, starting in the late 1950s, in time developed into Chinese suspicion and then rejection of the Soviet approach toward communism. "Restoration of capitalism," "embourgeoisement," and, more often, "revisionism" were China's accusations against Soviet development and policy reorientation after Stalin's death. For the Chinese leaders, especially Mao himself, the failure of socialist revolution in Russia was first of all caused by selecting wrong "successors." As Charles Ridley and Dennis Doolin point out, from the late 1950s "Mao began to show more and more concern for the kind of persons who would inherit his revolution."[86] Mao's concern resulted from his observation of the social transformation taking place in the Soviet Union. For Mao, "the revolutionary successor" issue in the Soviet Union was not just Stalin's failure to detect hidden traitors in the leadership but also, in a broader sense, the Soviet system's failure to produce a whole new generation of revolutionaries who would stand up against treason in the Kremlin. In other words, the "Soviet man" had been corrupted and had failed to carry on the revolution. This Soviet experience put Mao and other Chinese leaders on alert and affected Chinese domestic politics in the 1960s, given that by then most of the CCP's first-generation leaders were in their sixties, and the first young generation that had grown up after the revolution was approaching adulthood. To avoid the Soviet pitfalls in educating and selecting successors, therefore, became a priority of Mao's ideological and political agenda.

Chinese alertness to the issue of revolutionary successors was also sharpened by Western expectations of an ideological softening in China's future generations. Sometime in November 1963, Roger Hilsman, the US undersecretary of state, made a speech alluding to a "more sophisticated second echelon of leadership" in China and expressing hope that evolutionary development would "eventually profoundly erode the present simple view with which the leadership regards the world."[87] This comment did not escape the Chinese, who still remembered that John Foster Dulles, the US secretary of state in the late 1950s, had had a similar hope in the likelihood of "peaceful evolution" in future Chinese generations. "Peaceful evolution" thus had become an alerting phrase in the CCP's political language. The *People's Daily* responded to Hilsman's remark in February 1964, saying that it "amounts to a public declaration by US imperialism of its intention to promote 'peaceful evolution' in China."[88] In June 1965 the Ninth National Congress of the Chinese Communist Youth League was held in Beijing, and five top leaders (Mao Zedong, Liu Shaoqi, Zhou Enlai, Zhu De, and Deng Xiaoping) attended. The congress highlighted the danger that capitalist restoration and "revisionism" (referring to the Soviet Union) could corrupt the younger generations and called for launching new campaigns to "win over youth."

In August 1964, when commenting on "Khrushchev's phony communism and its historical lessons for the world," Mao listed five characteristics of the "revolutionary successors." Mao said that they must be "genuine Marxist-Leninists," "revolutionaries who wholeheartedly serve the overwhelming majority of the people," "proletarian statesmen capable of uniting with and working together with the overwhelming majority," "models in applying the party's democratic centralism," and "modest and prudent." Regarding the last characteristic, he noted that the successors must "guard against arrogance and impetuosity" and that "they must be imbued with the spirit of self-criticism and have the courage to correct mistakes and shortcomings in their work." This list of five characteristics ended with a more general qualification: "Successors to the revolutionary cause of the proletariat come forward in mass struggles and are tempered in the great storms of revolution."[89]

Years later, when the Cultural Revolution was sweeping across China and people looked back, many felt that they had failed to read the ominous implications in the phrase "tempered in the great storms of revolution."

In July of that same year, Mao talked with his nephew Mao Yuanxin—whose father had been a communist organizer and was executed by the enemy in the civil war—about the five characteristics. The elder Mao emphasized the relationship between these characteristics and the lesson of Soviet revisionism, once again clarifying that his emphasis on these characteristics was meant to prevent revisionism.[90] The record of this talk became an important source in further describing how a revolutionary successor should be cultivated. However, Mao Yuanxin's personal story constitutes an irony of the revolutionary successor. During his uncle's last years, he was entrusted by the elder Mao to be the commissar of the largest military region (Shenyang), which bordered the Soviet Union in Manchuria. More importantly, his uncle appointed him to be the Politburo secretary, relaying the leader's directives to the members of the Politburo and conveying information back to him. Unfortunately Mao Yuanxin did not pick the right horse in the power race. He allied himself with the Gang of Four and thus ruined his career as a successor. After his uncle's death, he was arrested along with the Gang of Four.

New Models of the Individual

Against this background, the first half of the 1960s witnessed an upsurge in models for the new man. As the *People's Liberation Army Daily* proclaimed: "The Mao Zedong era we are in is also an era of heroes. A succession of outstanding men rise up from the people; a profusion of good men and good deeds marks the era."[91] Many Chinese newspapers used the phrase "a constellation of heroes" to hail the sudden emergence of models for the new man. Often when the story of one hero was still unfolding in the news, it was quickly eclipsed by another. The intensive coverage and the succession of such models undoubtedly suggest a well-coordinated campaign to create and promote them.

The campaigns to exalt and emulate models were a modern hagiolatry in many ways. They often started by extensively promoting publicity of models, with lengthy reports in newspapers (often running many pages or continuing as a series over several days), publications of their diaries (always carefully selected or even rewritten) and of accounts about them provided by their close comrades, and in many cases leaders' commendations of them. Selectively narrated and often exaggerated to suit the party's ideological needs, these profiles of the heroes were larger than life and even unrecognizable to many who knew the individuals well. Following this publicity phase was the public emulation, marked by a flood of biographies, poems, songs, pictures, cartoons, movies, and plays based on the models' stories, as well as exhibitions of the heroes' personal items and sometimes the renaming of schools, work or army units, and even newborn babies after the models. Mass rallies were also held in which participants took a pledge to "learn from" the models or to "live and work" like them. Attendance at study sessions on model-promotion materials was required for everyone, and attendees were asked to make individual plans on how to emulate the heroes, often starting with "the most immediate and insignificant matters," such as offering assistance to a sick comrade, making a small donation, or extending work hours for a day to help clean up the workplace.

The Young Soldiers

The People's Liberation Army (PLA) took a leading role in generating this wave of models for the new man. The rise of the PLA as the most active and important political force came in the early 1960s, as Lin Biao—one of the ten marshals who replaced Peng Dehuai as defense minister after the latter criticized Mao's Great Leap Forward in 1959 (though in a manner of remonstrator)—launched a campaign to apply Mao's thought as a guideline to even routine business. By defending Mao's authority in the aftermath of the Great Leap Forward, Lin became Mao's staunch political ally and later his designated successor. Under Lin's leadership, the PLA initiated and implemented a number of radical moves in China that eventually led to the Cultural Revolution. Among these moves, the creation and promotion of models for the new man—most of whom were young soldiers—were the most conspicuous and popular.

The first and the most important hero was Lei Feng. In 1963 the name of Lei Feng, a sublieutenant and a truck driver in the army, suddenly made headlines in every newspaper and magazine. According to the official account, Lei was born in the early 1940s, and his parents and siblings, who had been abused by Nationalists, landlords, and the Japanese Army, all died. Lei, who had been left as an orphan when liberation came, was brought up by the local party organizations. As the most conspicuous figure in the "constellation" of models, Lei Feng distinguished himself by comparing his party loyalty to a child's love of its mother, a relationship deeper than an ideological commitment and class consciousness. Lei's affection for the party and the leader, made known in his posthumously publicized diary, was often more than political. For example, one day he got up "particularly happy," because the night before he had "dreamed of our great leader, Chairman Mao." This happened to be the same day of the party's fortieth anniversary. In the words of Mary Sheridan, such a passion was "romantic in an adolescent vein."[92] As Lei himself put it, "I am like a toddler, and the party is like my mother, who helps me, leads me, and teaches me to walk. . . . My beloved party, my loving mother, I am always your loyal son."[93] Lei also had a favorite metaphor, which likened revolutionary soldiers to screws—humble but indispensable and, above all, dutiful. Although Wu Yunduo was perhaps first to use this metaphor, as early as the 1950s, it was Lei Feng who made it more popular than ever.

For ordinary people, however, Lei Feng's renown was largely attributed to his countless good deeds, inspired by his diligent study of Mao's thought. Official propaganda described Lei as very frugal, saving every penny of his meager stipend as a soldier, but generous in making donations, often anonymously. On weekends and holidays he never took a break from work but instead would go to nearby train stations to help old passengers or women carrying children and to sweep out platforms and waiting rooms. His most bizarre good deed was washing the socks of his fellow soldiers at midnight while they slept soundly.

Lei Feng died in a traffic accident when on duty, and political instructors in his army unit quickly moved to commend his good deeds. But when the army's higher ideological and propaganda agencies became involved, they decided that Lei's value as a model consisted of more than just a number of good deeds. Ultimately, Lei's story drew the attention of Mao and other top leaders. In March 1963, Mao issued a directive: "Learn from Comrade Lei Feng." Seven other leaders—including Liu Shaoqi, second in the leadership; Zhou Enlai, the premier; and Deng Xiaoping, the general secretary of the party—also issued directives commending Lei. Chinese newspapers published calligraphic versions of the directives, accompanied by editorials and lengthy reports. In the "Learn from Comrade Lei Feng" campaign, Mao's thought was highlighted as the only ideological source that had inspired Lei. As Luo Ruiqing, chief of the general staff of the army, put it, Lei Feng "constantly studied Mao's works, did exactly what Mao teaches, strictly followed Mao's words at every moment, with a single goal in his mind: to be one of Mao's good soldiers." Luo also said that Mao's thought was Lei Feng's "weapon, wheel [referring to Lei Feng's job as a truck driver], and food."[94]

The campaign to emulate Lei Feng was the most popular one among countless others of the same nature, and an individual's performance in such a campaign could have an impact on his or her future, so much so that it became stressful to many. According to Anita Chan, who in the late 1970s interviewed many young students who had grown up in the 1960s:

> In classrooms where students were competing to get into the [Communist] Youth League and through that into a university, Lei Feng's type of good

deeds provided concrete standards by which league members could appraise the political performance of would-be candidates. The writing of diaries and the circulation of them for public criticism, above all to league members, became an important way to show activism; so too did the secret washing and mending of classmates' clothes and sheets and anonymous cleaning of windows and sweeping of floors. Teenage activists often became hard-pressed to think of new and ingenious ways to outdo each other.[95]

But Lei's moral, saintlike image became tainted after the mid-1980s, when the Maoist puritanical spell over Chinese society started to dissipate. People began to learn some facts about Lei Feng that were incompatible with the qualities of the new man of the 1960s and therefore had never been released before. For example, Lei Feng had an imported watch and a large piece of fine woolen material ideal for making a business suit, both of which would have been regarded as luxurious in a time when millions suffered from hunger. In addition, Lei had a bank balance of hundreds of Chinese yuan. There was nothing suspicious in these possessions in terms of their sources, because Lei had worked in a factory for several years before joining the army and that job may have been rewarding enough to finance them, given Lei's frugality. But many people could not help but wonder what was in his mind, as a model for the new man, when he accumulated these assets. One additional fact made Lei's image more sophisticated than that in the official propaganda: he had had a couple of romantic encounters with women he had worked or studied with. Such things would have been considered perfectly normal in the lives of everyone else, but not in Lei Feng's. The party thus modified Lei's profile in the 1980s by adding and acknowledging his "human" side.

Wang Jie, a miner and a squad leader, was another model created one year after Lei Feng was introduced. Born into a middle-class peasant family, Wang was always aware of his family's class origin (which was not as pure as Lei Feng's) and therefore regarded thought reform as a serious daily under-taking. As a result of such a constant ideological purification, he ultimately sacrificed his life: he covered an accidentally discharged grenade with his body to save his comrades' lives at a training session.

A selection of entries of Wang Jie's diary was published, reflecting a mind more sophisticated and self-critical than that of Lei Feng, perhaps resulting from the party's preference. Wang pondered every day on what was appropriate and inappropriate in his behavior as well as in his thought, through critical reflection from the perspective of "Mao's good soldier." In addition, his diary showed how he was inspired by other heroes. As he suggested: "Study such heroes as Dong Chunrui, Huang Jiguang, Qiu Shaoyun,

An Yemin [PLA soldiers who had died in action], and Lei Feng, etc. Use their exemplary deeds as a mirror, and never cease self-examination."[96]

Lei Feng and Wang Jie were two early models from the army in the first half of the 1960s. There were more young PLA soldier models. Liu Yingjun, at the cost of his own life, saved children from the wheels of a wagon drawn by runaway horses. Ouyang Hai pushed a horse loaded with ammunition beyond a railway track and saved the train, but he was hit by the train and died. Mai Xiande, a navy sailor who was wounded and paralyzed in a battle with the Nationalists, overcame his pain and disabilities in the hospital with spiritual power drawn from Mao's thought.

The campaign of exalting these young soldiers as models in the early 1960s illustrated some new characteristics of the new man, distinctive from the old models created in the war years and the 1950s. The first distinction was that Mao's personality cult rapidly overrode the party's role in their ideological development. In these models' diaries, we can see a tendency to project Mao's influence, while the party's role faded away to the background. For example, in Lei Feng's diary (61 entries altogether), Mao was not directly quoted, although some vague references to his "works" were made, and his name was mentioned eight times. The party, however, was mentioned 24 times. In Wang Jie's diary (116 entries), Mao was quoted 25 times and mentioned 59 times, and the party was frequently mentioned. In Liu Yingjun's diary, among 27 entries, 11 quoted Mao's directives, and 22 were devoted to studying Mao's thought, while the party was seldom mentioned.[97]

In addition to being an ideological guideline, Mao's thought was taken as a criterion for self-criticism and even as a source of spiritual power. For instance, Liu Yingjun wrote in his diary that every time he read Mao's "The Foolish Old Man Who Removed the Mountains," "I find a new source of inspiration, and new progress begins to show." After making a contrast between the foolish old man and himself, especially his tendency to succumb to difficulties, Wang Jie continued: "With the foolish old man standing as an example, I feel that my confidence and determination increase a hundredfold." This combination of Mao's personality cult with ideological education and self-examination appeared frequently in the later diaries, and over time it developed into a dominant pattern in mass emulation of models and thought reform.

The second distinction was conscious and constant thought reform through everyday self-examination and reflection. The long journey of becoming a new man was paved by inward self-denial and self-perfection. For instance, Wang Jie once felt guilty and confessed in his diary about using deception to get an official honor. The honor was given to the soldier who was the first to get to the assembly line in an early-morning drill. Wang

Jie overheard the company commander talking about the upcoming drill and stayed up all night for the signal, which was not expected by others. Afterwards this "deceptive trick" nagged at him, and he felt he had fooled the whole company. "From now on," he wrote, "I shall deal correctly with the issue of honor and be a nameless hero." Publicizing diaries of the models was thus quite effective in educating others, because it showed the "human" side of the heroes and therefore shortened the distance between them and their emulators. The diaries were also "more didactic and more 'soul-searching,'" as Sheridan has pointed out.[98] In the Cultural Revolution, such conscious personal efforts at self-examination and thought reform applied to everyone. As Lin Biao once suggested in a hyperbolic yet vivid tone, everyone should "consciously make revolution in the depths of his soul."[99]

The third distinction was the emphasis on the endurance of pain and hardship, even in ordinary work conditions, as a means to temper the revolutionary determination of new men and to prepare them for the ultimate test: sacrifice of their life. Many stories told how these heroes intentionally made their daily work tougher and even into an ordeal, in order to temper themselves, so much so that sometimes they even rejected receiving medical treatment or taking a rest when they were facing physical pain or extreme fatigue. Ouyang Hai, for instance, persisted at his work even after his hands were accidentally burned. He hid the wounds with gloves that enabled him to continue construction work without his comrades spotting his injury. It was believed that when war and other life-or-death trials were absent, intentionally enduring pain could be an alternative means to testify to one's revolutionary resolve and commitment. The final sacrifice was not a momentary righteous impulse but the result of discipline through daily ordeals. Mao himself was especially concerned about this issue. In the talk with Mao Yuanxin mentioned above, he chided his nephew for his fondness for comfort and fear of difficulty. Mao used the sacrifice of Yuanxin's father to educate his nephew, saying that if he continued to live in relative comfort, he would get down "on both knees and beg" the enemy for his life if he someday were to face the same test his father had.[100]

The Exemplary Cadres

In addition to young soldier models, the party also needed models for cadres, given that the bureaucracy had grown ever since 1949 and that the party wanted to avoid the Soviet experience of the formation of a new elite class in a time of peace and economic development. The party found its ideal cadre model: Jiao Yulu. Jiao was appointed as the party secretary of Lan Kao County (in Henan Province) in 1962, a year when millions were still suffering from the consequences of the Great Leap Forward. As soon as he arrived in that barren place, which was threatened by encroaching desert, Jiao made inspection tours on foot and bicycle and started planting trees as a greenbelt project to prevent more lands from being engulfed by desert. Jiao died eighteen months later from liver cancer. Apparently his hard work had precipitated the development of the cancer, and he had suffered tremendously from the pain. But according to the official account, Jiao never left his work for medical treatment. However, his story was not publicized until February 1966, two years after his death, and some people speculated that the party had waited to see whether his project worked out. Compared with many of his contemporary cadres, Jiao was a highly sympathetic hero, for he had not just preached to others to sacrifice but had set himself as an example and shared their hardships and sorrows.

In February and March of 1966, the *People's Daily* published three editorials, calling on cadres to "learn from Jiao Yulu." One of these editorials was titled "To Be a Better Revolutionary in the Second Half of One's Life." It established Jiao as a model for the cadres who had joined the revolution before 1949 and who were becoming accustomed to an easy life and office work during peacetime. Another editorial warned:

> Individual thought reform is just like sailing upstream; you either keep going upward or are forced to retreat downward. . . . If a revolutionary has undertaken profound thought reform in the first half of his life, that only means [he has created] a well-prepared ground for his continuous thought reform and should not excuse him from ceasing to do it. The correct attitude, as some comrades have said, is, "So long as you live, so much you should study, reform, and devote yourself to the revolution."[101]

Jiao's publicity, however, seemed somehow deflected from the main lines of the campaign of model building and emulation in a subtle way. The problem was that there was less emphasis on Mao's personality cult in the propaganda campaign for Jiao—Mao and his thought were mentioned, but less than in the campaigns promoting the young soldiers. Sheridan has speculated that Jiao's publicity was part of an effort made by Liu Shaoqi, the head of state and a potential competitor for power in Mao's eyes. The state bureaucracy might have wished to balance the campaign by celebrating the young soldiers, and to draw public attention away from the naive personality cult of Mao, toward the real economic predicament of the country. One piece of evidence supporting this speculation was that the PLA, after Jiao's publicity, immediately publicized more stories of young soldier models, in an even stronger tone that those in Mao's cult. In this regard, Mai Xiande's case is illustrative. Mai was a sailor who was seriously wounded in a naval engagement with the Nationalists. Sustained by Mao's teaching, he continued to fight until victory was secured. According to official propaganda, when nurses in the hospital showed him Mao's picture and read Mao's quotations to him, Mai suddenly regained consciousness from a deep coma. The story added a miraculous feature to Mao's personality cult. This intense new campaign to some degree overshadowed Jiao Yulu's image.

To what extent Liu and his associates might have sought to take this opportunity to cool down the fanaticism of Mao's personal cult is a matter for further research, but the campaign celebrating Jiao's was indeed quickly redirected from tackling economic problems to applying Mao's thought. As a matter of fact, the editorials about Jiao in the *People's Daily* were full of references to Mao, and the Xinhua News Agency published a timely brochure entitled "What Mao Says Is What Jiao Yulu Did." In the brochure the editors compared Jiao's words and deeds with Mao's teaching, by presenting quotations from Mao followed by an associated story of Jiao. In one example, Jiao always sent notes to colleagues reminding them of upcoming meetings, and he did so because Mao had said that "only if you are informed in advance will you have an effective meeting."[102]

Workers

Wei Fengying, a female worker-turned-engineer at the Northeastern Machinery Manufactory, was a prominent model for Chinese workers. According to official accounts, she began to study Mao's works in 1954 and transformed herself from an ordinary worker to an exemplary one. Wei often started her work earlier than others and left later, and many times she gave up opportunities for promotions and salary increases. When she was pregnant, she did not tell her supervisor but continued working, wearing a thick jacket covering her belly. She was so devoted to her work and technological innovation that during her courtship she was unable to make "nine out of ten" dates, and in four years she and her boyfriend had watched only half of a movie together, because she felt the urge to leave the theater midway through the movie in order to complete an unfinished work project. She was described as "Mao's good worker, the model of studying and applying Mao's thoughts, the pioneer of the industrial front, a spearhead of technological innovation, a good example for all workers."[103]

In comparison with Xiang Xiuli, Min Shuofu, and Ma Xueli—the new-man models for workers in the 1950s—Wei was more conscious of ideological self-education and self-reformation. As she once put it, "Although I was born into a worker's family, I was exposed to bourgeois ideas, so I need thought reform as well." When she was a young girl, she told others, she had worn white shirts to work, spent time combing her hair, and soaked elm bark in water and then applied the liquid to her hair to make it shine—an alternative to shampoo and conditioner. "I wanted to look like a pretty girl," she said. Then she was criticized by her foreman, who said that such behavior was dangerous: "Today you want elm-bark water, and what will you ask for tomorrow?" After studying Mao's works, her class awareness was raised, and she realized that she must "consciously use Mao's thoughts as a weapon and constantly fight the awareness of 'Me'": "As long as I am alive, I will fight the awareness of 'Me' forever." She even organized her whole family (eight people, including her mother-in-law) to study Mao's works regularly, even though no one among them was of bourgeois origin. Her famous motto was "We should be a radish with red skin and a red core, rather than having red skin but a white core." "Red skin" here referred to a working-class origin and appearance, while "red core" referred to genuine revolutionary spirit resulting from conscious thought reform and self-education.[104] Wei was later promoted to membership in the Central Committee of the CCP in the Cultural Revolution.

Conclusions Regarding the Individual Models

The campaign to promote new models for individuals originally conformed to the guidelines of Mao's five characteristics of revolutionary successors. But in time these characteristics were upstaged by the preeminence of Mao's personality cult, which was much less intellectually and ideologically sophisticated and mainly embodied by young, naive soldiers of low rank in the army. Jiao Yulu was an exception; his rank was at the county level in the civilian order, equivalent to the regiment in the military.

The emphasis on the young generation and people of low rank may have reflected Mao's political analysis that the party and state bureaucracy had been corrupted, with many cadres taking the "capitalist road" and becoming "China's Khrushchevs." Reeducation, or thought reform, would do very little good to change "China's revisionists," such as these. Instead it would be necessary and inevitable to topple the entire hierarchy. The only hope for a communist new man thus lay in the young generation, which, despite a lack of revolutionary experience, was "a piece of blank paper" on which he could write and paint. The Cultural Revolution, in this sense, was a revolution in which a young generation overthrew and replaced the old one under Mao's inspiration.

Collective Models for the New Man

While the individual models of the new man dominated China's political horizon, the nation also witnessed a surge of collective models in the early 1960s. These collective models were designed for almost every social occupation and emulated by every work unit, such as factory, commune, school, hospital, department store, and even kindergarten. The leaders of these exemplary units were often promoted as individual models as well, but their more important value was their role in turning their work units into a collective model.

"In Industry, Learn from Daqing"

Daqing, an oil field in northeastern China that was developed in the early 1960s, became a collective model for industry. Up to that time, China's oil supply had relied very much upon the Soviet Union. As the Sino-Soviet ideological dispute intensified, the political importance of energy self-reliance became more pressing for Beijing. But China was lacking in almost everything entailed in opening a big oil field: technology, experience, equipment, experts, minimum facilities for life in the wilderness of Manchuria (known as China's Siberia), and even the confidence that China did have significant oil deposits, given that Western and Russian geologists had declared that China was poor in oil. It was against this background that the official propaganda portrayed Daqing's success as a revolutionary miracle created by the new man armed with Mao's thoughts—and against all odds.

Though China was poor when measured by material means, it was rich in spiritual terms, and it was this spiritual power that guaranteed Daqing's success. Numerous legends circulating at the time recounted how Mao's thought had been transformed into material power and sustained the oil workers even at the most difficult times. At one crucial moment, for example, when the workers and cadres were facing extremely low temperatures and lacked food and shelter, a timely airborne delivery brought them hundreds of newly reprinted works by Mao: "On Contradiction" and "On Practice." These two philosophical pamphlets were believed to have "methodological value" for all kinds of work, from military campaigns to surgical operations. The workers and cadres studied the pamphlets overnight (though they had studied them before), and their difficulties soon subsided.[105]

The 32111 Drilling Team was promoted as exemplary of the new man in Daqing, embodied by Wang Jingxi and his fellow workers, who attributed their achievement to the application of Mao's thought in the first place. Wang was a typical Mao worshiper. He once said that the most unforgettable event in his life was meeting Chairman Mao. He was uneducated but became literate when he was middle-aged through hard study, motivated by a single goal: "'Learning' a word is like 'removing a mountain.' I want to remove all mountains from my way to see Chairman Mao."[106] This proclamation clearly showed the influence of Wang's study of Mao's famous essay

"The Foolish Old Man Who Removed the Mountains." But for Wang, the influence of Mao's teaching went far beyond ideological and moral aspects, as illustrated by the title of Wang's speech at a national conference on industry and transportation in 1966: "Relying upon Mao Zedong's Thought, We Will Take Over This Giant Oil Field as Quickly as Possible!"[107] Armed with Mao's thought on self-reliance, Wang and his comrades "demystified" foreign geological theories such as the notion that China was poor in oil, and despised those Western-educated Chinese scientists who were skeptical about China's capability to be oil self-reliant. "I don't believe that all oil is deposited under foreign countries' ground" was Wang's famous proclamation. For Wang, technological and operational innovations were not merely a technical issue but a political one as well. He claimed that in order to achieve energy self-reliance as quickly as possible, Chinese workers must not be bound by those "foreign" doctrines or listen to those "experts" who always looked in "thick and foreign textbooks" for solutions to practical problems. He defied those doctrines and often adopted unconventional operational procedures and steps to achieve desirable results—for example, drilling a well at almost a right angle (a technically difficult and dangerous position). In his speech, he said that the most important lesson was, "As long as we do what Mao teaches, there is no difficulty that we can not overcome." The Daqing experience, which was widely applied during the 1960s and 1970s, therefore was summarized as "Let politics take command and reform people's thought," an essential Maoist slogan.[108]

It would be difficult for a sensible observer to believe that Mao's thought could play a miraculous role in solving technical problems involved in an oil field, although no one would deny its possible effect in boosting Chinese workers' morale, given the overall fanatical atmosphere of the Mao cult. However, it would be more credible to say that Mao's discourse encouraged some heroic acts. One of the legends held that Wang and his fellow workers used their bodies to mix up components for concrete in order to save the oil field. One day, according to the official account, one of the oil wells suddenly erupted, posing a serious threat to the neighboring wells. The only way to put down the eruption was to pour concrete into the well, but the concrete mixer was not functioning well. At that crucial moment, Wang, the leader of the drilling team, plunged himself into the concrete pool and stirred the concrete components with his body. In imitation of him, many workers did the same, and the eruption was stopped. That act made Wang an instant hero and gained him the nickname "Iron Man." For this and other exemplary acts, Wang and his team were named the Heroic 32111 Drilling Team.

The Daqing oil field, and more specifically Wang Jingxi and his Heroic 32111 Drilling Team, were officially established as a model for China's industry. Mao issued a directive in 1964: "In industry, learn from Daqing." A campaign based on the directive was soon set in motion. Numerous delegations made pilgrimages to the oil field to study on-site, and at the same time the speakers from the oil field toured the country to introduce the "Daqing experience," or "Daqing spirit." Related books, songs, plays, movies, and poems flooded the official propaganda machine, and many workers and work units were renamed after Wang and his team in honor of their achievements.

"In Agriculture, Learn from Dazhai"

Almost at the same time that Daqing was in the headlines of national and local newspapers, Dazhai, a productive brigade in Xiyang County, Shanxi Province, gained extraordinary national prominence as a collective model for rural development. Located in the Taihang Mountains, Dazhai was a village endowed by nature with little favor. The soil there was arid and infertile, rainfall was insufficient, and nowhere was there a piece of field flat and broad enough for stable cultivation. For hundreds of years, Dazhai's villagers had barely survived. In the mid-1950s, however, the villagers—under the leadership of Chen Yonggui, the party secretary of the brigade—embarked on a number of tremendous efforts to transform the environment, and by the mid-1960s the appearance of the village and its surroundings had been changed. According to official accounts, what enabled them to achieve such extraordinary success was, first of all, the replacement of their "small-peasant mentality" with a "collective and socialist consciousness," thus transforming the private farmers into socialist "new men" in the countryside.

Like the history of Daqing, Dazhai's development was also a record of legends and heroic deeds of the socialist new man, mixed with miracles brought about by Mao's cult. In the early and mid-1950s, the formation of a cooperative required Dazhai's peasants—like farmers everywhere in China—to pool their lands, draft animals, and tools to lay a foundation for collectively owned property. Based on the value of their collectivized property, each family would be rewarded proportionally from the cooperative when the harvest came. The methods and procedures of property evaluation therefore became a focus of attention and, in some cases, apprehension. Chen Yonggui, the village's party secretary and a Mao worshiper who studied his hero's words every day, according to official accounts, deliberately undervalued his mule and his pig at half the price. Every villager knew that

Chen's mule was the strongest in the village and that his pig was pregnant, so the prospective baby pigs should have added to the pig's value. By setting himself as a model of selflessness, Chen led his fellows to enter the cooperative earlier than most villages in the province, and its establishment was announced intentionally on the anniversary of Mao's birthday.[109]

The formation of the cooperative enabled the peasants to fight the unfavorable natural elements collectively. Under Chen's leadership, the peasants built up dikes and dams and dug canals to form an irrigation network. They also leveled mountains to build terraced fields and reservoirs. Dazhai's approach—mass mobilization and collective work—drew attention from the leaders of the county and even the province. In 1958, during the Great Leap Forward and the people's commune movement, Xiyang County, inspired by Dazhai, organized its peasant labor force into a "cooperative production army" (discussed above), and this pattern of labor division and labor drafting was later followed by many provinces and counties in their own development projects.

In the campaign for people's communes, Chen Yonggui led the people of Dazhai to establish the first such commune in Xiyang County. In the early years of the 1960s, when hunger hung over millions of Chinese peasants, Dazhai again made itself a model. In the spring of 1960, when the market prices for food and forage were soaring, Dazhai sold its chaff (a supplementary food at the time) and forage to neighboring brigades at surprisingly low prices, helping them to survive. Meanwhile, when many provinces and counties were affected by a trend to retreat to individual farming, which had been proven more effective in promoting production but was regarded as a setback on the road toward communism, Dazhai persisted in its collective farming and maintained its commune.

In the summer of 1963, Dazhai suffered a massive flood, which destroyed 90 percent of the houses and caves (traditional Chinese residences in some northeastern mountainous areas). It also washed away most of the irrigation systems built up in the previous years. Chen Yonggui planned to reconstruct all that had been destroyed and once again appealed to mass mobilization, collective work, and sacrifice. Because Dazhai had been celebrated nationwide as a model rural community, it received many letters of sympathy from all over the country. Every day before work, Chen read one of those letters to the peasants to boost their morale. When the county government sent relief packages to Dazhai, Chen and the brigade's party committee decided to pass them on to other villages also suffering from the disaster.

At the beginning of 1964, the Central Broadcasting Station and the *People's Daily* publicized Dazhai's story. The broadcast station prepared a series of programs under the title "Learn from and Emulate Dazhai." The *People's Daily* started off its contribution to the propaganda campaign with a long report on February 10, 1964, entitled "The Road of Dazhai," accompanied by an editorial with a banner headline, "The Model of Construction in Mountainous Areas with the Revolutionary Spirit." The most important lesson people could learn from Dazhai, according to the *People's Daily*, was to make efforts to overcome egoism, to build up collectivism in people's minds, to integrate individuals into the community, and to change people's thought and mentality completely. That spring a central government delegation was sent to Dazhai to further inspect and confirm the stories. Soon the party decided that Dazhai deserved more honor and should be regarded as a "red flag" in agriculture. In December, Zhou Enlai, the premier, praised Dazhai in his report to the People's Congress, with details and statistics reflecting Dazhai's heroism and success. He pointed out three things in Dazhai that deserved to be learned by the people: "the principle of politics in command and ideology above anything, the spirit of self-reliance and hard work, and the love of collectivity and country with a communist consciousness."[110]

Four days later, Mao, in a rare move, invited Chen Yonggui, who was attending the People's Congress in Beijing as a representative from his province, to his birthday dinner. The array of special guests at the dinner clearly indicated Mao's thinking on China's political life. In addition to Chen Yonggui, there was Xing Yanzi, a young woman representing urban youth who had voluntarily settled in the country and "integrated" with the peasants. There was also Qian Xuesen, a prominent atomic scientist who had returned to China from the United States in the mid-1950s and had become one of the most important figures in developing China's nuclear arsenal. But that day he had been invited to Mao's birthday dinner for another reason, which Mao praised while they were wined and dined: "Qian Xuesen rejected payments for his articles and never let his family use his government car. That is very good."[111] Chen, Xing, and Qian were seated at the dinner table with Mao, while at another dinner table sat some top leaders, including Liu Shaoqi and Deng Xiaoping. Liu and Deng in particular had been attempting to introduce or restore some material-incentive measures to recover agriculture in the wake of the Great Leap Forward, and for this they were later condemned as "taking the capitalist road." According to Chen Yonggui's biography, the atmosphere at the dinner was uneasy, and only Mao was talking. With historical hindsight, people today may well interpret that occasion as an ominous sign of the great divergence in the inner circle of the leadership: Mao was using the dinner to show his preference for the new-man spirit over material incentives in solving China's economic problems.

Then Dazhai gained its national prominence. After "Learn from Comrade Lei Feng" and "In Industry, Learn from Daqing," Mao had found a collective model for China's peasants. His directive "In Agriculture, Learn from Dazhai" became a new ideological catchphrase. The ideological and economic importance of the "Dazhai road" can be illustrated by the following: "For a country as large and as backward as China, where is the way out for agricultural development? Relying upon state investment? It is obviously unfeasible. The people in Dazhai have found the answer for the country: putting Mao Zedong's thought in command, holding to the principle of 'ideology first,' and carrying forward the spirit of self-reliance and hard work."[112]

Pilgrims poured into this small mountain village of eighty families. The central government even had to order the army to dispatch helicopters and planes to drop food and clothes in a winter emergency in 1966, when thousands of pilgrims were starving and freezing on the road to Dazhai.

The campaign to emulate Dazhai lasted for more than ten years (until the end of the 1970s). Numerous villages, brigades, communes, and counties, deemed to have succeeded in adopting Dazhai's approach, were honored as a "Dazhai-style" village, commune, or county. Chen Yonggui, the leader of Dazhai, though he did not have even an elementary school diploma, was promoted into the CCP's Politburo and appointed as deputy premier, in charge of agriculture for the whole country. In the 1970s he attempted to change the basic economic accounting unit in rural areas from brigade to commune, which meant a higher level of public ownership, and thus one step closer to communism. For many, the proposed change sounded like a return to the Great Leap Forward. But his effort failed, as China had been suffering from the Cultural Revolution for years, and the mentality and dynamism of the Great Leap Forward and the early stage of the Cultural Revolution no longer existed. In early 1978 Chen visited Cambodia and was impressed by the Khmer Rouge's agricultural reconstruction plan, which virtually dismantled village and family, putting everyone in collective units. For Chen, it was a shame that in a matter of two years or perhaps just one year the Khmer Rouge, the little brother of Chinese communists, had achieved what China had failed to do, despite its much longer history of socialist revolution. Chen was sidelined and almost forced to retire (although honored as a labor hero till his death) after Mao's death, when Deng Xiaoping reemerged with his reforms to dismantle the people's communes and restore private farming. For the rest of his life, Chen was embittered and deplored the demise of the socialist spirit he long had championed, from the 1950s to the 1970s.

The Whole Country Must "Learn from the People's Liberation Army"

One way in which Daqing and Dazhai were distinctive from traditional or conventional industrial and agricultural management was that many of their most important engagements were organized in a military manner, as discussed in the case of Dazhai and Xiyang County's labor division and regimentation. This was even more true in Daqing. The entire undertaking of opening up the oil field was called *hui zhan* in Chinese, meaning "great battle." It was an adoption of a Maoist strategy in the civil war (concentrating as much military power as possible to gain an advantage over and to overwhelm and annihilate the enemy) by mobilizing and organizing massive manpower and technology to achieve certain goals that otherwise might take decades to accomplish. Therefore, Dazhai and Daqing, as models for agriculture and industry, were essentially associated with the army and its methods.

In addition to the adoption of military methods and strategy, starting in the early 1950s, some army units had been honored as collective models symbolizing the continuation of wartime spirit in peacetime. The Exemplary Eighth Company on the Nanjing Road was perhaps the most prominent one. Nanjing Road was the center of the commercial and entertainment district in downtown Shanghai before 1949, symbolizing all the vices of colonialism and capitalism in the communist perception of "old China." After the Liberation, a PLA company of the Shanghai Garrison was stationed in the district, but before long, the soldiers and officers found they were surrounded by all kinds of dazzling lures. The official propaganda later described the company's situation as a typical "test" for all Chinese communists as they took over cities. Sustained by upholding revolutionary Puritanism and maintaining the highest alertness, the soldiers and officers proved that they were tough and incorruptible. Though surrounded by the most upscale clothing stores, they continued to hand-sew their worn-out socks and shirts, for example. The company was named the "Exemplary Eighth Company on the Nanjing Road" by Mao and was held up by the party to teach its members how to remain immune from all forms of influence from the old social environment, impervious to "sugar-coated bullets," as Mao once put it.

To popularize the outstanding conduct of the company, the party's artists created a play (later adapted into a movie) titled *The Guards under Neon Lights*. In it a platoon leader of peasant origin is dazzled by the comfort and luxury on the Nanjing Road and slackens his revolutionary alertness, especially under the influence of a pretty young lady who turns out be an imperialist spy approaching him on purpose. When his peasant wife comes to visit him, he appears to be indifferent and throws away her hand-sewn socks. But with the help of the vigilant political officer of the company, he undergoes thought reform and pulls himself back before falling into the abyss. In a peculiar way this scenario highlighted the binary perception of the city and the countryside, a key issue of social environment in creating the new man: cities were permeated with vice and danger, whereas the countryside was pure and indispensable for political education and moral redemption. "Guards under neon lights" thus became the popular symbol of revolutionary vigilance and incorruptibility.

After the early 1950s the exemplary role of the PLA became increasingly prominent. The emergence of the young heroes in the early 1960s, such as Lei Feng, Wang Jie, and Ouyang Hai, can be viewed as a continuation of this exaltation, though with new dynamics and under new circumstances. One of the most laudatory official acclamations of the PLA's model value came on February 1, 1964, when the *People's Daily* published an editorial appealing for "emulation of the PLA." The most important role the army played as a collective model was its contribution to Mao's personality cult. Lin Biao, the defense minister then and the most enthusiastic advocate in promoting Mao's cult, claimed that the army must become "a gigantic school of Mao's thoughts." He issued a directive to the soldiers and officers: "Read Mao's books, listen to Mao's words, do what Mao teaches, and be Mao's good soldiers." At that time, "Mao's good soldiers" was virtually synonymous with all exemplary members of the army. Lin made another proclamation about the power of Mao's thought in transforming the human mind and the material world as well: "It is essential to imbue the workers and peasants with Chairman Mao's thought through the creative study and application of his works. Only so can the mental outlook of the working people be changed and spiritual forces be transformed into enormous material strength."[113]

The army created a set of values and priorities in performing its daily routine, and they were later introduced beyond the barracks. These were highly ideological and grouped under numerical phrases to aid memorizing and reciting, a typical method in Chinese learning of classics. For example, there were "four goods" and "four firsts." The "four goods" required that an army unit be good at (1) political and ideological work, (2) the three-eight working style, (3) military training, and (4) assurance of the well-being of soldiers. The "three-eight working style" included these instructions: (1) keep firmly to the correct political orientation, (2) maintain an industrious and simple style of work, and (3) be flexible in strategy and tactics. The "four firsts" referred to making the study of Mao's thought and other relevant ideological development the top priority. One example of "emulation of the PLA" was the establishment of a political department in all municipal, cultural, and industrial administrations to intensify ideological education. The political department was a PLA-style ideological and political administrative branch, set up in the army during wartime to politically educate soldiers, monitor officers, and maintain morale. Another striking example of "emulation of the PLA" was the adoption of military-style organization, especially in schools. For example, during the late 1960s and the early 1970s, in elementary schools, class two of the third grade was renamed as the second squad of the third company, and a class of a grade in middle schools was similarly renamed.

The PLA had been under Soviet influence since the mid-1950s, as it strove to develop itself into a modernized standing army, rather than a guerrilla force. One result was that the PLA adopted the Soviet system of military ranks and titles, with marshal at the top and corporal at the bottom. In the mid-1960s, however, in the increasingly intensified atmosphere of antirevisionism, the system was regarded as an example of the corrupting Soviet influence, which had compromised the PLA's Red Army egalitarian tradition by replacing it with a rigid hierarchy. Apparently such a system was no longer compatible with the image of the collective model for the new man. On May 22, 1965, therefore, the Standing Committee of the People's Congress issued a resolution to abolish this system. The resolution specified the style of military uniform, which would show no conspicuous signs of rank and title in the military or the security force. The only noticeable symbol of rank was that the uniforms of the officers above a certain level had four pockets, whereas soldiers and low-rank officers wore two-pocket uniforms.

REVOLUTION IN EDUCATION IN THE 1960S

As we have seen, China's education underwent radical experiments during the years of the Great Leap Forward but failed to achieve the anticipated results, and the authorities had to retreat in the early 1960s. By the mid-1960s, Mao began to initiate a new offensive against the existing education system. One goal of this new educational revolution was essentially associated with the creation of the new man: to bring up practical-minded and pragmatically trained laborers, and not intellectuals, bureaucrats, or technocrats, as had come to be emphasized in the Soviet Union.

During the spring festival of 1964, Mao gave a speech on education at a meeting with some of the party's Central Committee. While conceding that "the line and orientation" of the education system were in general correct, he insisted that the methods were wrong. In his opinion, the period of schooling was too long, and the syllabus should be "chopped in half." Students should have more time for learning outside the classroom—by which Mao meant military training and physical labor. Once again, he named Ben Franklin and Maxim Gorky as examples of the "self-taught" and added that "Watt was a worker, yet he invented the steam engine."[114] He complained that students knew nothing about the cultivation of rice, mustard, wheat, or millet. A widespread story of the time regarding Mao's attitude toward formal education alleged that Mao had told his own children: "You go down to the countryside and tell the poor and lower-middle peasants, 'My dad says that after studying a few years, we have become more and more stupid. Please, uncles and aunts, brothers and sisters, be my teachers! I want to learn from you.'"

In another talk in August of the same year, as a major part of educational reform, Mao asked for an immediate "going down" by university students and faculty:

> Professors, assistant professors, administrative workers, and students should all of them go down, for a limited period of five months. If they go to the countryside for five months or to the factories for five months, they will acquire some perceptual knowledge. Horses, cows, sheep, chickens, dogs, pigs, rice, sorghum, beans, wheat, varieties of millet—they can have a look at all these things. If they go in the winter, they will not see the harvest, but at least they can still see the land and the people. To get some experience of class struggle—that's what I call a university.[115]

When Mao heard from his nephew that people in educational institutions thought that the students and faculty in science and technology should spend less time participating in these campaigns than their peers in humanities and social sciences, Mao said:

> That is wrong; the class struggle is your most important subject, and it is a compulsory subject. . . . Your institute should go down to the countryside to carry out the "four cleanups"; from the cadres to the students, all of you should go, and not one should remain. . . . If you don't carry out the four "cleanups," you won't understand the peasants, and if you don't carry out five "antes," you won't understand the workers. Only when you have completed such a course of political training can I consider you a university graduate.[116]

The "four cleanups" was a campaign waged in the countryside to fight corrupted cadres and intensify socialist ideological education in 1964 and 1965. Numerous cadres, intellectuals, and university students in cities were involved in it as they were organized into "work teams" and sent down to participate in the campaign, through which they would be "reeducated" as well.

Apart from his suspicion and contempt toward formal or institutional education, Mao had a special distaste for humanities and social sciences. In his opinion, all of these subjects could be learned outside the classroom, and society would serve as the campus. In his plan to simplify the curriculum and send down the students and faculties, these subjects and departments bore the brunt. For example, in his talk at the spring festival of 1964, when he highlighted the imminence of sending down students and faculties, he treated students of humanities and sciences differently: "I am referring to the humanities. Students of natural science should not be moved now, though we can move them for a spell or two. All those studying the humanities—history, political economy, literature, law—must every one of them go."[117] Later in the Cultural Revolution, after all universities and colleges had been closed for two years and the party was considering reopening some of them, Mao said that higher education should to some degree be restored, but humanities and social sciences were excluded—only physics and engineering colleges were allowed to operate.

During the early 1960s, the Jiangxi Communist Labor University became a model for educational reform, being consistent with Mao's line. The university had been established under the inspiration of Mao's ideas. Its campus was set up in a mountainous area in Jiangxi Province, where Mao had led a guerrilla war decades earlier. It was not only a university, as the name implied. Rather, it was a more comprehensive political and educational system, consisting of primary and middle schools and a university. The whole curriculum was greatly simplified and reduced, in order to meet the immediate needs of agricultural and industrial production. All subjects had to be directly useful in neighboring factories and especially communes. A major part of the faculty consisted of part-time educators who came from the communes and factories, without any degrees or formal educational background. The time spent in "practical learning" was almost equal to classroom learning.

This school system was criticized by the educational bureaucrats for its "blooming without bearing fruits." When Mao heard of the bureaucratic opposition to this educational innovation, he wrote a supportive letter to the Jiangxi Communist Labor University in which he said: "I wholeheartedly support your venture. Your schools, including your primary and secondary schools, and universities, are following the principle of part-time work and part-time study, hard work and hard study, and costing the government nothing to run them. . . . They are good schools indeed."[118]

Mao's letter was later published by newspapers and initiated a campaign to establish educational institutions similar to the university in Jiangxi.

The Cultural Revolution: An All-Out Effort to Create a New Social Environment for the New Man

From 1966 to 1976, China experienced the Great Proletarian Cultural Revolution ("CR" hereafter), the most turbulent period of its history. The goals of the CR have been discussed ever since it started. Many would agree that the most important historical factor was a combination of Mao's fear of losing power to more practical leaders and his desire to continue the revolution under his banner to prevent China from becoming "revisionist." From the perspective of the creation of the new man, however, the CR was launched as an all-out effort to produce a more revolutionary social environment, a crucible in which the new man could be tried and tempered. When the CR was initiated, the party's Central Committee declared that it was "both broader and deeper than any revolution before" because it was going to "touch people's souls."[119] An editorial in the *People's Daily* in 1968 remarked that in the "unprecedented" CR, "all proletarian revolutionaries must dare to touch not only others' souls but also their own."[120] As a catchphrase, "touching souls" thus characterized the CR's radical approach toward transforming human nature and remolding the human mind. The meaning of the phrase in Chinese suggested a direct and forceful alteration of people's innermost being, which could often have painful and traumatic effects upon the most tender part of the human psychology.

The Red Guard: Violent Variation of the New Man

The most conspicuous phenomenon of the early stage of the CR was perhaps the Red Guard movement, which unleashed shocking violence and destruction. Typical Red Guard behavior seemed like vandalism on a national scale that spared almost nothing in the quest to "Destroy the Four Olds" (old ideology, culture, habits, and customs). It included but was not limited to burning books, scrolls, and paintings and destroying temples, statues, monuments, tombstones, and even furniture—in a word, any tangible signs of tradition and culture. It was not novel at all to fight against and eradicate cultural and religious symbols, time-honored customs, and even folkways established prior to the revolution in communist history; the Bolsheviks' iconoclastic and vandalistic campaigns, aimed at destroying the old Russian culture, formed a known predecessor. The Red Guards went much further, however, by searching people's houses and seizing or destroying anything inconsistent with the values and doctrines of the CR. But the most appalling Red Guard behavior was beating and killing people senior to them, the most radical form of "touching people's souls." According to Wang Youqin—who witnessed the Red Guard atrocity in Beijing when she was in middle school and has devoted her life since the late 1970s to collecting evidence of Red Guard violence—there were at least thirty-five verifiable cases of teachers and school administrators—along with victims of other social occupations and ordinary citizens—who were beaten to death in Beijing by Red Guards in August 1966, at the summit of the Red Guard terror.[121] In one case teenage girls beat their physical education teacher—a strong middle-aged man—to death with belts and sticks. They also attacked their classmates of "bourgeois origin" and in some cases brutally killed them. Nationwide, the number of victims of the Red Guard terror has been difficult to estimate, in part because of the prevalent anarchy of the time and in part because of the government's cover-up. On many occasions, humiliation and torture preceded the killing and made the suffering unbearable. For example, many victims were forced to kneel down on broken glass, to parade around while wearing "high hats" or with heavy items hanging from their necks, and to confess in public to crimes they had not committed or to their most private affairs. Therefore, in addition to the killings, many victims of the Red Guard terror committed suicide to put an end to their agony.

Members of the Red Guard belonged to the first generation born after 1949 and therefore had been brought up by the system to become new men. Why did many members—or at least many of the most politically active ones—of this generation display such a propensity for violence and even sadism? To what extent was this shocking trait of the generation "born in the new society and grown up under the red flag"—often the official portrait of the "after-Liberation" generations—associated with the education of the new man?

Psychologically, the Red Guard terror may be interpreted as an extreme example of the outburst of antisocial and antiauthoritarian tendencies common to teenagers and youth in many societies.[122] But in the context of Maoist China during the 1960s, the Red Guard terror was apparently more a direct result of the regime's political socialization than of the rebellious spirit of the young against their elders in general. The relationship between the Red Guards' violence and the education they had received has been discussed by many scholars. Anita Chan pointed out that "the root of the extremism does seem to have lain with the program of political socialization that the party had sponsored," especially a "Manichean worldview" that sees the world as polarized and allows nothing humanly sympathetic or even neutral to the enemy. Jing Lin examined how education prior to the CR had developed "non-critical and categorical thinking" among teenagers and young adults that led them to respond blindly and fanatically to Mao's call for eliminating class enemies.[123] Xu Youyu, an important liberal intellectual since the 1980s, and also a Red Guard, provided a number of insights for understanding the Red Guard character, emphasizing the "de-humanizing" aspect of China's education prior to the CR: "Humanity was treated as a typical bourgeois and revisionist concept, while maternal love, tenderheartedness, and compassion were all regarded as corrosive to the revolutionary fighting spirit. Human relationship was defined as either comradeship or class enmity."[124] Xu provided further analysis:

> There were yet two more factors in pre–Cultural Revolution ideology that had great impact on Red Guards. First, since students were said to be born with bourgeois sentiment, which meant they tended to be gentle and temperate and lacked revolutionary resolve and straightforwardness, in order to show their revolutionary stand, students applauded being rough-spoken and often intentionally put on airs of hooliganism and even banditry. The outrageous behavior of beating people by the first groups of Red Guards in the early stage of the Cultural Revolution was therefore a combination of inhumanity and showing off. Second, according to revolutionary ideology, one's political stand was most important, while method and specific manner were all secondary concerns. For example, you had to hate and struggle ruthlessly against those identified as class enemies. This was the main point. Those unnecessary beatings or even beating people to death were designated as "failed to carry out policies appropriately," and they were thought insignificant and minor problems.[125]

Therefore, Red Guard violence and brutality were indeed inherently associated with the pre-CR education or political socialization, which was essentially designed to shape the Chinese or Maoist version of the communist new man. As a matter of fact, in the early 1960s and prior to the CR, the official propaganda had projected the consciousness of intense "class hatred" of those models of the new man. For example, Lei Feng, the most celebrated model who was often described as soft-spoken or even timid, was also described as being keenly aware of the distinction between "love and hatred" in ideological terms. The famous lines in his diary advocated the treatment of enemy "as relentlessly as the harshest winter." One of his poems called upon people to "seize enemies' whips and flog them in return." The "enemies" here, however, were a broad category that in peacetime was understood to include political and ideological foes rather than armed soldiers.

The Red Guard atrocities revealed the dark and even malignant side of the social engineering of creating a new man—using class hatred to justify political violence against unarmed and helpless people—and this justification was further reinforced by the denial of the universal humanity based on social classification. As Xu Youyu put it, "In the Cultural Revolution, all of the Red Guards' brutal behaviors were allowed in the name of class struggle. They had no compassion for their victims, and they dared to whip their teachers and fire at their classmates. All of these people were under attack because they were thought to be 'class enemies.'"[126]

Such justification for political violence inflicted upon unarmed victims can be found in Mao's works as early as 1927, when he defended peasants humiliating, struggling, and even killing rural elites with the famous lines, "A revolution is not a dinner party, or writing an essay, or painting a picture, or doing embroidery; it cannot be so refined, so leisurely and gentle, so temperate, kind, courteous, restrained, and magnanimous. A revolution is an insurrection, an act of violence by which one class overthrows another."[127] The above words of Mao were the ones most widely circulated and most frequently quoted by the Red Guards during the CR, when they subjected their victims to physical abuse and even tortured them to "touch their souls."

Mass Resettlement and Heavy Labor: A Forceful Approach toward the Goal of the New Man

Mass resettlement, both permanent and temporary, from cities and urban-centered institutions—such as government offices, schools, hospitals, research institutions, and arts and literature entities—to the countryside was another conspicuous CR phenomenon. The ideological purpose of the resettlement was inherently associated with the goal of the new man: to uproot targeted groups socially and culturally and to plunge them into a new social and physical environment. Mao believed that since 1949 the "Four Olds," the main residue of the social environment of the old China that had hindered the growth of the new man, had not only persisted under the new regime but also found a new home in bureaucratic and revisionist development. All of these vicious elements were highly concentrated in the cities and in urban-centered institutions. Mao had revealed his antiurban and anti-intellectual proclivities in his thoughts on education in the late 1950s and early 1960s. Now in the CR he went further, urging a large portion of urban population—mainly students, cadres, intellectuals, and professionals—to be "sent down" to the countryside to be reeducated through physical labor and less comfortable living. The ancient curse of urban vice—the Babylonian—had reverberated in Christian tradition and utopian socialism, as well as in Russian populism in modern history, but it was in communist China and later in Cuba that such an anathema was targeted in an institutionalized manner.

The May Seventh Cadre Schools

The May Seventh Cadre Schools were a major project in this massive resettlement. They were a new reeducational device for members of the party and the state apparatus, which included almost all occupations of nonphysical work during Mao's time. From 1968 to the mid-1970s, thousands of such schools were established in China's countryside and millions of cadres and intellectuals participated in undergoing reeducation for several years through extensive ideological studies, self-criticism, and, most of all, heavy physical labor.

Behind the resettlement efforts was an anti-intellectual tradition that exalted physical labor as a venue for creation and virtue while despising intellectual work as a source of idleness and even vice. As was discussed earlier in this chapter, this tendency had appeared in various ideologies such as utopian socialism and populism in world history. People whose occupations were not directly associated with physical labor or firsthand knowledge were often deemed ignorant, parasitical, and even guilty by such ideologies. In a sense, this simplistic and binary view regarding physical and mental work challenged economic and intellectual specialization, the very fundamental institution of civilization, which had become much more ramified and sophisticated during the course of industrialization, urbanization, and, in general, modernization. Chinese intellectuals were familiar with this ideology long before the CR. For example, when they embraced the Marxist discourse on the role of the working class as a historical agent in the New Culture Movement (the late 1910s) and the May Fourth Movement (early 1920s), they went on to almost deify laborers. Li Dazhao, one of the founding figures in China's intellectual enlightenment and later communist movement, even questioned intellectuals' qualifications for praising the working class. As he put it, "The intellectuals who do not have to do any form of manual labor are not even qualified at all to say that 'workers are sacred.' The class of intellectuals, who do nothing but are fed well, should be expelled in the same way we expel capitalists."[128] Chen Duxiu, another key figure like Li in those movements, delivered a speech to a union of transportation and hotel workers in Shanghai in 1920, saying: "We are anxiously expecting those who are not engaged in physical labor to admit their useless inferiority, while those physical laborers realize their value and dignity. . . . It is time for us to reverse the order of an ancient Chinese proverb: 'Those who work mentally rule, and those who work manually are ruled.'"[129] Guo Moruo, a known revolutionary poet, once expressed in a rather farfetched manner the intellectual's sense of guilt before the working people. He wrote in one of his early poems, composed during the years of the May Fourth Movement, that as a young intellectual who had completed his study abroad and returned to China, on the shore of Lake Xi Hu (West Lake, a famous resort site in Hangzhou, Zhejiang Province) he saw an old peasant tilling the field. The young intellectual suddenly felt the urge to "kneel down before him / calling him 'my father' / licking off the dirt on his feet."[130] This tradition of celebrating manual labor and redeeming the guilt of nonmanual laborers to some extent catered to the CCP's policy of reeducating intellectuals through manual labor decades later.

The name of the May Seventh Schools derives from Mao's famous May Seventh Directive (1966), in which he proposed that distinctions between different occupations be broken and that everyone be involved in political and economic activities as well as military training, in addition to the activities entailed by their own occupational duties. The campaign for the May Seventh Schools officially started on October 4, 1968, when the *People's Daily* published a report introducing the way Heilongjiang Province had carried out Mao's directive by establishing a cadre school (named Liuhe May Seventh Cadre School) in a rural area. Cadres in the provincial government had been sent to that school to participate in agricultural work and to be reeducated. On the same day, the newspaper also published Mao's directive regarding this school: "The practice of sending a large number of cadres down and letting them participate in agricultural labor is an excellent opportunity for the cadres' reeducation. All cadres, except those too old, sick, and disabled, should do so."[131] Before long the May Seventh Cadre Schools were established as a nationwide reeducation system. Since China at that time allowed no freelance occupations, and the government assigned jobs to intellectuals, scientists, and artists and paid them according to their administrative ranks equivalent to certain levels of party or government officials, the category of "cadres" in this sense included all people who were involved in non-physical-labor occupations.

The description of an early model for such schools provides an example of how life in the May Seventh Cadre Schools started, with facilities less than rudimentary, and how physical labor and ideological education were integrated. The school was located in Anqing County, Heilongjiang Province (in Manchuria), at the foot of Xiaoxinanlin, a mountain range known for its long and snowy winter from October to April. Upon their arrival the first night, in cabins made of hay and brushwood and illuminated by oil lamps, the cadres held their first meeting for ideological study:

> The responsible cadre announced the key points for their work in this school. First, study Mao Zedong thought and use it to guide individual conduct in order to eliminate the bourgeois world outlook and replace it with a proletarian one. Second, study politics, practice military skills,

integrate with the masses, and criticize the bourgeoisie. Third, establish a school with bare hands, and equip it with all necessary facilities.[132]

To what extent did the cadres, intellectuals, and artists who responded to the call and left the cities really feel guilty and conscientiously accept such reforms? An official account of the time, though often exaggerated, held that at least many of them in the first months were prepared and resolved to face ideological and physical tests. The cadres and students were called May Seventh Fighters and were organized into military-style units (squads, platoons, companies, and battalions) to be assigned laborious and often back-breaking tasks such as clearing land, constructing roads and dams, building houses and mills, and finally, cultivating crops on virgin soils, often without the help of mechanical tools. In order to achieve the maximum result of being cut off from the old environment (that is, the urban lifestyle), the schools often did not allow supplemental food (such as canned food, candy, and cookies), soap, shampoo, skin lotion, or even medicine to be brought in or sent from cities. In some cases, these "luxuries," when found, were confiscated and exhibited as evidence of resistance against thought reform. Wang Meng, a novelist and later, in the 1980s, a party intellectual at the ministry level, had experience with reeducation through working and living with peasants in the late 1950s and the 1960s that even questioned the necessity of brushing one's teeth. As he recalled, "Some writers even self-criticized for their habit of brushing their teeth, because peasants did not think that was necessary. When I was working in the countryside, some peasants asked me, 'Is there shit in your mouth? Why do you dig your mouth with a shit-scoop [i.e., toothbrush] every day?'"[133] Under such circumstances, the physical endurance of hardships became the most tangible and measurable indicator of the effectiveness of thought reform, so much so that many decided to endure unnecessary discomfort or pain. One example was the treatment of mosquito bites. In many rural and forest areas the mosquito stings could cause problems much worse than swelling and itchy bites, but many May Seventh Fighters refused to apply medical ointment on the bites because "the peasants never use that."[134]

The case of Bai Shuxiang, a famous ballerina, exemplified the extent of hardship and physical labor entailed by ideological reeducation in the May Seventh Schools. Bai, a devoted artist, was found to be still practicing her dance in secret after being sent to the May Seventh School. Her ballet shoes were subsequently confiscated and taken as evidence of "recalcitrant resistance against thought reform." The school then assigned Bai duties typical for a male peasant: feeding pigs and horses and collecting animal waste in pigsties and cowsheds in the winter with bare feet. Afterward, her reeducators were content to see that her feet had been reshaped and her stature was no longer ideal for stage performance.[135] The reformation of her appearance thus indicated her identity transformation: she was no longer a fragile bourgeois ballet dancer but a tough proletarian husbandry worker.

The self-denial and even self-torturous scenarios in thought reform, such as forgoing treatment for mosquito bites, had its counterpart in the history of thought reform in North Vietnamese communism, which borrowed theories and practices in reeducating cadres and intellectuals directly from China during the late 1940s. Mountains and forests in Vietnam were notorious for various poisonous insects and insect-borne diseases, and for that reason many communist guerrilla soldiers and cadres fell sick, died, or survived with chronic recurrences. Bearing such health problems thus came to represent suffering and glory, as a result of going through what amounted to revolutionary redemption. Tran Duc Thao, a leading French-educated Vietnamese philosopher whose study of phenomenology (*Phenomenology and Dialectical Materialism,* 1951) gained him high esteem in the West, deliberately contracted malaria by sleeping in the jungles without a mosquito net. Tran had returned to Vietnam from France in 1951 to join the revolution. In the campaign of Vietnamese thought reform, he concluded that in order to make up what he had missed while in Paris and to show his sincerity, he had to do something extraordinary. He thus risked his life in this act, and that enabled him to be accepted by the Vietnamese communists. But Thao was later disappointed with the party-state reality of postcolonial North Vietnam, and during the 1956–1957 liberalization movement, inspired by de-Stalinization in the communist world, he stood up against many specific policies, from land reform to the control of intellectuals, just as many Chinese intellectuals of the time responded to Mao's calling to "Let one hundred flowers blossom, and let one hundred schools contend."

Tran was forced to publicly condemn himself in early 1958, when Ho Chi Minh launched a campaign similar to the "antirightist" campaign in China, and remained silenced for the rest of his life.[136]

Such stories of engaging in thought reform by undertaking dirty, stinky, and even potentially harmful work and living circumstances had a parallel in some other communist movements under Chinese influence. One example can be found in the Malayan communist movement. From the 1960s to the 1980s, the Malayan communists set up their bases in the jungles of southern Thailand, along the Thai-Malayan border. During the years of the Chinese CR, Malayan communists—who listened to the Voice of Malayan Revolution, which was set up in China's Hunan Province and broadcast CR messages every day—followed the Chinese model of thought reform and adopted many specific Chinese practices. According to Lin Mei, a female party member who grew up in the city of Singapore with some degree of education,

> Under that kind of atmosphere, people often thought that if you wanted to be progressive and revolutionary, you ought not to mind dirt, stink, and physically hard work. I myself was very conscious of hygiene and health. But some comrades from poor countryside families thought I wasn't revolutionary enough. Their idea was that if our revolutionary faith was firm, we ought to have the courage to pick up chicken shit with our bare hands.

In each of their compact barrack rooms, there was a container for night soil. She suggested that it be emptied every day, but her comrades said that peasants often waited until the container was full and then brought it out to use as manure, so why couldn't she stand the smell? They said people like her, with an urban and educated background and sensitive to an unhealthy environment, were "stinky ninth category"—a humiliating term for intellectuals commonly used during China's CR but originating in the Yuan dynasty (1271–1368). The dynasty was established by the nomadic and militant Mongols, who did not respect Confucianism and subsequently despised the Han intellectuals, placing them at the bottom of their social hierarchy, between prostitutes and beggars. To prove her revolutionary faith, therefore, Lin picked up chicken droppings with her bare hands, which resulted in skin diseases; when she became sick, she did not seek medical assistance but only took some painkillers. Years later she found out that, because she did not go to a doctor in time, she had developed some serious medical problems.[137]

Rustication of Educated Urban Youth

Another massive resettlement of city dwellers to the countryside was targeted at educated urban youth, officially called Up to the Mountains and Down to the Villages. Most of the rusticated, or sent-down, youth had just graduated from high school or even junior high school, only a small number consisting of university students or graduates. The movement of rustication of educated urban youth started much earlier than the May Seventh Cadre Schools, and it expected the sent-down youth to settle permanently in the country, instead of for a defined term, as with the May Seventh cadres. Behind such differences was a practical consideration of the employment problem in cities.

China's employment problem began to appear in the early 1950s, as the private sector drastically dwindled along with the progress of nationalization. In the meantime, free-market labor disappeared because the government had assigned work for everyone in cities and towns. This social transformation enabled the government to implement a planned economy and secure its own economic priorities on the one hand, but on the other hand the government was left with the burden of providing enough jobs for people living in urban areas. Mao himself was fully aware of this problem, and he once said, "Generally speaking, the whole country's six hundred million people are all under our command. . . . The choice for urban youth is to go to school, to the factory, or to the countryside and frontiers. We have to make arrangements for them."[138] According to the *People's Daily*, jobless teenagers and youth began to create serious juvenile delinquency problems in some cities as early as 1953.[139]

Facing this situation, the party began to encourage youth to participate in agricultural work as a way out. On December 3, 1953, the *People's Daily* published an editorial entitled "Organize High Elementary School Graduates to Participate in Agricultural Work," along with an investigative report on Penglai County, Shandong Province, where the local government had organized students to participate in agricultural work as part of the effort to solve the employment problem.[140] But soon the government began to address the same issue from an ideological perspective so as to evade the real cause of the problem while trying to solve it. In 1954 the Central Committee of the Youth League, the Ministry of Education, and the Department of Propaganda of the party's Central Committee each issued documents calling upon graduates to go to the countryside. These documents pointed out that "ideas of the old society" were still influencing the youth, as reflected in the contemptuous attitude toward physical labor. As a remedy for the problem, these documents advocated integration of education with labor, and with agricultural labor in particular, as an approach to reeducate the youth. Therefore, as Ding Yizhuang pointed out, "The cause for the campaign was initially economic, but in time it began to be overshadowed by ideology. The propaganda and mobilization of sending educated youth to the countryside were, from beginning to end, so ideologically charged that people tended to ignore the real economic motive of the campaign."[141]

Beginning in January 1958, China implemented a household registration *(hukou)* system to separate urban residents (that is, residents of cities and county towns) from rural dwellers as a major means of social control and institutional exclusion to limit the size of the population benefiting from government welfare.[142] Under this system the latter were not allowed to migrate to cities, and the former would lose their residential permission (along with all kinds of rations and educational and medical benefits) if they chose or were forced (often as a result of political purge or legal punishment) to relinquish their registered status. This modern-day, nationwide segregation system had a significant impact on almost every aspect of Maoist China's political, economic, and social life, and to a great extent today's China is still struggling with that legacy. What should be emphasized here is that the implementation of this system made the rustication movement more difficult to carry out. Before the 1960s the urban youth settling in the countryside did so largely voluntarily, but after the implementation of the household registration system, the loss of urban residency seemed too costly for many, especially after the great famine in the countryside between 1959 and 1962. Therefore in the 1960s the government had to increase the pressure on youth to make them feel more obligated to make the move. The youth were told that they ought to integrate with peasants by passing through three tests in villages: work (heavy physical labor, often under harsh conditions), life (simple and rough), and affection (developing a sentimental attachment to peasants). One purpose of this approach was to find and celebrate models of the socialist new man who had given up their reliable—if not necessarily comfortable—urban life and committed themselves to the socialist construct in the countryside, through which they themselves would be reeducated. Two female models may exemplify the ideal of the new man (and new woman) the party desired.

Xing Yanzhi was one of the earliest models of sent-down youth. In 1958, after graduating from junior high school, Xing left Tianjin, her hometown, and settled in the Dazhong Commune, Baodi County (one of Tianjin's suburban counties). The village where she started her new life was very poor and suffering hunger as a consequence of the Great Leap Forward shortly after her arrival. Undaunted and determined to change the village, Xing organized the girls and young women as "stormtroopers" to "save themselves by production." In the daytime they cut holes in the thick ice of the frozen river to catch fish, and in the evening they wove reed curtains for sale. Xing's efforts quickly drew official attention, and her name began to appear in provincial and national newspapers. At age twenty, Xing was promoted as a national model for the youth who responded to the party's call and devoted themselves to "socialist construction in the countryside." Xing was showered with countless official titles and honors. On December 24, 1964, she was invited to attend Mao's birthday dinner, seated beside him along with three other models for the new man, among whom was Dong Jiagen, another sent-down youth model. Dong was known for his saying, "Physical labor is a furnace, and I am a piece of ore. I am determined to be tempered into a piece of stainless steel." The other two were Chen Yonggui, the party secretary of the Dazhai brigade, and Qian Xuesen, a nuclear scientist, both introduced earlier in this chapter.

As a young girl, Xing attracted admirers nationwide, but the local party's organization decided that her husband ought to be a local man. In Xing's words, "I could not even think about anyone beyond the village, because I was a model of 'striking roots in the villages.'" With the party organization as a matchmaker, Xing married the leader of her village brigade, a typical farmer six years older than she. Decades later, when Xing was interviewed, she recalled no romance but "fidelity" in her marriage. She bore two sons but had no photos taken with them; her explanation was she was always too busy to spend time with them.

Hou Jun was another well-known model of rusticated youth. Born into an intellectual's family in Beijing, she gave up her college education opportunity, canceled her Beijing residential registration in 1962 when she was nineteen, and settled in Baodi, the same county where Xing Yanzhi became famous. The village she settled in was extremely poor: the soil was saline, and there was no electricity or even wells. Collected rain was the only source of drinking water. When the famine was at its worst in the early 1960s, as Hou recalled many years later, corn kernels were the only available, but limited, source of food. For several months she had to reduce her number of daily meals to two (breakfast and lunch only) to ensure that she had enough food to sustain work in the daytime, but she went to bed early with an empty stomach in the evening. Many of her fellow rusticated young friends fled back to the cities to share their parents' rations, but Hou persisted and organized the village girls to engage in productive work. The next spring, she was visited by Huang Zhongying, a well-known female journalist on her way to interview Xing Yanzhi, who had become a noted model. The result of Huang's visit was the discovery of another model, established in a lengthy report titled "A Special Girl," copublished in July 23, 1963, in the *Chinese Youth Daily* and the *People's Daily*. In the report, Hou Jun's reeducation through rustication was succinctly described: "Her ideology was formed as her hands blistered and hardened." But Hou was able to make her own choice in marriage. Her best friend had gone to the village with her but later fled back to Beijing, but the girl's younger brother admired Hou and moved to the village to help her after his sister's desertion. They soon lived together, sharing their meager food rations, and the young man became part of the "roots" Hou had struck in the village.

Compulsory "Up to the Mountains and Down to the Villages" Movement

Before the CR, the campaign of sending educated urban youth to the countryside was largely based on voluntarism, urged on by official propaganda.

But in 1968, after millions of the Red Guards had completed their task of "destroying the Four Olds" in the cities, the government began to force large numbers of urban youth to go to the countryside, and the official policy allowed each family to have only one child remaining in the city. Behind this compulsory domestic migration were basically two practical concerns. The first was the old problem of employment, which had been aggravated by the decline of economic production in the CR. The second was political. As Ding Yizhuang pointed out, the atmosphere in schools was politically charged following the rebellion against pre-CR authorities, and students became restless: "When the students were no longer needed by the political struggle, anyone with common sense would be able to see the potential destructive force among the millions of youth who clustered in cities with nothing to do."[143] In fact, beginning in late 1967, the cases of gang fighting and vandalism increased in many cities, and the government had to initiate campaigns to round up the loiterers.

But these practical concerns were addressed in a highly ideological tone that often made people forget any mundane motivation. As Mao declared in 1968, "It is necessary for educated young people to go to the countryside to be reeducated by the poor and lower-middle peasants." This call, combined with the May Seventh Directive, initiated a nationwide resettlement movement. From 1968 to 1975, about fifteen million youths were relocated from cities to the countryside. The government set forth a national plan to designate destinations for them, especially from the biggest cities. For example, those from Shanghai, the city that had been influenced the most by the "old society," were to go to Heilongjiang and Yunnan, the northernmost and southernmost provinces, respectively, while those from Beijing, the city with heavy bureaucratic influence and much everyday convenience, were to go to Inner Mongolia and Shanxi Province, both known for barren soil and harsh living conditions. For those individuals refusing to leave the city, there would be no job, ration card, or health insurance; a neighborhood committee (a grassroots political and social organization) would make frequent visits to their homes; and their parents would face pressure from their work units until the children left home in disgrace.

From 1968 to 1976, numerous models were created to promote the movement, and many of them sacrificed their lives during the rustication. Jin Xunhua, for example, an educated youth from Shanghai who was sent down to Heilongjiang Province, died in his effort to save timbers from a flood and became an instant national hero. A collective model of dedication and sacrifice were the youth sent down to a farm named Niutianyang, in Shantou, Guangdong Province. Niutianyang was on the coast, and to make rice production possible, it had been walled off by dikes, developed by the army and the sent-down youth, who were organized as militia and engaged in both military training and agricultural production.[144] The farm had a glorious history. Mao's May Seventh Directive had been originally issued in response to a report on the Niutianyang experience. Mao's idea was that people of every occupation should be engaged in some kind of productive work, just as the army was in Niutianyang. In July 1969 a strong tropical storm struck Guangdong Province, and Niutianyang bore the brunt of it. When the leaders of the military and the sent-down youth received warning of the storm, they decided not to evacuate but to protect the farm by reinforcing the dikes with human bodies. For them, the storm was a rare opportunity to demonstrate the revolutionary dedication of the new man empowered by Mao Zedong's thought, which was believed invincible. The decision was strongly supported by the soldiers and the youth. The result of the confrontation between the new man and the storm was tragic: the farm was destroyed, and 553 soldiers and 83 youths perished. Afterward, however, a propaganda campaign was launched to promote their "heroic spirit," and a book was published under the title *The Hymn to Heroes Who Fear No Difficulty nor Death*.[145]

Similar to thought reform through hard labor and living in a primitive or unhealthful environment, the Up to the Mountains and Down to the Villages movement had resonated as well in some radical social movements under Chinese influence. In Singapore during the second half of the 1960s, Barisan Sosialis (The Socialist Front), a pro-China leftist party, called on its followers among intellectuals and students (most of whom were ethnic Chinese) to "integrate with the masses of workers and peasants sentimentally, to love what they love, to hate what they hate, to share their pains and their joy, and to breathe with them and take their fortune and plights as your own."[146] To accomplish this goal, they organized "up to the mountains and down to the villages" activities, sending members of the party and associated organizations to factories, construction sites, and especially "vegetable, pig, and fish farms." Some of them went to pineapple and rubber plantations in neighboring Malaysia, which was much less urbanized but historically and culturally tied to Singapore. Some leftist student associations at the National University of Singapore organized their members to go to pineapple plantations in Selangor and Johor in western and southern Malaysia to "integrate" with peasants. A poet wrote a piece titled "Holding Hands," in which an intellectual's hand with tender palm and slim fingers was held by a worker's coarse, strong hand, symbolizing the "integration" between intellectuals and working people. But unlike its Chinese prototype, this movement was voluntary, and most of the activities were held during breaks in study and work. Ironically, in time, the movement's political and ideological purpose was gradually forgotten, and many participants viewed it as a weekend excursion or even a "cheap country tour."[147]

POSTSCRIPTS

The idea of a new man, a morally perfect person, served as a model for Chinese society and became embedded in the Chinese culture. The concepts of human malleability and the role of social environment in shaping human nature were not alien to Chinese history either. But they became part of the discourse of nationalist ideology in the early twentieth century; indeed, in the second half of the century, they became a prime target of the Chinese communist revolution, as Mao aspired to surpass the Soviet Union in both economic and ideological terms. The idea of new men—or "Mao's good soldiers"—was created to perpetuate the revolution and generate an economic miracle, born from the utter selflessness and dedication of such new men.

But the all-out effort to create the new man began to lose its momentum in the early 1970s, as the radical policies of the Cultural Revolution became increasingly more unbearable to the entire society, people longed for normalcy, and Mao's cult was undermined by the failure of many of his policies, especially the desertion in 1971 of Lin Biao, his successor and the major advocate of the directive to "be Mao's good soldiers." After Mao died in 1976, as economic reforms engulfed China and normal human life was restored, the ideal of the new man faded away into Maoist China's history and increasingly distant from China's reality. In today's China, political socialization is still very much ideologically charged, but the basic goal is no longer to create a new type of human being but to shape a citizen who accepts the party's legitimacy and is patriotic, above all other less politically defined civil obligations. The historical process of how the image of the new man faded away from Chinese political life requires another focused study and can only be summarized here in this brief manner.

Three

"Let Them All Become Che"
Creating the New Man in Cuba

As the most important communist revolution of the 1960s, especially in terms of its influence in the Third World, the Cuban Revolution presented its own type of "new man." From 1959 to the mid-1960s, the revolution underwent a rapid and drastic transformation, from a self-proclaimed radical nationalist/democratic revolution to a socialist and communist revolution. For many historians, the Cuban Revolution is a particularly intriguing case, compared with many other socialist or communist revolutions inspired or directly supported by the Soviet Union and China. The Cuban revolutionaries claimed their Marxist ideology and sided with the communist world rather late (almost two years after taking state power), but their transformation toward socialism and communism was much more radical and hurried. The historical moment at which Fidel Castro, Che Guevara, and other leaders began to embrace Marxism, perceive their revolution as socialist, and prepare measures to lead their revolution toward communism has been a subject of discussion since the early 1960s. This question is also important for a broader understanding of revolutionary movements and radical social transformation in the twentieth century.

While analyses of sociopolitical policies provide substantial ground for our understanding of the issue, an analysis of the revolutionary political culture is particularly relevant in Cuba's context. Because the socialist transformation in Cuba was less planned than in other countries and was carried out within a much shorter time, state imposition of the new social system was more forceful and had to be installed by indoctrinating people with new beliefs, values, symbols, and patterns of behavior. In this regard, a consciousness of a "new man" in Cuba was more inherently entailed by the establishment of a new system. As Richard Fagen has observed:

> Almost from the beginning the key mechanism of change has been seen not in this or that specific institution, policy, or program, but rather in the fundamental transformation of the sociopolitical character of the Cuban citizen. . . . During the 1960s the formation of a "new Cuban man" became

so central to revolutionary rhetoric and action program as to constitute the ideological and operational mainspring of the revolution. . . .

It is worth stressing that although the new man thesis was not formally articulated until after the Revolutionary Government had been in power for a number of years, the operation of the revolutionary system has almost from the outset depended on such a model of change.[1]

In such a transformation, characterized by emphasis on the new man, the Cuban leaders were facing a difficult choice between the Russian and Chinese models. Ideologically Castro and Guevara, in particular, were in affinity with the Chinese, who emphasized people's consciousness and devotion and relied upon mass mobilization and concentration of resources in economic development, as opposed to the Soviet model, which was based on a sound economic foundation, a technocracy, and stimulation of individual incentive. But Cuba's monocrop economy and its confrontation with the United States limited its choice of international allies. As a result, Castro followed an eclectic approach. He made Moscow his economic supporter and international ally and broke with China in 1966, while in domestic affairs he rejected the Russian model and adopted policies similar to those of Mao's in the Great Leap Forward and the Cultural Revolution. Castro's goal was to telescope the transformation from socialism, which was just starting in Cuba in the early 1960s, to communism in a matter of several years. To reach this goal, the creation of the new man in Cuba became just as crucial as it was then in China and was placed in the center of Castro's political agenda. From 1968 to 1970, following an escalation of years of revolutionary rhetoric and the intensification of institutional changes, Castro launched the Revolutionary Offensive, essentially the Cuban equivalent of a combination of China's Great Leap Forward and its Cultural Revolution, in which Cuba's new man was tried and tempered.

José Martí and the Early Expectation of the New Man

As in China, the new man was expected in Cuba long before the communist revolution. As early as the late 1880s, José Martí, the father of Cuban nationalism, expressed views similar to those of his Chinese counterparts, on the relationship between the creation of a new Cuban national character and the redemption of the nation.

Having struggled many years for Cuba's independence and frustrated by what he viewed as political defects of the Cuban people, Martí came to a conclusion similar to that of his contemporary Chinese intellectuals: that unless the whole nation's moral and political character was reformed, the goal of full independence would never be achieved. As John M. Kirk points out:

> Essential to Jose Martí's new approach to political life in a liberated Cuba were the innovations that he hoped to introduce in what can be termed the human dimension of the Republic. Marti was well aware of the pressing need for sweeping political reforms in the Patria, but also realized that in order for them to be successfully instituted it would be necessary from the outset to inculcate into every Cuban citizen certain moral qualities which together would result, he hoped, in a heightened moral consciousness and would eventually lead to the formation of a "new man."[2]

For Martí, the struggle for independence was on the one hand a fight against the Spanish colonialists, but on the other hand it was also the need for consistent education of the Cuban people. The most urgent educational task was to inject a measure of confidence in the minds of the people and convince them that they had the potential to build an independent nation. The lack of national confidence—a national inferiority complex—was largely a consequence of enduring colonialist rule; many Cubans were accustomed to thinking of themselves as inherently devoid of the capability of uniting as a nation, as the Spanish had derogatorily categorized them. This colonial mentality was a major psychological obstacle impeding the Cubans on their way to independence. For Martí, therefore, the cultivation of national confidence, or *dignidad* (dignity), was one of the most important requirements for independence. The Cubans would not only have to convince themselves of their ability to form an independent nation but also be proud of their distinct *cubanidad* (Cubanness). As Martí put it, "Does Cuba have to be a tavern, an idle beer parlor of San Jeronimo? Or will it be an independent, industrious, Latin American nation? This and nothing less is Cuba's task."[3] Such dignity and self-respect were to be extended from the national level to the individual level, meaning that Cubans should treat each other in a humanitarian way. As Martí once told the Cuban exiles living in Tampa, what he wanted for the first law of a new Cuba was "the worship of the full dignity of man by all Cubans."

To inspire his countrymen toward a national spiritual regeneration, Martí's political discourse was full of moral preaching. In addition to *dignidad*, he proposed *sociabilidad* (sociability) in his political thought, a term referring to "a reawakened social conscience supported by totally selfless conduct." For him, selflessness meant complete devotion to the public interest, and he persistently emphasized this notion in his speeches. As he put it, "Our life on this earth is essentially only an obligation to undertake good works."[4]

According to Martí, people were absolutely obligated to dedicate their talents and abilities to society. Their abilities represented only "a debt that has to be paid" to society: "The Creator issues them, and men are to collect the resulting advantages." An inability, or intentional refusal, to pay off this debt was equivalent to a crime. Therefore Martí saw laziness as a real and heinous offense. As he put it, "Laziness is nothing less than a public crime. Just as people do not have the right to be criminal, so too they do not have the right to be lazy. Not even indirectly should society assist those who do not contribute directly by working. . . . We should detest all lazy individuals and oblige them to take up a clean useful life."[5]

Martí had lived in the United States for many years, and he knew that, for many Cubans, America symbolized wealth and liberty. But for him, in a moral sense, America was a pitfall Cuba should avoid in its future, although in some rare cases he praised US industrialist-philanthropists such as Peter Cooper, because for him they symbolized the converse side of American life: hard work, generosity, and humanitarian love. As Martí once put it,

> Here you can see this general crudity of spirit that afflicts even expansive,
> delicate minds. Everyone fighting for themselves. A financial fortune is the
> only objective of their lives. . . . There is not sufficient soul or spirit in this
> gigantic nation, and without that marvelous coupling, everything is bound
> to collapse (in any nation) tragically. . . . It is necessary to shake these souls
> from their status as spiritual dwarfs.[6]

Martí's plan for social reform was founded largely upon a moral basis. It was highly idealistic, and for some it seemed out of touch with reality and could be compared only to the ideals of Cervantes' stereotypical character, Don Quixote. The philosophical foundation of this idealism, or quixotism, was Martí's firm belief in people's essential virtue and perfectibility, which to some critics seemed impractical. As he once answered to a Cuban exile asking why he pursued such sublime goals, "There is no one who does not have some moral worth . . . you only need to know how to find it."[7]

In the final analysis, as Kirk points out, we can understand the essence of Martí's thought only if we grasp his notion of the relationship between the creation of the new man and the success of the revolution:

> The key to understanding this deeply rooted idealism, which in the modern
> era seems somewhat incongruous, lies in Martí's fundamental concept of
> the new man, whom he obviously interpreted as a being with boundless
> potential. . . . Without this necessary moral foundation it is quite probable
> that the more radical of his plans would have come to naught; conversely

with the creation of what Marti envisioned as a "new revolutionary man," the revolution would have had an excellent chance of surviving.[8]

However, the new man Martí was yearning for cannot be regarded as a predecessor of the new man that Castro and Guevara were endeavoring to create more than half a century later. As Carlos Ripoll points out, the efforts to create a new man in Cuba in the 1960s not only resulted from Castro and Guevara's unrealistic attempt to achieve "the simultaneous creation of socialism and communism," which went far beyond Martí's blueprint for his country, but also were made at the cost of individual freedom, which was so essential to Martí's ideology. As Ripoll puts it,

> Marti did write of his hope that man would one day become a "new king" enriched physically and spiritually by the opportunity to use his energy and intelligence to the fullest, in accordance with his nature and "without fear or delay." But it is ludicrous to suggest . . . that Martí's ideal for the future development of the human race can be equated with the Castroite program for creation of the "new man," for that program rests on compulsory channeling of the individual's energies and abilities, on a timetable dictated by the state and in an atmosphere of fear. The Cuban Marxist-Leninist process of forced perfection of man is wholly at odds with Martí's views, which call for acknowledgment of human frailties and eschew attempts to suppress them or wish them away.[9]

Ripoll reinforced his argument by citing Martí's words: "Whoever seeks to improve man should not try to do so by eliminating his evil passions but rather should count them as a very important factor and try not to work against them but rather with them."[10] On another occasion Martí defended individual interest and development as opposed to public good. As he put it, "It is natural and human for a man to think constantly of himself, even in his acts of greatest abnegation, to attempt to reconcile his personal advancement with the public interest, and to serve the latter in a way that will benefit the former, or not harm it very much."[11]

Therefore, although the conceptualization of the new man was indeed an important part of Martí's nationalist ideology, his emphasis on individual freedom and his caution regarding the state's imposition of reform or reshaping the individual are evident to any attentive reader. The Castroist regime has long proclaimed that Martí "signified" Castro and that Castro "fulfills" Martí in a historically teleological interpretation, according to Enrico Mario Santí.[12] But as Ripoll showed, and as I will discuss later in this chapter, the differences between Martí's conceptualization of the new

Cuban and the Castroist-Guevarian "new man" engineering are significant and cannot be ignored.

Martí's dream of the new man was embodied in some revolutionary heroes of his time, such as Antonio Maceo, the legendary hero known as the Bronze Titan. Like Martí, Maceo died in Cuba's second war for independence and was thought to be an incarnation of revolutionary virtues. As one of his biographies describes him:

> For twenty-seven years—his entire adult life—all of his thoughts and actions were conditioned by the cause of Cuban independence. He sacrificed everything—his family and countless opportunities to lead a life of ease and luxury—to the cause. Continuing resolutely toward his fixed goal, suffering insult and criticism because he was a man of color, sustaining twenty-five wounds, he fought bravely and brilliantly for his country. . . . Neither bullets nor sickness stopped him.[13]

Martí was not the only one raising the issue of the "new man" among Cuban nationalists of his or later times. To the contrary, the new *cubanidad* concerned or even obsessed many of them. As Fagen concluded, "the transformation of Cuban man into revolutionary man is at the heart of Cuban radicalism."[14] For example, Diego Vicente Tejera (1848–1903), a political activist and a prolific essayist with a socialist tendency, believed that Cubans needed a new socialist spirit that could be developed only through education. He also believed that enlightened intellectuals should assume the responsibility for teaching ordinary people, especially workers. From 1897 to 1899, Tejera gave ten public conferences (lectures) for the Cuban exile community in Key West, Florida, in which he emphasized cultivating a new Cuban character and capability. For example, in the first conference Tejera spoke on "Education in Democratic Societies," which focused on raising people's class consciousness and development of a sense of public life. In the second conference, entitled "The Cuban Capacity," he repudiated myths that Cubans—especially the peasants—were religiously fanatical and culturally ignorant. Instead he pointed out their literary and artistic abilities and their tradition of scientific observation. For him, all of these qualities would pave the way for their political enlightenment, entailed by the new *cubanidad*. In the sixth conference, "Cuban Indolence," he urged Cubans to abandon the mentality of the colonized, to overcome political indifference, and to realize their potential for collective life.[15]

In addition to the new *cubanidad* discourse, Cuban nationalist ideology also displayed a disposition of voluntarism that stressed the importance of political determination and activism—a "subjective" factor—rather than the socioeconomic circumstances—the "objective factor"—required for the success of revolution. As Sheldon Liss points out, "Non-Marxist Cuban intellectuals who study and pursue radical revolutionary objectives are idealists for whom thought takes precedence over material reality, while their socialist counterparts regard material reality as more important than ideas."[16] Unrestricted by the classical Marxist doctrine of indispensable socioeconomic conditions for revolution, the radical non-Marxist nationalists tended to take direct actions and engage in armed struggle in the hope that a handful of dedicated guerrilla fighters would kindle a revolutionary fire among the people. Also, after the revolution, they tended to believe that economic problems would be resolved through education and emulation and that people would let moral incentive lead them. All of these ideas would find their equivalent in the policies carried out by Castro and Guevara in the 1960s.

MALLEABILITY AND ENVIRONMENTAL DETERMINISM: CUBAN LEADERS' CONCEPTS OF HUMAN NATURE

Like the Russian and Chinese communists, the Cuban revolutionary leaders' basic conception of human nature derived from the principles of environmental behaviorism: people's consciousness and psychology were completely at the mercy of the social environment. They believed that all undesirable aspects of human nature, such as egoism, individualism, political indifference, and even laziness and tardiness, were by no means inherent to human nature. Rather, they were simply the results or remnants of the old social environment in which bourgeois ideology, colonialist contempt for physical labor, and lack of incentives for workers affected the Cuban people's attitude toward their work even after the revolution. As Castro put it, "Man comes from capitalism full of selfishness; man is educated under capitalism amidst the most vicious selfishness as an enemy of other men, as a wolf to other men." It was "the principle of the jungle," he asserted.[17] Guevara spoke of the same issue. Under capitalism, he believed, "the alienated individual was bound to the society as a whole by an invisible umbilical cord: the law of value."[18] In socialist society, although the environment had been changed, the vestiges of the old societies would remain for a period, continuing to affect people's attitude toward society and work. As Guevara once put it, "we are all children of that environment," and the masses were "not pure."

As was mentioned earlier, Martí saw both sides of the Cuban people. On the one hand, he acknowledged the many negative aspects in their consciousness and psychology, such as lack of confidence, lack of mutual respect and self-esteem, and, for some, a problem of idleness. But on the other hand, he seemed to have a boundless faith in his people's innate virtue and believed in their human perfectibility and creativity. We can find similar contradictory stands in Castro's words. He emphasized defects of the Cuban people as much as Martí did, attributing them to the infection of the old society; but on many occasions he expressed an almost infinite faith in their potential to be reformed and reshaped to make history. Colombian novelist Gabriel García Márquez, one of Castro's closest friends, once marveled that Castro had "the nearly mystical conviction that the greatest achievement of the human being is the proper formation of conscience and that moral incentives, rather than material ones, are capable of changing the world and moving history forward."[19]

Associated with his belief in human malleability, Castro also developed his own theory of human evolution. He once talked to a group of young Americans about the "biological evolution" of human beings. According to him, the evolution from larvae and fish to human had stopped some two to three thousand years ago, and people now were not smarter than those of Aristotle's times. "The humanity we have known up until now is a pre-historic humanity, a savage humanity," he said, and not until all social evils are eliminated will humanity leave prehistoric times and will the real history of humanity begin.[20] This evolutionary interpretation of human history seemed to suggest the importance of the Cuban Revolution in regard to the whole evolutionary process of the human species, thus corresponding to the so-called *Homo sovieticus* (discussed in the introduction).

Guevara's view of human nature was almost identical to Castro's but was often expressed in analogies that reduced human nature to mechanical devices. For example, Guevara wrote, "I believe the simplest way is to acknowledge his unfinished nature. He is an unfinished product."[21] On another occasion he mentioned the revolutionaries as a conscious cog in a wheel, albeit "a happy cog." The cog analogy was apparently identical to the Stalinist metaphor and was remarkably similar to the metaphor of the revolutionary screw, popular in China. A more philosophically sophisticated Guevarist vision of the new man, as Michael Lowy points out, was that a revolution was authentic only if it made efforts to transform people, and this transformation was "the dialectical negation of the individual of capitalist society."[22] Lowy, with sympathy for the Guevarist stand, concluded that for Guevara "what is utopian is not envisaging the possibility of a 'new man,' but rather believing in an eternal and unchanging 'human nature.'"[23] A very popular slogan in Cuba—"We cannot conceive a new society without a new man"—originally derived from Guevara. In his "Man and Socialism in Cuba," Guevara claimed that the new man Cuba was going to create would not be like the nineteenth or twentieth century's man but would belong to the twenty-first century. After Guevara's death, Castro pronounced that Che himself had personified the new man, and "Let them all become Che!" came to be the most frequent ending for his numerous speeches.

The intense and entrenched Castro-Guevarist belief in human malleability and the role of social environment in reshaping human nature has led some authors to go beyond Enlightenment thinking and Marxism, as discussed in chapter 1, to explore its roots. Some of them have found religious, emotional, and even physiological influence in Castro's and Guevara's unique life experiences. Thomas Dalton, for example, noticed that Castro had attended Colegio de Belén, an elite Jesuit high school in Havana, and "was impressed by the priests' strong character, austerity, and self-discipline" and "admired their compassion, fairness, and sense of justice."[24] Dalton suspected a possible connection between the Jesuit education and Castro's ideas about reshaping the human mind. Thomas Aquinas, the theologian authority for the Jesuits, believed that "a sense of justice cannot be acquired solely by reasoning . . . but must involve an existential act to overcome physical and emotional barriers." Based on this, Dalton suggested: "Castro would have found this ethic appealing because it encouraged an experimental attitude. It suggested that human nature could be reshaped under socialism by a concerted application of new scientific methods to change the psychological and social circumstances of existence."[25] Guevara, who had suffered from asthma since his childhood, later spent many years studying medical science and subdued the difficulties brought about by this disease with his strong will, especially when he was on revolutionary duty. Dalton emphasized his "fascination with the psychosomatic dimensions of allergies" and his "strong interest in understanding factors that weaken or contribute to the breakdown of the human immune system, making the individual susceptible to diseases." Dalton went on to suggest, "These formative experiences and interests help explain Guevara's insistence that a new person would have to be created with intestinal fortitude strong enough to immunize him or her against the deforming forces" of everything obstructing the growth of the "new person."[26]

The Cuban leaders' conviction of human malleability was echoed among ordinary Cubans. An American interviewer reported that a Cuban teacher told her: "We cannot accept the idea that it is inevitable for Man to be evil. We believe we can develop in youth the goodness which Man contains—and that will be the New Man. He might develop naturally, just as there has been a historical development which took Man from communalism to feudalism to capitalism and now to socialism. But why wait? I think we must create him."[27] A more sophisticated response, instead of a simple conviction, regarding the new man was given by a Cuban woman who had lived in France and worked for the Cuban division of UNESCO in the early 1970s. She pondered the role of heredity and environment in determining ideological development and then drew a conclusion identical to the official one, not only of communist Cuba but of other communist regimes as well—that is, it was necessary to create an environment favorable for the growth of the new man:

> Now there is much discussion as to how we are to develop the "new man," and whether the heredity or environment are the basic factors in his development. It seems to me that if heredity is the determining factor, we would have to kill off all the ugly, stupid, and bad people, which is clearly impracticable. Conversely, if we brought up twenty children in the same environment as Fidel or El Che, I doubt we could produce twenty Castros or twenty Guevaras.
>
> To me, the most logical theory accounts for both heredity and environment. Some people are born potentially tall or short but their environment will determine whether that potential is fulfilled. The same holds true for emotional and intellectual qualities. I believe that environment encourages or else frustrates and stunts the development of a hereditary trait. So it seems to me that what we must do is create an environment, especially in the schools, that accommodates only favorable hereditary traits. Then we may see the "new man" emerge in our society.[28]

REVOLUTIONARY CONSCIOUSNESS AND VOLUNTARISM: THE NEW MAN CAN CREATE A REVOLUTION

Ever since Lenin, the issue of revolutionary consciousness (or class consciousness) overcoming individual spontaneity has been considered the key in making the revolutionary and new man. This thesis is revisionist, given the classical Marxist premise that socioeconomic change should precede ideological and political ones, or "superstructure" has to be determined by "infrastructure." But the history of communist revolution everywhere has been the antithesis of this doctrine, especially in the case of the Cuban revolution.

A key element in the Cuban revolutionary ideology was the belief in revolutionary consciousness and, based on that, revolutionary voluntarism resulting from the direct revolutionary experience. The belief was that the human will could triumph over socioeconomic circumstances, that a handful of revolutionary vanguards could inspire and arouse ordinary people with their dedication and self-sacrifice, and that revolutionary enthusiasm and devotion could overcome otherwise insurmountable obstacles. In other words, revolutionary voluntarism promoted the belief that conscious and dedicated human action was the premise for making a revolution. This Castro-Guevarist belief was thus a greatly radicalized version of the Leninist doctrine of revolutionary vanguardism.

The emphasis on consciousness and subjective will was in essence a response to the classical Marxist formula for judging whether there was a "revolutionary situation"—that is, a balance between subjective and objective factors. Subjective factors were the revolutionary vanguard's determination and willingness to sacrifice, whereas objective factors were social and economic conditions that favored such a revolution. Castro was well aware of this Marxist doctrine, and so were the Cuban communists, the People's Socialist Party, or PSP, who had been under Moscow's control ever since the party's establishment in the 1930s. The Soviet Union judged economic and social development in Latin America to be noncapitalist, and therefore a revolution—a socialist one in particular—was out of the question. Following this line, the Cuban communists, like their fellow Latin American communists, were engaged only in legal and parliamentary activities. But the Castroists, from the very beginning (1956), believed that direct actions, based upon the will, determination, courage, and morale of the vanguard, could awaken and educate the people. In other words, the revolutionary vanguards could create, rather than await, a revolutionary situation.

Castro had spoken of this issue many times. Yes, there should be a balance between subjective and objective factors, he said, but such a situation happened too rarely. What usually happened was that the objective factor was ripe, while revolutionary will was insufficient or simply absent. On the other hand, according to the Cuban experience, "When the objective factors are not quite perfect, but the subjective will is there, the revolution has every chance of success."[29] He said that when he had begun to be involved in the revolutionary activities at Havana University, very few students understood and supported the revolution—"only thirty out of five thousand students," or less than 1 percent, as he put it. But these few revolutionary students succeeded in injecting and spreading revolutionary awareness among the masses, just as Lenin had hoped in his *What Is to Be Done?* Had the revolutionaries given up their efforts and just waited "with folded arms," excusing themselves with unripe objective circumstances, the revolution would never have happened.

Guevara was more empathetic about this revolutionary voluntarism. In "Man and Socialism in Cuba," his main theoretical work, he argued that from the Moncada attack on, the "man" was the basic factor of the revolution. The revolution, he said, "was carried out in two different environments:

the people, an as-yet unawakened mass that had to be mobilized, and its vanguard, the guerrilla, the thrusting engine of the generator of revolutionary awareness, and militant enthusiasm."[30] In other words, "this vanguard was the catalyst that created the subjective condition necessary for victory": "The vanguards have their eyes on the future and its recompenses, but the latter are not envisioned as something individual; the reward is the new society in which human beings will have different characteristics: the society of communist man."[31]

In *The Second Declaration of Havana,* an official announcement of Cuban revolutionary ideology made in February 1962, Cuban leaders further expressed their faith in "the initial struggle by small combat units" and "the invincibility of those first nuclei" capable of eventually arousing mass support. "It is the duty of every revolutionary," the declaration stated, "to make the revolution. It is known that the revolution will triumph in America and throughout the world, but it is not for revolutionaries to sit in the doorways of their houses waiting for the corpse of imperialism to pass by."[32]

Given this experience and the interpretation of the victory of the revolutionary war, one can understand without much difficulty why Cuban leaders were so convinced that consciousness and will were more determinative in making a revolution than favorable social and political conditions. For them, "subjective" efforts took precedence over "objective" conditions, and ripe revolutionary situations were "created" rather than "awaited." The ordinary people, they believed, would be inspired by the vanguard's actions and would overcome their political apathy, standing up for their own interest.

This emphasis on consciousness and, subsequently, on revolutionary voluntarism became the most important ideological resource of the 1960s, when the Cuban communists faced enormous difficulties in making Cuba a tropical utopian communist society. They realized that their country was lacking in almost every "objective" element required for a transformation to socialism and communism, but they not only dismissed the classical Marxist doctrine and the Soviet experience but were even proud of such dismissal. For them, it was just another opportunity to make history. For that purpose, they even attempted to modify the Marxian definition of communist society, in which the maximum affluence of material goods was inexorably the premise. For instance, Castro once said that communist society would be a society in which "man will have reached the highest degree of social awareness ever achieved," and Guevara said, "Man is the conscious actor of history. Without the consciousness which encompasses his awareness as a social being there can be no communism."[33]

In analyzing the dynamics of the Cuban Revolution, Fred Judson addressed the power of "social [revolutionary] myth." Judson noticed that "the revolutionary consciousness" was the basis of the "dedication and discipline of groups." He divided "revolutionary consciousness" into two parts: rational (historical analysis of the necessity and justification of the revolution) and nonrational (faith and belief in victory, emotional identification with the cause of social revolution, and a belief that social regeneration would be made possible by insurrection and revolution).[34] The nonrational part was essentially a "revolutionary myth" that created and sustained conviction. Judson believed that, especially in the case of the Cuban Revolution, "the non-rational elements of revolutionary consciousness are crucial."[35] Borrowing from George Sorel, he observed, "The power of social myth lies in its ability to 'overcome the probabilistic world of scientific fact,' the limitations of logical premises. . . . It conjures up the vision of some final struggle."[36] In the case of Cuba, the nonrational aspect of revolutionary consciousness offset the rational one (which emphasized the objective conditions), and thus the revolution was to be triumphant against all odds. It was exactly in this sense that Castro and Guevara developed and justified their revolutionary voluntarism.

CULTIVATING A REVOLUTIONARY CONSCIOUSNESS IN THE EARLY YEARS OF THE REVOLUTION

After taking over state power, the revolutionary leaders intended to immediately inject a revolutionary consciousness—the new *cubanidad* as expected by Martí, but designed much more to serve the particular regime's political agenda—into the population as a key element in transforming it before a socioeconomic restructuring occurred. As Tzvi Medin points out in his study of the development of revolutionary consciousness in Cuba:

> Clearly, without socioeconomic restructuring (e.g., nationalizations, cooperatives, state farms), the formation of social consciousness as it was carried out in Cuba would have made no sense at all, but the important point is that social consciousness did not begin to take on its new aspect in reflection of the new socioeconomic structure; rather, it was being molded from above in a process parallel to the development of the new social economic system. It was a case of explicit and conscious development by the revolutionary leader, not a superstructural reflection of economic conditions or the automatic reproduction of a consciousness that already predominated.[37]

Medin said that Cuba's postrevolutionary experience provided "a patent illustration of the power of political and military elite in a modern state" to directly influence the "popular consciousness." He argued that "in 1959, the alternatives of radical reformist populism or socialism remained exclusively in the hands of the revolutionary leaders (and, ultimately, of Fidel Castro)," and they chose to create revolutionary consciousness in the masses "by means of a conscious and explicit policy to that effect."[38] In other words, the road to socialist revolution in Cuba was chosen consciously by the leaders almost from the beginning (1959), rather than being a result forced mainly by confrontation with the United States. One piece of important evidence was the leaders' intention to inject revolutionary consciousness into the people and the political means they used to implement that policy. As Medin argues,

> It was not until April 16, 1961, that Castro declared the revolution to be socialist, and the problem of consciousness then began to be placed in a Marxist-Leninist perspective. But even from the beginning, during the two and a half years that the revolutionaries were in power before the official declaration of socialism, explicit efforts were made to create revolutionary consciousness, reflecting the leaders' very clear view of its importance.[39]

It was in this sense that a number of important questions about the Cuban Revolution were inherently interconnected: the nature of the revolution (when it became socialist), the new man (the clear vision of and forceful efforts to create the new man as part of the socialist agenda), and the confrontation with the United States (whether the confrontation forced the revolutionary leaders to take the socialist road, or the socialist policies led to or intensified their anti-American tendency). The question regarding the nature and transformation of the Cuban Revolution (nationalist, democratic, or socialist) from the perspective of Sino-Cuban connections is discussed further below.

As soon as the revolutionaries secured their political control over the island, they made a series of efforts to change people's consciousness, similar in some ways to the efforts of the Chinese communists in their thought reform campaign of the early 1950s. Fagen used the phrase "salvageability of pre-revolutionary man" to refer to "redirection and resocialization sufficient to turn the individual into a useful and loyal citizen."[40] Castro made a statement demanding elimination of those ideological and cultural forces that were obstructing the revolution, very similar to the denunciation of the "Four Olds" by Mao and the CR radicals. The obstructions, as Castro listed them, were "the force of custom, of the way and habits of thinking and looking at things that prevailed in a vast section of the population."[41] Castro even warned the officers of the rebel army, many of whom had joined the war only for democracy and freedom and were completely unprepared for socialism. As he put it, "They had developed as officers, but they had had no opportunity to gain a political grounding."[42] An example of early actions toward this goal was the establishment of the Instituto Cubano del Arte e Industria Cinematográficos, based on a law passed in March 1959, which stated: "The cinema constitutes, by virtue of its characteristics, an instrument of opinion and formation of individual and collective consciousness, and it can contribute to the depth and clarity of the revolutionary spirit and help to sustain its creative vitality."[43]

But it was the Literacy Campaign of 1961 that marked the large-scale state engagement in indoctrinating a new consciousness and making a new man. In September 1960, Castro announced to the United Nations General Assembly that Cuba would become "the first country in the Americas to be able to claim that it has not a single illiterate inhabitant" by the end of the next year. The world was taken by surprise, given Cuba's extremely low literacy rate and its very limited educational resources, and above all the exodus of teachers after the revolution. On Cuba's revolutionary calendar, 1961 was designated as "the year of education," and in that spring the government closed all secondary and preuniversity schools, mobilizing and organizing teachers, students, and some workers in cities into militarized units, called brigades, to be sent to the countryside to eliminate illiteracy in one year. The official number of literacy workers may have been as high as 271,000 (Cuba's total population was close to seven million at the time), although the actual figure might be lower.[44]

In the history of the twentieth century, state-initiated literacy campaigns, especially in underdeveloped nations, were inherently associated with the establishment of a new national and cultural identity. Therefore the texts that were used often reflected the perspectives of a particular regime or its leaders. For example, Turkey's literacy campaign was headed directly by Atatürk in the 1920s, and those in Africa in the 1960s were headed by Julius Nyerere (Tanzania) and Kenneth Kaunda (Zambia). However, the Cuban campaign was so politically driven and ideologically charged, made possible by its military-like structure and "combat spirit," that the goal of literacy seemed to be either compromised or reduced to serve the political goal.

The excessive political/ideological nature of the Literacy Campaign was typically reflected in its literacy texts. Most of them were simply Castro's speeches and government statements or revolutionary legends. The texts were often organized into groups under given themes, most of which started with quotations of Castro's, with a few from Martí. In *Manual for the Alphabetizer*, for example, the first twelve themes were listed as "The Revolution," "Fidel Is Our Leader," "The Land Is Ours," "The Cooperatives," "The Right to Housing," "Cuba Had Riches and Was Poor," "Nationalism,"

"Industrialization," "The Revolution Is Converting the Barracks into Schools," "Racial Discrimination," "Friends and Enemies," and "Imperialism." "Democracy," the sixteenth theme, started with Castro's definition: "Democracy is this system, in which a rifle is given to any citizen who is ready to defend a just cause."[45] Even topics that were usually nonpolitical were saturated with politics. The theme "Health," for example, started with Castro's quotation, "Today our people are receiving the assistance of hundreds of doctors who are struggling to improve conditions in the nation."[46] Arithmetic problems and exercises were often of a political nature as well. For instance, one question read: "On December 2, 1956, Fidel Castro and 81 other expeditionaries disembarked near Belic, at Las Coloradas beach, facing the Sierra Maestra. By land and by sea the forces of the tyranny bombarded them; 70 men lost their lives. How many expeditionaries from the 'Granma' began the epic struggle for the liberation of Cuba?"[47]

Fagen observed that in the campaign "civic training," or making a new Cuban, was more important than literacy itself. The first method for achieving this goal was "political education," which "involved furnishing and refurnishing the minds of the students with the historical, ideological, and political images which the regime felt were appropriate to the new social order."[48] The second method "involved interactive aspects of the recruitment, publicity, and teaching processes themselves":

> The first type—direct participation—involved the literacy worker and
> the students in their interaction; each was to learn from the other. The
> second type—indirect participation—involved (at least potentially)
> the entire population. The citizenry in general was to be imbued with
> national consciousness and mobilized, made aware, made proud, and made
> productive by associating itself with the campaign against illiteracy and all
> the related symbolism.[49]

In fact, it was the second method—interaction between teachers (people from cities, or *alfabetizadores*) and students (peasants, or *alfabetizantes*) and the involvement of the whole citizenry for the purpose of "national awareness"—that distinguished the Cuban Literacy Campaign from most other literacy efforts and thus deserves more attention. Here the learning was mutual, as Castro clearly stated to the teachers: "You are going to teach, but at the same time you will learn. You will learn much more than you will teach." He said that the peasants would teach them "the why of the revolution better than any book" and "what is a healthy, sound, clean life; what is upright morality, duty, generosity, sharing the little they have with visitors."[50] In other words, the teachers had knowledge and were conversant with the government's policies, but the students might be superior in terms of their sincerity in embracing revolutionary ideology, their moral uprightness, and their frugality simply by virtue of the way they lived and worked. The campaign obviously was expected to achieve not only literacy for peasants but also a certain type of ideological transformation for urbanites (intellectuals and students) as well. Ana Serra has pointed out that the Literacy Campaign "called for a form of identity crossing between the volunteer teachers of the city and the peasants: the city instructors were called to *become* the peasants and the peasants were incited to *become* teachers." In the campaign, Serra notes, "the Sierra acted as liminal space where class barriers or differences between country and city were allegedly blurred: isolated from the rest of the world, teachers and peasant students were said to interchange roles and gradually fuse their identities into that of the New Man."[51]

Here we can clearly see a historical parallel between the Cuban Literacy Campaign and the Chinese efforts toward ideological transformation of intellectuals and students, such as thought reform and the rustication movement. But in another sense the Cuban campaign was similar to the Red Guard movement as well, because the Cuban students suspended their studies, responded to the leader's call, and were empowered to change society. At that moment they were transformed from the educated to the educators and assumed cultural and political responsibilities usually taken only by adults. It is not difficult to understand the feeling of glory and mission among those who registered for the campaign.

Despite the fanfare of government propaganda and initial excitement and euphoria among the participants, the countryside experience of individual *alfabetizadores* often became difficult and even painful. The brigades were sent to villages and then broken into groups, with individual *alfabetizadores* ultimately living with designated *alfabetizante* families. The *alfabetizador* conducted a survey on literacy rates in the immediate community and then engaged in teaching. The first glimpses of the villages and small rural communities were often overwhelming to the campaigners in the extent of their backwardness, deprivation, and isolation. But what made the experience even more difficult was the encounter with the villagers on a daily basis, which was accompanied by misunderstanding and mutual alienation, sometimes charged with hostility. For many *alfabetizadores*, the eight-month literacy mission was very stressful. For example, a fifteen-year-old female *alfabetizador* suffered from tension and nervousness while living with a hostile peasant family and was even beaten badly one time by the boys of the family. Like the Russian populists and the Chinese rusticated youths, she also found that, contrary to what she had been told to expect, she could hardly find anything she would love to learn from the peasants ideologically or morally. For example, the peasants were so biased against blacks that when they heard she was going to conduct literacy surveys in black families, they were all shocked and tried to stop her. Instead of "learning from peasants," the real ideological and political impact that the literacy mission had on many youth was the endurance of physical and psychological difficulties and the fortification of revolutionary will. For many of them, the experience was also taken as one step toward joining the revolutionary elite and attaining personal excellence. In fact, the girl in this example was later admitted to the University of Havana and became an active student leader who always saw the revolution as her own cause.[52] In general, the campaign was a special form of political socialization that to a great extent succeeded in transforming the Cuban youths from individual students into collective political activists who identified themselves with the goal of the new regime, the embryo of the new man—instead of their having a national citizenship identity, as cultivated by political socialization in many societies. Therefore, the demystification of a supposed morally and politically superior peasant did not have a significant impact on the campaigners or lead them to question other official doctrines.

Some other aspects of the Cuban Literacy Campaign served the goal of the new man as well. For example, the whole campaign was launched as a nationwide military mobilization and carried out in a military manner; 100,000 student teachers were ranked as campaigners and organized into Conrado Benitez Brigades; 35,000 teachers formed Schoolteacher Brigades; and 15,000 other workers formed Fatherland or Death Brigades. They received intensive training and took orders from the government; many of them wore berets, military uniforms (olive green pants and boots), or identical blue jeans; and they were dispatched to designated countryside locations and worked together like army units. In fact, the "brigade" as the major organizational form for civilian tasks was just an extension of the wartime manpower organization and practically the only form of managing human resources that the revolutionary leaders were familiar with. Additionally, the Literacy Campaign's use of military forms "set a precedent of militarism that would steadily intensify over the next thirty years," as Sheldon Liss observed, and "over time this militaristic mentality came to dominate policy making concerned with cultural change."[53]

To conclude, as Fagan pointed out, the Literacy Campaign demonstrated that "in Cuba we have a classical example of a revolutionary regime taking positive and massive action for the express purpose of creating the type of citizenry which the leadership feels is necessary for the functioning of the system."[54] In time the techniques invented for the campaign would be applied to many other efforts targeting the creation of the Cuban new man.

The CDR: An All-Encompassing Mechanism for Creating a Participatory Identity for the New Cubans

The Cuban Revolution differentiated itself from most other communist revolutions, especially in its early stage (the 1960s), with its mass participation and its less bureaucratic and institutionalized approach toward fulfilling the regime's sociopolitical agenda. The mass participation was mainly manifested by various organizations, among which the Committee for the Defense of the Revolution (CDR) was the most prominent. This organization is often introduced as a showcase of the Cuban people's political activism and their willingness to "participate," but an examination of the essential functions of this peculiar Cuban innovation illustrates the regime's intention to create a nationwide participatory identity for the new Cubans.

The CDR was established in September 1960, a time of intense vigilance against the subversion of the revolution by real and alleged internal and external threats. The original purpose was to mobilize and organize Cuban people at the grassroots, or neighborhood, level to discover hidden enemies. But as Fagen points out, the revolutionary vigilance soon became "only one of many purposes" of the CDR.[55] CDR activities and responsibilities could include "coordination, organization, administration of finance, revolutionary instruction, vigilance, popular defense, education, public health administration, urban reform, provisioning (distribution of scarce goods), voluntary work, propaganda and cultural instruction, sports and recreation, and the furtherance of international peace."[56] The CDR's meticulous concerns even included disciplining defiant children and overseeing some domestic matters, and it therefore became popular, as delinquency problems plagued many families. Some of the CDR's functions were associated with ideological education, especially so-called revolutionary instruction, which required organizing seminars and study circles in neighborhoods to introduce socialist ideology and government policies. This function was particularly important during the 1960s, when drastic social changes were introduced by the regime.

But these broadly defined responsibilities were actually just the surface role of the CDR in the revolution. The CDR's importance, rather, lay in its being a broad-based organization with open membership that enabled the regime to engage virtually everyone in nationwide, coordinated sociopolitical activities. As Castro himself once put it, "it is the organization that permits those citizens who cannot belong to any other organization to work for the revolution."[57] Those who already belonged to certain types of organizations (the party, a youth league, or simply a work unit) were still obliged to enroll in the CDR. Therefore the CDR was an all-encompassing organization that left no one outside the regime's ideological, political, economic, cultural, and social framework, and by doing so it created a nationwide "new Cuban" identity that transcended regional, occupational, gender, and age differences. This identity stood as the individual participated in all kinds of activities, and it created a sense that the individual was integrated into a larger national community through action. It was in this way that the CDR contributed to the formation of the new man in Cuba.

CAUGHT BETWEEN CHINA AND THE SOVIET UNION: A DIFFICULT CHOICE

The relationship between the Chinese and Cuban revolutions of the 1960s is a remarkable story of a complicated ideological, political, and diplomatic engagement in the context of world communism and the cold war that can be examined from various perspectives. But it may be legitimate to say that the theme of creating the new man, and its importance in both revolutions, provides a unique standpoint in linking them together.

From the very beginning, Cuba's admission into the communist world came with a tough assignment—to balance itself between China and the Soviet Union—and as the tension and hostility between Beijing and Moscow escalated, this situation inevitably forced Cuba to make a choice between the two communist giants.[58] However, Cuba's acrobatics between China and the Soviet Union was not just diplomatic, attempting to ensure economic and military support from both Beijing and Moscow. To a greater extent, the split between Beijing and Moscow had an ideological and political impact on Cuba's approach toward communism in general, and specifically was associated with the question, what type of people was the revolution attempting to create?

China showed great interest in the Cuban Revolution from the very beginning, and details of that interest were made available only recently. Immediately after Fidel Castro's guerrilla force entered Havana on New Year's Eve 1959, China realized the significance of this political change only ninety miles from the US coast, and an editorial note in the *People's Daily* hailed it as a victory for the nationalist and anti-imperialist movement.[59] This assessment of the Cuban Revolution would remain officially unchanged until April 1962, when Castro declared its socialist nature. In the immediate years after taking state power (1959 and most of 1960), Castro's government attempted not to associate itself with world communism too early and too officially; it even maintained its diplomatic relationship, established by the Batista government, with nationalist Taiwan, until the fall of 1960. It did this for a number of reasons: strong anticommunist sentiment in Cuba and Latin America; Castro's claim that his revolution was merely nationalist and democratic; and the US response to it. The PRC had no official diplomatic relations with any Latin American country at the time. Therefore the only possible official channel between Havana and Beijing was China's Xinhua News Agency ("XNA" hereafter), whose reporters were permitted entrance to some Latin American countries. In December 1959, Cuba officially approved China's application for the establishment of XNA's Havana branch. The branch was also a propaganda apparatus that disseminated materials reflecting China's official stand, largely through its Spanish version of XNA's daily reports and commentaries.

Two events in the summer of 1959 marked the early development of Sino-Cuban relations without official diplomatic recognition. One was that Che Guevara secretly contacted Chinese diplomats when he was representing the new Cuban government and visiting some non-Western countries (including Morocco, Egypt, and Indonesia). Guevara was urging the Chinese to purchase Cuban goods in the future if Cuban-US economic relations deteriorated. The Chinese, after reporting to Beijing, immediately promised to do so.[60] Another event occurred on July 13, when Raul Castro, Fidel's brother and the minister of armed forces, met Yao Zhen, the head of the Chinese journalist delegation. Raul told the Chinese that Cuba would sever its diplomatic ties with Taiwan, but before doing that, it would like to have an "important Chinese cadre" in Havana to represent Beijing.[61] Receiving this message, Beijing decided to send an envoy to Cuba. On August 19, Mao wrote a directive on the telegram Yao Zhen had sent from Havana. The directive was issued to Zhou Enlai and Chen Yi (the foreign minister) and suggested sending a "comrade who has a strong political sense and is at the rank equivalent to minister plenipotentiary or chargé d'affaires, but in the name of the head of or journalist of the XNA."[62]

Castro and his July 26 Movement were a totally new political phenomenon in world communism. As a matter of fact, the reputation of Castro and his July 26 Movement as a democratic and nationalist revolution were established by Western and American news agencies.[63] When Castro entered Havana, the question "Who Is Fidel Castro?" puzzled not only Chinese leaders but their diplomats and intelligence agents as well. Chinese leaders soon found that they were dealing with two kinds of revolutionaries. One was Castro's July 26 Movement, which carried out the revolution and controlled the government but had no official ties with the international communist camp. In addition, the movement had insisted that its ideology was nonsocialist and non-Marxist, in order to win over Western public opinion—particularly that of Americans—and to isolate the Batista government among Cubans who would support a nationalist and democratic revolution but not a socialist or communist one. The second kind of revolutionaries the Chinese leaders were dealing with was the Cuban communists—the People's Socialist Party, or PSP. The PSP had contributed little to the revolution, instead toeing the Soviet line of nonviolent revolution in Latin America, but it had connections with Moscow and Beijing.[64] The party realized its mistake after December 1958 and was doing its best to incorporate itself into the new regime. Therefore, for the Chinese, the fundamental questions were whether the Cuban revolution would develop into socialism and who would be in charge if such a transformation happened.

The answers to these two questions became clearer as more and more socialist-oriented policies were adopted in Cuba (nationalization of principal industrial and financial institutions in particular) in 1959 and 1960. In the meantime the Sino-Cuban connection, developed through two channels, gradually convinced the Chinese leaders of the socialist and communist nature of the Cuban revolution.[65] One channel was the XNA (before the diplomatic recognition of the two countries in September 1960), which dealt with the Cuban government and the Fidelistas. The other was the International Liaison Department of the Chinese Communist Party (established in 1952 to oversee party-to-party affairs, especially with communist parties that were either not in power or underground), which dealt with the PSP. The two questions were finally answered in the spring and early summer of 1961. In April, after the defeat of the Bay of Pigs invasion, Castro declared the socialist and communist nature of his revolution. In July the Fidelistas, the PSP, and the Revolutionary Directorate (Directorio Revolucionario, a small but active student organization that participated in the overthrow of Batista) announced unification and formed the Integrated Revolutionary Organizations (Organizaciones Revolucionarias Integradas), with Castro as the first secretary and the Fidelistas dominating the Central Committee.[66]

As soon as the socialist direction of the Cuban Revolution was confirmed and Castro's role became uncontested, the Chinese moved quickly to consolidate their relationship with the new ideological base and to woo Castro himself. The first book in Chinese introducing the Cuban Revolution, entitled *Heroic Cuba*, lavished praise on Castro. The book was a collection of articles written by Chinese journalists and other visitors to Cuba. The first article was a portrait of Castro, entitled "The Great Helmsman of the Cuban Revolution," incorporating a title used only for Mao in China at the time.[67] Recognizing its unfavorable position in its competition with the Soviet Union to win over Havana, the official line regarding China's policies toward Cuba was "to be patient and cautious."[68] In other words, anything that might push the Cubans toward the Soviets ought to be avoided. Before Shen Jian, the first Chinese ambassador to Cuba, set off for Havana, in April 1961, Zhou Enlai and Chen Yi directly instructed him, and their most important point was that the Chinese "must understand Cuba's situation."[69]

Economically China stretched itself to the limit to accommodate Cuba's needs, in particular for food and everyday necessities, despite its own woeful situation in the aftermath of the disastrous Great Leap Forward. In November 1960, two months after the official recognition, Che Guevara led an economic delegation to China, meeting with Mao, Zhou Enlai, Chen Yi, and other Chinese leaders. In the Sino-Cuban treaty signed by Guevara and Li Xiannian, China's deputy premier, China provided Cuba a long-term, interest-free loan of 240 million old rubles (US$60 million) for five years (1961–1965).[70] When a Cuban trade delegation visited China in February 1963, Zhou Enlai told the Cubans, "The loan was just a form of aid. If you are not able to pay it back when it is due, you may well postpone it. If once again you cannot make it, you can once again postpone it."[71] It was understood by the Cubans that if they were not able to return it, then the Chinese would accept the situation, for Guevara often said, gratuitously: "It is unbelievable there is such a loan in the world: interest-free, no due date, and not even responsibility for paying it back."[72] It was this experience that in part contributed to Guevara's recognition that China, rather than the Soviet Union, better represented the selfless spirit of the new man. Guevara's 1961 visit also secured a Chinese purchase of one million tons of Cuban sugar, in exchange for China's rice, the major item Cuba wanted to obtain from China.[73] In order to compete with the Soviet Union, China promised to buy Cuban sugar at the rate fixed between Cuba and the Soviet Union, whatever it was. When the international sugar price went up, the Soviet Union raised the rate from 4.11 cents to 6.11 cents per pound, and China immediately adopted the same rate.[74] After tornadoes struck Cuba in October 1963, China, whose own people were still suffering from hunger, immediately provided 5,000 tons of grain and 3,000 tons of pork, plus medicine, cloth, shoes, and stationery to Cuba. Zhou Enlai and Li Xiannian directly coordinated this aid project and ordered different provinces to make contributions. According to the official Chinese history of foreign policy, in the first half of the 1960s the cash value of trade between China and Cuba stayed at a level of US$150 million annually, and in 1965 it peaked at US$224 million.[75] By 1965, Cuba's trade with China was second only to its trade with the Soviet Union, amounting to 14 percent of the island's total foreign trade.[76]

China also advised on Cuba's economic development, based on its own experience of the transformation from a self-claimed democratic/nationalist revolution to a socialist revolution. For example, in October 1963, Bo Yibo, the director of China's Central Planning Committee, wrote an article for *Cuba Socialista* (a party organ, similar to China's *Red Flag*), introducing the Chinese experience of socialist industrialization.[77] China even ventured to suggest that Cuba change the island's single-crop exportation economy. As early as September 1960, Zeng Tao, the director of the XNA Havana branch, began to discuss this issue with Carlos Rafael Rodríguez, a member of the PSP's Politburo who had kept close ties with the July 26 Movement and later became Cuba's economic leader. The discussion took place at a prolonged dinner. When Rodríguez complained about Cuba's food shortage, Zeng said he "took the opportunity to suggest that Cuban peasants should learn how to grow grains" instead of growing only sugarcane. Zeng told him that, based on China's experience, it was not just an economic issue but a political one as well, because, without grain, a socialist country could not maintain its independence. But Rodríguez obviously preferred the idea of "socialist labor division," an economic doctrine endorsed by the Soviet Union and meaning, in Cuba's case, to export sugar in exchange for food and other necessities from other socialist states. Zeng went further, introducing Mao's self-reliance doctrine, but that did not impress Rodríguez at all. Instead, Rodríguez suggested that China import more Cuban sugar and export more rice and other necessities to Cuba.[78]

A similar but more serious discussion took place between Shen Jian, the first Chinese ambassador to Cuba, and Guevara in the aftermath of the 1963 tornado disaster and the consequent Chinese assistance. Shen talked to Guevara and suggested that Cubans cultivate as many crops as possible in order to achieve self-reliance in their food supply. Guevara accepted the suggestion and asked Shen for technical support. Shen immediately cabled Beijing to send rice experts to Cuba, helping to change the country's agricultural structure.[79] The advice and assistance China provided regarding the Cuban economy not only reflected its concerns over the economic importance of Cuba's food production in the revolution but also formed part of the Sino-Soviet competition in the Caribbean island. The Chinese understood that the monocultural nature of the Cuban economy was the main reason for Cuba's reliance on Moscow. A more diverse economy would bring about more flexibility for Cuba's international stand.

In addition, China sent numerous cultural and mass organization delegations to Cuba within a rather short period. These delegations came from trade unions, women's federations, youth leagues, among them scientists, artists and writers, model workers and peasants, gymnasts, and so on to represent the new Chinese people and to show the spirit and enthusiasm generated by socialism.[80] The Cubans arranged for all of these Chinese delegations to witness the revolutionary enthusiasm manifested in Cuban mass rallies, workplaces, schools, and families. The Chinese were also invited to participate in volunteer work.[81] The representatives of the Chinese new man were impressed by what they had observed in Cuba, and upon their return home, they told the Chinese people that a new type of Cuban was emerging after the revolution. One example widely publicized in China was the story of a 106-year-old woman who became literate and politically enlightened by participating in Cuba's Literacy Campaign in 1960.[82] After visiting some of Cuba's new communities—designed by the government to bring up a new generation by combining work, education, and residence—the Chinese concluded, "The Cuban government is taking all measures to cultivate the new generation. This is a difficult but grandiose plan."[83] All of these cultural activities helped to create and intensify in Cuba an atmosphere of revolutionary participation and celebration. This atmosphere was characteristic of the Cuban revolution in the early 1960s, as part of the euphoria that reflected the revolution's popularity. In the later 1960s this celebratory atmosphere remained essential in boosting people's morale, especially when the Cubans had to face the grim reality of rationing for everything. In return, Cuba sent similar delegations to China, with the youngest one, a child delegation, led by Castro's eleven-year-old son.

Although Cuba obviously seemed to benefit from such economic and cultural relations much more than China did, what China received in return was significant. In the late 1950s and early 1960s, China was struggling to achieve oil and energy self-reliance in order to put an end to its dependence on the Soviet Union for those supplies and technologies. Shen Jian, the first Chinese ambassador, visited Cuba's oil refinery not long after he arrived in Cuba. Cuba was the experimental site for some American technologies, particularly oil refining and communication. The refinery Shen visited had been built in 1958, one year before the revolution, by adopting advanced American technology. Shen asked the Cuban government for its blueprint and other data, and the Cuban government provided him the whole package of information about the refinery, at the request of Che Guevara. As the author of the official history of China's foreign relations acknowledged, "China's first large-scale refinery facilities were established with the help of Cuban technology."[84] Ironically, this recognition came just recently. From the 1960s to the 1980s, according to official propaganda, it was new men like Wang Jingxi, inspired and armed with Mao Zedong thought, who had enabled China to become self reliant in oil and oil-related technologies. No mention was made of the importance of Cuban-imported American technology in this achievement.

From the very beginning of the establishment of connections between Cuba and the communist world, Havana was fully aware of its predicament of being caught between China and the Soviet Union. From 1960 to early 1965, Cuba's standpoint was to maintain neutrality so as to keep both Chinese and Soviet support as much and as long as possible, in hopes that the two would someday bridge their ideological differences. The official Cuban standpoint regarding the Sino-Soviet quarrel can be found in Guevara's statement in August 1963: "The Sino-Soviet quarrel is, for us, a sad development, but since the dispute is a fact, we tell our people about it and it is discussed by the party. Our party's attitude is to avoid analyzing who is right and who is not. We have our own position, and as they say in the American films, any resemblance [presumably of Cuba to either contestant] is purely coincidental."[85] Cuba's neutral standpoint was used by Beijing and Moscow in turning the island into their propaganda battlefield. From 1960 to 1964, both nations disseminated propaganda materials in Cuba that reflected their point of view (largely by selling the text of their news reports and pictorial magazines in Cuban bookstores and sending them to government offices through Cuban post offices). The Chinese were much more aggressive in sending out such materials directly to the home addresses of many Cuban political and military cadres. The Cubans did nothing to restrain this propaganda warfare, but in their own publications they made no comments on the Sino-Soviet debate. When they translated and reprinted Chinese and Russian materials, they omitted the mutual accusations.

As the Sino-Soviet polemics intensified, like most other socialist countries, Cuba was increasingly forced to choose sides. From 1961 to 1965, Cuba struggled with this difficult situation but eventually, in early 1966, had to choose Moscow as its main international ally and economic/military supporter, resulting in an open polemic and denouncement of China and even of Mao personally. Cuba accused China of cutting rice exportation to Cuba and disseminating subversive materials among Cuban political and military personnel to overthrow Castro and of assisting the US blockade of Cuba, while China retorted that Cuba had joined the international anti-China "chorus" orchestrated by imperialism and revisionism. The Sino-Cuban split was apparently caused by the Sino-Soviet rift, as part of the divergence in global communism. Although for many communist parties or countries such a choice was difficult or painful, Cuba's situation was further complicated by its own ideological disposition. The Sino-Cuban mutual accusations were short-lived; after early 1966, there was no more exchange of any words between China and Cuba.

The metaphor "Castro's stomach is in Moscow, but his heart in Beijing" was drawn by K. S. Karol, based on his firsthand observation of the true feelings of the Cubans about China.[86] Karol was a Polish-born, Soviet-educated intellectual who was disappointed with Stalinism and lived in

Paris during the 1960s. He made trips to China and Cuba in the second half of the 1960s, in search of a new communism. Afterwards he provided rich stories and observations of Cuban attitudes toward China and Russia, also with some comparisons between China and Cuba. According to him, both China and Cuba demonstrated a strong tendency to find a new approach toward communism, different from the Russian one. In front of him, the Cuban leaders made no effort to conceal their aversion to the Russians, while conceding their material reliance upon Moscow. On the other hand, they displayed strong interest in what China had been doing since the Great Leap Forward and in the ongoing Cultural Revolution. Karol's stomach-and-heart metaphor clearly referred to Cuba's economic need for Russia and its ideological affinities with China.

Karol visited China in 1965 and shortly thereafter published a book entitled *China, the Other Communism*, in which he praised China's social experiment based on egalitarianism, moral incentive, and antibureaucratic efforts. He saw these efforts as a countermodel to the Soviet regime. After he arrived in Cuba in 1967, he found that one chapter of his book had been published as a brochure by the Culture Committee of the State, under the title "The Elusive Proletarian Culture," and distributed among the cadres of certain ranks. The chapter focused on "certain key postulates of the Chinese experiment—its egalitarian approach, its refusal to use material incentives." When he asked the Cubans he met, they told him that they were also deeply impressed by China's political fervor, and they thought the Chinese were plainly far better revolutionaries than the Russians. No one had wanted to mention the debate between China and Cuba two years earlier. In contrast, Karol noticed that Cuban criticism of Russia was almost overt in private discussions:

> In fact, the breach between Havana and Moscow was much deeper than
> Cuban pronouncements abroad seemed to suggest. The language used
> by the Castroists at home was full of phrases reminiscent of Chinese
> arguments. They used the term revisionism as an obvious reference to the
> U.S.S.R. and its allies abroad. Even merchandise from eastern Europe
> was commonly described by this title (such as trucks and blades of poor
> qualities).[87]

When Karol met with Castro, the Cuban leader asked him about what was going on in China, and laid out the different positions of Cuba, China, and Russia: "The Chinese may be doing interesting experiments, but we are trying to go much further than they have. Money remains at the core of their social program, even though [their] sights are set on equality, while Russians deliberately encourage differences in income. We intend to get rid of the whole money myth, rather than tamper with it. We want to abolish money altogether."[88]

Karol also emphasized that Che Guevara was the most outspoken critic of the Soviet Union among the Cuban leaders. His criticism was largely directed at Russian economic policies, with a deeper concern about the revisionism and restoration of capitalism caused by such policies. According to Karol, during Guevara's last visit to the Soviet Union (in 1963), he invited a group of Russian students to the Cuban embassy to discuss the issue. He made a rather stunning remark on Soviet economic reform:

> I know it only too well. It was used in Cuba before the Revolution and is widespread in the foremost capitalist countries. And frankly, what you tell me about the profitability of enterprises under a market economy is neither a novelty nor a great secret. Capitalism knows all about this type of profitability. There is just one snag in this system: when all enterprises vie for profits, you have unrestrained competition followed by anarchy and finally by an irresolvable crisis. Then there is nothing to do but to make a revolution and thereby restore reason to society.[89]

René Dumont, a French Marxist economist who worked as a consultant in Cuba and argued with Guevara on the issue of material and moral incentives (introduced later in this chapter), further pointed out the relationship between Guevara's vision of the new man and his criticism of the Soviet Union. To Dumont, Guevara seemed to be looking for

> a sort of ideal vision of the Socialist Man, who would become a stranger to the mercantile side of things, working for society and not for profit. He was very critical of the industrial success of the Soviet Union, where, he said, everybody works and strives and tries to go beyond his quota, but only to earn more money. He did not think the Soviet Man was really a new sort of man, for he did not find him any different, really, than a Yankee.[90]

On the other hand, Guevara openly praised communist China and the Chinese people, who he concluded had been inspired by Mao's thoughts and were so willing to sacrifice. During his first trip to China in 1960, he lauded the people's communes as a socialist model for the newly independent countries. He concluded that the Chinese were more politically conscious. The Chinese technicians in Guevara's ministry worked for free, while the Russians requested salaries and housing from Cuba. Guevara thought that the Chinese showed a "truer" socialist "morality." As he put it, "Sacrifice is fundamental to a Communist education. The Chinese understand that very well, much better than the Russians do."[91] Indeed, as Liss points out, Guevara "concurred with Mao's contention that one immediately constructs a revolutionary conscience or else runs the risk of holding to capitalist incentives, as he thought had occurred in the Soviet Union."[92]

Though the Cubans tried to avoid openly irritating the Russians with their criticism, sometimes they could not help but go beyond beating around the bush. For example, in March 1967, *Granma Weekly Review* published a long editorial entitled "The Struggle against Bureaucracy: A Decisive Task," allegedly written by Armando Hart, the organization secretary of the party's Central Committee. The editorial, which regarded the emerging bureaucracy in Cuba as a sign of the danger of the restoration of capitalism, described "a special stratum of men whose relations to the means of production and political decisions place them in the leadership" and stated that "they have a bureaucratic mentality, a bureaucratic concept of administration, seeking comfort and privilege." These words were very similar to a Maoist denunciation of the cadres who were taking the "capitalist road" at the same time in the Cultural Revolution. In explaining whence Cuba was infected by this bureaucratic disease, the editorial pointed to the Soviet Union almost directly: "In the first few years of the revolution there was the introduction of some administrative systems and organizational procedures, copied from countries of the socialist camp, that were weighted down with bureaucracy."[93] And at that time, the editorial said, the Cubans were lacking "a sense of criticism" for filtering out negative aspects of the socialist camp's influence. This analysis was also similar to China's condemnation, after its split with the USSR, of the Soviet bureaucratic influence on its own political and administrative systems in the early years of the PRC.

Cuba's criticism of the Soviet Union at times even led to questioning the real nature of the Soviet system. For example, Cuban president Osvaldo Dorticós Torrado once declared that "we have our little heresy," in reaction to the Soviet conception that "the abundance of consumer goods was the only problem to solve" on the way toward communism. He continued, "Ever since 1962 . . . Russians have spoken less and less of communism and more and more of profits and the restoration of the market mechanism." He made these comments in a conversation with Karol, and the latter was struck by the similarities between criticisms of the Soviet Union made by him and Mao.[94]

The Cuban criticism of Soviet revisionism was facilitated by a historical analysis, which linked Soviet economic policies in different times of Soviet history. In April 1965, when Guevara visited Cairo, he gave an interview in which he clearly indicated that there was a long tradition of compromising communist principles in exchange for economic growth. The earliest example of such compromise was Lenin's New Economic Policy, and the latest one was "Liberman's experiments." He condemned "the production law," which was dominant in Soviet economic policymaking. According to Guevara, Yugoslavia, which then allowed a certain amount of non-Stalinist or noncommunist economic factors to exist, was "in imminent danger of walking toward capitalism," while the Soviet Union and its satellites had not "finally abandoned the possibility of returning to capitalism if we take the matter from the general historical point of view."[95]

Although there is much less evidence on the Chinese side showing Beijing's interest in what was going on in Cuba or even trying to compare the two countries, Cuba's defiant attitude toward Russia did not completely escape Mao. As early as 1964, Mao commented, "Revisionism is being rebuffed everywhere. . . . In Cuba they listen to half and reject half; they listen to half because they cannot do otherwise, since they do not produce oil or weapons."[96]

All of the evidence of the Cuban critique of the Soviet Union and the affinity with China led to one conclusion: in the 1960s, in addition to the Chinese, the Cubans were also disillusioned with the political and economic changes in the Soviet Union. One thing they particularly did not like in the Soviet Union was the negative ideological impact on the new man brought about by Soviet economic policies. Having been alerted to Soviet revisionism as China was, Cuba also wanted to avoid the Soviet pitfall, namely the compromise of revolutionary principles for the sake of economic expediency.

MORAL INCENTIVES VERSUS MATERIAL INCENTIVES: A DEBATE ON THE DYNAMICS OF CREATING THE NEW MAN

When Dorticós commented that since 1962 the Russians had "spoken less and less of communism and more and more of profits and the restoration of the market mechanism," he was referring to the Soviet discussion on economic incentives and the market mechanism. This debate, as discussed in chapter 1, had a great impact on almost every socialist nation. In most Eastern European countries, it brought about a relief from the strict Stalinist command economy and justified reformist requests for more autonomy for managers and more material incentives for individual workers. But in China it was criticized as revisionist because it caused a concern that such a reform would unleash the worker's desire for material rewards and therefore undermine the consciousness of the new man. As Peter Clecak, a contemporary Western Marxist sympathetic to China, observed in 1969:

The Chinese regard such arguments for material incentives as dangerous rationalizations. Material incentives, they contend, may initially appear to be nothing more than efficient and temporary means of enriching the socialist community. But when self-interest becomes the chief incentive to physical and mental activity, economically rational means subvert socialist and communist ends, eroding instead of building the foundations of a future society. The society purchases material enrichment at the heavy price of moral and spiritual impoverishment of its members. The primary emphasis on personal gain imposes a nearsighted mode of social vision; neglecting the whole of social reality, the "successful" man must magnify those parts relevant to his immediate personal ends. Life is inevitably privatized; individuals withdraw into their narrow spheres of activity.[97]

In Cuba, discussion about the Soviets caused similar confusion and was echoed by division and debate among Cuban economic leaders. The Cubans responded to the discussion with a sense of urgency due to their country's worsening economic situation. Beginning in 1962—shortly after the implementation of the large-scale state intervention in the economy, the nationalization of principal industries and financial institutions, and the exodus of managers, technicians, and skilled workers, as well as America's embargo—production declined significantly. In late 1962, most important daily consumer goods, such as rice, meat, oil, eggs, chicken, and so on were rationed. When the impact of the debate in the Soviet Union reached Cuba, the leaders were divided into two opinions on the causes of their economic problems and how to promote production. One group was represented by Carlos Rafael Rodríguez, who was then the chief of the National Institute for Agrarian Reform, and Marcelo Fernández, the minister of foreign trade. Like reform-minded Soviet economists, they believed the traditional socialist economy was overcentralized and command-based, out of touch with consumers' needs reflected in the market, and driven by collectivist consciousness and political goals. The stagnation and even decline in Cuban production could be understood only from this perspective. Therefore they were in favor of some reformist Soviet approach, such as a self-managed budget system, which meant loosening state control, giving more latitude to middle or lower economic leaders and managers about what to produce and how to sell, and establishing worker pay based on labor quotas. This group was called the Economists, according to Bertram Silverman, but the term had been coined earlier by Lenin, with a negative implication.

On the other side of the debate was Che Guevara, the head of the National Bank and the Ministry of Industry. Guevara was the main thrust behind Cuba's nationalization and establishment of a socialist economy, and he was appointed exactly for that purpose. According to Cuban revolutionary legend, at a meeting regarding the nomination of a National Bank director, when Castro asked "Who is a good economist?" Guevara immediately raised his hand because he misheard the word "economist" as "communist." But he was appointed anyway. Instead of adopting noncommunist methods, the Guevarist solution for economic problems was something similar to Lenin's War Communism in the early 1920s, which disregarded material incentive, rationed daily necessities on an egalitarian basis, and promoted volunteer labor. He insisted that for communists it was compulsory to persist in the socialist nature of the economy by sticking to overall state planning, central budgeting, an egalitarian way of determining workers' incomes, and enhancing people's revolutionary enthusiasm and socialist consciousness as their work ethic.

Although the debate involved several major economic issues, it was the one between material and moral incentives that crystallized the nature of the entire debate and its implication for creating the new man. As part of this international communism concern, Cuba's debate involved foreign communists who were in Havana to help socialist transformation. Some European Marxist economists, as advisers to the Cuban government, participated, and their observations provided interesting perspectives. Among them, the Frenchmen Charles Bettelheim and René Dumont joined the side opposed to Guevara, while Ernest Mandel, a Belgian, stood behind him. The two sides carried out their polemic publicly, through newspapers and magazines such as the *Roy* and *Revolution* and through policies adopted in their respective ministries.

The debate touched two key issues of the Cuban Revolution. The first was the tension and balance between subjective efforts and objective circumstances, the classical theoretical question of the revolution. The reason the Economists supported conciliation with capitalist methods was that the lack of a substantial economic and technological foundation in an underdeveloped country like Cuba placed significant constraints on the transformation of economic and social institutions. They further argued that socialist morality could not be imposed by political pressure and executive measure but could be introduced only by education and indoctrination. As Charles Bettelheim observed, "The decisive factor in changing man's behavior lies in the changes rendered to production and its organization."[98] In other words, political slogans and ideological discourse could do little to change people's entrenched mentality and behavior while the production and organization of society remained at a relatively low level. Therefore it was quite clear that, for these Economists, at least at that moment, the existing unfavorable circumstances presented an insurmountable obstacle to the subjective revolutionary resolve.

The second issue pointed to a more specific question: material incentive versus moral incentive. If the society lacked sufficient economic efficiency to convert itself to a higher stage of development, and the consciousness of the workers had not been promoted to a level at which work was not for money but for contribution, then material incentives should be allowed to pragmatically increase production.

The implications of the debate went far beyond economics. It was a matter of life or death for the project of making the Cuban new man, as Guevara instinctively sensed. For him, the odd smell from his opponents' proposals was so discernible, the consequences of such proposals so grave, that he could not treat it as a purely economic discussion. As Liss points out,

> Che Guevara knew that the Cuban revolutionary government inherited many potentially corrupting capitalist ways alien to the revolution, including material incentives. In utopian fashion he defined value according to moral or social or human worth, not supply and demand. To him, work was more valuable in human terms than in terms of economic efficiency. He construed economic man as a monster created by capitalism and believed that the economic system should serve society—that money was no part of human life.[99]

René Dumont had traveled extensively around the country and found that the most serious problem in agriculture was that the workers on state farms didn't feel they were owners of the property and therefore were not motivated, relative to private farmers. He suggested that, in order to give the workers a real sense of co-ownership, they should be paid for their overtime labor to maintain the farms and the equipment during the off-season. Guevara rejected the idea. He insisted that what Cuban workers needed was not a sense of ownership but a sense of responsibility.[100]

Guevara was not rejecting everything his opponents recommended. He was not suggesting imposing the same communist methods in the private sector, and sometimes he compromised by allowing some forms of prizes and compensation in his own ministry to differentiate those who worked more from those who worked less. But he certainly rejected using such rewards in the public sector as a basic driving force. His fundamental concern was that if the proposals of his opponents were fully applied, the efforts to create the new man would be in vain. When his opponents quoted some classical Marxist remarks emphasizing the importance of an economic base, he retorted by reminding them of Cuban experience: the triumph of the Cuban Revolution had been achieved not by mature social conditions but by the mature consciousness of the vanguard. In his principal work, "Man and Socialism in Cuba," written as a manifesto of his stance in this debate, Guevara attributed the victory of the revolution to the "heroic attitude" of the vanguards, instead of favorable objective circumstances. He made it clear that "one of our fundamental tasks from the ideological standpoint is to find the way to perpetuate such heroic attitudes in everyday life."[101] To effectuate this, "society as a whole must become a huge school."[102] In other words, for Guevara, a "heroic attitude" would be the only remedy for Cuba's ailing economy, and it would not bring about any side effects to the growth of the new man.

In contrast to his opponents' proposal to utilize material incentives, therefore, Guevara urged and organized massive campaigns of voluntary labor to promote production, accompanied with a socialist emulation movement. Following his example, the cadres and workers in his ministry often stayed longer at their work after dark and sacrificed their weekends and holidays. When Guevara felt compelled to award those of his enthusiastic disciples and winners of emulation or competition with certain forms of material benefits, he was often reluctant to grant or announce such rewards to the champion workers publicly. Instead he preferred to give the rewards to the winners after ceremonial commendations and away from public view.

The debate over material and moral incentives came to an abrupt end in early 1965, when Castro, who had kept silent during the whole polemic, said that the revolutionary's task was not philosophical argument. His was a vague statement showing no favor to either side but only indicating his disapproval of the ongoing debate. Castro was obviously concerned about the debate's unsettling effects on the party leadership's unity. The polemical articles quickly disappeared from all publications, but the plaguing production problem remained unsolved. What were Castro's true feelings and thoughts about the debate? To learn that, people would have to wait for two years, when he was about to plunge Cuba into a fervent political campaign, the Revolutionary Offensive. At that time the debate was mentioned in Cuban newspapers and in his speeches, in which he praised Guevara, who had disappeared from Cuba's political scene. For example, in one of *Granma*'s editorials (March 1967), the author not only denounced the idea of "material incentive" but also regarded it as a major threat to the realization of the ideal of the new man:

> If we allow certain categories characteristic of the capitalist system to survive . . . if we take the easiest way out, using material interest as the driving force in the socialist construction, if merchandise is held up as the central core of the economy, if the presence of money remains omnipotent

within the new society, then selfishness and individualism will continue to be predominant characteristics in the consciousness of men and we shall never arrive at the formation of new man.[103]

Nothing, however, more explicitly expressed Castro's standpoint on the issue of material versus moral incentives than his speech responding to Soviet suppression of the Prague Spring. On August 24, 1968, three days after Moscow and its satellites invaded Czechoslovakia to crack down on liberalization, Castro made a lengthy speech, televised nationwide, to endorse the invasion, but he also took advantage of this event to lecture the Russians by pointing out the connections between their economic reforms and the bourgeois liberalization in Czechoslovakia. He asked how such circumstances could arise in a country such as Czechoslovakia and then answered himself, beginning by quoting a *Pravda* analysis of the situation in Czechoslovakia: "But this statement is very interesting. It says: 'Unfortunately, discussions concerning economic reform in Czechoslovakia developed on another basis. That discussion centered, on the one hand, around a global criticism of all development proceeding from the socialist economy and, on the other, around the proposal to replace the principles of planning with spontaneous mercantile relations, granting a broad field of action to private capital.'" Castro then asked a serious question:

> Does this, by chance, mean that the Soviet Union is also going to curb certain trends in the field of economy that are in favor of putting increasingly greater emphasis on mercantile relations and on the efforts of spontaneity in those relations, and those [trends] that have even been defending the desirability of the market and the beneficial effect of prices based on that market? Does it mean that the Soviet Union is becoming more aware of the need to halt those trends? More than one article in the imperialist press has referred jubilantly to those trends that also exist within the Soviet Union.[104]

For Castro, it was quite clear that events in Czechoslovakia symbolized the failure of Soviet reform, if such a reform was meant to perfect socialist economy. The Soviet failure conversely proved that Cuba's stand was correct. Castro went further, indicating that in Cuba the new man was growing in a healthy environment, while people in Czechoslovakia and the Soviet Union had been corrupted by compromises with noncommunist elements. As he said triumphantly:

> There are thousands of young people ever ready to go anywhere as technicians specialized in different fields, thousands of young people

stating their willingness to go fight wherever they are needed. Our constant problem here is that everyone dreams of someday being permitted to leave the country to help the revolutionary movement wherever he may be needed.

In other words, the internationalist conscience of our people has developed, [and] the communist conscience of our country has developed day by day.[105]

SOCIALIST EMULATION AND VOLUNTEER LABOR: THE INSTITUTIONALIZATION OF MORAL INCENTIVE

While the debate on material and moral incentives was still ongoing, Che Guevara championed campaigns to institutionalize moral incentive and social conscience, among which the implementation of communist voluntary work and socialist emulation and volunteer labor stood out as the major campaigns. In the terminologies of the socialist governments, voluntary work was defined as "communist" because the participants expected no material compensation, whereas emulation, because it often involved work beyond regular assignments but carried certain rewards, was deemed "socialist"—"to everyone according to his contribution."

Communist volunteer labor originated under War Communism in the early years of Soviet Russia, as an extraordinary measure to solve the problem of labor shortages. "Communist Saturday volunteer labor," as Lenin called it, remained part of the regular schedule of political and work ethics education for Soviet students and workers throughout the 1950s. In China, especially during the Great Leap Forward, it was frequently used for the same purpose. But only in Cuba did volunteer work become an institutionalized measure to promote production without the cost of labor compensation. Socialist emulation also originated in the Soviet Union, and in the 1930s it was an important stimulation for the realization of industrialization. For many workers, socialist emulation provided opportunities to make extra income, because the emulation was often based on work quotas and a significant contribution beyond the quotas would bring the individual corresponding compensation. In fact, Soviet labor heroes significantly increased their income by surpassing their work quotas and were granted other material benefits such as vacations, housing, and special treatment with regard to health care and shopping, thus constituting a stratum of worker elite. In China before the Cultural Revolution, labor heroes received extra compensation as well, but not as much as their Soviet counterparts did. In Cuba, however, emulation was institutionalized not only to promote production but to reduce labor costs as well; therefore material rewards for extra work in the 1960s were low and were gradually reduced or became merely symbolic.

In order to coordinate emulation on a national scale, the Ministry of Labor formed the Executive Committee for Emulation and established provincial and local administrations in 1962. The duties of this committee included setting the criteria for the evaluation of emulation, assigning individual quotas, and recording attendance in every workplace. The forms of rewards for the winners in emulation were gradually changed from material and substantial rewards, measured in cash, to moral and symbolic ones, such as public commemorations, medals, buttons, diplomas, plaques, certificates, honorable mentions in factory or farm bulletins, and banners such as those celebrating May Day, the Hundred-Year Struggle, the Heroes of Moncada, and the Heroic Guerrilla Awards. The highest honor was the yearly Hero of Labor awards bestowed by the party's leaders at mass public gatherings.

When emulation started in the early 1960s, the winners could have cash prizes, but the government preferred to give them consumer goods with cash value instead. The idea behind such alternatives was to limit the use of money and eradicate the "dollar sign" in the workers' mind. On many occasions winners were honored with neither cash nor consumer goods but with vacations and travel to the Soviet Union and Eastern European countries. In 1966 the cash prize was completely abolished, and prizes of consumer goods were gradually reduced in value. Instead of material rewards, winners were given more and more symbolic honors, as mentioned above.

Although the hostility toward money was nothing new in world communism, in Castro's and Mao's revolutions this hostility developed to the near abolition of money.[106] For Castro, money was a necessary transitory instrument but completely incompatible with the goal of the new man, and therefore its use ought to be limited as much as possible. Thus he proclaimed in 1968, as the Revolutionary Offensive had just been set in motion, "We will not develop a socialism mentality and a communism with a dollar sign in the minds and hearts of men and women."[107] As Fagen observed, "The feeling against the role of money in society extends well beyond a simple rejection of extra pay for extra work. What is called into question by Castro and his followers is nothing less than the exchange and distributive functions of the monetary system."[108] In reality, the use of money in Cuba from the mid-1960s to the very end of the decade was indeed significantly limited. By the summer of 1968, when the Revolutionary Offensive was under way, education, medical care, local phone calls, burials, sports events, and some housing were free. In addition, most daily necessities were rationed, and extra money, in theory, could buy nothing. A moneyless society was almost on the horizon.

Castro's repugnance for money and Cuban efforts to create a moneyless society had their equivalents in China. Mao, like Castro, personally detested money and said it was the "dirtiest stuff" in the world, even though cash had been officially named "people's money" *(ren ming bi)*. According to people close to him, Mao "never wanted to touch money," and he ordered cash to be put into envelopes so he would not see the "dirtiest stuff" when it was inevitably involved in some situation—he often gave money to his relatives and old friends and to his attendants when they left him. In China there are two interpretations of Mao's hatred of money: one takes it to be part of his moral and spiritual qualities; the other dismisses it as nonsense, because Mao simply did not have to touch money, as everybody else did. As a matter of fact, the amount in Mao's personal bank account was astronomical: more than 130 million Chinese yuan when he died in 1976, according to one recent source. At the time, a monthly salary of 100 yuan would be considered a rather decent income and enough for a family of four. Mao's enormous bank balance mainly resulted from royalties for his works published in multivolumes, with millions of copies and an obligation for everyone to buy them.[109] As for the role of money in China under Mao, first of all, a household registration system separated people living in cities and towns from peasants, with the former guaranteed similar low-cost benefits as in Cuba, and the latter excluded from these benefits. In addition, most consumer goods were rationed. Therefore the place for money in society was very limited. In the mid-1970s, however, the Maoist ideologues still launched a campaign attacking money as "bourgeois legal rights." At about the same time, under Maoist influence but going much further, the Khmer Rouge totally abolished money after entering cities (see chapter 4). Eric Hoffer, an American social thinker, had an insightful observation in this regard:

> Whoever originated the cliché that money is the root of all evil knew hardly anything about the nature of evil and very little about human beings. The monstrous evils of the twentieth century have shown us that the greediest money grubbers are gentle doves compared with money-hating wolves. . . . A society without money will be largely preoccupied with managing people. There will be little social automatism. Sowing, harvesting, mining, manufacturing, etc., will become burning national problems.[110]

Volunteer work was another major method used to institutionalize moral incentive. As early as 1961, volunteer work was introduced to Cuba by its leaders, Guevara in particular, and soon became part of workers' regular schedules. Although the economic value of volunteer work was clear to all Cuban leaders, for Guevara its most important aspect was that it demanded sacrifice on a daily basis and thus was a gradual process toward the goal of the new man. With his advocacy, such practices were introduced to other ministries as well. Guevara promoted the campaigns by his own example—he often went to construction sites, state farms, and cane fields on the weekends or holidays. He considered volunteer work and emulation as the people's tasks not only in their working hours but also during their spare time:

> Every worker at every factory must be conscious that emulation is something more than a competition during a given period. It's a vital part of our nation's work. . . . All of you should engage in emulation on all levels: shop to shop, department to department, factory to factory, enterprise to enterprise. . . . Emulation should be part of the worker's day-to-day discussions during the hours he's not working. That would really mark the triumph of emulation.[111]

Volunteer work was organized by every unit in all kinds of social occupations but was also often launched as a national campaign, lasting for a certain length of time. In April 1967, for example, 250,000 people participated in various types of volunteer labor for at least two weeks, some for six weeks, by donating their after work hours and weekends. It was called the Giron Fortnight and became an annual campaign commemorating the defeat of the Bay of Pigs invasion. A more conventional form of volunteer labor was routine or random overtime work without pay, sometimes two hours per day, sometimes more. The workers who undertook more volunteer work could gain the same honorable and nonmaterial prizes that models in socialist emulation were awarded.

EDUCATION: THE MAIN INSTRUMENT FOR MAKING THE NEW MAN

As in the Soviet Union, and China in particular, education was a major vehicle in Cuba's social engineering to create the new man. Since the early 1960s, Cuba's education system experienced fundamental reforms and reconstruction. The integration of ideology with knowledge, work with study, social and political participation with classroom activities, and eventually school with society was the goal of such a transformation. Gaspar Jorge García, the secretary general of the Trade Union of Education and Scientific Workers, once outlined the goal of the new education: "What is proposed is to train active and conscientious builders of the Communist society. . . . It will be achieved to the degree that old educators are reeducated and a new mentality is created, a new socialist mentality."[112]

Like Mao, Castro also often regarded himself not only as a political leader of a revolutionary regime but also as a teacher and a moral mentor of the nation. As he once put it: "I have always had a great addiction to education. My plan, which was not original, was to universalize study as well as work. The alternative would be to have an intellectual elite and a group that does not study, which would always perform hard manual labor. People talked about it and gave it attention, but Cuba was the first to put it into practice."[113] In addition, Castro had a particular interest in and vision of early education. When he was in the Sierra Maestra in 1958, he revealed his future educational plan to a French reporter:

> I shall create agricultural units for each 25,000 inhabitants. . . . These units will have a training center for the children, since it is harder to teach the old than the young. . . . The children will be housed and fed, clothed and educated, and by their own work they will make these centers self-supporting to the point where they will be able to amortize the plant and machinery, which will belong to the state.[114]

On March 13, 1959, one month after he became prime minister, Castro summoned a group of university students to join *Meet the Press*, a regular television program in which Castro announced and explained his policies of social reform. He asked the students, rather than the faculty, to remake the curriculum and reform the structure of the university. He told them that the old higher education was an evil environment in which young Cubans had been corrupted. His attack on the old education was full of moral indignation: "Who was ever taught to be honest here? To be decent? Who ever set a good example? How are the schools going to teach anything under a rotten system that is more interested in defrauding than teaching? What could a child learn from a criminal teacher?"[115]

Guevara also advocated an educational revolution that would eventually eliminate distinctions between work and study, and between society and school. As he put it, "Education is increasingly integral, and we do not neglect the incorporation of the students into work from the very beginning."[116]

Innovations in Early Political Socialization

Educational changes took a priority in the Cuban leaders' political agenda from the very beginning of the revolution and were often combined with the general task of political socialization of the young generations. This prioritization was evident in a number of significant innovations made as early as 1960. The Schools of Revolutionary Instruction (Escuelas de Instrucción Revolucionaria) were the earliest. Initiated in January 1961 but secretly conceived much earlier, this school system recruited students of age fourteen and above to be trained as the future party functionaries; therefore it was a training center for the political elite. The candidates were handpicked by the government, and there was no competition for admission. Castro once explained the purpose of the schools as "the ideological formation of the revolutionary, and then, by means of the revolutionaries, the ideological formation of the rest of the people."[117] Given its purpose of preparing students for future leadership posts, this innovation combined revolutionary vanguardism, early consciousness cultivation, and future political privilege. The very existence of this school system suggested a profound irony of the Cuban Revolution: the revolution was carried out in the name of social equality, but access to the leadership posts in the society was limited to a small minority of people chosen by the government at a very early age. With its center in Havana and branches all over the island, this school system developed rapidly under the government's auspices. In only one year it established twelve regional schools, and one national institution, with twelve thousand students. By 1963 it had two hundred local schools, seven provincial centers, and nine national institutions, and the numbers of students increased accordingly.[118]

Another early educational innovation was Training for Teachers of Elementary Schools. In 1960 hundreds of teenage students—most ages thirteen and fourteen, with some as young as eleven—were recruited by the government and sent to Minas del Frío in the Sierra Maestra, which had been the site of Guevara's headquarters during the guerrilla war. The very first lesson for the students was to build their classrooms and dormitories with their own hands. In the following years, a training center, formally named the Vocational Center in Minas del Frío, was developed. By 1967 it had become a "school city," with a capacity of up to eight thousand students. The center had about forty buildings divided into zones and nuclei for organizational purposes. Life there was highly regimented. The students were organized into brigades named after heroes and heroines who had died in the guerrilla war, and the routine schedule resembled the activities in barracks. A *Granma Weekly Review* reporter vividly described life in the center:

> Early each morning, students gather before their respective dormitories to salute the flag and sing the Cuban national anthem. . . . Following this ceremony, the professors say a few words about the previous day's activities

and discuss news of some current national and international events. A Minas del Frío student should know what is going on in Cuba and in the world, and he must learn to analyze the facts critically.[119]

The teachers, who lived with the students as supervisors, came from the Frank País Pedagogical Institute at the University of Oriente and from the Makarenko Pedagogical Institute in Tarara, near Havana.[120] The students would spend two years at the vocational center and another two years at the Manuel Ascunce Domenech School at Topes de Collantes, also in a mountainous area.[121] The final two years of the program were spent in the Makarenko Pedagogical Institute.

The integration of teacher training with leadership preparation was a particular goal of this school system, through which the party and state expected to fuse the ideological and pedagogical development of future generations. As one government document pointed out, the purpose of creating this school was "to solve the problem of the rural school through the formation of a new type of teacher: one who is able to share the life of the country people, educate children in the communist concept, and serve, at the same time, as a revolutionary leader in the rural community in which he works."[122]

Radical Changes in Elementary and Middle Education

The primary and intermediate education systems also underwent fundamental changes. As a former student of Catholic schools, Castro had unpleasant memories of his early school years. In 1967, when he dedicated a new school building, he said: "The school we know was a type of prison, where a child was forced to be from morning until afternoon. . . . The result was that the student was traumatized and viewed school as a misfortune, a punishment, a jail."[123]

After Castro took power, his plan for elementary and middle schools was quickly put into practice. During the 1960s, there were two main projects for the type of school that Castro had envisaged. The first project was to replace day schools with boarding schools. This project was ushered in by the state-sponsored nurseries built in the early 1960s. The purpose of the public nursery system was twofold: to free women from child care so that they would be able to work, and to separate children from their parents and put them under state supervision in the early stages of the development of their consciousness. In the first half of the 1960s, numerous boarding schools were built across the country. Castro personally took a great interest and care in this project. On January 28, 1967, he delivered a speech at the inauguration of one such school at San Andrés de Caiguanabo. San Andrés was the first of the three pilot plans for organizing everyday life within a new community designed and constructed by the government. A three-hundred-student boarding school and five day nurseries were built, with another three smaller schools and five day nurseries being built. Castro said that the children's lives should be "perfectly organized" and that "under this system, the infant may attend a children's nursery from the age of one month on, that is, beginning when the mother's maternity leave is up and she returns to her job." Then he elaborated the next step for children with meticulous consideration:

> When they reach school age, their lives will be organized around the school. They will receive an education, recreation, and food. They will enter school on Monday and return home on Friday, perhaps on Saturday. We have to see which is better: to go home on Friday, or to give Saturday over to sports activities in general at the school and have the children return home at midday on Saturday.[124]

In the same speech, he suggested that the boarding school system would eventually involve the entire educational process, from elementary school up to university.

What were the educational principles of these boarding schools? Although Castro assured his audience that "these children will receive a comprehensive education," the major goal was the combination of labor with education, starting at a very early age: "Even if they are just six and in first grade, they will know how to grow lettuce, how to produce a head of lettuce. . . . They will do whatever they can, but the most important thing is that as soon as they can reason, they will begin to develop the idea of how material goods are produced."[125]

This plan was not devised to satisfy children's curiosity about nature but rather to develop in them "a noble concept of work." The context in which the combination of work and study was emphasized changed over time as a result of changes in the historical situation. Before and shortly after the revolution, the plan was part of the concept of the romanticized utopian society in which everyone would participate ideally, even from a very early age. But shortly after the new regime began to implement a socialist economic mechanism, it faced a discrepancy between the ideal and reality and became obsessed by the inefficiency, absenteeism, tardiness, theft, and all kinds of delinquency problems among workers. Castro attributed these problems to the influence of capitalism and colonialism. Under these circumstances, the early fusion of work with study was regarded as a measure to inculcate the socialist work ethic into the future generation so as to prevent these problems.

Another project in primary and secondary education, called School Goes to the Country, was an attempt to integrate the urban education system with agricultural work in particular. The project was tested in the province of Camagüey in 1966 and then spread all over the country for all junior and senior high schools from the following year onward. The project moved all students and teachers, as well as all necessary teaching materials and equipment, from cities to the countryside. As one report noted, it "sets up camp at a farm and, for six weeks, combines productive work with study, physical education, sports, and recreation."[126]

The motivating factor for this project was originally economic, as a *Granma* editorial explained: "The farm work of over 140,000 students and teachers is an extraordinary contribution." But the more important purpose was its role in educational reform, as summarized in the *Granma* report:

1. To achieve continuity in studies within the new productive work plan so that production may be maintained and regular school promotion will not suffer.
2. To move away from a strongly theoretical framework, as expressed in books, lectures, and theoretical works, in order to give meaning to the concepts: "linking the school with life," "theory together with practice," and "education" together with "productive work."
3. To apply planning for polytechnic education to the sector of agricultural production.
4. To strengthen the character of schoolchildren to conform with socialist moral standards, and to contribute in the long run to education in the family.
5. To strengthen the ties between the city and the countryside, between manual labor and intellectual labor.
6. To contribute to the improvement of teaching personnel, on both a theoretical and a practical basis, as defined by the revolutionary nature of the plan.[127]

Like the Schools of Revolutionary Instruction and the teachers' training centers, the sites for the School Goes to the Country were also selective. The locations had to have suitable "geographic and human pictures." The "geographic picture" meant it should have some types of major products for students to work on, such as sugarcane, cattle, ores to be mined, forests, fruits, and so on. The "human picture" referred to the regional revolutionary history, especially "the biography of martyrs whose names have been given to people's farms, sugar mills, departments, etc."

This nationwide movement was extensively covered by the Cuban press, radio, and television. After one year's experimentation, *Granma Weekly Review* hailed the program as "a powerful instrument for the moral and ideological formation of our young people," noting that "through work, character is built, will is strengthened, creative activities are channeled, [and] true discipline is cemented," and that the process "develops collective tendencies and eradicates individualistic ones."[128]

A further goal of this project was to make the students feel obliged to link their future careers with the practical needs of the country. In other words, they were to learn to put their societal obligations before personal preferences in their career choice. According to *Granma,* the students learned firsthand about living conditions of the workers and peasants and became "acquainted with the problems to be solved through the application of science and technology." This awareness would help students choose their disciplines when they entered the colleges and universities. The subordination of individual interests to collective demands, one of the new man's major characteristics, was therefore implanted in the minds of the young generation.

To further promote a "socialist attitude" toward work, in May 1964 the government adopted Resolution 392 on polytechnic education, with an emphasis on the integration of work with study. The resolution stated that the building of a new society required a new attitude toward life, which was "love for work and respect for the worker." This new attitude, however, could not "occur spontaneously as the result of a complex process." Polytechnic education was therefore designed to provide the "constant and natural conditions of life" in which work was an essential element. Further, the function of such an education was not only ethical but also epistemological, because "education based on experience of life is the most effective."[129] This resolution signaled an educational reorientation that was to be implemented in the years to come.[130]

Higher Education

Cuban higher education also underwent a fundamental transformation after the revolution. The guidelines for its transformation were to reduce or even eliminate the subjects and curriculum of theoretical and advanced studies, as well as arts, humanities, and social science. The existence of anything that did not have immediate application in production or could hinder ideological education in political socialization would be difficult to justify. Like Mao, who had an intense aversion to intellectuals and doubted that professors had real knowledge, so did Castro, whose anti-intellectualism was often reflected in his sardonic stories about "professors." One such story was about a professor of the "University of the School of Agronomy of Havana" who went onto the rocky peninsula to plant sixty-seven hectares of citrus.[131] Castro coined a term—"the agronomists on the sidewalk"—to refer to such professors, meaning that they lived in the cities and had grown nothing. Also like Mao, Castro envisaged a future with no tangible or institutional barriers between school and society. As Castro put it, "In the future, practically every plant, agricultural zone, hospital, and school will become a university. . . . One day we will all be intellectual workers!"[132]

But what made Castro a little different from Mao was that he not only stressed the ideological and pedagogical purposes of the educational revolution but also clearly illustrated its pragmatic aim and necessity. In this sense he combined the roles of Mao and Liu Shaoqi in China. Castro on numerous occasions told Cubans that, as an underdeveloped country, Cuba could not afford to provide all children with free and full-time education. The students—or at least a large portion of them—had to earn their right to education by integrating their study with physical labor. In a 1972 speech aimed specifically at the Basic Secondary School programs, Castro said that Cuba had about 3.5 million young people needing education. "In this situation," he explained, "we have no alternative. . . . [I]n addition to being an infrangible pedagogical principle, a social and human necessity, it is further a necessity for our country's development."[133]

The first significant move in higher education, after the revolution, was to reduce the number of universities, because Castro thought that advanced and theoretical studies were overrepresented in Cuba and were wasting educational resources. As a result, the number of universities was reduced from seven to three (University of Havana in the west, University of Las Villas in the central area, and University of Oriente in the east).[134] In those three that survived, the curriculum and enrollment were reoriented toward more practical goals. From 1959 to 1967, among the entire student population, students declined from 25.3 to 7.1 percent in social sciences and from 4.3 to 2.1 percent in humanities, while enrollment increased from 19.7 to 26 percent in education, from 13 to 23.7 percent in engineering and architecture, and from 4.7 to 10 percent in agricultural science. The most striking decline was in the discipline of law: the percentage of law students declined from 11.2 to 0.8 percent—that is, there were six thousand law students in 1959 but only two hundred in 1967.[135] The autonomy of the universities was abolished shortly after the revolution, the faculty were purged and reappointed, a political requirement for student enrollment was implemented, and historical and dialectical materialism was required and consisted of about 12 percent of the curriculum. Castro also wanted to introduce a cleavage between students and the older generation of faculty, as he said in his talk with students of Havana University in March 1959: he wanted students to teach the professors what was right.[136]

The second half of the 1960s marked the peak of educational reforms. As physical labor became an essential part of elementary and middle education, it also took a prominent role in higher education. Regular schedules were frequently interrupted by calls for massive volunteer labor in cane fields, construction sites, or other places where the human resource was lacking. The government also established the Worker-Peasant Faculty to provide workers and peasants with part-time study programs at the secondary education level to prepare them for college.

At the same time, Castro proposed a more pragmatic and technological higher education. On May 13, 1969, he talked to students of the University of Havana about future universities. Communist Cuba, he told them, would be built on mechanized industry and agriculture, and therefore a technical education would be necessary for everyone. Most courses that were currently being taught in universities would be offered in technological institutes, while universities would remain as research centers for practical postgraduate instruction. All university students would be trained either in fields or factories, learning science in the laboratories, medicine in the hospitals, agriculture on the state farms, animal husbandry at the livestock-breeding centers, and so on. The liberal arts as a curriculum would vanish from the universities and in the future could be picked up only through individual reading.

The integration of study with work was also reflected in the policies toward qualification for admission. One important change was the enrollment of a large number of workers and peasants, after several years of preparation in the Worker-Peasant Faculty. This policy not only changed the composition of the student body but also had a significant impact on the curriculum. Herbert Matthews, an American sympathizer of the Cuban Revolution, revisited Cuba in 1972 and closely observed such changes. According to him, "A worker is brought to the university not to study books while he leaves his work, but to study as he continues working, contributing his practical knowledge to the university—he teaches as he learns, and in the factory he teaches the university student who comes to work there."[137] This description could just as well have been used to identify the "worker-peasant-soldier" students in the state-run universities and the worker-students in the factory-run colleges of China. Like their Chinese counterparts, prospective students in Cuba needed to have a "report" from a mass organization, especially the Committee for the Defense of the Revolution, to prove their revolutionary attitude for their admission.[138]

Integration of work with study also took place at the institutional level. The universities set up work centers in factories and mines, directly linking research and teaching with practical productive needs. For example, all three major universities set up such work centers in the Moa Bay and Nicaro nickel plants. There were also a number of educational hospitals where teaching and study were combined with clinical practice.[139] According to José M. Millar, the rector of Havana University in the early 1970s, the university had been a place apart from the general society before 1959, but after the revolution it became "an integral part of the revolutionary economy and social system." He announced that in the future the university would be "a vast complex of schools, factories, farms, mines, hospitals, et cetera, where students are workers and workers are students." The essence of this educational revolution was "the total socialization of education through integration of work and study."[140]

Castro once specified the kind of person that Cuban higher education was to bring up: "an engineer, an agronomist, a soil technician, a livestock specialist."[141] Or, as Fagen noted, such a person would be a "technologically trained and sensitive man."[142] As far as the entire higher education system was concerned, Castro also predicted an entire integration of school with productive units, as discussed earlier. These changes and proposals coincided with Mao's anti-intellectual idea that only technological and mechanical colleges were necessary, while the social sciences and humanities had to be pared down and learned through participation in class struggle and productive work.

From the 1960s to the early 1970s the Cuban educational system experienced revolutionary changes that were as sweeping and radical as those in China. Castro was fully aware of the significance of this revolution, as he once proudly said, "People talked about it and gave it attention, but Cuba was the first to put it into practice."[143] As mentioned earlier, Castro had dreamed of an educational revolution even before he came to power, but he acknowledged that his plan was not original. This acknowledgment indicated that he had been exposed to some thoughts about educational reforms or revolutions and the consistency between those ideologies and his own innovation. If the essence of educational revolution in China was "open-door schooling," then its Cuban equivalent was Castro's announcement that in the future every productive unit would become a university and José M. Millar's vision of a "total socialization of education" would be realized.[144] The product of this new educational system in both cases was even more similar to the Chinese: a practical-minded, technically oriented, and intellectually unsophisticated communist new man.

MODELS FOR THE NEW MAN: INDIVIDUAL AND COLLECTIVE

In Cuba, just as in China, the 1960s witnessed a surge of revolutionary models of the new man, created for the purpose of mass emulation. The Cuban leaders' conception of human nature (malleable and subject to the social environment) and their revolutionary voluntarism (the vanguard could inspire ordinary people) laid the theoretical ground for modeling and emulating, while ideological, practical, and economic needs reinforced the demand for such models.

Individual Models

The individual models of the Cuban new man were guerrilla war heroes and heroines, volunteers, work heroes, and other exemplary figures who championed revolutionary consciousness. To honor them, especially in the case of martyrs, many communities, schools, factories, and farms took their names. The anniversaries of their deaths were often commemorated with mass rallies and volunteer work drives.

The most venerable guerrilla war hero was Frank País, one of the underground commanders of the July 26 Movement in Santiago de Cuba, who had been killed by Batista's forces. *Granma Weekly Review* once called him the "symbol of Cuban youth." The Pedagogical Institute at the University of Oriente, whose graduates undertook the training of elementary schoolteachers, was named after him. The revolutionary martyr in the shrine next to País was Camilo Cienfuegos, a legendary guerrilla commander who died in an aircraft crash shortly after the 1959 victory. Guevara once wrote that "there was never a man . . . comparable to Camilo," who had been "a complete revolutionary, a man of the people, an artist of the revolution, sprung from the heart of the Cuban nation."[145]

In peacetime, the models were mainly workers who either exceeded the labor quota or devoted themselves to voluntary labor. For example, in Guevara's Ministry of Industry, there was a labor hero named Arnet, who worked 1,607 hours in six months. The figure means that he had constantly worked about nine hours a day for six months without a day off and without extra pay.

Castro often took the opportunity to exalt labor heroes and to associate their achievements and spirit with a more general topic: the creation of new

Cubans. One such occasion was his visit to the Cuban Steel Plant on February 23, 1967. In his address to the workers, he first emphasized that the job of all revolutionary organizations was to develop revolutionary consciousness; he then selected and glorified more than twenty workers who had done "outstanding work in production." Among them some had "worked a minimum of 16 hours daily, and on four occasions labored 24 consecutive hours," and they had accumulated 100 to 200 hours of voluntary work but did not collect overtime pay. After naming and introducing them one by one before the crowd, Castro said, "The example of those who worked overtime without receiving extra remuneration is not to [suggest] that all workers can do so. It is to demonstrate how a new conscience is created."[146]

The most venerated model for individuals, however, was Che Guevara himself, the chief advocate and personification of the new man. In the official Cuban account, Che's name is surrounded by an aura of nearly saintlike acts of dedication. For instance, he was appointed to be the manager of the Cuban National Bank and the minister of industry at the same time, but he rejected the salary for the former ($1,000 per month) and accepted only the latter salary ($200 per month). Every weekend, whenever he was free from his leadership duty, he performed volunteer work and urged his subordinates to make the same commitment. He never abused his privileges, such as allowing his family to use his government car, even when his children had a medical emergency. His resignation of his leadership position to sacrifice himself in the guerrilla war for the sake of the revolution characterized his personification of the new man.

As Matthews once pointed out, "Cuban socialism was the projection of Che's own fanatical, dedicated, self-sacrificing personality. He never seemed to realize that his standards were superhuman."[147] Indeed, some stories suggested an arbitrary nature in his conduct when urging his subordinates to adopt the new man's moral standard. Cadres and clerks in his ministry often felt compelled to participate in volunteer work at the cost of their family time and personal lives, if they wanted to remain in Guevara's good graces. In the prevailing atmosphere, it would seem odd for someone not to show up for volunteer work while most of his or her colleagues and co-workers were in Guevara's sight. The following story illustrates Guevara's attitude toward others in this regard. One day before Guevara went to a meeting, one of his friends saw that he was not wearing a watch that was needed in such meetings, so the friend lent his own watch to Guevara. It was a fine watch with a gold wristband. Later Guevara went up to this friend and handed him a Cuban National Bank receipt, acknowledging that the gold wristband had been donated to Cuba's gold reserve.[148]

One factor that may well have contributed to Guevara's departure was his disillusion with the feasibility of bringing up a new man during peacetime. As more and more evidence showed Cuban workers' reluctance to sacrifice and work hard in their daily assignments, Guevara became increasingly critical of their lack of revolutionary awareness, but he realized that "in moments of extreme danger, it is easy to activate moral incentives." After Guevara's death, the regime took him as a perfect model for the new man. Castro repeated on many occasions that Che symbolized the new man, and asked Cuban youth to "become Che," so much so that even in preschool care centers visitors would find a sign on the wall: "Shaping Men in Che's Image."[149]

Collective Models

As in China, the collective models chosen to exemplify the new ethics and new life of the new man in Cuba were engaged together in a productive task and often lived in the same community. The most outstanding collective model was the Isle of Youth (originally named the Isle of Pines), sixty miles from the main island and about the size of Delaware. The island had been under direct American control from 1899 to 1925, but when the United States obtained Guantánamo, it relinquished control of the island. After it was returned to Cuba, the island was used for incarceration, of political prisoners in particular. Castro himself had been imprisoned there after the failure of the Moncada attack. During his time there, he took advantage of the facilities and regulations of the prison system to organize the Abel Santamaría Academy in honor of a comrade who was captured and killed by the government army after the Moncada attack. The academy was perhaps Castro's first attempt to politically educate his followers based on his understanding of and preference for revolutionary ideologies. Castro developed a curriculum that included Marxist texts and Soviet literary works such as *That Is How Steel Was Tempered.* This historical experience earned the island a remarkable value in educating young generations in the postrevolutionary years.

In 1966 a hurricane devastated the island, and thousands of youth from the Young Communist League were shipped there to help clean up the debris. An idea emerged from this act: to build a new youth community on this historical island and make it a symbol of the new Cuba. Castro approved the project, and the island was handed over to the Young Communist League. Within a few years, more than fifty thousand young people had settled on the isle (originally it had only eight thousand residents), where they started a variety of agricultural and industrial projects. One of the main goals was to replace Israel as the world's leading exporter of citrus by the mid-1970s, and another was to develop a cattle industry to provide milk and meat, which were traditionally imported from Canada and the United States. Infrastructure services and facilities such as housing, schools, hospitals, and recreation centers were all built by the youth for the common good of the community.

A sign in the island's capital town indicated the aspiration of the construction and experiment on the island: "Why shouldn't this island be the first site of communism in Cuba?"[150] On this island, the communist principle "From everyone according to his ability, to everyone according to his needs" was implemented. The rank of salary had nothing to do with a worker's skill, education, working hours, or quotas but was based on the number of members in the worker's family. Most consumer goods and services, including housing, were free. Money became more useless there than anywhere else in Cuba, except on the occasions when people went to the recreational center for fun. Revolutionary enthusiasm on the island was high. As one official there noted, "Each man makes his daily contribution without watching the clock."[151]

The official propaganda portrayed the island as a new way of life: collective work and collective life, with all people making contributions to their fullest potential, and the state taking care of everyone. Essentially, what was established on the Isle of Youth was a completely new social environment, deliberately designed so that the new man could grow, free from any vestige of the old Cuba. It materialized the ideas of environmental determinism from the Enlightenment and became a communist enclave in socialist Cuba. Every year people from all over the country formed brigades going to the island to participate in the projects there and also to be educated. Camps were established so that children from the main island could live there for several months and be immersed in this new environment. The island was also used as a showcase of Cuban communism for the benefit of foreign visitors. Castro himself frequently brought his foreign guests there, sometimes celebrating his birthday in this massive laboratory for the new human species he had designed and cultivated. He would repeatedly tell his guests that Havana and other Cuban cities they were familiar with did not represent the new Cuba, whereas those new towns and this island in particular really did.

Pinares de Mayarí, a mining area developed in the middle of the 1960s, was another collective model. There were about seven thousand volunteers, of which young women made up the majority, and they worked and lived together with free food, clothing, and housing. Their salary was determined by their family size. In general, it was another Isle of Pines on a smaller scale, and it too was used as an educational center for Cubans and a showcase for foreign visitors.

In addition to model communities and settlements such as the Isle of Youth and Pinares de Mayarí, migratory "brigade" units were sent to places where difficult or urgent tasks emerged. The military origin of their name indicates the nature and the organization of these labor-army units. The Youth of Steel Brigade was one of them. In 1966, seven hundred university students and three hundred professors responded to Castro's call to enhance the labor force by forming such a brigade. They undertook tasks such as building coffee plantations in rocky, weed-covered, wild fields. According to a *Granma* report, the brigade was a "busy human beehive, singing and laughing while working with communist spirit." In the breaks, as they lay on the ground "under a warm sun, the students review[ed] their lessons." Therefore, it was also regarded as part of the reform of higher education, combining work with study. After the coffee plantation project was completed, they were shifted to a highway construction site. The Youth of Steel Brigade was a typical vanguard work unit, and it was imitated by other labor groups all over the country.

The Discrepancy between the Ideal of the New Man and the Reality of Workers' Attitudes

Cuban social engineering in creating the new man, notwithstanding its magnitude, persistence, and especially the official bravado, was far from successful. One problem the leaders encountered was Cuban workers' attitude toward their work. The party's forceful efforts, such as political education, model emulation, and volunteer work, failed to transform the majority of Cubans into enthusiastic worker bees represented by vanguard or model workers. To the contrary, the fanfare and bombardment from newspapers, magazines, and TV with stories about the devotion and even the work mania of model Cubans could not conceal the grim reality. In time, deficiencies in organization and work ethic problems in Cuban workers were openly discussed in the Cuban press as well as in the leaders' speeches. Starting from the early 1960s, accusatory epithets such as "individualists," "parasites," "antisocial elements," and "loafers" were frequently used by the government to condemn workers who had an improper attitude toward labor.

From the perspective of a liberal-democratic system and an individual-centered society, the Cuban workers could hardly be blamed for their lack of motivation to work, not to mention the negative elements of Cuban cultural tradition that had plagued Martí more than a half century earlier. In addition to numerous volunteer hours and even days, the Cuban workers had to sacrifice a large portion of their wages to the revolution. For example, the Four Percent Voluntary Contribution for Industrialization was enacted into law in March 1960. In Cuba and most other socialist countries, of course, the adjective "voluntary," in reality, offered no justification for anyone to stay away from the drives. In addition, 1 percent of their salary was deducted for union fees and 2 or 3 percent for "volunteer" contributions to aid disaster victims, finance national campaigns, build monuments, and so forth.[152] Many people groaned. One activist critically described the reaction as "What? Take four percent out of my wages as long as I live? How am I going to manage?"[153] In reality, many such people chose not to work as much as they could or found excuses not to contribute by saying that they were studying and therefore not working full-time. Other factors also diverted Cuban workers' money and time. For example, gambling had been popular before the revolution. After 1959 the government allowed some forms of it to exist and benefited from it until the Revolutionary Offensive, which abolished all forms of gambling. It was one of the odd contradictions in the Cuban Revolution, indicating the extent to which the most rhetorical communist revolutionaries had to compromise with reality when facing serious socioeconomic limits.

When Guevara advocated socialist emulation and emphasized that "work should be a moral necessity," he also acknowledged that many workers "see having to work every day as an oppressive necessity, a necessity one tries to avoid."[154] The reason was, according to him, that when the old society was torn down, the workers had not developed a new attitude of obligation to work. They thought that the factory was "still under the old boss, . . . still the way it was in the past," and according to Guevara, such thinking was "precisely the reflection of the old society in the consciousness of men who are building a new society."[155] In a letter he acknowledged that "man has still not transferred all the coercion surrounding him into conditioned reflexes."[156] On another occasion he remarked, "Man still needs to undergo a complete spiritual rebirth in his attitude toward his work, freed from the direct pressure of his social environment though linked to it by his new habits. That will be communism."[157]

Castro was also vexed by the workers' attitude toward their jobs. When speaking at the Twelfth Workers Congress of the Cuban Federation of Labor, he complained, "A completely socialist consciousness has not yet been formed. Many workers did not see work as a means of creating social wealth, of creating benefits for all. They did not see that work was their fundamental duty." One year later he noted that "we see in many towns the loafers who produce nothing."[158] Like Guevara, he also attributed this defect to the remnants of the old social environment, for example, the attitude of the elite during Spanish colonialism who disdained physical labor; slavery, under which the laborers had hated their work; and, most importantly, the influences of foreign capitalism.

This concern about the workers' attitudes toward their daily assignments was reflected in the communications of many rank-and-file officials. In a letter, one confused official wrote: "I don't understand these people. . . . At the time of the Bay of Pigs invasion, these peasants took up their guns and enthusiastically hurried to their posts, ready to lay down their lives. . . . A few months later, I saw them dozing in the fields, shirking work. Why, I ask myself, are they ready to die for the Revolution, but not work for it?"[159] K. S. Karol also witnessed Cuban workers dozing under trees during working hours and relaxing beside broken machines instead of repairing them.

The Cuban leaders found that moral persuasion and ideological indoctrination were not sufficient to maintain discipline and improve economic efficiency. They had to take measures beyond educational methods. For example, in 1962 the government introduced an identification card for laborers who were working in the state sector. It was a fourteen-page booklet containing records of place of employment, type of work performed, attendance, punctuality, volunteer labor, work speed, and political attitude. This card was required when workers wanted to apply for or change jobs. In 1964 the government enacted the Law of Labor Justice. According to Carlos Rafael Rodríguez, the president of the National Institute for Agrarian Reform, sanctions under this law would be applied "[in order] to correct anti-social attitudes, negligence, laziness, and to those who . . . manage to work less than the eight hours established for all kinds of work."[160] Other measures included compulsory service in rural areas for some professions, especially medical doctors. For example, a regulation requiring medical graduates to work in the countryside for three years was implemented as early as 1960, and a similar three-year requirement for army service was announced three years later. In addition, rehabilitation centers that combined political education with forced labor were built for workers who failed to comply with the labor law, failed to meet the work quota, or were frequently absent.

THE REVOLUTIONARY OFFENSIVE: AN ALL-OUT EFFORT TO CREATE THE NEW MAN

The so-called Revolutionary Offensive was the climax of Cuba's social engineering to create the new man. It lasted for more than two years, from early 1968 to June 1970, and was a nationally organized and coordinated campaign affecting every aspect of society. The offensive set a goal of producing ten million tons of sugar for the next year (1968–1969), which was three to four million tons more than the average production figure of the 1960s. But this economic goal was set for a higher social and ideological purpose: to galvanize the people with an intensified revolutionary militancy in a mock war situation and thereby to mobilize the whole country to its fullest potential. It came with the hope of clearing out—once and for all—the remnants of the old social environment that were still corrupting the Cuban people and impeding the growth of the new man.

The dynamics of this nationwide campaign were multiple. The shortage of almost all consumer goods worsened in the second half of the 1960s, and the Cuban economy grew even more reliant on Soviet aid. Castro planned to exchange the additional sugar produced by the campaign for consumer goods and industrial materials in the international market and consequently to create more opportunities for his ideological and political independence from Moscow. Politically, Castro, like Mao, wanted to find a new way—different from the Soviet one—toward communism. To this end, both of them adopted a pattern of rapid social transformation by breaking with bureaucratic convention and relying on mass mobilization. In China, Mao began to emphasize the "mass line" (direct reliance upon the masses) in the late 1950s and attacked bureaucracy in the early 1960s, culminating in the Cultural Revolution, which virtually destroyed the existing bureaucratic apparatus. Cuba's bureaucracy was not as well established as China's, and Castro had been able to directly address the people in mass rallies and to launch various campaigns by using his charisma. But he still felt confined by bureaucracy and wanted to find a more direct and effective approach to mobilizing the people. Ideologically, the Cuban leader found that, ten years after the revolution, the people's consciousness was still far from satisfactory, as shown in workers' attitudes toward their jobs. In order to intensify ideological indoctrination and implement harsher discipline, the regime needed to create an atmosphere of state emergency and even put the country into warlike conditions.

The first step of this campaign was to identify and wipe out social elements and eliminate social "worms," as Castro put it, which caused ideological contamination, corrupting many workers and resulting in delinquency. On March 13, 1968, he gave a long speech at the University of Havana, declaring the beginning of the campaign.

Based on a survey conducted by the Municipal Administration of Metropolitan Havana, Castro concluded that the main source of political and ideological contamination sprung from the proprietors of various stands on the streets. He presented detailed data from the survey, asserting that the proprietors were guilty of a number of charges: lack of legal authorization, bad sanitary conditions, and being neither integrated into revolutionary organizations nor participating in volunteer work, even though most of them were in good physical condition. The more serious charges were exploitation of their employees and possession of illegal supplies (bought on the black market or in the countryside at premium prices or simply stolen from state-owned stores).[161]

But the most immoral influence of the street businesses was that they lured and distracted many workers from their daily paid or volunteer work. In fact, most of these proprietors were former workers who had abandoned their jobs or people who simultaneously worked for both state and private businesses but took more care of the latter. This delinquency was not only an important reason for economic inefficiency but also the most visible source of ideological corruption. According to the survey, most of the proprietors possessed a counterrevolutionary attitude or antisocial manner, and the highest percentage of requests for permission to leave the country—largely to go to the United States—also came from these people.

"Gentlemen," Castro announced, "we did not make a revolution here to establish the right to trade!"[162] Following his speech, a campaign against the remaining small private businesses began. The Committee for the Defense of the Revolution, the Cuban mass organization empowered to exercise authority, especially at the neighborhood level, launched nationwide actions to confiscate the stands and shut down the bars, including those owned by the state, which were thought to have been the sites of illegal and alluring gatherings. The proprietors were rounded up and sent to workplaces such as cane fields and construction sites. Within a week, the privately owned small businesses that had survived the nationalization in the early 1960s disappeared. In addition, many artisans and self-employed workers were also gradually incorporated into the state sector. Gambling was abolished as well.

Eliminating the proprietors was the first step in a nationwide cleanup of the remnants of the old society, for the well-being of the new man. As Castro later said, "We are little by little sanitizing our environment, cleaning it up, creating a country that is really a country of workers."[163]

In the atmosphere of the Revolutionary Offensive, the old debate on incentives was regenerated; three years after the debate had been abruptly put to an end, Castro found that there was no way he could bypass this crucial issue. This time he raised it in a solemn, philosophical manner: Was human nature malleable? Was the ideal of the new man realistic? Castro, while condemning all kinds of social "worms," announced his "faith" in humankind again, as he declared:

> The concept of socialism and communism, the concept of a higher society, implies a man devoid of those feelings [i.e., nonsocialist thoughts], a man

who has overcome such [self-centered] instincts at any cost, placing above everything his sense of solidarity and brotherhood among men. And this brings to mind the famous topic of incentives. For a long time they were theoretically discussed, and the question appeared to be one of method, but, in our opinion, it is a much more profound question.[164]

In the same speech, Castro announced that even though all efforts to "improve" people failed in the end, "we will never renounce our faith in mankind." Echoing him, an editorial in *Granma* once again asserted the faith that people could be made better and could work harder: "Our revolutionary ideas are based on the deep conviction—confirmed in practice—that men are capable of working more and better when they are inspired by social and historical objectives."[165] Another Cuban magazine, *Bohemia,* quoted Castro as saying: "If it is admitted that man is incapable of learning, of developing *conciencia,* then those brainy economists will be proven right: the revolution will fail."[166] Although Castro still stuck to his "faith" in human malleability and the power of revolutionary ideology in reshaping people, his impatience and frustration, caused by the slow growth of the Cuban new man and the sometimes stubborn resistance of Cuban workers, reached the point that he even extended the category of "exploiters" to include some workers. As he put it,

> Capitalism was a pyramid of exploitation, a pyramid where those on top exploited those below them, and so on. . . . And often it spreads even among the workers, for there were workers who had salaries five times as great as the ones who cut sugarcane. . . . Capitalism, on principle, established this ladder of exploitation, and it is clear that capitalism has to be pulled out by the roots.[167]

With this analysis—putting some workers into the category of exploiters and capitalists—Castro believed that he had found a deeper cause hindering his moral crusade to create the new man among Cuban workers.

The launching of the Revolutionary Offensive involved the regimentation of the entire country. Synthetic war conditions were created, with civilian life organized on military rules and production tasks treated as combat missions. Despite a decade of running the country in peacetime, Castro and most other leaders were still uncomfortable with a routine and regulated statecraft process and found that military methods were the most effective way to carry out the party's political and economic plans. A *Granma* editorial in March 1967 blamed bureaucracy for all the undesirable qualities of society, such as corruption and degeneration of the revolutionary spirit, lack of political initiative, labor delinquency, and economic inefficiency. The editorial made comparisons between the Algerian and Vietnamese revolutionary armies and the Guatemalan government army: the former did not have bureaucratic organizations, but they were much more efficient than the latter even though it had been well equipped and trained by Americans. The Cuban rebel army was another telling example. The editorial thus concluded: "It is possible to overcome bureaucratic ways of organization. There are organizational forms that are far more efficient than bureaucratic ones. . . . In socialism, the incorporation of workers via the militias—the revolutionary origins of the armed forces—and the system of an army of technically trained cadres . . . makes possible an army free of the evil of bureaucracy."[168]

An even more important function of the simulated war and regimentation, however, was that they created a sense of emergency and stimulated individuals to ignore or suppress their personal needs and engage in collective efforts. In fact, Guevara had envisioned the necessity of militarization of the country in peacetime and regarded it as an effective way to create the new man. As he put it: "In moments of extreme danger, it is easy to activate moral incentives; to maintain their effectiveness, it is necessary to develop a consciousness in which values acquire new categories. Society as a whole must become a huge school."[169] As mentioned earlier, one may even deduce that Guevara's departure from Cuba and his return to guerrilla warfare resulted in part from his disillusionment with the prospect of creating a new man in peacetime.

In terms of labor organization and work efficiency, regimentation and militarization meant organizing the labor force into military units, dispatching them with orders, and imposing harsh discipline similar to that in the military. As *Granma* put it, "It is necessary to wage a day-by-day campaign against absenteeism, carelessness, low-quality work; and all other factors that affect productivity adversely."[170] A state of emergency had proven to be very effective in stimulating morale and reducing bureaucratic red tape during the days of the invasion of the Bay of Pigs. Once again, Guevara was the one who advocated applying such extraordinary measures to everyday life. As Robert M. Bernard pointed out:

> Guevara was deeply impressed by the moral and emotional forces thus released. He noted that during the four-day Bay of Pigs state of emergency, industrial output did not decline; bureaucratism with what Guevara called its "jungle of paper and red tape" was reduced; production problems and decisions were solved and made by each individual with remarkable alacrity and initiative, and absenteeism disappeared.[171]

Based on such experience, Guevara urged that the great example of mobilization, caused by the military emergency, be made permanent. In this sense the militarization implemented in the Revolutionary Offensive could be viewed as a nationwide test of what he advocated.

Castro's home province, Oriente, can be used as an example of the militarization of this campaign. Before the sugarcane season started, military officers were sent to take charge of work units, and all civilian cadres were required to attend a short training course supervised by these officials. A military roster to organize manpower and check attendance was established, and "by bringing the roster up to date, it was possible to determine the exact number of persons who could be mobilized and organized into each battalion, in detail."[172] All labor forces were organized into two strategic groups: front line and rear echelon. The front line was on the scene of work sites, primarily in sugarcane fields, and it was commanded directly by the front line's command headquarters, led by the chief officer (usually the first secretary of the local party committee) and his general staff. Rear echelon command headquarters, located in the cities, were led by the second secretary of the local party committee.

Before the sugar harvest season officially started, Oriente Province operated an exercise to test this military system. According to *Granma*, "organizations worked systematically and dynamically, using military methods to create the conditions for a mobilization of 90,000 people, overcoming countless difficulties and securing the best use of the resources at hand."[173] To create an authentic wartime atmosphere and stimulate workers' "battle spirit," daily work began with the sound of combat alarm, and some factories were even intentionally blacked out at night for a moment when an air raid siren sounded.

Women were organized into brigades to take work positions left by men who went to "the front." The brigades of women also maintained surveillance on all kinds of "antisocial elements." Children were mobilized by the Pioneers Union and supervised by the Communist Youth League. They were also organized and sent to various "battlefields" to deliver messages, greetings, and letters. This activity was regarded as a special "form of political and ideological education for them."[174]

When the harvest season came, the entire country was plunged into a simulated war situation:

A state of alert has been announced. The troops are ready. Battalion commanders give last-minute instructions. The civil defense communications system . . . is set to transmit all front-line reports to the command post. . . . Communications in the mountain zones will be carried out by messengers on muleback or by runners. . . .

In the cities, the drivers check their trucks and take a final look at their instructions: no passing on the highway, keep your distance, no parking on hills. . . .

The political instruction department will supply the troops with materials such as field newspapers and bulletins. . . . Political instructors and activists in battalions, companies, and platoons will participate in these activities. Other activities are planned for places whose conditions do not permit printing and broadcasting.

The men and women who worked out this project and the troops participating in it will be given a great send-off at every departure point. . . . Families and friends, bands, and entertainers will give a rousing farewell to those who march to the front.[175]

Such nationwide mobilization and militarization of production and everyday life lasted for almost two years, until the summer 1970, when Castro acknowledged the failure of the goal for the ten million tons of sugar.

In addition to the would-be new men and new women in real action, the Revolutionary Offensive also produced a number of fictional models in literary works. Miguel Woodward's celebrated novel *Sacchario* (1970) was one example. The novel relates how young Cubans become new men as they participate in the campaign for ten million tons of sugar. The term "Sacchario," as Ana Serra has suggested,

> reveals how the novel wants to give shape to the identity figure of the worker ("saccarius") whose life is intimately connected with the sugarcane, and to Cuban tradition in its stories which, like syrup ("saccharum"), is distilled from the plant. Because of his connection to the Cuban sugar tradition, Dario [the protagonist] appears to be an amalgam of collective stories and can be likened to the syrup extracted from Cuban sugarcane.[176]

Dario represents the Cubans who came of age when the revolution took place, and the novel is an account of his emergence as a revolutionary Everyman and his "development from a potential revolutionary to a full-fledged one." As the hero devotes himself to the campaign, he acquires a new identity, which "becomes a metaphor for the highest point in the history of Cuban nationhood that, according to the text, is embodied in the collective effort of the Sugar Campaign." Throughout the novel, the "contrast between 'the old Dario' and 'new Dario' is constant," revealing how the campaign transforms his ideology and gives him a new identity.[177]

In summary, the Revolutionary Offensive, like China's Cultural Revolution, was apparently an all-out push to intensify efforts made in previous years for the transformation of the society and its people. To change completely the parts of the social environment that were thought to impede the growth of the new man was a major purpose in both campaigns. As Castro put it when the Revolutionary Offensive started: "We will bring up human beings devoid of selfishness, devoid of defects of the past, human beings with a collective sense of effort, a collective sense of strength."[178]

This proclamation reverberated in "The Declaration of Cuban Students," published on July 26, 1968:

> The Formation of the New Man . . . cannot be reduced to a slogan. Che viewed it as the result of an integral, multi-faceted formation in constant critical relationship with the society which this man will both forge and be forged by. Such men will be as varied and complex as the society of the future, but absolutely equal in their duties and in their prerogatives as human and social beings.
>
> The building of that society, of the conditions which generate these men, is our historical task.[179]

POSTSCRIPT

As in China, the idea of a new man came long before communist revolution in Cuba and was embedded in the nationalist discourse—a premise for national redemption, as José Martí believed. The peculiarity of the Cuban Revolution in 1959 facilitated the ideological and political rationale for putting this idea into practice as a prime goal of the regime, as Castro aspired to achieve a quick triumph of communism on the island. The idea of the new man—or "Let them all become Che," as the slogan of the time proclaimed—was created to precipitate communism and to offset the economic and technological shortcomings of the nation with revolutionary consciousness and sacrifice. In comparison with China's experience, Cuban efforts to create such a new man progressed more rapidly and reached the summit in the late 1960s, as Castro launched his Revolutionary Offensive, in purpose and chronology a parallel to Mao's Cultural Revolution.

But just as Mao's drive for the new man lost its momentum in the early 1970s, a historically synchronized setback occurred to Castro's similar aspiration. In July 1970—in front of a mass rally—Castro acknowledged the failure of the effort to achieve the ten million tons of sugar, the key project in his Revolutionary Offensive. The failure of the production goal was also an indication of the failure of the whole "offensive," because the apparently unrealistic goal was believed to be achievable by the dedication of the new men, who themselves would be tempered in the crucible of the campaign. The year 1970 thus marked a watershed in the history of the Cuban Revolution, indicating Castro's recognition of the infeasibility of building communism on the island in any immediate future. From that point onward a "revolutionary institutionalization" gradually developed, to adopt the Soviet style of organization and management and to abandon or downplay many policies and approaches based on voluntarism and the belief in revolutionary consciousness. Accordingly, the "new man" rhetoric was significantly toned down and has often been manifested defensively—to fend off foreign and imperialist ideological influence rather than to create a new human species. Since the 1990s, as Soviet communism declined and China drifted further away from Maoist communism, Castro's Cuba stands almost lonely as a leftover of 1960s revolutionary fanaticism. As in the case of China, the course of the image of the Cuban new man as it faded away into history requires another major study.

Four

The Global Impact of the
Communist New Man

This survey of the Soviet Union, China, and Cuba has outlined the attempts to create a new man in the world communist revolution and has profiled the major characteristics—real and fictional—of such a new man. However, the historical horizon on which this new man emerged in the twentieth century can be further broadened by examining his influence in other countries, many of which had similar revolutions while many others did not. This chapter looks at the global impact of the communist new man from three perspectives. The first is the similar efforts in remaking people in the Soviet Union, China, and Cuba. The second is the admiration of the communist new man by some Westerners who became alienated from their own societies and sought alternative social systems. The third is the favorable perceptions of the communist new man by some Third World leaders, who were seeking ideas and methods for developing their own countries and for nation building despite many obstacles and were inspired by the alleged selflessness and sacrifice of people in communist countries.

VARIETIES OF THE REVOLUTIONARY
NEW MAN IN OTHER COUNTRIES

The description of the new man in Russia, China, and Cuba can be enriched by studying political efforts in many other similar communist regimes or revolutions that were heavily influenced by these three prototypes but nevertheless had their own peculiar experiences and distinctiveness. Such a study is helpful in understanding the three major cases in a broader context. In some instances, especially in countries with a strong premodern social setting, the term "new man" can be reduced in its meaning to a much less philosophically and intellectually sophisticated level and is attached to implications that are alien even to its predecessors in the Soviet Union, China, and Cuba.

The most immediate sphere of influence of the "Soviet man" was, of course, in Eastern Europe after the Second World War, when a number of countries were kept behind the "iron curtain" and became laboratories for the new man experiment. John Kosa, a Hungarian native who experienced the initial years of Soviet rule but escaped to the West in 1949, devoted himself to research on the measures and policies designed for turning young Hungarians into communist new men. It is noteworthy that Kosa had lived under the new regime for only three to four years, but what he experienced in this new man project gave him sufficient courage to risk an escape. Kosa recalled the beginning of the new man experience:

> Our first impression was that the party, with the repetitiousness of a stubborn child, claimed to know everything better than anybody else, claimed always to be right and asserted that the citizen can be right only to the extent of his agreement with the party. Soon we had to realize that this was more than a pose of self-aggrandizement; the party as a political power wanted to accomplish much more than a poseur or a braggart wants. It wanted to change us, the sundry citizens of the country, to transform us into images to its liking; it wanted to rebuild our inner selves in the way that an old piece of furniture is rebuilt.[1]

Kosa assessed that, by the end of the Second World War, the plan for the new man had succeeded in the production of the "first generation," or the "Soviet man," and now it was time "to apply the same formula to the citizens of the freshly conquered countries, to form a second generation of Soviet man out of Albanians, Bulgarians, Czechoslovakians, Germans, Hungarians, Poles and Rumanians." The national, ethnic, and cultural diversities involved in this "tremendous task" were so great that it seemed that "the idea of the one and common Soviet mold [was] the unrealistic product of a doctrinaire mind." But, as Kosa put it, "The Communist planners . . . were little concerned about academic arguments and just as little concerned about the significance of national diversity. They believed that the Hungarian or Bulgarian, as well as the Kazakh or Georgian, would with his peculiarities represent one variety of the same general species, the Soviet man."[2]

In the 1960s and 1970s, as the Soviet approach toward communism involved increasingly more material incentives and relied upon the infrastructure of an industrialized society, and as more revolutionary movements developed in societies with a premodern character, the Chinese approach began to attract more followers in the world's communist and radical social movements. One example is the Naxalites, who were Indian communists led by Charu Mazumdar. Under a strong Maoist influence, the Naxalites launched their armed struggle in West Bengal in the late 1960s. One of their most important revolutionary strategies of class struggle, adopted from the Maoist peasant revolution, was to "annihilate" the rural elite physically. To accomplish this, they encouraged peasants to kill the doomed ones by using primitive tools or even bare hands. The logic, explained by Sanjay Seth, was that, in a society like India where the "oppressed" people's sense of inferiority and subordination was so entrenched because of the caste system, rebellion against the oppressor demanded tremendous courage and psychological ascendance. The transformation from a submissive peasant to a conscious revolutionary thus demanded a dramatic and violent act of participation that would transform and empower. "If annihilation was a dramatic way of challenging the power and prestige of feudal elites," Seth writes, "conversely it was also important to the peasant creating a new sense of self" because "[i]n killing his oppressor he at one stroke effaced his subordination *and* created, or created the space for, a new identity for himself." In other words, Seth concludes, "killing the landlord could help the peasant define himself anew; and the greater the violence and display with which he did it, the greater the distance he put between himself and his previous identity as a subordinate." Seth's interpretation is supported by Mazumdar's own words. As the latter put it, "Only by waging class struggle—the battle of annihilation—[will] the new man ... be created," and this new man "will defy death and will be free from all thoughts of self-interest."[3]

The Khmer Rouge, the Cambodian communists, is a more illustrative example. The development of the Cambodian communist movement was from the very beginning overshadowed by Chinese communism, especially by the Cultural Revolution's influence. Pol Pot visited China several times during the CR, and his longest visit, in 1965 on the eve of the CR, lasted for three months. Zhang Chunqiao, Chen Boda, and Yao Wenyuan, the most aggressive Maoist CR ideologues, explained to him the essence of Maoist revolutionary ideology, especially the necessity of the CR. Seeking advice for Cambodian socialism, Pol Pot met with Mao in person in June 1975, shortly after the Khmer Rouge took over the country. Mao told him, in his idiosyncratic way, in his late years, of exaggerating the danger of "revisionism" that China was "unqualified" to guide or criticize the Khmer Rouge, because "we are now a capitalist country without capitalists, as Lenin once said." Mao told him that this was so because China had preserved many institutions that protected social inequality.[4] Pol Pot may well have taken this to mean that Mao was acknowledging that China had not solved the problem of preventing revisionism or capitalist restoration and that the CR was encountering significant resistance. Some new materials reveal that it was Zhang Chunqiao, the theoretical mastermind of the Gang of Four (the most radical Maoist ideologues), who drafted the constitution for Cambodia's new regime during Pol Pot's 1975 visit. The constitution was promulgated in 1977, at the peak of the Khmer Rouge's social experiment.[5] Pol Pot once again visited China in 1977. During that visit, although Mao had died and the Gang of Four had been purged, Pol Pot made a high-profile pilgrimage to Dazhai, the collective model of the Chinese new man, accompanied by Chen Yonggui, the Maoist model for peasants. Pol Pot's visit apparently signified his support of the Maoist CR line, which was being abandoned by the post-Mao CCP leadership.

In those circumstances, Dazhai became the link between the remaining Maoists in China and the extremist Maoists outside China. Chen Yonggui, sensing the prospect that Maoist CR theory and practice would be denounced altogether, developed a close ideological affinity with the Khmer Rouge. He visited Cambodia in 1978. Many Khmer Rouge members actually did not know his name, but they were all very impressed by the legend of the Chinese new men in Dazhai, so they simply told each other, "Dazhai is coming." Accompanied by Pol Pot wherever he went, Chen was very excited to see the Khmer Rouge's extremist policies in pushing the country into communism. Later, when he returned to China, he told his close friends with a sigh: "Marx, Lenin, and Mao, they all failed to accomplish communism, but in Cambodia they made it." He added that "how they jumped to communism is worth our study."[6]

This historical context may help better understand the new man question in the Khmer Rouge regime. The Khmer Rouge coined the terms "new people" and "base people." The new people were also called the April 17 people, referring to those who had lived in the major cities until the Khmer Rouge entered in April 1975. By comparison, people who had lived in the Khmer Rouge's "liberated areas" were called base people, because they had been reeducated to some extent and thus were treated less harshly. Therefore in this case the term "new people" indicated the status of people who were still to be reshaped rather than otherwise. These Cambodian "new people" were shortly afterward forced to evacuate the cities and walk to the countryside, where they were subject to "thought reform" combined with heavy labor. The result was that millions perished from exposure, exhaustion, malnutrition, disease, and mass murders.

The Chinese influence in the Cambodian process of remaking people is apparent in many Khmer Rouge policies. Thought reform was one of them. The "new people," who were separated from their families, sent to the countryside, and forced to engage in intensive ideological studies combined with backbreaking work, were frequently asked questions such as these: Are you still thinking of your family? Are you really with the revolution? Do you really feel happy when you work, or is work just something you have to do? But the Khmer Rouge went much further, driven by the "lesson" taken from China's development. Altered by Mao's apocalyptic words and having witnessed the loss of momentum of China's revolutionary fanaticism in the mid-1970s and the halt of its Cultural Revolution, the Khmer Rouge concluded that the Chinese failure in perpetuating revolution was caused by their preservation of all old social institutions, even though they had made tremendous efforts to reform them. The old social institutions consisted of family, money, market, education, and most of all, the space containing all of them—the cities. As the Khmer Rouge deduced, they were major elements of the old social environment, and the Chinese experience had proven that they were essentially unchangeable. The Khmer Rouge thus abolished those institutions—instead of reforming them—from the moment the KR entered the cities, in order to create a totally new social environment for the sake of the new man. One result of dismantling these institutions was that it helped recruit young followers, some even teenagers, for the Khmer Rouge, because now they had no school to attend or family to be part of. Many Khmer Rouge soldiers were alarmingly young, often under fifteen years old, and the AK-47s they carried seemed larger than the soldiers themselves. But these young recruits often proved to be the most ferocious and ruthless combatants and executioners. Yet even this aspect of the Khmer Rouge case has a Chinese precedent: in the history of Chinese communism, there were numerous *hong xiao gui* (little red devils) who were much younger than the age of maturity but proved to be the most loyal members of the movement. Recruited by the party in the late 1920s and early 1930s, and without family or formal education, many of them survived the wars and went on to bear the stars and bars of generals in the 1950s.

By destroying these institutions, the Khmer Rouge believed they would avoid the pitfall of Maoist revolution, just as Mao had believed that by launching the CR and other political campaigns, the revisionism that had overtaken the Soviet Union ten years earlier would have no chance in China. Just as the Chinese and Cubans despised the Russians for their corruption by material incentives, some of the Khmer Rouge became critical of the Chinese. One example was their disapproving attitude toward the Chinese experts working in Cambodia, who used the foreign currency they were paid during their service to buy household electronics at customs when they returned to China. Additionally, when a Chinese engineer asked how much the construction of a reservoir had cost, the Khmer Rouge answered proudly: "That was made by our people. In Cambodia we do not use money."[7]

Under the influence of Castroism, the Nicaraguan Sandinista Revolution around the 1980s was another example of the new man discourse and practice, and perhaps the last one sponsored by a revolutionary government. The Sandinista Revolution had a peculiar moralist character, due to its liberation theology influence and its highly emphasized promise of an equitable society. According to an American interviewer, many Sandinista activists clearly articulated the relationship between the construction of the new society and molding of the new Nicaraguans. And sometimes they even talked about the "New Man project." One young activist so described the difficulties in creating the new man: "There is no 'New Man'—only talk about him, and little pieces of him here and there. We are no doubt closer to this collectivist idea than before. But the egoist remains very strong. Many kids my age are concerned about nothing but shirts, pants, how they look, and a lot of them just want to breakdance all day."[8] In the Nicaraguan context, what opposed the values of the new man was—along with other elements of the old social environment common to all societies prior to socialism—machismo. It was an entrenched mentality and pattern of behavior, represented by "hard drinking, excessive gambling, womanizing, and wife beating," which many believed had been cultivated and reinforced as a result of Spanish colonization. The creation of the new Nicaraguan was therefore a fight between two sets of values, as Lancaster observed:

> Just as certainly, men—even educated, involved, revolutionary men—have been markedly slower to change their habits. Two sets of values coexist, compete, and more than occasionally blur: the ideals of machismo, with its cult of aggressive masculinity, defined as a mode of sexual and physical conquest; and the ideals of the revolutionary New Man, who is envisioned as hardworking, devoted, and family oriented.[9]

The cases of the Hungarians, the Naxalites, the Khmer Rouge, and the Sandinistas are telling examples of the universal appeal of the concept of the new man in identity transformation and character building carried out by communist or other radical social movements, regardless of their distinctive social and cultural backgrounds.

THE COMMUNIST NEW MAN IN WESTERNERS' EYES

The twentieth century was a time when Western societies were facing challenges, from both inside and outside, that questioned or even denunciated liberal, democratic values and the capitalist system, starting at the end of the First World War, peaking in the 1930s, and recurring in the 1960s. The experiment with socialist or communist ideas thus became an alternative model for many Western intellectuals, social activists, and even clergymen. For these people the communist new man stood as a sharp contrast to their fellow countrymen who, according to them, had been spoiled by self-centered ethics and material comfort, devoid of any lofty or spiritual meaning. Their perception of the communist new man thus not only reflected their wishful thinking about communist regime but also, or even to a greater extent, reflected the social problems in the West.

The Soviet New Man in Western Eyes

As a better-or-worse alternative, the emerging Soviet new man drew significant interest from many Westerners, especially intellectuals and social activists, in the 1920s and 1930s, when their own societies were experiencing cultural and social disorientation and uncertainty in the postwar years, and the devastating economic and political crisis of the 1930s. Although their observations of the Soviet experiment with human nature at times evoked a somewhat mixed feeling of caution and excitement, a more favorable response and approving tone, reflected especially in numerous travel accounts, seemed more common. The observations of these sensitive and perceptive Westerners often captured the most distinctive characteristics of the Soviet new man, as opposed to what they had been used to in their own societies. Some examples of such observations may well illustrate the impact of the Soviet experiment in the West and the connections between the Enlightenment tradition and ongoing social engineering.

The on-the-spot observation of the Soviet state in its inception (1920) by well-known British philosopher and antiwar activist Bertrand Russell has been an important source in this regard. With the expectation of a new future, in contrast to war-torn Europe, Russell discovered to his chagrin something fundamentally wrong in the mind-set of the Soviet leaders. The Bolshevik outlook on life was established in particular on a belief that "human nature can be transformed by force," and the leaders were acting accordingly. For Russell, this could mean only "centuries of darkness and futile violence."[10] A less-known but more interesting observation of the Bolshevik regime in its early stage was made by René Fueloep-Miller, a German author who witnessed the revolution. With caution and anxiety, his *Mind and Face of Bolshevism*, first published in German in 1926, provided an insightful psychological and sociological analysis of the looming new Russians. Fueloep-Miller pointed out one of the most important aspects of Soviet social engineering: elimination of the awareness and expression of individuality. For him, the new Russian was a "collective man," a "million-headed impersonal mass," a "titanic, many-membered body," "a mighty and powerful organism" that had "swallowed up all the individual cries, the joyful or angry words." Such a creature was strange, alien, and ominous to anyone outside the experiment, but as Fueloep-Miller observed, "those . . . who firmly believe in the Revolution proclaim with ecstatic rapture that this sinister-seeming being is the great achievement of the century, the 'new man'; such will be the aspect of that creature of the future which is called upon to take the place of the individual, and, from now on, to reign in his stead."[11]

The contemporary sociopsychological theories of Le Bon and Freud interpreted this sudden emergence of a "collective man" as something regressive and primitive. As Fueloep-Miller put it, both of them emphasized "the decline of individual initiatives, a reciprocal leveling of the most valuable qualities of the individual in favor of their joint mass reaction, and, therefore, a retrogression to primitive psychological conditions." But in contrast to these Western European views, the Bolsheviks saw this "collective man" as "a 'superior category,' a higher, more valuable form of organization of existence, the realization of which is worth any sacrifice."[12]

In addition to the replacement of individuality with collectivity, an "external man" also replaced the "inner man," through participatory and ritualistic activities such as festivals, demonstrations, meetings, parades, and so on. Fueloep-Miller observed: "For only in external human beings can be found the elements from which real collectivity can be manufactured; the inner life is so infinitely differentiated, so inextricably bound up with the nature and vicissitudes of the individual, that an association of all, of the kind aimed at by the Bolshevists, can be attained only through the multiplication of the external functions."[13] As for the question of why such a "passionate protest against the value and significance of the individual personality, so hard for the Western European to understand," was accepted by the Russians, Fueloep-Miller provided a classical explanation from a historical perspective. As he put it, "The Russian has never been able to perceive the ultimate development of humanity except in a collective form, in a conception of the collectivity, of the 'people,' into which even the Russian idea of God has always been retransformed."[14]

In contrast to Miller's Cassandra-like tone, many Westerners observed the Soviet experiment with profound interest, optimism, and even elation, amidst the criticism of their own society. Ella Winter, an American journalist who visited the Soviet Union in the early 1930s, was impressed by the Soviet experiment aimed at changing human nature. As she stated in her book *Red Virtue—Human Relationships in the New Russia,* in the long chapter entitled "Designing a New Man," "The New Man is planned as the new society is developed." In another chapter, "One of the Five Million" (with "five million" referring to the five million Russian youths and "one" referring to a model), Winter portrayed a typical Soviet new man. Sergei Davidovitch, a twenty-two-year-old Komsomol organizer working for the State Planning Committee in Moscow, had participated in numerous political activities, especially the forced collectivization, the fighting, and the killing of many kulaks. He possessed nothing and dressed as simply as he lived. He slept little and occasionally did not sleep at all, especially when he had to prepare reports for the committee. He kept himself informed about the latest political news at any time and "would walk for hours in the snow to give news of the latest political move, the latest governmental pronouncement." He could tell at a glance if the people he met were "ours or not." His most adored hero was one of his comrades who had killed many white soldiers. After encountering and observing him closely, Winter concluded, "The major problems of life, problems that torture many people for years, were for him settled," or more exactly, "these things were just naturally known."[15]

Frankwood E. Williams, an American authority on mental hygiene and adolescence in the first half of the twentieth century, was deeply obsessed by the rising cases of "human relations" problems in the United States, such as mental problems, juvenile delinquency, parent-child tension, and divorce, and attributed them to the capitalist system. After visiting the Soviet Union twice in the early 1930s, he published *Russia Youth and the Present-Day World,* in which he announced that Soviet Russia had explored solutions for the sorts of problems plaguing the West, with remarkable success. A Soviet mental hygiene authority told him that for three months he had searched Moscow's hospitals for a new case of manic-depressive illness for his classroom teaching, but he could find none. Williams himself visited many hospitals, clinics, museums, parks, schools, nurseries, factories, collective farms, and so on. Although the Soviets' technology and facilities were far from desirable by US standards, Williams finally concluded that the secret of the Soviets' success was that, unlike in the US, where such problems were individually solved through a clinical approach, in Russia the efforts were made at the "mass" level for the "social relief of anxiety," as a Soviet mental hygiene expert explained to him.[16] In other words, in Russia there was a coordination for mental health and psychological wellness that involved everyone—physician, nurse, teacher, worker—who could "contribute to the one undertaking that has meaning for them all." Williams noted that the same was true for artists, dramatists, musicians, and writers.

In a chapter entitled "Can Russia Change Human Nature?" Williams revealed a more profound basis for Russia's success. He asserted that the success in controlling mental problems resulted from Russia's systematic efforts to change human nature, which had been assumed in the West to be impossible. Williams emphasized the role of "setting" in shaping and reshaping human nature, arguing that in the West people were used to only one social setting, which was capitalist and exploitative, and that human nature, when shaped under this setting, had been assumed to be unchangeable. Such a belief in unchangeable human nature was actually a fiction, according to Williams. In Russia, by comparison, people were creating a new setting, a collective and communist one that had resulted in significant changes in human nature and in turn had helped reduce mental problems. This argument indicated the influence of the environmental determinism of the Enlightenment. In the context of the Great Depression of the 1930s, Williams declared, "The greatest evil in the world today is the keeping up of the fiction in regard to man," and he complained that since the beginning of the New Deal, nothing had changed toward reshaping human nature. Until Westerners changed their concept of man, Williams predicted, "our best brains can do no more than attempt to devise and cure mere symptoms that arise from time to time."[17]

Sidney and Beatrice Webb, orators of the Victorian socialists and the Fabians and perhaps the most vocal Soviet sympathizers during the 1930s in Great Britain, visited the Soviet Union in 1936 and were equally impressed by the Soviet new man. Their book *Soviet Communism: A New Civilization?* contained a long chapter entitled "The Remaking of Man," in which they distinguished Soviet society from Western society: "In no direction does the purpose and policy of the Soviet government stand in sharper contrast with the purpose and policy of any other administration than in its attitude towards the character and habits of the citizens at large."[18] The slogan they spotted on the wall of the Moscow Sports Club concisely summed up the purpose of the Soviet state: "We are not only rebuilding human society on an economic basis; we are mending the human race on scientific principles."[19] The Webbs correctly pointed out that Lenin and his associates believed that human nature was mutable, and that the basic purpose of the revolution and the government was to remove the people's "social heritage" that had been bequeathed from the old social environment. It was this "ultimate reason" that justified the Bolsheviks' ruthless elimination of all kulaks, capitalists, and petit bourgeois.

A specific thesis regarding the new man, that the Webbs developed in their book, was the comparison between Bolshevik morality and Christian ethics. The Bolshevik repudiation of all religious beliefs naturally raised concerns in the West: in the absence of religious ethics, which had served as an important part for the foundation of secular moral standards, how could the Bolsheviks establish a moral society? The Webbs argued, however, that the Bolsheviks were creating an effective substitute: a sense of universal individual indebtedness. It meant that in the Soviet Union everyone was born in the debt of the state and the party. For example, life without exploitation and oppression was at the cost of numerous martyrs' sacrifices; the meaning and direction of life were revealed and pointed out by the party; and education and jobs were provided by the state. The individuals reciprocally were obliged to serve the state and the party to their best and even had to be ready to lay down their lives. Therefore this concept of the universal individual indebtedness in Soviet society led its citizens on their road to redemption, as the concept of original sin did in Christian societies.

The Webbs were also drawn to Soviet polytechnic schools, institutions experimenting with the idea of completely integrating work with study, and felt that those were a "gigantic exercise" applying British educator Samuel Butler's principle to "learn in doing." Soviet schools were put into "a constant and intimate association with the neighboring factory and country" and "must be understood as a deliberate attempt to bring school closely into contact with adult life and practice."[20] As for the political organization systems, the Webbs provided detailed descriptions for every organization for certain ages and concluded that their purpose was mainly educational rather than political. They even attended the Seventh All-Union Conference of Komsomols and then said: "It was impossible not to be impressed with the enthusiasm and energy, the joy of new freedom and the eagerness for improvement of this exuberant youth."[21]

The Chinese and Cuban New Men in Western Eyes

By the 1960s the Soviet Union had lost its attractiveness for a great number of Western intellectuals and other people, for basically two reasons. One was that the despotic nature of Stalinism was revealed in de-Stalinization and further exposed in the crackdown of the Hungarian Revolution (1956). The other was that the modernization and bureaucratization of Soviet society and associated social changes (discussed in chapter 1) reduced the romanticized and moral expectations of the system among Westerners who had felt alienated in a similar, though much more advanced, society. Many of them therefore turned to China and Cuba. The 1960s and early 1970s were times when Western societies were tormented by social protests, and witnessed a surge of Western travelers to China and Cuba to observe the social experiments firsthand, while others who closely followed their reports looked up to these two countries with hope and admiration. Paul Hollander has offered an explanation for the intellectuals' enthusiasm for and fascination with the communist societies in this context. According to Hollander, the rejection of the intellectuals' own societies was closely linked with their embrace of the communist countries, and such a phenomenon was not unique in that century:

> Not surprisingly, my inquiry found that alienation from one's own society and susceptibility to the attractions, real or imagined, of others are very

closely linked. The late 1920s and early 1930s proved an excellent example. Then, as in the 1960s and early 1970s, Western intellectuals responded to the crises and problems of their society with intensified criticism and a surging interest in alternatives. The Soviet case offered the most hopeful alternative to the economic and social chaos of the first period. In more recent times the problems of Western societies were less economic and more spiritual and political in nature. In the 1960s and early 70s the putative emptiness of affluence and material comforts provided the broad background against which specific causes for discontent and social criticism came to be projected: Vietnam, race relations, corporate capitalism, consumerism, or the bureaucratization of life. More generally, I contend that in recent times the increasing strains of secularization played an important part in predisposing many intellectuals to admire such societies as China under Mao and Cuba under Castro.[22]

Against this general background, how the state treated its people and how the people responded to it in different social settings were major concerns in these intellectuals' minds. While Westerners were assumed to be spiritually corrupt and materially spoiled, having no sense of the collective or any other sublime purposes transcending individual interests, communist society offered a contrasting example. As Hollander put it, "It comprises the achievement of or the striving for 'wholeness,' the sense of identity and community, meaning and purpose in life."[23]

In the works of these intellectuals, the main focus was the qualities of the people who lived under these regimes and had been created by their new social environment—their new attitude, their transformed character, their high spirit, single purpose, boundless faith, and infectious enthusiasm. In many cases we can find a revival of interest and fascination demonstrated in the Western intellectuals' literature of the 1930s, as a result of their travel to the Soviet Union.

The Chinese New Man in Western Eyes
For many Western visitors, China in the 1960s and early 1970s represented a fond dream of tenacious and admirable efforts to change human nature. Visitors were very perceptive about anything related to the Chinese people, who were experiencing a course of ideological and moral transformation. As Arthur Galston, an American scientist, put it: "Visiting China . . . made me wonder whether 'human nature' as we know it in the competitive West is the only course of development model possible for mankind. It reawakened some of my youthful idealism and made me question some

of the deep-rooted cynicism prevalent in our society."[24] Peter Worsley, a British social scientist, felt the same way about "the Chinese attempt to transform human values and personal relationships at the level of everyday life, to challenge assumptions that certain models of behavior are naturally 'entailed' under conditions of industrial or city life."[25]

The Chinese model of the new man had many merits and virtues. First and probably most important was, according to Hollander, the sense of participation and wholeness and the absence of alienation in "a society permeated by singleness of purpose."[26] A typical articulation of this perception was that of Carol Tavris, an American psychologist: "Most of all, you leave diversity and controversy, the hallmarks of America, to be wrapped in a uniformity of belief and single-mindedness of purpose."[27] Staughton Lynd and Tom Hayden, two noted American social activists in the 1960s, were under the same impression: "Walking before breakfast . . . we passed a group of women energetically singing before starting a day's work. Everywhere is the pulse of purposeful activity."[28] Ruth Sidel, an American social work specialist, expressed a similar observation: "People go about their daily work with a purpose and even a sense of mission," as well a "sense of participation and commitment to an ideal greater than one's self."[29] Such purposefulness and commitment even seemed to have a magical function of healing and providing resistance to physical pain. When a group representing the Committee of Concerned Asian Scholars saw an old woman doing a job collecting metal pieces, her hands covered with cuts from the work, they asked her if the wounds were painful. The old woman answered: "When you are working for the revolution, it doesn't hurt."[30]

Some intellectuals were deeply moved by and even felt jealous of how the revolution had changed people's minds and characteristics. Lois Wheeler Snow, an American actress, expressed such a feeling when she heard a Chinese actress tell of how she and other actors and actresses had been reeducated through working and living together with peasants and workers and serving them with their artistic performance on the worksites. They felt that only since then had they been truly happy, because they felt completely integrated with the working people. Encountering these new artists, Snow said: "Envy stole over me as I listened to these young people who belong to a society that has gained their wholehearted dedication."[31]

High morality was another essential character of the Chinese new man. As Harvard Chinese history professor John K. Fairbank observed, the Chinese Revolution had not only been materially progressive "but also a far-reaching moral crusade to change the very human Chinese personality in the direction of self-sacrifice and serving others." In this regime, moral behavior was simply another manifestation of "political conduct." He confirmed the relationship between model emulation and the high moral level among the masses; China was governed "by exemplary moral men, not laws." His conclusion was that "Americans may find in China's collective life today an ingredient of personal moral concern for one's neighbor that has a lesson for us all."[32]

Such high moral standards were so prevalent that they appeared to have changed the foundation of sexual relations: "The Chinese have succeeded in fundamentally altering the notion of attractiveness by simply substituting some of these revolutionary attributes for the physical ones."[33] When Chinese women were asked what was the most important qualification of the man they wanted to marry, the answer was "correct political thinking." As a result of the politicization of sexuality, "relations seemed free of jealousy and infidelity."[34] Associated with this de-emphasized sexuality, Chinese women showed little "superficial" interest in fancy dresses, and they wore no makeup. An associated issue, but one having a more substantial influence on human life than sexuality, was the breaking up of families. The mass relocation of millions of people, forced to move from cities to rural areas, amazed the Western intellectuals. For example, some members of the Committee of Concerned Asian Scholars concluded that Chinese people seemed willing to be separated for years from their families.

When most of these intellectuals made their way to China, the Cultural Revolution was turning China upside down. For many of these intellectuals, however, the CR was neither social turmoil nor human tragedy but "a society-wide spiritual renewal." Joshua Horn, a British physician who had settled in China, made a bold and confident prediction: "History may see it as the harbinger of the emergence of Communist Man."[35] One example was an observation regarding a May Seventh Cadre School, made by the first Western communist allowed to visit such a school. Maria Antonietta Macciocchi, a member of the French Communist Party, visited China in the fall of 1970 and was invited to visit the school, which was forty miles from Beijing. She drew a picture of the school, which she included in her book *Daily Life in Revolutionary China.*

The school had been built by the cadres themselves in "an abandoned camp, a sort of uninhabited cemetery" in 1968. It was designated for cadres and intellectuals from the Eastern District of Beijing. The principles of the school were characterized by three elements: the style of Yan'an, perfect unity with the masses, and the leading of a simple life in the service of the revolutionary cause, fearing neither hardship nor death.[36] The pupils were divided into the following groups: the old leaders who had fought in the war against

Japan and the war of liberation, activists of working-class and peasant origin, and the "three-door cadres" (out the door of the family, through the door of the school, and then through the door of the party organization). There were also young instructors, middle school teachers, state administration employees, party staff workers, and trade unionists. The categories showed that in cities virtually no one with educated, executive, or managerial background could escape being sent down to the countryside to receive such reeducation.

A main target of reeducation was the old cadres who used to be dedicated revolutionaries but who, after entering the cities and taking offices, "become lazy [and] take it easy" and for whom "the revolution becomes just a memory."[37] After moving into the school and undergoing reeducation, they had "rediscovered" their revolutionary style of life and "recaptured" the youth of their earlier days. As a sign of their spiritual rejuvenation and as a result of their "souls" having been "touched," their attitude toward heavy, dirty physical labor changed. For example, the visiting Macciocchi was told:

> In the spring of this year we organized teams of comrades from the school; they went into the Eastern District of Peking to collect garbage and drain the sewers with buckets and carts. When one does this sort of job, one loses any sort of bureaucratic attitude, any notion of hierarchy. It isn't easy, especially at first. The disgust, the shame at being recognized as a former leader, the fear that other people are talking about your errors—even the fear of disease—all that does exist.[38]

One personal account described such distaste at first and the complete conversion at last. A former deputy mayor was put to work in the sanitation department of his district, picking up the dirt and garbage and shouting, "Bring your garbage here!" as he went by—the classic cry of the garbageman. But he was ashamed because everyone had known him—the important man who made speeches to crowds, who had power. Then he asked himself, "Why can't I shout 'Bring the crap here' as freely and naturally as the garbagemen do? Because I am accustomed to a comfortable life, because in a way, the revisionist influence is eating away at me." After analyzing and condemning himself, the cadre was able to overcome his distaste and shout loudly: "Bring your garbage here!"

As a sign of the soul being touched, most of the cadres and intellectuals seemed to have profoundly changed their attitude toward physical labor, according to the cadre who escorted Macciocchi and related this example to her:

Comrade Chen was head of the Ministry of Health in the Eastern District of Peking. When a peasant came in from the country she would disappear; she avoided all contact with him, for she had a horror of dirt. She is here. Since entering the school she has changed so much that she even lived with a peasant woman who had just given birth and was seriously ill. Not only did she give her injections and provide her with the necessary care, she even disposed of her excreta and washed her. And she nursed her like this for several nights.[39]

The cadre then concluded: "An offensive must be launched against notions of dirt, ugliness, danger, fear of death, if one wants to make the revolution within oneself."[40]

Macciocchi's observations indicated that, like many others, this cadre acknowledged that in the May Seventh Cadre Schools the political, psychological, and physical pressures were often extremely high. But he thought that the endurance of such a hardship would temper the cadres and intellectuals as a necessary step of reeducation.

The Cuban New Man in Western Eyes

In Cuba, Western intellectuals found the same basic characters of the communist new man as they discovered in China. But in comparison with the Chinese, the Cuban new man had some distinctive characteristics in these Westerners' eyes. One particular attraction was that the leaders themselves were perfect examples of the new man. Standing in contrast to senior, dignitary, and much less public Chinese leaders who walled themselves off in the secluded and mysterious imperial Zhongnanhai, the leaders in Havana were young, imposing, energetic, and charismatic in the way they inspired their people, interacted with foreigners, and, in some cases, even were self-sacrificing. Paul Hollander's observation may be enlightening. Hollander argued that modern, secular, and commercialized Western society had stripped intellectuals of any heroic admiration—a combination of hero worship and charismatic fascination—but now they had found alternatives embodied in Castro and Guevara. For example, noted American writer Norman Mailer, when referring to Castro's visit to New York, expressed his admiration for the legendary guerrilla leader:

So, Fidel Castro, I announce to the city of New York that you gave all of us who are alone in this country . . . some sense that there were heroes left in the world. . . . It was as if the ghost of Cortez had appeared in our century riding Zapata's white horse. You were the first and greatest hero to appear in the world since the Second War. . . . You give a bit of life to the best and most passionate men and women all over the earth.[41]

The intellectuals were deeply impressed by the power of charisma that Castro used to arouse his people. Abbie Hoffman said, "When he is tall and straight, the crowd immediately is transformed."[42] His dedication was obvious, and it reaffirmed his power and appeal, as Elizabeth Sutherland noted: "He seems, first of all, utterly devoted to the welfare of his people—and his people are the poor, not the rich. When he speaks, it is as if his own dedication and energy were being directly transfused into his listeners with an almost physical force."[43] One particular detail that fascinated many Western visitors was the Cuban leaders' tirelessness, especially their sleeplessness (a habit formed in the guerrilla war years). Many Western intellectuals who were granted access to Castro and Guevara often had midnight conversations with them. For example, Jean-Paul Sartre, who had many such occasions, labeled them "night watchmen" and said it seemed that the Cuban leaders had totally overcome some basic human needs.[44] As Hollander pointed out, "powerful, dynamic, and heroic renaissance men exercising iron-willed command over their body and mind, tirelessly reshaping their society—this was the exciting vision many Western intellectuals, such as Sartre, were ready to embrace." Hearing of Guevara's death, Sartre made a comment, widely spread later, that Che was "the most complete man of his time."[45]

Some visitors also found that Cuba had much in common with what excited them about China, in particular a deep sense of purposefulness and community. As Kirby Jones and Frank Mankiewicz observed,

> Castro's Cuba is prosperous and its people are enthusiastic, reasonably content and optimistic about the future. Perhaps the overriding impression of three trips to Cuba is the enthusiasm and unity of the Cuban people. They are proud of their accomplishments and sing songs about themselves and their country that reflect this self-pride. . . . The people work together and work hard for what they believe to be the good of their neighbors and therefore their country.[46]

For Barry Reckord, who was obsessed with the lack of the sense of a harmonious community and a common cause of the time, this was a kind of new Cuban man: "The society is moral even if the individual is not. Men are more just, more human in a collective sense."[47]

The experience of the Venceremos Brigade in this regard is a telling example of the perception of the new man in Cuba. The brigade was an organization of American and some Canadian youths and intellectuals who went to Cuba seeking political inspiration through participating in work (cane cutting) and political rallies, visiting Cuban families, making pilgrimages to revolutionary historical sites, and especially listening to Castro's speeches. One of the fundamental purposes for many members going to Cuba was to "find different human natures in different social systems." They blamed the American social environment for their being individualistic and selfish; as they put it, "the American system of values prevents us from achieving our revolutionary goals" and "interferes with revolutionary potential." For them the trip to Cuba was "consciousness-raising," because only in a totally new social environment could the consciousness of the new man be cultivated. In the book *Venceremos Brigade: Young Americans Sharing the Life and Work of Revolutionary Cuba,* the editors emphasized that all materials in the book reflected a theme of collectivism versus individualism.[48]

For many members of the Venceremos Brigade, visiting Cuba became a process of reeducation. Through this trip, they felt that they had cultivated a sense of purposefulness and community—the essential character of the communist new man, something they felt did not exist in their own society. This essential character was solidarity—all members were inspired by the same revolutionary goal, and this common goal made them ignore all divisions in American society, such as race, gender, class, and education. In other words, they broke all the social boundaries that had separated them from one another in the United States and were united by a single purpose.[49] Among brigade members, those who were most self-critical were white Americans, who were "paralyzed with shame and despair over the values which a competitive, individualistic and racist middle-class culture had instilled in them." It was a self-hatred that, for some members, "deepened the gloom that surrounded any prospect of a white revolutionary culture."[50]

It is not coincidental that when Castro went to the brigade's camp and talked to the members, the subject of creating the new man stirred their minds. According to Castro, "Man is capable of doing great things. But this evolution stopped in a specific moment in history or in prehistory," and "the humanity we know up until now is a prehistoric humanity, a savage humanity." Thus it was implied that his revolution was an attempt to create a human being that for the first time in history would be real and civilized. The brigade members pointed out with admiration that "through his leadership Cuba is developing whole generations of Fidel," and "we are now entering into the era of the true human history—the New Man [era]."[51]

It is worth noting that there were some similarities between the Venceremos Brigade and China's Up to the Mountains and Down to the Villages movement. Of course the Chinese movement consisted entirely of

Chinese and was largely compulsory, whereas the American brigade incorporated foreigners and was spontaneous, but the purposes, the motives, and many activities were identical. The fundamental similarity was that both movements were seeking a way of reeducating urban youths and youths who had grown up in a more materially comfortable social environment. The purpose was to instill or cultivate revolutionary consciousness through backbreaking labor, to make the educated recognize their guilt of social or racial origin and physical incapability as the result of an easy or luxurious life, and to try to integrate them with the peasants and workers by abandoning their old habits of urban life and their detesting of physical labor. In a word, both movements were trying to turn the participants inside out, to make communist or revolutionary new men out of young urban material.

RESPONSES FROM THIRD WORLD LEADERS

The twentieth century was also a time of decolonization and independence in which many leaders of newly independent countries were seeking approaches to give their economies a great push for modernization and their people a new identity—a sense of belonging or new community—for nation building. Because the Western approach toward that goal could in no way be imitated, and because the most important resource was neither the existing economic and technological wealth nor foreign investment and aid but their own population, such leaders were forced to seek ideological inspiration from socialist countries. They were inspired by the alleged Chinese and Cuban successes in mobilizing and organizing the masses to contribute to the construction of their countries, to the extent that they agreed to reduce and suppress or in some extreme cases to abnegate their material needs and individual interests, so that the state could control and distribute as many resources as it needed for its development. The communist new man, therefore, marked a transformation of people's mentality and attitude.

The appeal of world communism to former Western colonies as they strove for independence arose in the early 1920s, as Lenin formed the Comintern to spread revolution in Asia by exploiting anti-imperialist and nationalist movements there. The Soviet experience of transforming and engaging backward Russians and especially non-Russian minorities in "socialist construction" attracted some nationalist leaders in Asia. For example, Jawaharlal Nehru of India paid close attention to the Soviet policies in central Asia and Caucasia that were aimed at developing the economy and changing social settings through literacy campaigns and ideological education. For Nehru, the level of social development and the peoples' political awareness in these Soviet republics were almost the same as most parts of his own country, so if the Soviets could do that, then why not India in the future? He expressed his admiration of the Soviet Union in *Glimpses of World History*, a compilation of letters written to his daughter for her history education while he was in jail in the early 1930s.

The 1950s and 1960s was a remarkable time for worldwide decolonization and national independence and thus for the appeal of the Chinese and Cuban new men in the Third World. One particular source of the influence of the communist new man in the Third World was the presence of Chinese and Cuban servicemen in these countries, who were sent out on a mission of internationalism. For the newly independent Asian and African countries in search of a new social system, China and Cuba presented an efficient and successful model for countries with historical backgrounds similar to their own. As Castro once said, "From our own experience we know . . . that there will be no economic development in any underdeveloped country without socialism, without centralizing all the resources of the economy and channeling them in the needed direction."[52] The contrast in size and population of China and Cuba was immense, but both of them shared a colonial past and a revolutionary experience, and even more important was that both of them claimed to have successfully built a new nation and gained international recognition in the absence of Western aid. These successes were admirable to many Third World leaders who were seeking methods both for attaining material progress and establishing an ideological and moral foundation for national unity and citizenship education.

From the perspective of some Third World leaders, one essential secret of such success was that the two countries had injected a martial spirit and a sense of discipline among the masses, paving the way for large-scale mobilization and even regimentation. In other words, China and Cuba had found a way to educate the ordinary people into accepting a new concept, reformulating the relation between individuals and society. Without this achievement, all other successes would have been inconceivable. It was within this context that the communist experiment seemed appealing to some Third World leaders.

Cuba attracted attention initially in Latin America and the Caribbean and later in Africa, particularly in Angola and Ethiopia, where Cuban aid workers and troops became important in military interventions and civilian projects as well. The motivations and outcomes of the Cuban involvement in these regions were multidimensional and complicated, often a mix of a service to the Soviet global strategy and the expansion of Cuba's international influence, justified by offering assistance to peoples who were fighting colonialism, racism, and warlordism. Notwithstanding the motivation, many Africans appreciated Havana's assistance and admired ordinary Cuban servicemen's contribution and sacrifice, seeing that as a quality of the new Cubans. South African civil rights leader Nelson Mandela once revealed this aspect of the African perception of the Cuban help, which has been used by the Cuban government as an example of the international recognition of its success in making dedicated new citizens.[53]

The Chinese model drew attention in Southeast Asia, India, and several African countries. An outstanding example was the admiration of China—for its material as well as moral strength—in Tanzania under Julius Nyerere, the founding figure of that country's independence. As the *Nationalist*, Tanzania's government newspaper, pointed out, China "has all the characteristics of a truly big POWER. It has a powerful independent industrial base interwoven in a self-sustaining socialist economy; it has united conscious, hard-working people alive to their responsibilities and ready to sacrifice, build and defend their country, and finally China has the 'BOMB': today's symbol in the world's realpolitik."[54]

Nyerere realized that material achievement could not be an overnight miracle and that Tanzania was not ready for such rapid modernization. As he put it, "Our tools are as old as Mohammed, we live in houses from the times of Moses." He also said that "while the Americans and the Russians are going to the Moon, we Africans are dancing," and that "they are sending rockets into outer space while we are eating wild roots."[55] On the contrary, as the essential resources of social change, people's spirits and minds could become more determined through ideological education that did not need a sound material basis. And in this regard the Chinese could serve as a model for his people.

Before turning to China in search of a model, Nyerere had already noticed that there was a characteristic distinction between the people of the "East" (socialist countries) and the "West" (capitalist countries). When medical students in Dar es Salaam went on strike to demand better conditions, Nyerere noticed that only two students did not participate. These two had spent years trained in Russia and East Germany. Nyerere suspected that they represented "a difference in attitude." As he put it, "The West is just too individualistic. . . . All the textbooks of Western countries talk about rights, rights, rights, and no duties. . . . And duty is usually defined as 'obey the law'—the minimum." On the contrary, he observed, "In the Eastern countries, there has been a reaction to this. A reaction, I think, that works like a pendulum; to strike a balance, you must swing each way. . . . [T]he Eastern countries have African needs: a stress on duty."[56]

With this generally favorable view toward the socialist countries, Nyerere especially regarded those with a colonial background as more suitable models for Tanzania. He once asked: "Why should Tanzania not learn from the agricultural communes of China? Their experience could promote thoughts and ideas about our own rural organization, provided that we go to learn, proceed to think—not to copy. Why can we not learn from the Korean success in rural transformation in comparison with continuing difficulties in other Communist countries? Do the Cuban experiments in adult education have nothing to teach us?"[57] More specifically, Nyerere was interested in how these socialist countries successfully reshaped people's minds and uplifted their morality, thus transforming the ill-educated and politically apathetic masses into well-organized manpower, willing to contribute everything to nation building. As George T. Yu put it:

> Still another appeal of the Chinese model can be found in the political, moral, and social imperfections perceived in Tanzanian society but accepted as eradicated in contemporary China. Tanzanian elite deplore what they regard as the lack of spirit, the "conspicuous consumption," and the absence of discipline and organization in their own society. This attitude can be found among the government officials, the intellectuals, and the locally based administrators faced with the daily realities of governing. All perceive the need for some form of martial spirit, political and social mobilization, and regimentation if Tanzania is to complete the task of nation-building. In the Chinese model, the Tanzanian finds the spirit, frugality, and organization he seeks.[58]

Nyerere made two visits to China. The first was in 1965, when China was mobilized in the campaign of model emulation and Mao was gathering the momentum for the Cultural Revolution. The second was in 1968, at the peak of the Cultural Revolution. Nyerere's Chinese hosts made special arrangements for him, escorting him to see communes, factories, schools, and everything that could showcase the new China and the new Chinese people. Nyerere was deeply impressed. At the farewell banquet on the eve of his departure from Beijing, he was full of praise for the spirit of the Chinese masses: "On my first visit I said in Shanghai, after I had witnessed the revolutionary spirit of your people, that I wished all the people of Tanzania could come to China and witness for themselves what a determined people can do. Today, after the cultural revolution, the spirit of the people of China is even greater than before."[59]

He acknowledged that Tanzania could learn much from China, and even considered the possibility of cultural revolution:

> If we really want to move from national independence to the real independence of the people, and if we really want to make sure that

the African revolution will ever move forward, and not degenerate into neocolonialism, then I say that we should learn from you. Indeed, from what I have seen of China in 1965, I must say that if you found it necessary to begin a cultural revolution, in order to make sure that the new generation would carry forward the banner of your revolution, then certainly we need one.[60]

Nyerere was especially moved by the Chinese people's sense of frugality. As he told his Chinese hosts, "The conscious and deliberate frugality with which your people and your Government efficiently and joyfully conduct their affairs was a big lesson for me and through me for my people. I believe we should begin to apply that lesson."[61] Compared to Dar es Salaam, Chinese cities such as Beijing, Nanjing, and Shanghai had very few cars. There was an anecdote about this comparison of automobiles and its influence on Tanzania. When asked by Nyerere how many cars the Chinese Foreign Ministry had, Chen Yi, the Chinese minister, answered that the ministry had only ten. After Nyerere returned to his own country, the "ten cars" story was spread, and in the Tanzanian parliament a debate ensued, demanding a reduction in the number of imported Mercedes-Benzes. Considering the plain and uniform Chinese style of dress, Nyerere even felt that Tanzanian people in Dar es Salaam looked like millionaires because of their gaily colored clothing.

The Chinese people's discipline and their devotion to their work were other characteristics that Nyerere considered relevant to his own people. Combined with this impression was the obvious success of a highly effective, organized society. When Nyerere made an inspection tour of the Tanzanian construction sites of the Friendship Textile Mill and the Tan-Zan Railway, both financially and technologically supported by China, he was fascinated by the high enthusiasm and efficiency demonstrated by the Chinese technicians and workers who were working there. He called his people's attention to this phenomenon and "pondered how he could instill the zest for hard work and disciplined cooperation into his own people."[62] As he put it: "Disciplined work is essential, and here once again our Chinese technicians have set us a great example."[63]

However, it cannot be assumed that Nyerere chose China as the only model for his country. On the contrary, his attitude was eclectic and utilitarian. For him, Israel, Norway, and Denmark were also successful models for cooperative work. But there is no doubt that when it came to China, what he expressed was not only interest but also deep admiration and fascination. From China, what Tanzania could learn was much more than just some organizational methods; it could learn the means to morally uplift its entire population. As an editorial in the *Nationalist* commented, "We would like to ask the people of the entire world to do a little more serious soul searching about the People's Republic of China."[64] Although Nyerere never directly referred to the systematic social engineering of creating the new man in China, his impression and perception of that country and the comparisons he made between the Chinese and his own people revealed the influence of the Chinese new man experiments upon him and Tanzania, at a very critical time in the building of the new Tanzanian nation.

Conclusion

On the threshold of the third millennium, the fate of mankind depends on an answer to the question: is it possible to transform human nature?
—Mikhail Heller, *Cogs in the Soviet Wheel*

Immanuel Kant once contemplated that "out of the crooked timber of humanity no straight thing was ever made."[1] After completing the writing of the preceding chapters, I feel that no other statement in the history of human self-reflection—to the best of my knowledge—is more concise yet effective in expressing my sentiments at this moment. Like many of his Enlightenment contemporaries, Kant was fond of the Chinese civilization, especially its philosophy, so much so that Nietzsche once dubbed him the Chinaman of Königsberg. It remains unclear whether Kant had ever read Xunzi, the intellectual hybrid of Confucianism and Legalism, to the extent that he came to know Xunzi's belief that rulers must use harsh measures to straighten out the human materials (which he likened to warped lumber).[2] If Kant did, we have an interesting example of a cross-cultural inspiration in regard to remaking human nature; if he did not, then the point becomes even more intriguing: how is it that these two philosophers, separated by two millennia and nurtured in two completely different cultures, came to use words so nearly identical to express such a similar concern?

For me, Xunzi was simply justifying the state's coercion of human nature. Although he did not trust human nature, he did have faith in the government. The question of whether the rulers themselves might also have a twisted mind did not concern him; therefore the possibility that their moral and political enforcement might only lead their people further astray was unthinkable. But Kant sounds more reflective, and he indeed was more conservative than many of his Enlightenment colleagues, as far as the extent to which the environment could refashion human nature was concerned. For him, some "inner fastness" of the human mind could not be conditioned. Whatever the basis was for his "crooked timber" metaphor, I believe he was referring to both the materials and the craftsman. The materials were like warped timber, arousing dissatisfaction or even loathing at the prospect of straightening them out; even if the craftsman's mind was better formed than his materials, nothing outstanding and enduring could be expected to result from this experiment.

In this sense, the history of the communist "new man" experiment started with the impulse justified by Xunzi's sanguine belief, but in the end it got closer to Kant's pessimistic observation, especially as more and more shocking episodes about the moral quality of many communist leaders have been revealed and entered our historical awareness. From a vantage point of living in the postcommunist era, apparently we have no reason to believe that, after decades of state engineering to reshape human nature, the Russians, Chinese, and Cubans are now morally better than most peoples in the world. Even in the 1930s and the 1960s, when those governments were claiming that the new man was being born and many in the West believed that was so, the image of the new man was still essentially a hyperbolic sketch consisting of more wish and fiction than reality, as the previous chapters have shown.

But the task of a historical study is not simply to announce the failure of the creation of the new man or to denounce such efforts and enforcements as arbitrary, tyrannical, or even inhuman; it is acknowledged, though, that a historian's approach cannot be entirely objective or value-free, and that a certain degree of moral evaluation is always inevitable as long as the subject involves human intent and action to forcibly change others' lives. In this regard, the communist experiment has no lack of harsh critiques. Even the most revered communist hero, Che Guevara, who set himself apart from most communist leaders by establishing himself as an example of self-sacrifice, receives judgments such as "Guevara's desire for the development of the New Man, I believe, comes from his need to control the lives of others, [and] his urge to power."[3]

Throughout my research and writing of this book, I have come to believe that, like many other massive but futile and even harmful human endeavors, the goal of making people better or more virtuous—based on faith in human malleability and perfectibility, justified by ideological, moral, or spiritual concepts, and accomplished through political coercion—is one of the fundamental human passionate impulses that has fascinated or, perhaps to a greater extent, obsessed a great number of the most intellectually and politically capable people throughout world history. It is just like many other human impulses, but essentially it is associated more with human relations and can be satisfied only with changes in others' lives on a large scale, instead of merely quenching one's own psychological or corporeal desires within one's own individual life or immediate social sphere. This impulse has been reflected intellectually in numerous ideas in different cultures, but has more frequently and more intensively been manifested in modern times, as radical social transformation created tensions between the society and the individual, and as prominent intellectuals and politicians had more power to address their ideas and to materialize them through state policies, often in the name of nation building and national identity formation.

Therefore I propose to conclude the historical narratives of the communist experiment with human nature in two dimensions: metaphysical and empirical. In the metaphysical dimension, I will present some observations made by other authors and relate them to the Russian, Chinese, and Cuban cases. This connection will help position the assessment of these experiments in world history from a philosophical and psychological perspective. In the empirical dimension, I will briefly compare the historical contexts and particular traits of the communist new men in several cases, especially the similarities between the Chinese and Cuban new men, through which a connection between the new man project and the socioeconomic condition will be established. My hope is that this reflection between these two dimensions achieves a balanced accounting and avoids overstating either of them—that is, seeing these endeavors as the result of purely whimsical and even megalomaniac human ambition regardless of their context, or attributing them to entirely pragmatic and specific socioeconomic drives that defy any profound philosophical and psychological interpretation.

METAPHYSICAL DIMENSION

The phenomenon of the new man, as both an ideal and a reality in many communist countries in the twentieth century (as well as noncommunist regimes), has drawn the attention of sensitive intellectuals of all types, and many of them have viewed it from a broader temporal and spatial perspective. For example, when thinking critically about the Enlightenment and its sociopolitical implications, Michel Foucault pointed out that "the claim to escape from the system of contemporary reality so as to produce the overall programs of another society, of another way of thinking, another culture, another vision of the world, has only led to the return of the most dangerous traditions," and he mentions, more specifically, "the programs for a new man that the worst political systems have repeated throughout the twentieth century."[4]

I will start with the observation of Isaiah Berlin, who was one of the most vocal defenders of liberalism and individual freedom against totalitarian/authoritarian power in the twentieth century and whose work is particularly pertinent in interpreting the communist efforts to create a new man. Berlin approached the issue through tracing the history of the ideas of the new man;

his comprehension was profound, even though ideologically he apparently opposed the people he tried to understand.

For Berlin, any fanatical desire to remake people was a malignant development of some particular ideas expressed in the Enlightenment and in Romanticism. As he put it, "Many of the seeds planted in the eighteenth or nineteenth century have flowered only in the twentieth."[5] For him, in a sense, even communism was "doctrinaire humanitarianism driven to an extreme." In his *Freedom and Its Betrayal: Six Enemies of Human Liberty,* he listed Helvétius and Rousseau as the top two adversaries of human liberty and stated that their doctrines contained the seeds of advocacy and justification for the forcible alteration of human nature in the name of collective and sanctified goals.[6] Berlin further illustrated the temptation and justification of such an impulse to remake people:

> I may conceive myself as an inspired artist, who moulds men into patterns in the light of his unique vision, as painters combine colours or composers sounds; humanity is the raw material upon which I impose my creative will; even though men suffer and die in the process, they are lifted by it to a height to which they could never have risen without my coercive—but creative—violation of their lives.[7]

Berlin also noticed how the power of science in changing human life aroused the desire to change human nature based on some "scientific principles." For him, the attitude of the new-man social engineers toward human beings was identical with that of scientific experimenters to their lab supplies. As he put it, "The task of realizing it [changing human nature] must be entrusted to technically trained believers who look on the human beings at their disposal as material which is infinitely malleable within the confines revealed by the sciences. Stalin's remark that creative artists are 'engineers of the human soul' is a very precise expression of this spirit."[8] To reinforce his conclusion, Berlin also quoted Nikolai Bukharin's remarks on "molding communist humanity out of the human material of the capitalist period."[9]

It is worth noting that, just as the conceptualization of the new man was a contribution made by the Russian intelligentsia, its antithesis—the skepticism and criticism of this idealized man and of the sociopolitical process entailed by the molding of such a person—appeared originally in Russia as well, even before the term new man was coined in the 1860s. Alexander Herzen, a prominent Russian social thinker sensitive to any type of oppression and imposition, was disturbed by the embryonic development of this notion among Russian and European radicals and criticized it from a liberal perspective. In exile in Western Europe and witness to the revolutionary tempest of 1848, Herzen was defending human liberty on two fronts—against both the old-style absolutist monarchy, which had gripped Russia for centuries, and the radicalized ideologies that were sacrificing the current generation in the name of "progress in the future."[10] More specifically, Herzen was anxious, in an apocalyptic manner, about the radical intellectuals and revolutionaries' impatience with ordinary people's lack of political consciousness, as well as their contempt of people's philistinism, which would naturally lead them to embrace the idea of reshaping people. As he put it,

> You are angry with people for much that they haven't done, because you think them capable of all those admirable qualities for which you have educated yourself or have been educated; but they for the most part didn't have that education. . . . Why we should expect from everyone we casually meet model virtues and unusual understanding, I do not know. Probably because of a tendency to idealize, to judge from above.[11]

The communist experiment with human nature actually received wide attention from various authors, which, if not as focused as Berlin's, might be episodic but inspirational to a certain extent. For example, Eric Hoffer, a twentieth-century American social writer whose work was concerned largely with mass movements and political power, had some insightful observations as early as the 1950s. As he observed, "The radical has a passionate faith in the infinite perfectibility of human nature. He believes that by changing man's environment and by perfecting a technique of soul forming, a society can be wrought that is wholly new and unprecedented." Hoffer also wrote: "To ripen a person for self-sacrifice he must be stripped of his individual identity and distinctiveness. . . . The most drastic way to achieve this end is by the complete assimilation of the individual into a collective body."[12]

If the above observations were made from a distance or even from an apocalyptic perspective, then Hu Ping's contemplation of the issue would enrich the panel with profound analysis embedded in firsthand experience. Hu once pointed out the connections among the idea of human malleability/perfectibility, the concept of the new man, the forceful measures for implementing the plan for the new man, and its outcome. Hu argued that the communist perception of human nature and the forceful measures used by the new-man social engineering were superficially paradoxical. In theory the communists believed that maladies in people were all results of external influence and that "as long as a new social system is established, people will become new men of noble desire and will become well-rounded," but in reality they had to resort to forceful measures to implement those new ideas.[13] A more profound understanding of this paradox was, as Hu believed, a cynical view of ordinary people. Hu argued that, from the very beginning, the communists never believed in a peaceful approach to social change, and that this was indicated by "their disappointment in people and their frustration with so-called selfishness, obscuration, and cowardliness of people," for "if people had not been so politically indifferent and watched the injustice with folded arms," the rulers would not have been able to hold the power. In this regard, Hu believed that the Chinese communists were particularly good examples of his argument. Their road to power had been extremely long and treacherous, and they were many times in a desperate struggle for survival. Therefore, Hu concluded, "it is quite understandable that they felt abandoned, distressed, and resentful. This experience made them prone to a dark view of people and human nature . . . but they often camouflaged their disappointment in and loathing of the people with idealistic doctrines such as the revolutionary vanguard and the proletarian dictatorship."[14]

In this book, chapter 1 examined the origin and development of the idea of the new man from the Enlightenment, in which the belief in human malleability and perfectibility facilitated environmental behaviorism (or environmental determinism) and in turn justified the state's coercion of certain values onto ordinary people, not just to make them behave but to remold them. The cases of the Soviet Union, China, Cuba, and many other revolutionary regimes and movements have detailed the realization of such an idea in various forms. From a more philosophical and psychological perspective, Berlin, Hoffer, and Hu Ping in particular, as well as Herzen, provided insights helpful in understanding the deeper roots of radical ideologies being in human emotion and human impulse. In this sense, rational sociopolitical thinking, or revolutionary ideology, is accompanied or reinforced by a psychological complex of irrational compulsions associated with the desire to control and manipulate other people's lives. In world history, the cases of a ruler imposing his or her will upon the ruled and justifying that imposition by various reasons were not rare, but it is only in the regimes discussed in this book that such manipulation became massive and enduring state endeavors with significant impact on ordinary people's thinking and lives.

EMPIRICAL DIMENSION

The idea of the new man that originated in the Enlightenment and was developed thereafter has been tested in socialist countries. To what extent did the ideal become reality? If we acknowledge that the worldwide communist revolution has failed to create a society sustainable in terms of its self-proclaimed ideological and socioeconomic goals, then the aspiration of a new man, who was believed to be capable of perpetuating the revolution against all odds, was never the reality, because if it had been, the revolution would not have failed. Another way to argue that the new man was never the reality is to emphasize a simple fact: in all stages of its development and even in terms of models, the new man was always a complex of fictional and real figures, of legends blended with facts, and it may be true that the fictional and mythical elements constituted a larger part in the complex.

But just as very few things in history are pure in their definition or their commonly perceived roles, the fact that the new man was never a historical reality does not constitute a reason to dismiss him as a phantom or an illusion. Instead, the historical reality of the new man should be perceived more from the perspective of to what extent the efforts to create him were associated with and affected the ideological development and socioeconomic policies in those countries where he was conceived and nurtured. In this sense, the new man did emerge as a sharp contrast to the national character prior to the revolution and to his contemporaries in other parts of the world. Even more so, while demonstrating similar political and moral qualities, the new men who arose in different countries had their own distinctive traits, cultivated in differing ideological and socioeconomic cradles.

The "Soviet man," as the prototype of the communist new man, embodied some basic qualities of the communist new man—ideological conformity, political loyalty, devotion to the party, selflessness, and self-sacrifice—but all were based on a single, more integrating quality: the replacement of self-awareness and spontaneity by class consciousness and guided action. The Soviet Union created a number of institutions such as party schools, the Young Pioneers, and the Communist Youth League and mechanisms such as model emulation and the use of literature and art to fashion an ideal, though fictional, type of new man. The Soviet man took shape in the 1930s as a robust socialist builder, but in the meantime, as the country was undertaking quick industrialization, economic efficiency became a priority, and to an extent compromised some traits of the new man. As a result, the tough aspect of the Soviet Man softened as material incentives and individual interests crept in, education and experience overshadowed revolutionary consciousness, and a party-government bureaucracy generated a new social elite. This tendency continued to develop and finally manifested itself in the early 1960s when many young Russians expressed their awakened self-consciousness and economic debate on material incentives stirred heated ideological debate about the approach toward communism globally.

In the 1960s a more radical and thoroughgoing social-engineering project of creating a new man proceeded in China and Cuba. Mao and Castro, as well as Guevara, were fervent believers in human malleability. Alerted by the Soviet lesson and driven by economic needs, the Maoist and

Castroist regimes took as a primary target on their political agendas the creation of an incorruptible new man, who would perpetuate revolutionary militancy in peacetime and create economic miracles with political devotion. In order to forestall the Soviet revisionist pitfall in their own countries, they launched nationwide campaigns as their most intensive efforts in social engineering—the Chinese Cultural Revolution and the Cuban Revolutionary Offensive. Through these campaigns, they aspired to create an entirely new social environment that would not only clean up all traces of the old society but also break up the bureaucratic system and elite culture that developed after the revolution. The Cultural Revolution and the Revolutionary Offensive might be interpreted from various perspectives, but from the environmental determinist perspective, which could be traced back to the Enlightenment, they were the most radical and grandiose experiments aimed at creating a new environment for the new human species. The Chinese new man, identified as "Mao's good soldiers," and the Cuban new man, described by the slogan "Let them all become Che," thus stood as landmarks at the end of the long pursuit—since the Enlightenment—for an ideal human type.

The ideological and political parallels between China and Cuba were so remarkable that Castro once had to claim his originality in 1969, when asked about the similarities between China's Cultural Revolution and Cuba's Revolutionary Offensive: "If we did something similar to the Chinese Communists, it was an accident of history."[15] The similarities between communist China and Cuba of the 1960s have drawn some attention from scholars. For example, Carmelo Mesa-Lago in the early 1970s put China and Cuba into the same category of socialist countries "characterized by emphasis on ideological development (the goal of a New Man, classless society, egalitarianism, etc.), a mobilization regime, and anti-market tendencies."[16] On the contrary, the priority of the Soviet Union and its satellites was material—rather than moral—development. For that purpose the Soviets and many Eastern European countries introduced economic reforms that resorted to moderate material incentives and the market mechanism. As a response to this trend, Mesa-Lago noted, "the Chinese and Cubans complained that the use of material incentives and market mechanisms was a regressive step in the path towards communism and the development of a New Man, thus supporting moral incentives and egalitarianism." For Mesa-Lago and many others, what set China/Cuba apart from the Soviet Union/Eastern Europe was a difference between "utopians" and "pragmatists"—the former impatiently wanted to press "square people into round holes" immediately, whereas the latter were willing to temporarily "adjust the hole" to the people. Mesa-Lago also synchronized the political events taking place in China and Cuba in the second half of the 1960s. As he put it, "The efforts of the Great Proletarian Cultural Revolution in China and of the Revolutionary Offensive in Cuba have been fairly similar. This seems consistent with the similarities of their systems."[17] Contrary to the expected results, the similar "excessive emphasis on mobilization, moral incentives, and egalitarianism" in the two campaigns brought about the same negative consequences, such as "a slowdown of labor effort, absenteeism, and declines in output and productivity."[18] Like Mesa-Lago, Richard Carson also wrote, in the early 1970s, "Indeed, the Mao-Guevarist 'road to communism' places much more emphasis on a transmutation of human nature so that man is no longer self-seeking."[19]

A more recent and specific comparison between Mao and Castro was made by William Ratliff, who even challenged their "Marxist" stock:

> Each was inclined to look at the world through fundamentally anti-Marxist glasses. Judging by their statements and policies, neither leader accepted Marx's conviction that the political and social superstructures of a society flow from the economic substructure, but rather believed that the economic system must and can be changed by the communist party's prior ideological and political transformation of the masses into "new men." These convictions were most clearly manifested in Mao's Cultural Revolution and Castro's Revolutionary Offensive, the former evidently an important inspiration for the latter. These revolutionary experiments reflected the two leaders' greater attention to subjective rather than objective conditions, to moral over material incentives, to guerrilla-oriented Sierra Maestra (and Yenan) mentalities with their fundamental skepticism toward the institutionalization of a revolution.[20]

Therefore, after more than two centuries of development from Enlightenment ideals to socialist realities, the new man became the fundamental momentum and the centerpiece of the major radical policies and institutional innovations in China and Cuba, from educational reforms and mass model emulation to militarization, antiurban and anti-elite culture, promotion of moral incentives, and so on. The social engineering was carried out through economic projects, even though such projects were supposed to have a practical orientation and to be assessed only by productive efficiency. The drive behind Chinese and Cuban formation of the new man was particularly reinforced by each leader's self-proclaimed role of being their nation's moral mentor; they had that desire long before they became national authorities, and it may not have had much to do with their revolutionary ideology at that moment. Rather, it was a profound disposition of their personalities. People may argue that many Third World leaders, eager to inculcate progressive ideologies or simply modern knowledge in their people, once sought the same position of national mentor—for instance, Kemal in Turkey in the 1920s and Nyerere in Tanzania in the 1960s. But these nationalist leaders were far less philosophically articulate and politically powerful than Mao or Castro in carrying out their respective educational projects.

The "communist new man" was set as the ultimate goal claimed by each communist country, but only in China and Cuba did the regimes regard it as an immediate goal, approach it with enduring enthusiasm, and subject all dimensions of society to it, at least within a certain length of time. If in the Soviet Union the new man was created for the purpose of constructing socialism, then in China and Cuba the new man stood at the center of policies, and the economic projects were regarded as a process in which the new man was to be tempered. When conventional educational efforts seemed to have failed in protecting the growing new man from corruption, the two regimes staged unprecedented nationwide campaigns as their ultimate measures to accelerate the maturation of the new man.

But the aspiration of reshaping human beings was not unique to communist revolutions. It was one of the components of the Enlightenment and had deep roots in the Western intellectual and political tradition. The communist experiments of creating a new man coincided with Western social and cultural crises in the 1930s and 1960s and therefore attracted many Western intellectuals who felt alienated in their own societies and were seeking a spiritual and moral alternative. During the 1960s the Chinese and Cuban experiments also coincided with a wave of decolonization, and some Third World leaders were inspired by the new man's high spirit and dedication, which they thought could provide the moral foundation for their own nation building and citizen education.

The implication and impact of creating a communist new man, therefore, went far beyond the communist movement itself and constituted a world historical phenomenon.

Notes

All translations from Chinese materials with pinyin titles are this author's unless otherwise noted.

INTRODUCTION

1. I use "new man" rather than "new people" because the former is a historical term. In Russian, Chinese, Spanish, and many other languages used in communist countries, the terms for the new human model may differ in implying gender (in some instances specifically associated with women, the term "new woman" was in place); they were all translated into English as "new man" by those who used the terms themselves and by Western authors from the 1920s to the 1960s.

2. Quoted in Mikhail Heller, *Cogs in the Soviet Wheel: The Formation of Soviet Man* (London: Collins Harvill, 1988), 43.

3. For thought reform, see chapter 2 in this book and Robert Jay Lifton, *Thought Reform and the Psychology of Totalism* (New York: Norton, 1969). For brainwashing, see Edward Hunter, *Brainwashing in Red China: The Calculated Destruction of Man's Mind* (New York: Vanguard, 1951); Hunter, *Brainwashing: The Story of Men Who Defied It* (New York: Farrar, Straus, and Cudahy, 1956); and Lifton, *Thought Reform*.

4. Hu Ping, *Ren de xun hua, duo bi yu fan pan* [Man's Taming, Evading, and Rebelling] (Hong Kong: Asia Science Publisher, 1999), 6–7.

5. Leon Trotsky, *Leon Trotsky on Literature and Art* (New York: Pathfinder Press, 1970), 158.

6. Quoted in Heller, *Cogs in the Soviet Wheel*, 27. It was Alexander Zinoviev's satirical novel *Homo Sovieticus* (London: Victor Gollancz, 1985) that helped make the phrase more known in the West, but with negative connotations—as a person created by the Soviet system who was politically indifferent and had no interest in his work.

7. For a full citation of Castro's comments, see Sandra Levinson and Carol Brightman, eds., *Venceremos Brigade: Young Americans Sharing the Life and Work of Revolutionary Cuba; Diaries, Interviews, Tapes, Essays, and Poetry by the Venceremos Brigade* (New York: Monthly Review Press, 1971), 164.

8. In *The "New Man" in Cuba: Culture and Identity in the Revolution* (Tampa: University Press of Florida, 2007), Ana Serra examines political speeches and award-winning novels during the formative years of the Castro regime and argues that Cuban writers during this period made important contributions to the image of the Cuban new man. The perspective of the book is literary criticism, grounded in poststructuralist theories, and thus differs from a historical work.

1. FROM THE ENLIGHTENMENT TO THE SOVIET NEW MAN

1. Nicholas Capaldi, *The Enlightenment—The Proper Study of Mankind: An Anthology* (New York: Capricorn Books, 1968), 18.

2. For a recent discussion on Locke's influence, particularly his *Treatise of Education* and *Essay on Human Understanding,* among British colonizers in India in the eighteenth and nineteenth centuries, see Peter Robb's article "Children, Emotion, Identity and Empire: Views from the Blechyndens' Calcutta Diaries (1790–1822)," *Modern Asian Studies* 40, no. 1 (2006): 175–201.

3. Capaldi, *Enlightenment,* 20.

4. Claude-Adrien Helvétius, "The Nature of Man," in Capaldi, *Enlightenment,* 125.

5. G. V. Plekhanov, *Essays in the History of Materialism* (New York: Howard Fertig, 1967), 85.

6. Isaiah Berlin, *Freedom and Its Betrayal* (Princeton, NJ: Princeton University Press, 2002), 15, 21.

7. Jean-Jacques Rousseau, *On the Social Contract* (New York: St. Martin's Press, 1978), 184.

8. Ibid., 68.

9. Ibid., 46, 54.

10. For example, see Zev M. Trachtenberg, *Making Citizens: Rousseau's Theory of Culture* (New York: St. Martin's Press, 1993).

11. Quoted in J. M. Thompson, *Leaders of the French Revolution* (New York: Barnes and Noble, 1968), 239.

12. Simon Schama, *Citizens: A Chronicle of the French Revolution* (New York: Alfred A. Knopf, 1989), 827–828.

13. J. M. Thompson, *Robespierre* (New York: D. Appleton–Century, 1936), 63.

14. Ibid., 63–64.

15. Schama, *Citizens,* 828.

16. Mona Ozouf, *Festivals and French Revolution* (Cambridge, MA: Harvard University Press, 1988), xi.

17. Ibid., 198.

18. Lowy, *Marxism of Che Guevara,* 21–22.

19. Karl Marx, *A Contribution to the Critique of Political Economy* (Chicago: Charles H. Kerr and Co., 1904), 11–12.

20. Karl Marx, *Poverty of History,* edited by C. P. Dutt and V. Chattopadhyaya (New York: International Publisher, 1936), 124.

21. Karl Marx, *Capital* (New York: Bennett A. Cerf and Donald S. Klopfer, 1936), 529–530.

22. Donald J. Munro, *The Conception of Man in Contemporary China* (Ann Arbor: University of Michigan Press, 1977), 10.

23. See Wang Ruoshui, *Wei ren dao zhu yi bian hu* [Defending Humanism] (Beijing: Sanlian Publisher, 1986). Wang, as a senior party intellectual and philosopher who became critical of Maoism after the Cultural Revolution, was a leading figure in the discussion on alienation under socialism. Wang was dismissed from his official post (deputy general editor of the *People's Daily*) and was expelled from the Chinese Communist Party (CCP) in the late 1980s for his heresy. He spent most of the rest of his life in the United States and died in 2002.

24. Quoted in Saul K. Padover, ed., *On the First International* (New York: McGraw-Hill, 1973), 113.

25. Vladimir C. Nahirny, *The Russian Intelligentsia: From Torment to Silence* (New Brunswick, NJ: Transaction Books, 1987), 87.

26. Ibid., 9.

27. Ibid., 70–71.

28. Ibid., 187.

29. Nikolay Gavrilovich Chernyshevsky, *What Is to Be Done? The Story about the New Man* (New York: Vintage Books, 1961).

30. Elizabeth A. Wood, *The Baba and the Comrade: The Bolsheviks and the Genealogy of the Woman Question* (Bloomington: University of Indiana Press, 1997), 25.

31. Quoted in Dmitri Volkogonov, *Lenin: A New Biography* (New York: Free Press, 1994), 20.

32. Quoted in Philip Pomper, *Sergei Nechaev* (New Brunswick, NJ: Rutgers University Press, 1979), 78.

33. Che Guevara, "Man and Socialism in Cuba," in Bertram Silverman, ed., *Man and Socialism in Cuba:—The Great Debate* (New York: Atheneum, 1971), 352.

34. Edward Shils, "The Intellectuals and the Powers: Some Perspectives for Comparative Analysis," in Philip Rieff, ed., *On Intellectuals* (New York: Anchor Books, 1970), 48.

35. Nahirny, *Russian Intelligentsia,* 123.

36. Maurice Meisner, *Marxism, Maoism, and Utopianism: Eight Essays* (Madison: University of Wisconsin Press, 1982), 83.

37. Maxim Gorky, *Untimely Thoughts* (New Haven, CT: Yale University Press, 1995), 74.

38. Quoted in Ella Winter, *Red Virtue: Human Relationships in the New Russia* (New York: Harcourt, Brace and Co., 1933), 10.

39. Maxim Gorky, "V. I. Lenin," http://aha.ru/~mausoleu/a_lenin/gorky_e.htm.

40. Max Eastman, *Trotsky: A Portrait of His Youth* (New York: Faber and Gwyer, 1925), 117–118.

41. Trotsky, *Leon Trotsky,* 158.

42. Joseph Stalin, "The Lenin Heritage," in Stalin, *Lenin* (New York: International Publishers, 1939), 353.

43. Quoted in Heller, *Cogs in the Soviet Wheel,* title page for the chapter "The Goal." For the reference for Stalin's toast, see Slava Gerovitch, "'New Soviet Man' Inside Machine: Human Engineering, Spacecraft Design, and the Construction of Communism," *Osiris* 22 (2007): 139.

44. Michel Foucault, "What Is Enlightenment?" http://philosophy.eserver.org/foucault/what-is-enlightenment.html.

45. Sinyavsky, *Soviet Civilization,* 115.

46. Frank S. Meyer, *The Molding of Communists* (New York: Harcourt, Brace and Co., 1961), 10.

47. Joost A. M. Meerloo, *The Rape of the Mind: The Psychology of Thought Control, Menticide, and Brainwashing* (New York: University Library, Grosset and Dunlap, 1955), 6.

48. Michael David-Fox, *Revolution of the Mind: Higher Learning among the Bolsheviks 1918–1929* (Ithaca, NY: Cornell University Press, 1997), 45.

49. Meerloo, *Rape of the Mind,* 6.

50. It was not until the mid-1950s, encouraged by the atmosphere of de-Stalinization, that Chinese scientists began to challenge the Soviet doctrines and claim scientific credibility for genetics. For the Chinese discussion on the topic, see L. A. Schneider, "Learning from Russia: Lysenkoism and the Fate of Genetics in China, 1950–1986," in Denis Fred Simon and Merle Goldman, eds., *Science and Technology in Post-Mao China*, Harvard Contemporary China Series, vol. 5 (Cambridge, MA: Harvard University Press, 1989), 45–68.

51. H. G. Wells, *Experimental Biography* (Philadelphia: Lippincott, 1967), 702.

52. David-Fox, *Revolution of the Mind*, 87.

53. R. D. Hess and J. V. Torney, *The Development of Political Attitudes in Children* (Chicago: Aldine, 1967), 7.

54. Stanley Allen Renshon, "Assumptive Frameworks in political Socialization Theory," in Renshon, ed., *Handbook of Political Socialization: Theory and Research* (New York: Free Press, 1977), 5.

55. Richard E. Dawson and Kenneth Prewitt, *Political Socialization* (New York: Little, Brown, 1969), 16.

56. Ibid., 17.

57. Quoted in *Great Soviet Encyclopedia* (1973–1983), s.v. "Russian Communist Youth League," 5:232.

58. Ibid.

59. Ibid., 234.

60. Ibid., "Russian Young Pioneers," 243.

61. The lyrics of the song are as follows: "The five-pointed star is rising over the earth / We proletarian children will build a new world / Forward boldly, you Leninists! / The commune is your watchword / let each of you fulfill the expectation of comrade Lenin / We shall relieve the communist youth. / We are the friends of every worker / The children of the world shall form one family / We will show life a new way, for the old have need of rest / We are children of communist heroes / the spirit of the warriors is strong in us / We will build the commune sooner with the aid of science / Labor and science shall unite to make us stronger / Books will be useful to us and make our work easier / With united strength we are resolved to master science and press on further / Come, you children, follow our fighting cry / We are free minds and not slaves / We are resolved to be tenacious and steadfast—like Il'ich Lenin."

62. Quoted in Helen Redl, ed., *Soviet Educators on Soviet Education* (New York: Free Press, 1964), 150.

63. For a reference to recent investigation on the alleged child-hero, see Catriona Kelly, *Comrade Pavlik: The Rise and Fall of a Soviet Boy Hero* (London: Granta Books, 2006).

64. Redl, *Soviet Educators*, 245.

65. George S. Counts, "The Repudiation of Experiment," in Robert V. Daniels, ed., *Foundations of Soviet Totalitarianism* (Lexington, MA: D. C. Heath and Co., 1972), 121.

66. Ibid., 123.

67. Ibid., 126.

68. Jeffery Brooks, *Thank You, Comrade Stalin!* (Princeton, NJ: Princeton University Press, 1999), 24, 26.

69. Ibid., 85.

70. Quoted in Sinyavsky, *Soviet Communism*, 45.

71. Alexsei Gastev, "We Grow out of Iron," in James von Geldern and Richard Stites, eds., *Mass Culture in Soviet Russia* (Bloomington: Indiana University Press, 1995), 3.

72. Vladimir Kirillov, "The Iron Messiah," in von Geldern and Stites, *Mass Culture in Soviet Russia*, 4.

73. Chen Jian, "Xun zhao ge ming zi lu" [The Road to the Revolution], in Chen Jian, ed., *Yu Chin Peng dui hua* [Dialogue with Chin Peng] (Kuala Lumpur: Centre for Malaysian Chinese Studies, 2006), 363–364.

74. For a news report on the TV series and the sensation it aroused, see Xinhua News Agency, "'Gang tie shi zen yang lian chen de' zai zhong yang dian shi tai bo chu" ["That Is How Steel Was Tempered" Is Showing on China's Central TV], http://www.chinavista .com/news/200002/guonei/ch022902.html.

75. For more on the discussion on Pavel Korchagin and Bill Gates, see "Pavel and Gates: Who Is the Hero?" *People's Daily*, April 22, 2002, http://www.people.com.cn/GB/ shizheng/252/7955/7959/20020422/714386.html. The report describes the discussion and includes the major arguments published in *China Youth Daily* and *Beijing Youth Daily*.

76. Jiang Changbin's online article is titled "Zhi yi *gang tie shi zen yang lian cheng de* li shi bei jing" [Questioning the Historical Background of *That Is How Steel Was Tempered*], http://www.qinxiaojianqi.com/bbs/dispbbs.asp?boardID=108&ID=10489&page=5. For the academic discussion, see Zhang Zhongfeng, "Jing nian lai xue shu jie you guan *gang tie shi zen yang lian cheng de* zheng lun shu ping" [Introduction and Comments on Academic Discussions on *That Is How Steel Was Tempered* in Recent Years], *He nan shi fan da xue xue bao* [Study Journal of Henan Normal University] 5 (2002).

77. Quoted in Heller, *Cogs in the Soviet Wheel*, 201.

78. Alexandra Kollontai, *The Autobiography of a Sexually Emancipated Communist Woman* (New York: Schocken Books, 1975). The article "The New Woman" is included in the book.

79. Quoted in Heller, *Cogs in the Soviet Wheel*, 200–201.

80. Ibid., 202.

81. Barbara Evans Clements, "The Birth of the New Soviet Women," in Abbott Gleason, Peter Kenez, and Richard Stites, eds., *Bolshevik Culture* (Bloomington: Indiana University Press, 1985), 220.

82. For an introduction and analysis of the stratification in Soviet society produced in the early years of the cold war, see Alex Inkeles, "Myth and Reality of Social Classes," in Alex Inkeles and Kent Geiger, eds., *Soviet Society: A Book of Readings* (Boston: Houghton Mifflin, 1961), 558–573 (originally published as "Social Stratification and Mobility in the Soviet Union: 1940–1950," *American Sociological Review* 15 [1950]: 465–479); and Robert A. Feldmesser, "Toward the Classless Society?" in Inkeles and Geiger, *Soviet Society*, 573–582 (originally published as "Equality and Inequality under Khrushchev," *Problems of Communism* 9 [1960]: 31–39).

83. Mikhail Heller and Aleksandr M. Nekrich, *Utopia in Power* (New York: Simon and Schuster, 1982), 284.

84. Ibid.

85. Inkeles, "Myth and Reality," 561.

86. Harald Hallaraker, "Soviet Discussion on Enterprise Incentives and Methods of Planning," *Economics of Planning* 3, no. 1 (1963): 54. The quotation is Hallaraker's summary of Liberman's points. The same book has an English version of Liberman's article on pages 55–61.

87. See Janusz G. Zielinski, "Centralization and Decentralization in Decision-Making," *Economic Planning* 3, no. 3 (1963): 196–203; Zielinski, "Notes on Incentive Systems of Socialist Enterprises," *Economics of Planning* 7, no. 3 (1967): 258–265; Lars Porsholt,

"Socialist Market Economy in Czechoslovakia?" *Economics of Planning* 5, nos. 1–2 (1965): 87–93 (this article is a compilation of translations of two essays by two Czechoslovakian economists); and Ludek Rychetnik, "Two Models of an Enterprise in Market Socialism," *Economics of Planning* 8, no. 3 (1968): 216–231. For the Chinese promotion of its "socialist market economy" to Cuba and Castro's thoughts about it, see Yinghong Cheng, "Fidel Castro and 'China's Lesson for Cuba,'" *China Quarterly* 189 (March 2007): 24–42.

88. "The Action Program of the Communist Party of Czechoslovakia," April 1968. Quoted in Paul Ello, *Czechoslovakia's Blueprint for Freedom* (Washington, DC: Acropolis Books, 1968), 107.

89. Ibid.

90. For a brief introduction to Sun Yefang and the accusation, see Zhong gong zhong yang dang shi yan jiu shi [Research Department of the History of the Chinese Communist Party], *Zhong guo gong chan dang li shi da shi jie* [Chronology of the History of the Chinese Communist Party] (Beijing: Zhongdong Dangshi Publisher, 2006), 228.

91. Peter Clecak, "Moral and Material Incentives," *Socialist Register* (1969): 101.

92. Ibid.

93. Marc Slonim, *Soviet Russian Literature: Writers and Problems, 1917–1977* (New York: Oxford University Press, 1977), 383.

94. René Fueloep-Miller, *The Mind and Face of Bolshevism* (New York: Harper and Row, 1965), 315.

95. Quoted in Gerovitch, "'New Soviet Man' Inside Machine," 136.

96. Ibid., 136–137.

2. "BE MAO'S GOOD SOLDIERS"

1. Confucius, *Lun yu* [Analects], in Wang Xiangqian, ed., *Zhu Zi Jie Cheng* [Anthology of Classical Masters] (Shanghai: Shanghai Shudian Publisher, 1987), 1:274–275.

2. Xunzi, *Xunzi*, in ibid., 289.

3. Quoted in Gao Hua, *Hong tai yang shi zen yang sheng qi de: Yan an zheng feng de lai long qu mai* [That Is How the Red Sun Rose: The Origin and Development of the Yan'an Rectification] (Hong Kong: Hong Kong Chinese University Press, 2000), 423.

4. Philip C. Huang, *Liang Ch'i-ch'ao and Modern Chinese Liberalism* (Seattle and London: University of Washington Press, 1972), 63.

5. Ibid.

6. Chen Duxiu, "Xin qing nian" [New Youth], in *Chen Duxiu wen zhang xuan bian* [Selection of Chen Duxiu's Writings] (Beijing: Sanlian Publisher, 1984), 1:112–114.

7. Li Dazhao, *Li Dazhao wen xuan* [Selected Works of Li Dazhao] (Beijing: Renmin Publisher, 1984), 1:42–44.

8. Quoted in Li Yongtai, *Zhong xi wen hua yu mao ze dong zhao qi si xiang* [Mao's Early Ideological Development under the Influence of Chinese and Western Cultures] (Chengdu: Sichuan University Press, 1989), 98.

9. Ibid., 92–95. For more general studies on Chinese intellectuals in the 1910s and 1920s, see Vera Schwarcz, *Chinese Enlightenment: Intellectuals and the Legacy of the May Fourth Movement of 1919* (Berkeley: University of California Press, 1986).

10. Quoted in Li Yongtai, *Mao's Early Ideological Development,* 109.

11. Jane L. Price, *Cadres, Communists, and Commissars: The Training of the Chinese Communist Leadership, 1920–1945* (Boulder, CO: Westview Press, 1976), 45. For a more

recent study on this issue, see Hans J. van de Ven, *From Friends to Comrades: The Founding of the Chinese Communist Party, 1920–1927* (Berkeley: University of California Press, 1991).

12. Edgar Snow, *Red China Today: The Other Side of the River* (New York: Random House, 1972), 147.

13. Quoted in Hans J. van de Ven, *From Friends to Comrades*, 161.

14. Ibid., 162.

15. E. Snow, *Red China Today*, 167.

16. Mao Zedong, *Talks at the Yan'an Conference on Literature and Art* (Ann Arbor: Center for Chinese Studies, University of Michigan, 1980), 79.

17. Liu Shaoqi, "Ren de jie ji xing" [The Class Nature of People], in *Si xiang zhi nan* [Ideological Guidelines] (Hong Kong: Hong Kong Sanlian Publisher, 1949), 1.

18. Liu Shaoqi, *Zen yang zhuo yi ge hao de gong chan dang yuan* [How to Be a Good Communist] (Hong Kong: New Democracy Press, 1950), 4.

19. Ibid., 8.

20. Liu Shaoqi, "Class Nature of People," 5.

21. Mao Zedong, "Talks at the Yan'an Conference on Literature and Art," in *Selected Works of Mao Tse-Tung* (Beijing: Foreign Language Press, 1967), 3:73.

22. R. Price, *Education in Communist China* (New York: Praeger, 1970), 87.

23. Maria Hsia Chang, *The Labors of Sisyphus: The Economic Development of Communist China* (New Brunswick, NJ: Transaction Publishers, 1998), 22.

24. David E. Apter, "Discourses as Power: Yan'an and the Chinese Revolution," in Tony Saich and Hans van de Ven, eds., *New Perspectives on the Chinese Communist Revolution* (Armonk, NY: M. E. Sharpe, 1995), 193.

25. Qu Changchuan, "Lun ke fu ge ren zhu yi: Wo zai yan an zheng feng zhong de jin li" [On Overcoming Individualism: My Experience in the Yan'an Rectification], in Qiang Xiaochu, ed., *Hui yi yan an zheng feng* [Memoirs of the Yan'an Rectification] (Harbin: Heilongjiang People's Publisher, 1958), 21.

26. Apter, "Discourse as Power," 210.

27. Jerome Chen, ed., *Mao Papers: Anthology and Bibliography* (London: Oxford University Press, 1970), 11.

28. Mao Zedong, "In Memory of Norman Bethune," in *Selected Works of Mao Tse-Tung*, 3:337.

29. Mao Zedong, "Serve the People," in *Selected Works of Mao Tse-Tung*, 3:177.

30. Mao Zedong, "The Foolish Old Man Who Removed the Mountains," in *Selected Works of Mao Tse-Tung*, 3:272.

31. John Starr, *Continuing the Revolution: The Political Thought of Mao* (Princeton, NJ: Princeton University Press, 1979), 225.

32. Mao Zedong, "A Letter to Xu Teli," in Jerome Chen, *Mao Papers*, 5.

33. Gao, *That Is How the Red Sun Rose*, 399.

34. Zhang Xianling, "Hui yi yan an zheng feng" [Memoirs of the Yan'an Rectification], in Qiang Xiaochu, ed., *Memoirs of the Yan'an Rectification*, 23–24.

35. Cases of torture were common during the Yan'an Rectification. One source is the recently published memoir by Zeng Zhi, a female revolutionary who experienced the campaign and suffered from interrogation for a fortnight. In her memoir she gave vivid descriptions of various methods of torture and the stories of victims. See Zeng Zhi, *Yi ge ge min de xin chun zhe* [A Survivor of the Revolution] (Guangzhou: Guangdong Renmin Publisher, 1999.)

36. Kosa, *Two Generations of Soviet Man,* 56.

37. Ibid., 58.

38. Gao, *That Is How the Red Sun Rose,* 425.

39. Ibid., 525–526.

40. Ibid., 435.

41. Ibid.

42. Ibid., 423.

43. Chang, *Labors of Sisyphus,* 22.

44. Mao Zedong, "San da yun dong de wei da sheng li" [Great Victories of the Three Campaigns], in *Selected Works of Mao Zedong,* 5:65.

45. Wei Chengsi, ed., *Zhong guo dang dai jiao yu si chao 1949–1987* [Educational Thought in Contemporary China, 1949–1987] (Shanghai: Sanlian Publisher, 1988), 35.

46. Lin Zi, *Gong chan dang zhong guo de si xiang gai zhao* [Thought Reform in Communist China] (Hong Kong: Chuang Keng Publisher, 1953), 57–58.

47. Ibid.

48. Ibid., 61–64.

49. Jiang Nanxiang, "Yu kai de jie shou ren min zheng fu de an pai, beng fu jian she de zhan dou gang wei" [Cheerfully Accept the Assignment of the People's Government and Go to the Fighting Positions of Construction], in Propaganda Department of the Committee of the Youth League of Northwestern China, ed., *Fu cong zhu guo yao qiu, can jia zu guo jian she* [Obey the Fatherland's Demand: Participate in the Fatherland's Construction] (Lanzhou: Xibei Qingnian Publisher, 1952), 2.

50. Pavel Korchagin is the main character in the Soviet novel *That Is How Steel Was Tempered,* discussed in chapter 1.

51. Wu Yunduo, *Ba yi qie xian gei dang* [Dedicating Everything to the Party] (Beijing: Gongren Publisher, 1963), 4.

52. Shen Yan, *Min Suofu: An quan xin shi de yi mian qi zhi* [Min Suofu: A Model of Safe Driving] (Shanghai: Shanghai Renmin Publisher, 1956), 5.

53. Fang Shuming and Huang Jichang, *Xiang xiuli* [Xiang Xiuli] (Beijing: Zhongguo Qingnian Publisher, 1959), 36.

54. Hubei Provincial Committee of the Chinese Communist Party, *Ma xueli* [Ma Xueli] (Wuhan: Hubei Renmin Publisher, 1959), 6.

55. Mao Zedong, "Lun ren min min zhu zhuan zheng" [On People's Democratic Dictatorship], in *Selected Works of Mao Zedong,* combined ed., 1366.

56. John King Fairbank, *The Great Chinese Revolution, 1800–1985* (New York: Harper and Row, 1986), 282.

57. Wu Si, *Chen yong gui chen fu zhong nan hai: Gai zhao zhong guo de shi yan* [The Rise and Fall of Chen Yonggui: The Experiment of Reforming China] (Guangzhou: Huacheng Publisher, 1993), 2.

58. Qin Hongyi, "Mao zedong he liu shao qi zai nong ye he zuo hua wen ti shang reng shi de cha yi" [The Differences between Mao Zedong and Liu Shaoqi on Agricultural Collectivization], *Gunagxi she hui ke xue* [Guangxi Social Science Journal] 7 (2004): 120.

59. Department of the Study of Marxism and Leninism, Jinan University, *Dang de ba jie liu zhong quan hui xue xi cai liao* [Study Materials for the Party's Sixth Plenary Session of the Eighth Central Committee] (Guangzhou, 1959), 14.

60. Wu Si, *Rise and Fall of Chen Yonggui,* 44.

61. *People's Daily,* February 3, 1958.

62. It is noteworthy that about twenty years later (from 1975 to 1977), collective dining halls became the distinctive feature of Cambodian communism when Pol Pot carried out his project of collectivization. The Khmer Rouge considered the family dining hall as "the capitalist framework" and were proud of their achievement of abolishing it. They said that even "in those otherwise admirable countries," such as China, families still ate together and that "postponed the success of the revolution." See David P. Chandler, *Brother Number 1: A Political Biography of Pol Pot* (Boulder, CO: Westview Press, 1992), 126.

63. Department of the Study of Marxism and Leninism, *Study Materials*, 15.

64. Mao Zedong, "Xue sheng de gong zuo" [Students' Work], in Editing Group of Mao Zedong's Early Writings, Hunan Province Committee of the Chinese Communist Party, ed., *Mao ze dong de zhao nian wen gao* [Mao Zedong's Early Writings] (Changsha: Hunan Publisher, 1990), 450.

65. Xiao Yu, *Mao ze dong de qin nian shi dai* [Biography of Early Mao Zedong] (Taipei: Libai Publisher, 1987), 210.

66. Department of the Study of Marxism and Leninism, *Study Materials*, 32–33.

67. For a comparative study of the Chinese-Cuban educational revolutions in Maoist and Castroist regimes, see Yinghong Cheng and Patrick Manning, "Education in Revolution: China and Cuba in Global Context, 1957–76," *Journal of World History* 14, no. 3 (2003): 359–391.

68. Wei, *Educational Thought*, 2.

69. Zhou Quanhua, *Wen hua da ge ming zhong de jiao yu ge ming* [The Education Revolution in the Cultural Revolution] (Guangzhou: Gunagdong Jiaoyu Publisher, 1999), 425.

70. Mao Zedong, *Guan yu zheng que chu li Ren min nei bu mao dun wen ti* [On Correctly Dealing with Contradictions among the People] (Beijing: Renmin Publisher, 1959), 23.

71. Zhou Quanhua, *Education Revolution*, 465.

72. Ibid. "Associate doctorate" was a Soviet degree equivalent to a Master's in the Western academic hierarchy.

73. Wei, *Educational Thought*, 86–88.

74. Education Ministry of the People's Republic of China, ed., *Zhong guo jiao yu nian jian* [The Yearbook of Chinese Education], 1949–1981 (Beijing: Zhongguo Jiaoyu Publisher, 1982), 467.

75 Ibid.

76. *People's Daily*, April 13, 1958.

77. Ibid., July 30, 1958.

78. Ibid.

79. Quoted in Zhou Quanhua, *Education Revolution*, 447.

80. Mao Zedong, "Students' Work," 450.

81. Stuart Schram, ed., *Chairman Mao Talks to the People* (New York: Pantheon Books, 1974), 242–252.

82. For a brief introduction to this subject, see John Wellens, "The Anti-Intellectual Tradition in the West," *British Journal of Educational Studies* 8, no. 1 (1959): 22–28.

83. Anonymous, *Mao zhu xi zai Ren min zhong jian* [Chairman Mao among the People] (Beijing: Renmin Publisher, 1958), 62. Mao's idea was echoed by other leaders. For example, Tao Zhu, the party secretary of Guangdong Province, said that a benefit of the people's communes would be to combine the steelworkers' job with agricultural labor: "The steelworkers are very tired after working in front of the furnace every day. If they participated

in some agricultural labor when they are off duty, such a switch would refresh them, be good for their health, and be much better for their spirit." Department of the Study of Marxism and Leninism, *Study Materials*, 16.

84. Anonymous, *Er guo min chui pai wen xuan* [The Anthology of Russian Populists] (Beijing: Renmin Publisher, 1963), 65.

85. Gong Yuzhi, *Gong Yuzhi hui yi* [Memoir of Gong Yuzhi] (Nanchang: Jiangxi Renmin Publisher, 2008), 323. The appendix, "Some Materials about the Historical Development of the Soviet Educational Guideline," runs from page 367 to page 411.

86. Charles Ridley and Dennis Doolin, *The Making of a Model Citizen in Communist China* (Stanford, CA: Hoover Institution Press, 1971), 8.

87. William F. Dorrill, "Leadership and Succession in Communist China," *Current History* (September 1965): 133.

88. *People's Daily*, February 19, 1964.

89. Joint Editorial of *People's Daily* and *Red Flag*, "Guan yu he lu xiao fu de jia gong chan zhu yi ji qi zai shi jie lis hi shang de jiao xun: Jiu ping su gong zhong yang de gong kai xin" [On Khrushchev's Phony Communism and Its Lesson in World History: The Ninth Commentary on the Open Letter of the Central Committee of the Communist Party of the Soviet Union], *People's Daily*, August 3, 1964.

90. Schram, *Chairman Mao Talks*, 242–252.

91. *People's Liberation Army Daily*, editorial, November 23, 1964.

92. Mary Sheridan, "The Emulation of Heroes," *China Quarterly* (January–March 1968): 56.

93. Lei Feng, *Lei feng ri ji* [Lei Feng's Diary] (Beijing: Zhongguo Qingnian Publisher, 1965), 34.

94. Anonymous, *Lun lei feng* [On Lei Feng] (Beijing: Beijing Publisher, 1965), 4.

95. Chan, *Children of Mao*, 45.

96. Wang Jie, *Wang jie ri ji* [Wang Jie's Diary] (Beijing: Renmin Publisher, 1965), 27.

97. Mary Sheridan first noticed this pattern. See her article "Emulation of Heroes."

98. Ibid., 57.

99. Anonymous, "Xue xi wei ren min fu wu" [Study "Serve the People"], *Liberation Army Daily*, November 30, 1966.

100. Schram, *Chairman Mao Talks*, 245.

101. *People's Daily*, editorial, March 3, 1966.

102. Anonymous, *Xiang Jiao Yulu xue xi zuo mao zhu xi de hao xue sheng* [Learn from Jiao Yulu and Be Chairman Mao's Good Student] (Hong Kong: Hong Kong Sanlian Publisher, 1966), 33.

103. Anonymous, *Wei fengying—mao zhu xi de hao gong ren* [Wei Fengying—Chairman Mao's Good Worker] (Beijing: Renmin Publisher, 1965), 3.

104. Ibid., 7–20.

105. But it is ironic that it was Liu Shaoqi who decided to send Mao's works to the workers for inspiration. A few years later, in the Cultural Revolution, he was disgraced and died miserably as the number one "capitalist roader."

106. Wang Jingxi, *Du zhu xi de shu, ting mao zhu xi de hua, wei shi you shi ye er feng dou* [Read the Chairman's Book, Listen to the Chairman's Words, Strive for the Cause of the Proletariat] (Beijing: Shi You Hua Gong Shiyou Huagong Publisher, 1977), 5.

107. Ibid., 24.

108. Ibid., 13.

109. Wu Si, *Rise and Fall of Chen Yonggui*, 53.

110. "The Road of Dazhai," *People's Daily,* September 19, 1965.

111. Interestingly, it was Qian Xuesen who tried to persuade Qian Weichang (they were close friends) to leave China for the United States immediately before the Communists' takeover. (See the section "The Early 1950s: Thought Reform among Intellectuals and Students" above in this chapter.) Qian Weichang agreed to leave but afterward changed his mind. During the campaign of thought reform in the early 1950s, he revealed this incident, condemning himself and Qian Xuesen as well. Qian Weichang later was trusted enough by the party to be used as an example of a reeducated former bourgeois intellectual. He received several honorable official titles after that. However, when Qian Xueseng went back to China during the mid-1950s, as arranged by Zhou Enlai, the premier, and became a leading figure in China's nuclear project, Qian Weichang's fame was eclipsed by Qian Xuesen's, and, naturally, the story of persuading him to leave China was never mentioned.

112. "The Road of Dazhai," *People's Daily,* September 19, 1965.

113. Lin Biao, "Lin biao tong zhi zai qing zhu wu chan ji jie wen hua da ge min qun zhong da hui shang de jiang hua" [Comrade Lin Biao's Speech at the Mass Rally Celebrating the Great Proletarian Cultural Revolution], August 18, 1966. Reprinted in Anonymous, ed., *Ba wu chan jie ji wen hua da ge min jin xindao di* [Carry the Great Proletarian Revolution through to the End] (Beijing, 1966), 30.

114. Schram, *Chairman Mao Talks,* 213.

115. Ibid., 246.

116. Ibid., 213.

117. Ibid., 215.

118. Quoted in David Milton and Nancy Milton, eds., *People's China: Social Experimentation; Politics, Entry onto the World Scene, 1966 through 1972* (New York: Random House, 1974), 263.

119. Central Committee of the Chinese Communist Party, *Decision of the Central Committee of the Chinese Communist Party Concerning the Great Cultural Revolution* (Beijing: Foreign Language Press, 1966), 1.

120. *People's Daily,* editorial, July 19, 1968.

121. Wang Youqin, "Student Attacks against Teachers: The Revolution of 1966," *Journal of Chinese and International Affairs* (March–April 2001): 29–79. Wang also published a book in Chinese detailing the atrocities with firsthand materials (often interviews with witnesses and victims' relatives, co-workers, and friends). For reference, see Wang Youqin, *Wen ge shou nan zhe* [Victims of the Cultural Revolution] (Hong Kong: Open Monthly Publisher, 2004).

122. Anita Chan recorded a former Red Guard's account of students humiliating their authoritarian classmaster to release their pent-up complaints. "As long as he was the classmaster," the student said, "he was always in control of the students. Psychologically you could feel he was controlling you." But in the summer of 1966, when the CR turned the school upside down, his students—now the Red Guards—"grabbed" his collar and brought him to the classroom. When the rest of the class saw him, "immediately, their awe of the classmaster was gone. The teacher was shaking. He had never dreamt of this. He spoke with a trembling voice, no longer his former self." Chan, *Children of Mao,* 126.

123. Lin Jin, *The Red Guards' Path to Violence: Political, Educational and Psychological Factors* (New York: Praeger, 1991).

124. Xu Youyu, *Xin xin se se de zhao fan pai: Hong wei bin jing sheng shu zhi de xing cheng ji yan bian* [Rebels of All Stripes: A Study of Red Guard Mentalities] (Hong Kong: Chinese University Press, 1999), 36.

125. Ibid.

126. Ibid., 40.

127. Mao Zedong, "Hunan nong ming yun dong kao cha bao gao" [The Report of an Investigation of the Hunan Peasant Movement], in *Selected Works of Mao Zedong,* combined edition, 17.

128. Li Dazhao, *Anthology,* 1:44.

129. Pei Yiran, "Dang dai zhong guo gong nong gan bu yu zhi shi feng zhi mao dun de you lai yuhou guo" [The Origin and Consequences of the Contradiction between Worker-Peasant Cadres and Intellectuals in Contemporary China], *Dang dai zhong guo yan jiu* [Modern China Studies] 14, no. 2 (2007): 98.

130. Guo Moruo, "Zai lei feng ta xia [Under Leifeng Pagoda], in *Guo mo ruo wen xuan* [Selections of Guo Moruo's Works] (Beijing: Renmin Wenxue Publisher, 1982), 1:165.

131. "Hei long jiang liu he wu qi gan xiao de jin yan" [The Experience of Heilongjiang Liu He May Seventh School], *People's Daily,* October 4, 1968.

132. Zhao Feng, *Hong se niu peng—wu qie gan xiao de zheng shi gu shi* [Red Cowsheds—the Real Stories of the May Seventh Cadre Schools] (Xining: Qinghai Renmin, 1999), 5.

133. Pei, "Origin and Consequences," 101.

134. Ibid., 196.

135. Zhao Feng, *Red Cowsheds,* 8.

136. Shawn Macale, "Vietnamese Marxism, Dissent, and the Politics of Postcolonial Memory: Tran Duc Thao, 1946–1993," *Journal of Asian Studies* 61 (2002): 29.

137. Qiu Yihong, *Sheng min ru he liu: Xin, ma, tai shi liu wei nu xin de gu shi* [Life Is Like a River: Stories of 16 Women from Singapore, Malaya, and Thailand] (Selangor, Malaysia: Che Lue Zi Xun Yan Jiu Zhong Xin, 2004), 301–303.

138. Mao Zedong, "Zai sheng shi zi zhi qu dang wei shu ji hui yi shang de jiang hua" [Talk in the Meetings of the Party's Secretaries of Provinces and Autonomous Regions], in *Selected Works of Mao Zedong,* 6:339.

139. *People's Daily,* April 4, 1966.

140. When the party initiated a campaign, it was customary to publish an official guideline with a case example.

141. Ding Yizhuang, *Zhong guo zhi qing shi 1953–1968* [History of the Sent-Down Chinese Educated Youth: 1953–1968] (Beijing: Zhongguo Shehui Kexue Publisher, 1998), 12.

142. The law establishing the system, entitled Regulations on Household Registration in the People's Republic of China, was approved by the Standing Committee of the First National People's Congress in January 1958. For a recent study of the subject, see Fei-Ling Wang, *Organizing through Division and Exclusion* (Stanford, CA: Stanford University Press, 2003).

143. Ding, *History of the Sent-Down Chinese Youth,* 450.

144. The rustication had two forms. In one form, individual youths were sent to villages. In the other form, they were organized into paramilitary units and were sent to militarized farms, where they lived in barracks. Youths in Niutianyang belonged to the latter form.

145. For a detailed report on the Niutianyang incident, see Chen Mingyang, "Niutianyang de 'jing sheng yuan zi dan'" [The "Spiritual Atomic Bomb" of Niutianyang], published in commemoration of the twentieth anniversary of the incident in *Nanfang Zhoumo* [Southern Weekend], a weekly published in Guangzhou, July 30, 1999.

146. Zhu Chengfa, *Hong chao: Xin hua zuo yi wen xue de wen ge chao* [The Red Tide: Singapore's Chinese Left Literature under the Influence of China's Cultural Revolution] (Singapore: Lingzi Media, 2004), 127.

147. Ibid.

3. "LET THEM ALL BECOME CHE"

1. Richard R. Fagen, *The Transformation of Political Culture in Cuba* (Stanford, CA: Stanford University Press, 1969), 13.

2. John M. Kirk, *Jose Marti, Mentor of the Cuban Nation* (Tampa: University Press of Florida, 1983), 86.

3. Ibid., 87.

4. Ibid., 96.

5. Ibid.

6. Ibid., 90.

7. Ibid., 105.

8. Ibid., 201.

9. Carlos Ripoll, *Jose Marti, the United States, and the Marxist Interpretation of Cuban History* (New Brunswick, NJ: Transaction Books, 1984), 39–40.

10. Ibid., 40.

11. Ibid., 47.

12. Enrico Mario Santi, "Jose Marti and the Cuban Revolution," *Cuban Studies* 16 (1986): 146–147.

13. Philip S. Foner, *Antonio Maceo, The "Bronze Titan" of Cuba's Struggle for Independence* (New York: Monthly Review Press, 1977), 252.

14. Fagen, *Transformation of Political Culture,* 2.

15. Sheldon B. Liss, *Roots of Revolution: Radical Thought in Cuba* (Lincoln, NE, and London: University of Nebraska Press, 1987), 40–41.

16. Ibid., xxi.

17. Fidel Castro, "To Create Wealth with Social Conscience," in Bertram Silverman, *Man and Socialism in Cuba: The Great Debate* (New York: Atheneum, 1971), 361.

18. Guevara, "Man and Socialism in Cuba," 340.

19. Fidel Castro, *My Early Years* (New York: Ocean Press, 1998), prefatory page.

20. Levinson and Brightman, *Venceremos Brigade,* 164.

21. Guevara, "Man and Socialism in Cuba," 338.

22. Lowy, *Marxism of Che Guevara,* 28.

23. Ibid.

24. Thomas C. Dalton, *"Everything within the Revolution": Cuban Strategies for Social Development since 1960* (Boulder, CO: Westview Press, 1993), 20. The section is titled "The Jesuit Origins of Conciencia."

25. Ibid., 21.

26. Ibid., 23.

27. Elizabeth Sutherland, *The Youngest Revolution: A Personal Report on Cuba* (New York: Dial Press, 1981), 137.

28. Oscar Lewis, Ruth M. Lewis, and Susan M. Rigdon, *Four Women: Living the Revolution; An Oral History of Contemporary Cuba* (Chicago: University of Chicago Press, 1977), 102.

29. K. S. Karol, *Guerrillas in Power* (New York: Hill and Wang, 1970), 383.

30. Guevara, "Man and Socialism in Cuba," 338.

31. Ibid., 339.

32. Fidel Castro, *The Second Declaration of Havana* (New York: Pathfinder Press: 1962), 20–21.

33. Guevara, "Man and Socialism in Cuba," 336.

34. C. Fred Judson, *Cuba and the Revolutionary Myth: The Political Education of the Cuban Rebel Army, 1953–1963* (Boulder, CO, and London: Westview Press, 1984), 2.

35. Ibid., 3.

36. Ibid., 9.

37. Tzvi Medin, *Cuba: The Shaping of Revolutionary Consciousness* (Boulder, CO, and London: Lynne Rienner, 1990), 9.

38. Ibid., 9–10.

39. Ibid., 7.

40. Fagen, *Transformation of Political Culture*, 15.

41. Medin, *Cuba*, 7.

42. Ibid.

43. Ibid., 7–8.

44. Richard R. Fagen, *Cuba: The Political Content of Adult Education* (Stanford, CA: Hoover Institution, 1964), 11. Fagen's figure was based on a Cuban Ministry of Education report of January 1962.

45. Ibid., 24–53.

46. Ibid., 47.

47. Ibid., 63.

48. Ibid., 12.

49. Ibid.

50. Fidel Castro, "Castro Pledges 100 percent Literacy," 1961 speech, http://www1.lanic.utexas.edu.

51. Ana Serra, "The Literacy Campaign in the Cuban Revolution and the Transformation of Identity in the Liminal Space of the Sierra," *Journal of Latin American Cultural Studies* 10, no. 1 (2001): 313–332.

52. Lewis, Lewis, and Rigdon, *Four Women*. The girl's name was Monica, and the book devoted seven chapters to her personal experience (pp. 3–128).

53. Liss, *Fidel!* 26.

54. Fagen, *Transformation of Political Culture*, 13.

55. Ibid., 71.

56. Ibid., 80.

57. Quoted in ibid., 81.

58. For a more comprehensive diplomatic history of the Beijing-Havana-Moscow triangle in the 1960s, see Yinghong Cheng, "Sino-Cuban Relations during the Early Years of the Castro Regime, 1959–1966," *Journal of Cold War Studies* 9, no. 3 (2007): 78–114.

59. *People's Daily*, New Year editorial, January 1, 1959.

60. Huang Ziliang, *La ting mei zhou de zai fa xian* [Rediscovery of Latin America] (Beijing: Shijie Zhishi Publisher, 2004), 76.

61. Wang Taipin, *Zhong hua Renmin gong he guo wai jiao shi* [The Diplomatic History of the People's Republic of China] (Beijing: Shijie Zhishi Publisher, 1998), vol. 2, *1957–1969*, 489.

62. Mao Zedong, *Jian guo yi lai mao ze dong wen gao* [Mao Zedong's *Manuscripts since the Foundation of the PRC*] (Beijing: Renmin Publisher, 1996), 8:465.

63. For example, Castro's interview with Herbert Matthews of the *New York Times* in February 1958 was published in a three-part series and subsequently created an enormous sensation in favor of the Fidelistas in the United States.

64. There were some connections between the July 26 Movement and the PSP prior to the former's victory. The PSP sent delegations to visit Castro in the Sierra Maestra and

had representatives staying with the guerrillas, but they did not cooperate with Castro's forces in large-scale actions.

65. For example, in April 1960, when Qian Liren, the deputy director of the International Liaison Department of the Chinese Communist Party (ILDCCP), led a Chinese youth delegation to attend the Fourth Congress of the League of Cuban Socialist Youth (a PSP organization), he met Anibal Escalante, the PSP's executive secretary. In the meeting, as Zeng Tao (director of the XNA Havana branch) recalled, Escalante discussed the possibility of uniting three revolutionary forces—namely, the PSP, the Fidelistas, and the Directorio Revolucionario—into a single party. Escalante was apparently showing the Chinese the efforts his party had made to push Cuba toward socialism. Four months later, in August, Wu Xiuquan, a member of the CCP's Central Committee and one of the deputy directors of the ILDCCP, led a delegation to attend the PSP's Eighth Congress. Wu met Blas Roca, the PSP's general secretary, who told the delegation, "There is a 95 percent possibility that, together with the PSP, Castro will be taking the socialist road." Zeng Tao, *Wai jiao shen ya shi qi nian* [My Seventeen-Year Diplomatic Career] (Nanjing: Jiangsu Renmin Publisher, 1997), 19–20.

66. The name was changed to the United Party of the Socialist Revolution (Partido Unido de la Revolución Socialista) in 1963, and to the Communist Party of Cuba (Partido Comunista de Cuba, or PCC) in October 1965.

67. Tan Wenrui, "Gu ba ge min de wei da duo shou" [The Great Helmsman of the Cuban Revolution], in Anonymous, ed., *Yin xiong de gu ba* [Heroic Cuba] (Beijing: Shijie Zhishi Publisher, 1962), 1. The article was originally published in the *People's Daily*, November 2, 1962.

68. Wang Taipin, *Diplomatic History*, 491.

69. Shen Jian, "Wo de wai jia shen ya" [The Bygones of My Foreign Missions], in Wu Xiuquan and Liu Xiao, eds., *Wo de da si shen ya* [My Career as an Ambassador] (Nanjing: Jiangsu Renmin Publisher, 1993), 111. The Sino-Cuban diplomatic relationship was established in September 1960, but the Chinese ambassador was dispatched six months later, largely due to the time required for preparation of the legation on both sides. The XNA's Havana branch served as the governmental channel before the embassy was officially established.

70. "Facts on Sino-Cuban Trade," interview with a "responsible foreign trade official," *People's Daily*, January 10, 1966.

71. Wang Taipin, *Diplomatic History*, 196.

72. Shen Jian, "Bygones of My Foreign Missions," 121. This is the Chinese version of Guevara's words, and there may be the similar quotations in other sources.

73. Cuba's per capita rice consumption was much higher than that of the average Latin American country. Before the revolution, the United States was the rice provider for Cuba. Due to mismanagement and America's economic sanction, rice rationing was imposed in Cuba in 1962.

74. Wang Taipin, *Diplomatic History*, 495. According to this author, the first Chinese purchase of Cuban sugar was made in December 1959, in the amount of 50,000 tons. The second was made in July 1960, in the amount of 500,000 tons, which was a diversion of sugar originally intended for the Soviets. The third such purchase was made during Guevara's visit, in November 1960, in the amount of 1 million tons. Ibid., 490, 492.

75. Ibid., 495.

76. Damian J. Fernandez, "Cuba's Relations with China: Economic Pragmatism and Political Fluctuation," in Donna Rich Kaplowitz, ed., *Cuba's Ties to a Changing World* (Boulder, CO: Lynne Rienner, 1993), 19.

77. Bo Yibo, "The Socialist Industrialization of China," *Peking Review* 41 (October 11, 1963), 11.

78. Zeng Tao, *My Seventeen Years*, 21–22. Twenty-five years later, in 1986, when Zhen led a Chinese People's Congress delegation to Cuba, his request for visiting Cuban grocery stores was reluctantly granted, but his host, the chairman of the Cuban Foreign Trade Commission, frankly acknowledged that there was no comparison between food supply in China and Cuba. When Zhen went to one Cuban grocery store, he found there was very little to buy and that even sugar required a ration card. Zhen emphasized that such a food shortage was the result of ignoring his suggestion. But obviously Zhen's analysis was erroneous: China solved its food problem in the 1980s, not by sticking to the Maoist self-reliance doctrine, but by reintroducing nonsocialist incentives. During that 1986 visit to Cuba, Zhen met Rodríguez and found him to be very interested in China's economic policies, with many specific questions. In 1991 Rodríguez visited China and expressed an interest in China's economic reforms. In the early 1990s, Cuba began to introduce limited economic reforms, one notably allowing foreign tourists to visit the country.

79. Shen Jian, "Bygones of My Foreign Missions," 121.

80. One example was the Chinese art delegation—made up of ninety-eight top Chinese singers and all kinds of stage performers, including members of the Beijing Opera—that visited Cuba in 1961. The delegation stayed in Cuba for two months, giving performances in all thirteen provinces—from Havana to Sierra Maestra—which could be compared to China's revolutionary shrines such as the Jinggang Mountains and Yan'an. The performances of this delegation—even the Beijing Opera, which was often considered to be difficult for foreigners to appreciate—were received by the Cubans with enormous enthusiasm and became a national sensation. The delegation was deluged with praise from all Cuban leaders, extensive press coverage, and televised broadcasts.

81. For example, Zhang Baifa, one of Beijing's model construction workers in the 1950s and 1960s and the deputy mayor of Beijing in the 1990s, joined the Chinese youth delegation and participated in volunteer work at a construction site in the Sierra Maestra.

82. Sun Tingzheng, "Yi bai lin liu shui de lao fu zhai diao liao wen mang de mao zi" [One-Hundred-Six-Year-Old Woman Became Literate], *Guangming Daily,* July 26, 1961.

83. Wu Xiu, "Fang wen Gu ba de xue xiao he xin cheng shi" [Visiting Cuba's Schools and New Cities], *Guangming Daily,* December 21, 1961.

84. Wang Taipin, *Diplomatic History,* 496.

85. Herbert L. Matthews, *Revolution in Cuba* (New York: Scribner, 1975). Matthews was a senior journalist of the *New York Times* whose interview with Castro in early 1958 greatly enhanced the latter's popularity in the West. Therefore, he was to communist Cuba what Edgar Snow was to communist China.

86. Karol, *Guerrillas in Power,* 304.

87. Ibid.

88. Ibid., 384.

89. Ibid., 331–332.

90. Joe Lee Anderson, *Che Guevara* (New York: Grove Press, 1997), 479.

91. Ibid., 608. In 1965, as Castro was compelled to cool Cuba's relationship with China, apparently due to pressure from Moscow, Guevara had to leave Cuba. Exactly to what extent Guevara's overt pro-Chinese ideological stand contributed to his departure has been a question for historians. According to Wang Youping, the Chinese ambassador to Cuba from 1964 to 1969, he met Guevara nine times from June 1964 to March 1965. The last meeting was on March 26, 1965, when Castro began to make some public but insinuative criticism

about China's responsibility in the Sino-Soviet quarrel. (During a mass rally on March 13, celebrating the anniversary of a major student uprising against the Batista regime, Castro for the first time made insinuations critical of China's standpoint by referring to "Byzantine feuds." Castro also used the word "contraband" to refer to propagandistic materials that foreign communist parties had disseminated in Cuba, a comment that was obviously directed at China.) Wang was received by Guevara in the company of a Chinese textile delegation. When the meeting was over, Wang alone was asked by Guevara to stay in his office, and the two of them talked for more than an hour. According to Wang, Guevara looked blue and was coughing all the time and constantly using an inhaler to alleviate his cough (he had suffered from asthma since childhood). Although Guevara was short of breath, he did most of the talking in the meeting. He told Wang he was leaving Havana for the summer harvest in the Oriente Province, which later on became a pretext for his disappearance. He then began to praise the Chinese Revolution and Chinese culture and told Wang he admired the country. When Guevara smoked, he told Wang the pipe he was using had been bought in Beijing when he had visited China the previous month. Superficially, there was nothing substantial or imminent in this meeting, but there seemed to be something compelling behind Guevara's seemingly small talk. Wang observed: "The time Guevara spent with the textile delegation was much shorter than the time he spent with me, and he was talking all the time in the two meetings. My feeling was that his meeting with the Chinese textile delegation was a pretext. His real intention was to meet the Chinese ambassador [i.e., Wang himself]. At that time, Sino-Cuban relations were increasingly deteriorating, so any direct contact between a Cuban leader and the Chinese ambassador would be politically too sensitive. Therefore I think the meeting with the Chinese textile delegation just provided him an opportunity to meet me and say good-bye without raising suspicion among other Cuban leaders." Wang was proud that he had been the last foreign ambassador Guevara met with as a Cuban leader. Although Guevara was apparently the most pro-Chinese and anti-Soviet Cuban leader, Wang recalled that Guevara never talked to him about the Sino-Soviet division, neither did he touch on any sensitive issues in Sino-Cuban relations when they met, even privately. It seemed that Guevara had intentionally avoided any revelations of his personal views on such issues in front of the Chinese, who might have interpreted his words as evidence of the Cuban party's dissension. Wang Youping, *Wo zai qi ge guo jia de wai jiao shen ya* [My Career as an Ambassador in Seven Countries] (Nanjing: Jiangsu Renmin Publisher, 1996), 91–92.

92. Liss, *Roots of Revolution*, 166.

93. *Granma Weekly Review* (hereafter *"GWR"*), March 13, 1967.

94. Karol, *Guerrillas in Power*, 358–359.

95. *Al-Tali-ah* (Egypt), "Major Excerpts from an Interview with Ernesto Guevara (April 1965)," in Daniel Tretiak, *Cuba and the Soviet Union: A Growing Accommodation* (US Air Force Project, Rand Corporation, July 1966), 56–57.

96. Schram, *Chairman Mao Talks*, 198.

97. Peter Clecak, "Moral and Material Incentives," 106.

98. Silverman, *Man and Socialism in Cuba*, 4.

99. Liss, *Roots of Revolution*, 166.

100. Anderson, *Che Guevara*, 479.

101. Silverman, *Man and Socialism in Cuba*, 338.

102. Ibid., 343.

103. *GWR*, March 13, 1967.

104. *GWR*, August 25, 1968.

105. Ibid.

106. The Khmer Rouge officially abolished the monetary system. For a historical connection between the Khmer Rouge and Maoist China, as far as the money issue is concerned, see the conclusion in the present volume.

107. *GWR*, March 3, 1968.

108. Fagen, *Transformation of Political Culture*, 143.

109. For a recent reference on Mao's loathing of money, see Xu Yan, "Mao Zedong: Zhong guo de ju ren" [Mao: China's Giant], *Beijing Youth Daily*, April 18, 2001. A widely circulated scenario recounts that when Mao once unknowingly touched an envelope with cash inside, he acted as if his hand had been bitten by a snake. Afterwards Mao warned the secretary to never let his hand touch money again. For a reference about the amount in Mao's bank account, see Peng Xinting, "Mao Zedong de gao fei gai gui shui?" [Who Is the Legitimate Inheritor of Mao's Money?], *Nan Fang Dou Shi Bao* [Southern Municipal Daily], December 11, 2007. The article was written as part of the discussion over the legal issue regarding the inheritance of Mao's bank deposit.

110. Eric Hoffer, *In Our Time* (New York: Harper and Row, 1976), 37, 39.

111. Che Guevara, *Che Guevara and the Cuban Revolution: Writings and Speeches of Ernesto Che Guevara*, edited by Davis Deutschmann (Sydney: Pathfinder Press, 1987), 101.

112. Ibid., 29.

113. Fred Ward, *Inside Cuba* (New York: Crown, 1978), 95.

114. Robert E. Quirk, *Fidel Castro* (New York: Norton, 1993), 160.

115. Ibid., 136.

116. Che Guevara, *Venceremos! The Speeches and Writings of Ernesto Che Guevara* (New York: Macmillan, 1968), 391, 397.

117. Fagen, *Transformation of Political Culture*, 105.

118. *GWR*, June 19, 1966.

119. *GWR*, June 24, 1966.

120. Frank País was a celebrated revolutionary hero who died in the armed struggle against Batista. A. S. Makarenko was a well-known Soviet educator, introduced in chapter 1.

121. Manuel Ascunce Domenech was a hero who died in Literacy Campaign of 1961.

122. *GWR*, November 5, 1967.

123. *GWR*, January 30, 1967.

124. *GWR*, February 5, 1967.

125. Ibid.

126. *GWR*, July 3, 1967.

127. Ibid.

128. Ibid.

129. Ibid.

130. The time around 1965 has been recognized as an important turning point in postrevolutionary Cuba's educational development. For example, see Rolland G. Paulston, "On Cuban Education," in Carmelo Mesa-Lago, ed., *Revolutionary Change in Cuba* (Pittsburgh: University of Pittsburgh Press, 1971), 387; Gerald H. Read, "The Revolutionary Offensive in Education," in James Nelson Goodsell, ed., *Fidel Castro's Personal Revolution in Cuba, 1959–1973* (New York: Knopf, 1975); and Matthews, *Revolution in Cuba*.

131. Castro discovered such ignorance during one of his inspection tours in the early 1960s and used this story to discredit "professors." In a mass rally in 1967 he told people this story sardonically and repeated several times that the ignorant person was a "professor," a "real expert," and the "man who really knows." *GWR*, May 7, 1967.

132. Read, "Revolutionary Offensive"; Fidel Castro, *Fidel Castro on Chile* (New York: Pathfinder Press, 1982), 134.

133. Max Figueroa, Abel Prieto, and Raúl Gaul Gutierrez (Educational Department Center, Havana), *Experiments and Innovations in Education: Study Prepared for the International Bureau of Education*, no. 7 (Paris: UNESCO Press, 1974), 6.

134. Paulston, "On Cuban Education," 387–388.

135. Ibid., 389–391. See also Leo Huberman and Paul Sweezy, *Socialism in Cuba* (New York: Monthly Review Press, 1969), 43–44.

136. Quirk, *Fidel Castro*, 136.

137. Matthews, *Revolution in Cuba*, 344.

138. Eusebio Mujal-Leon, "Higher Education and the Institutionalized Regime," in Irving Louis Horowitz, ed., *Cuban Communism* (New Brunswick, NJ: Transaction Publishers, 1989), 416.

139. Matthews, *Revolution in Cuba*, 344.

140. Quoted in ibid.

141. *GWR*, August 7, 1967.

142 Fagen, *Transformation of Political Culture*, 142. Fagen also pointed out that Castro's fascination with science and technology even extended to nuts and bolts.

143. Ward, *Inside Cuba*, 95.

144. Read, "Revolutionary Offensive," 217; Matthews, *Revolution in Cuba*, 344.

145. *GWR*, January 11, 1967.

146. *GWR*, August 7, 1967.

147. Matthews, *Revolution in Cuba*, 240.

148. Anderson, *Che Guevara*, 503.

149. Ernesto Cardenal, *In Cuba* (New York: New Direction, 1972), 134.

150. Sutherland, *Youngest Revolution*, 216.

151. Robert M. Bernard, *The Theory of Moral Incentives in Cuba* (Tuscaloosa: University of Alabama Press, 1971), 124.

152. P. Oscar Lewis, Ruth M. Lewis, and Susan M. Rigdon, eds., *Four Men: Living the Revolution; An Oral History of Contemporary Cuba* (Chicago: University of Chicago Press, 1977), 133.

153. Ibid., 148.

154. Guevara, *Che Guevara and the Cuban Revolution*, 101.

155. Ibid., 167.

156. Julie Marie Bunck, *Fidel Castro and the Quest for a Revolutionary Culture* (University Park: Pennsylvania State University Press, 1994), 139.

157. Che Guevara, "Notes on Socialism and Man," *International Socialist Reviews* (Winter 1966): 21.

158. *GWR*, March 13, 1967.

159. Peter Schmid, "Letter from Havana," *Commentary* 40, no. 3 (1965): 57.

160. Lowry Nelson, *Cuba: The Measures of a Revolution* (Minneapolis: University of Minnesota Press, 1972), 120.

161. *GWR*, March 16, 1968.

162. Ibid.

163. *GWR*, March 23, 1968.

164. *GWR*, May 16, 1968.

165. Ibid.

166. Bernard, *Theory of Moral Incentives*, 125.

167. *GWR*, March 16, 1968.

168. *GWR*, May 19, 1967.

169. Guevara, "Man and Socialism," 343.

170. *GWR*, May 19, 1968.

171. Bernard, *Theory of Moral Incentives*, 125.

172. *GWR*, April 14, 1968.

173. Ibid.

174. Ibid.

175. Ibid.

176. Ana Serra, "The Historical Zafra and Nation Building in Revolutionary Cuba: Miguel Cossio Woodward's *Sacchario* (1970)," *Revista de Estudios Hispánicos* 37 (2003): 614–615.

177. Ibid., 615.

178. *GWR*, February 4, 1968.

179. Quoted in Sutherland, *Youngest Revolution*, 94.

4. The Global Impact of the Communist New Man

1. Kosa, *Two Generations of Soviet Man*, 5.

2. Ibid., 16

3. Sanjay Seth, "Indian Maoism: The Significance of Naxalbari," in Arif Dirlik, ed., *Critical Perspectives on Mao Zedong's Thought* (Atlantic Highlands, NJ: Humanities Press, 1997), 299.

4. Sheng Zhihua and Li Danhui, "Xi ha nu ke, Bo er bu te yu zhong guo" [Xihanuke, Pol Pot, and China, 1960–1970s], http://www.shenzhihua.net/ynzz/000032_2.htm.

5. Hu Ben and Huang Zhangjin, "Shen pan hong se gao mian" [Trial of the Khmer Rouge], *Feng Huang Zhou Kan* [Phoenix Weekly], Hong Kong, March 5, 2008, 28.

6. Wu Si, *Rise and Fall of Chen Yonggui*, 249.

7. Ben Kiernan, *The Pol Pot Regime: Race, Power, and Genocide in Cambodia under the Khmer Rouge, 1975–79* (New Haven, CT: Yale University Press, 2002), 121.

8. Roger N. Lancaster, *Life Is Hard: Machismo, Danger, and the Intimacy of Power in Nicaragua* (Berkeley: University of California Press, 1993), 147–148.

9. Ibid., 39–40.

10. Bertrand Russell, *The Practice and Theory of Bolshevism* (New York: Simon and Schuster, 1964), 43.

11. René Fueloep-Miller, *The Mind and Face of Bolshevism* (New York: Harper and Row, 1965), 1. The book was originally published in German under the title *Geist und Gesicht des Bolschewismus* in 1926 by Amalthea-Verlag, Zurich, Leipzig, and Vienna, and an English version was first published in the United States and England in 1927. The citations here come from the 1965 edition.

12. Ibid., 5.

13. Ibid., 11–12.

14. Ibid., 7.

15. Winter, *Red Virtue*, 122–130.

16. Frankwood E. Williams, *Russia Youth and the Present-Day World* (New York: Farrar and Rinehart, 1934), 15.

17. Ibid., 219–211.

18. Sidney Webb and Beatrice Webb, *Soviet Communism: A New Civilization?* (New York: Charles Scribner's Sons, 1936), 805. The question mark in the book's title was dropped when the second edition was published one year later.

19. Ibid., 806.

20. Ibid., 406.

21. Ibid., 328.

22. Paul Hollander, *Political Pilgrims: Western Intellectuals in Search of the Good Society*, 4th ed. (New Brunswick, NJ: Transaction Publishers, 1998), 7–8.

23. Ibid., 28.

24. Arthur W. Galston, *Daily Life in People's China* (New York: Crowell, 1978), 240.

25. Peter Worsley, *Inside China* (London: Allen Lane, 1975), 20.

26. Hollander, *Political Pilgrims*, 293.

27. Carol Tavris, "Field Report: Women in China," *Psychology Today*, May 1974, 43.

28. Staughton Lynd and Tom Hayden, *The Other Side* (New York: New American Library, 1966), 40.

29. Ruth Sidel, *Women and Child Care in China* (New York: Penguin Books, 1982), 168.

30. Committee of Concerned Asian Scholars, *China!* (New York: Bantam Books, 1972), 278–279.

31. Lois Wheeler Snow, *China on Stage* (New York: Vintage Books, 1976), 205. It is noteworthy that Lois Snow, the first wife of Edgar Snow (the author of *Red Star over China*), was a vocal sympathizer of Communist China in the West. But since the Chinese government cracked down on the democratic movement in 1989, she has become one of the staunchest supporters of China's pro-democracy movement and has involved herself in charitable activities helping the families who lost their relatives in the crackdown.

32. John K. Fairbank, "The New China and the America Connection," *Foreign Affairs*, October 1972, 35.

33. Orville Schell, *In the People's Republic: An American's First-hand View of Living and Working in China* (New York: Vintage Books, 1977), 45.

34. Shirley MacLaine, *You Can Get There* (New York: Bantam Books, 1976), 183.

35. Joshua Horn, *Away with All Pests* (New York: Monthly Review Press, 1969), 145.

36. Maria Antonietta Macciocchi, *Daily Life in Revolutionary China* (New York: Monthly Review Press, 1972), 88.

37. Ibid., 89.

38. Ibid., 90.

39. Ibid.

40. Ibid.

41. Quoted in Hollander, *Political Pilgrims*, 236.

42. Quoted in ibid., 238.

43. Quoted in ibid.

44. Jean-Paul Sartre, *Sartre on Cuba* (New York: Vintage Press, 1961).

45. Khwaja Masud, "Remembering Che Guevara," *International News*, October 9, 2006, http://www.thenews.com.pk/daily_detail.asp?id=27548; Dayan Jayatilleka, "Che's Visage on the Shroud of Time," *LankaWeb.com*, November 13, 2007, http://www.lankaweb.com/news/items07/141107-3.html.

46. Quoted in Hollander, *Political Pilgrims*, 257.

47. Barry Reckord, *Does Fidel Eat More?* (New York: Praeger, 1971), 24.

48. Levinson and Brightman, *Venceremos Brigade*, 16.

49. Ibid., 21.

50. Ibid., 164.

51. Ibid., 344.

52. Matthews, *Revolution in Cuba*, 240.

53. Nelson Mandela, "An Unparalleled Contribution to African Freedom," in Armando Choy, Gustavo Chui, and Moises Sio Wong, *Our History Is Still Being Written* (New York: Pathfinder Press, 2005), 179–182.

54. George T. Yu, *China and Tanzania: A Study in Cooperative Interaction* (Berkeley, CA: Center for Chinese Studies, 1970), 33.

55. William Edgett Smith, *We Must Run While They Walk: A Portrait of Africa's Julius Nyerere* (New York: Random House, 1971), 3.

56. Ibid., 18–19.

57. Yu, *China and Tanzania*, 38.

58. Ibid., 35.

59. Ibid.

60. Ibid.

61. Ibid., 36.

62. John Hatch, *Two African Statesmen: Kaunda of Zambia and Nyerere of Tanzania* (Chicago: Henry Regnery, 1976), 294.

63. Yu, *China and Tanzania*, 37. It must be added here that the influence of China's Cultural Revolution in Tanzania and many other African countries was a complicated matter. While Chinese revolutionary enthusiasm inspired Nyerere, the anarchic and rebellious spirit unleashed in the CR spilled over to African countries and disturbed the leaders. The Chinese workers and technicians in Tanzania not only "rebelled" against their own authorities (the embassy officials) but instigated Tanzanian workers and students (the "green guards," a Tanzanian student organization) to do the same to their own government. Nyerere was informed of the seriousness of the development by the Tanzanian intelligence. His second trip to Beijing in 1968 was in part for requesting the Chinese government to restrain such activities in his country. His meeting with Mao was unpleasant in the beginning as he criticized the indiscriminate "rebellion" against any authorities. But later Mao agreed with him and Zhou Enlai immediately ordered those most aggressive "rebels" in Tanzania back to China. For a reference of the incident, see Zhou Boping, *Fei chang shi qi de wai jiao shen ya* [Diplomatic Career in an Unusual Time] (Beijing: Shejie Zhishi Publisher, 2003), 20–26. Similar incidents also occurred in Zambia and some other African countries. When the Chinese diplomats, engineers and workers enthusiastically disseminated Mao's badges, the Little Red Books and other CR materials along with provocative slogans such as "To rebel is justified" and "The political power grows out of the barrel of a gun," the governments of their host countries were alerted and some diplomatic quarrels ensued, often resulting in the expulsion of the Chinese personnel involved in the events. Ghana even cut off official diplomatic relations with China. For a reference on the CR's negative influence in Africa and some other parts of the Third World, see Ma Jisen, *Wai jiao bu wen ge ji shi* [The Chinese Foreign Ministry in the Cultural Revolution] (Hong Kong: Chinese University Publisher, 2003).

64. Ibid., 96.

CONCLUSION

1. This is Isaiah Berlin's rendering from his notes taken at one of R. G. Collingwood's lectures. A more literal translation is "out of timber so crooked as that from which man is

made nothing entirely straight can be carved." Isaiah Berlin, *The Crooked Timber of Humanity* (London: John Murray, 1990), v.

2. See Xunzi, *Xunzi,* in Wang Xiangqian, *Anthology of Classical Masters,* 289.

3. Anthony Daniels, "The Real Che," *New Criterion* 23, no. 2 (2004), http://www .newcriterion.com/archive/23/oct04/che.htm.

4. Foucault, *What Is Enlightenment?*

5. Isaiah Berlin, *Four Essays on Liberty* (London: Oxford University Press, 1969), 31. It is Berlin's major contribution to discern and delineate the ideological tendency developed among those eighteenth- and nineteenth-century philosophers who prepared the path for various totalitarian regimes in the twentieth century. One of his concise arguments is as follows: "This conception of man, inherited from the Romantic movement, remains in us to this day: it is something which, despite all that mankind has lived through, we in Europe have not abandoned. For this reason, when Hegel and Marx prophesied inevitable doom for all those who defied the march of history, their threats came too late. Hegel and Marx, each in his fashion, tried to tell human beings that only one path to liberty and salvation lay before them—that which was offered them by history, which embodied cosmic reason" and those who failed to "adapt" themselves to the path or "realize" its "rationality" would be destroyed by "the forces of history." For Berlin, the manifestation of this ideological justification for imposing one's will on others in the name of "history" or universal law was "the faith of Lenin, of Trotsky, of Mao, for all I know of Pol Pot. Since I know the only true path to the ultimate solution of the problems of society, I know which way to drive the human caravan; and since you are ignorant of what I know, you cannot be allowed to have liberty of choice even within the narrowest limits, if the goal is to be reached." Isaiah Berlin, *The Crooked Timber of Humanity* (London: John Murray, 1990), 199, 15.

6. See the discussion of Helvétius and Rousseau in chapter 1 of this book.

7. Berlin, *Four Essays on Liberty,* 150.

8. Ibid., 29–30.

9. Ibid., 137. Bukharin's remarks and Berlin's comments are as follows: "'Proletarian coercion, in all its forms, from executions to forced labour, is, paradoxical as it may sound, the method of moulding communist humanity out of the human material of the capitalist period.' These lines by the Bolshevik leader Nikolai Bukharin, in a work which appeared in 1920, especially the term 'human material,' vividly convey this attitude." Quoted in ibid., 138.

10. Berlin, *Crooked Timber of Humanity,* 16.

11. Alexander Herzen, *From the Other Shore* (London: William Clowes and Sons, 1956), 103.

12. Eric Hoffer, *The True Believer* (New York: Harper and Brothers, 1951), 73, 61. The first quotation was also used as an epigraph by Fagen in his *Transformation of Political Culture in Cuba.*

13. Hu, *Man's Taming,* 232.

14. Hu Ping, *Quan ru bin—dang dai zhong guo de jing sheng wei ji* [The Cynicism Syndrome—Contemporary China's Spiritual Crisis] (Mountain View, CA: Broad Press, 2005), 10.

15. Matthews, *Revolution in Cuba,* 193.

16. Carmelo Mesa-Lago, "A Continuum Model for Global Comparison," in Mesa-Lago, ed., *Comparative Socialist Systems: Essays on Politics and Economics* (Pittsburgh: University of Pittsburgh Press, 1975), 96.

17. Ibid., 3.

18. Ibid., 115.

19. Richard Carson, "Property Rights," in Mesa-Lago, *Comparative Socialist Systems*, 334.

20. William Ratliff, "Cuban Foreign Policy toward Far East and Southern Asia," in George Fauriol and Eva Loser, eds., *Cuba: The International Dimension* (New Brunswick, NJ: Transaction Publishers, 1990), 207–208. Maurice Meisner, when analyzing the relationship between Marxism, Maoism, and Utopianism, briefly mentioned the antiurban tendency shared by Mao and Castro. He also noted that Frantz Fanon's neo-Marxism and Nyerere's African socialism bore the same character as well. See Maurice Meisner, *Marxism, Maoism, and Utopianism*, 72–73.

Selected Bibliography

In China during Mao's time, especially during the Cultural Revolution, authorship was regarded as a manifestation of "bourgeoisie individualism"; therefore many books were published either without authors' names or under a collective name such as a writing group or a work unit.

Anderson, Joe Lee. *Che Guevara*. New York: Grove Press, 1997.

Anonymous. *Er guo min chui pai wen xuan* (The Anthology of Russian Populists). Beijing: Renmin Publisher, 1963.

———. *Lun lei feng* (On Lei Feng). Beijing: Beijing Publisher, 1965.

———. *Mao zhu xi zai Ren min zhong jian* (Chairman Mao among the People). Beijing: Renmin Publisher, 1958.

———. "Pavel and Gates: Who Is the Hero?" *People's Daily,* April 22, 2002. http://www.people.com.cn/GB/shizheng/252/7955/7959/20020422/714386.html.

———. *Wei feng ying—mao zhu xi de hao gong ren* (Wei Fengying—Chairman Mao's Good Worker). Beijing: Renmin Publisher, 1965.

———. *Xiang Jiao Yulu xue xi zuo mao zhu xi de hao xue sheng* (Learn from Jiao Yulu and Be Chairman Mao's Good Student). Hong Kong: Hong Kong Sanlian Publisher, 1966.

———. "Xue xi wei ren min fu wu" (Study "Serve the People"). *Liberation Army Daily,* November 30, 1966.

Apter, David E. "Discourses as Power: Yan'an and the Chinese Revolution." In Tony Saich and Hans van de Ven, eds., *New Perspectives on the Chinese Communist Revolution,* 193–234. Armonk, NY: M. E. Sharpe, 1995.

Berlin, Isaiah. *The Crooked Timber of Humanity*. London: John Murray, 1990.

———. *Four Essays on Liberty*. London: Oxford University Press, 1969.

———. *Freedom and Its Betrayal*. Princeton, NJ: Princeton University Press, 2002.

Bernard, Robert M. *The Theory of Moral Incentives in Cuba*. Tuscaloosa: University of Alabama Press, 1971.

Bo Yibo. "The Socialist Industrialization of China." *Peking Review* 41 (October 11, 1963): 3–7.

Brooks, Jeffery. *Thank You, Comrade Stalin!* Princeton, NJ: Princeton University Press, 1999.

Bunck, Julie Marie. *Fidel Castro and the Quest for a Revolutionary Culture*. University Park: Pennsylvania State University Press, 1994.

Capaldi, Nicholas. *The Enlightenment The Proper Study of Mankind: An Anthology*. New York: Capricorn Books, 1968.

Cardenal, Ernesto. *In Cuba*. New York: New Direction, 1972.

Carson, Richard. "Property Rights." In Carmelo Mesa-Lago, ed., *Comparative Socialist Systems: Essays on Politics and Economics,* 321–340. Pittsburgh: University of Pittsburgh Press, 1975.

Castro, Fidel. "Castro Pledges 100 percent Literacy." 1961 speech. http://www1.lanic
.utexas.edu.

———. *Fidel Castro on Chile.* New York: Pathfinder Press, 1982.

———. *My Early Years.* New York: Ocean Press, 1998.

———. *The Second Declaration of Havana.* New York: Pathfinder Press, 1962.

Central Committee of the Chinese Communist Party. *Decision of the Central Committee of the Chinese Communist Party Concerning the Great Cultural Revolution.* Beijing: Foreign Language Press, 1966.

Chan, Anita. *Children of Mao: Personal Development and Political Activism in the Red Guard Generation.* Seattle: University of Washington Press, 1985.

Chandler, David P. *Brother Number 1: A Political Biography of Pol Pot.* Boulder, CO: Westview Press, 1992.

Chang, Maria Hsia. *The Labors of Sisyphus: The Economic Development of Communist China.* New Brunswick, NJ: Transaction Publishers, 1998.

Chen Duxiu. *Chen Duxiu wen xuan* (Anthology of Chen Duxiu). Beijing: Sanlian Publisher, 1984.

———. "Xin qing nian" (New Youth). In *Chen Duxiu wen zhang xuan bian* (Selection of Chen Duxiu's Writings), 1:112–114. Beijing: Sanlian Publisher, 1984.

Chen, Jerome, ed. *Mao Papers: Anthology and Bibliography.* London: Oxford University Press, 1970.

Chen Jian. "Xun zhao ge ming zi lu" (The Road to the Revolution). In Chen Jian, ed., *Yu Chin Peng dui hua* (Dialogue with Chin Peng), 351–390. Kuala Lumpur: Centre for Malaysian Chinese Studies, 2006.

Chen Mingyang. "Niutianyang de 'jing sheng yuan zi dan'" (The "Spiritual Atomic Bomb" of Niutianyang). *Nanfang Zhoumo* (Southern Weekend), July 30, 1999.

Cheng, Yinghong, and Patrick Manning. "Education in Revolution: China and Cuba in Global Context, 1957–76." *Journal of World History* 14, no. 3 (2003): 359–391.

Chernyshevsky, Nikolay Gavrilovich. *What Is to Be Done? The Story about the New Man.* New York: Vintage Books, 1961.

Clecak, Peter. "Moral and Material Incentives." *Socialist Register* (1969): 101–135.

Clements, Barbara Evans. "The Birth of the New Soviet Women." In Abbott Gleason, Peter Kenez, and Richard Stites, eds., *Bolshevik Culture,* 220–238. Bloomington: Indiana University Press, 1985.

Committee of Concerned Asian Scholars. *China!* New York: Bantam Books, 1972.

Confucius. *Lun yu* (Analects). In Wang Xiangqian, ed., *Zhu Zi Jie Cheng* (Anthology of Classical Masters). Shanghai: Shanghai Shudian Publisher, 1987.

Counts, George S. "The Repudiation of Experiment." In Robert V. Daniels, ed., *Foundations of Soviet Totalitarianism,* 117–128. Lexington, MA: D. C. Heath and Co., 1972.

Dalton, Thomas C. *"Everything within the Revolution": Cuban Strategies for Social Development since 1960.* Boulder, CO: Westview Press, 1993.

Daniels, Anthony. "The Real Che." *New Criterion* 23, no. 2 (2004). http://www.newcriterion
.com/archive/23/oct04/che.htm.

David-Fox, Michael. *Revolution of the Mind: Higher Learning among the Bolsheviks 1918–1929.* Ithaca, NY: Cornell University Press, 1997.

Dawson, Richard E., and Kenneth Prewitt. *Political Socialization.* New York: Little, Brown, 1969.

Department of the Study of Marxism and Leninism, Jinan University. *Dang de ba jie liu zhong quan hui xue xi cai liao* (Study Materials for the Party's Sixth Plenary Session of the Eighth Central Committee). Pamphlet printed by and circulated at the university. Guangzhou, 1959.

Ding Yizhuang. *Zhong guo zhi qing shi 1953–1968* (History of the Sent-Down Chinese Educated Youth, 1953–1968). Beijing: Shehui Kexue Press of China, 1998.

Dorrill, William F. "Leadership and Succession in Communist China." *Current History* (September 1965): 127–140.

Eastman, Max. *Trotsky: A Portrait of His Youth*. New York: Faber and Gwyer, 1925.

Editing Group of Mao Zedong's Early Writings, Hunan Province Committee of the Chinese Communist Party, ed. *Mao ze dong zhao qi wen gao* (Mao Zedong's Early Writings). Changsha: Hunan Publisher, 1990.

Ello, Paul. *Czechoslovakia's Blueprint for Freedom*. Washington, DC: Acropolis Books, 1968.

Fagen, Richard R. *Cuba: The Political Content of Adult Education*. Stanford, CA: Hoover Institution, 1964.

———. *The Transformation of Political Culture in Cuba*. Stanford, CA: Stanford University Press, 1969.

Fairbank, John King. *The Great Chinese Revolution, 1800–1985*. New York: Harper and Row, 1986.

———. "The New China and the America Connection." *Foreign Affairs*, October 1972, 31–37.

Fang Shuming and Huang Jichang. *Xiang xiuli* (Xiang Xiuli). Beijing: Zhongguo Qingnian Publisher, 1959.

Feldmesser, Robert A. "Toward the Classless Society?" In Alex Inkeles and Kent Geiger, eds., *Soviet Society: A Book of Readings*, 573–582. Boston: Houghton Mifflin, 1961. Originally published as "Equality and Inequality under Khrushchev," *Problems of Communism* 9 (1960): 31–39.

Fernandez, Damian J. "Cuba's Relations with China: Economic Pragmatism and Political Fluctuation." In Donna Rich Kaplowitz, ed., *Cuba's Ties to a Changing World*. Boulder, CO: Lynne Rienner, 1993.

Figueroa, Max, Abel Prieto, and Raúl Gaul Gutierrez (Educational Department Center, Havana). *Experiments and Innovations in Education: Study Prepared for the International Bureau of Education*, no. 7. Paris: UNESCO Press, 1974.

Foner, Philip S. *Antonio Maceo: The "Bronze Titan" of Cuba's Struggle for Independence*. New York: Monthly Review Press, 1977.

Foucault, Michel. "What Is Enlightenment?" http://philosophy.eserver.org/foucault/what-is-enlightenment.html.

Fueloep-Miller, René. *The Mind and Face of Bolshevism*. New York: Harper and Row, 1965.

Galston, Arthur W. *Daily Life in People's China*. New York: Crowell, 1978.

Gao Hua. *Hong tai yang shi zen yang sheng qi de: Yan an zheng feng de lai long qu mai* (That Is How the Red Sun Rose: The Origin and Development of the Yan'an Rectification). Hong Kong: Chinese University of Hong Kong Press, 2000.

Gastev, Alexsei. "We Grow out of Iron." In James von Geldern and Richard Stites, eds., *Mass Culture in Soviet Russia*, 3. Bloomington: Indiana University Press, 1995.

Gerovitch, Slava. "'New Soviet Man' Inside Machine: Human Engineering, Spacecraft Design, and the Construction of Communism." *Osiris* 22 (2007): 135–157.

Gong Yuzhi. *Gong Yuzhi hui yi* (Memoir of Gong Yuzhi). Nanchang: Jiangxi Renmin Publisher, 2008.

Gorky, Maxim. "V. I. Lenin." http://aha.ru/~mausoleu/a_lenin/gorkye.htm.

———. *Untimely Thoughts*. New Haven, CT: Yale University Press, 1995.

Guevara, Che. *Che Guevara and the Cuban Revolution: Writings and Speeches of Ernesto Che Guevara*. Edited by Davis Deutschmann. Sydney: Pathfinder Press, 1987.

———. "Man and Socialism in Cuba." In Bertram Silverman, ed., *Man and Socialism in Cuba: The Great Debate*, 335–410. New York: Atheneum, 1971.

———. "Notes on Socialism and Man." *International Socialist Reviews* (Winter 1966): 19–25.

———. *Venceremos! The Speeches and Writings of Ernesto Che Guevara*. New York: Macmillan, 1968.

Guo Moruo. "Zai lei feng ta xia" (Under Leifeng Pagoda). In *Guo mo ruo wen xuan* (Selections of Guo Moruo's Works), 1:165. Beijing: Renmin Wenxue Publisher, 1982.

Hallaraker, Harald. "Soviet Discussion on Enterprise Incentives and Methods of Planning." *Economics of Planning* 3, no. 1 (1963): 53–54.

Hatch, John. *Two African Statesmen: Kaunda of Zambia and Nyerere of Tanzania*. Chicago: Henry Regnery, 1976.

Heller, Mikhail. *Cogs in the Soviet Wheel: The Formation of Soviet Man*. London: Collins Harvill, 1988.

Heller, Mikhail, and Aleksandr M. Nekrich. *Utopia in Power*. New York: Simon and Schuster, 1982.

Herzen, Alexander. *From the Other Shore*. London: William Clowes and Sons, 1956.

Hess, R. D., and J. V. Torney. *The Development of Political Attitudes in Children*. Chicago: Aldine, 1967.

Hoffer, Eric. *In Our Time*. New York: Harper and Row, 1976.

———. *The True Believer*. New York: Harper and Brothers, 1951.

Hollander, Paul. *Political Pilgrims: Western Intellectuals in Search of the Good Society*. 4th ed. New Brunswick, NJ: Transaction Publishers, 1998.

Horn, Joshua. *Away with All Pests*. New York: Monthly Review Press, 1969.

Horowitz, Louis, ed. *Cuban Communism*. New Brunswick: Transaction Publishers, 1989.

Hu Ping. *Quan ru bin—dang dai zhong guo de jing shen wei ji* (The Cynicism Syndrome—Contemporary China's Spiritual Crisis). Mountain View, CA: Broad Press, 2005.

———. *Ren de xun hua, duo bi, yu fan pan* (Man's Taming, Evading, and Rebelling). Hong Kong: Asia Science Publisher, 1999.

Huang, Philip C. *Liang Ch'i-ch'ao and Modern Chinese Liberalism*. Seattle and London: University of Washington Press, 1972.

Huang, Ziliang. "The First Case of the Sino-Latin American Friendship." In Yu Wuzhen, ed., *The Diplomatic Experience of the New China*, 79–101. Beijing: Shijie Zhishi Publisher, 1996.

———. *La ting mei zhou de zai fa xian* (Rediscovery of Latin America). Beijing: Shijie Zhishi Publisher, 2004.

Hubei Provincial Committee of the Chinese Communist Party. *Ma Xueli* (Ma Xueli). Wuhan: Hubei Renmin Publisher, 1959.

Huberman, Leo, and Paul Sweezy. *Socialism in Cuba*. New York: Monthly Review Press, 1969.

Hunter, Edward. *Brainwashing in Red China: The Calculated Destruction of Man's Mind*. New York: Vanguard, 1951.

———. *Brainwashing: The Story of Men Who Defied It*. New York: Farrar, Straus, and Cudahy, 1956.

Inkeles, Alex. "Myth and Reality of Social Classes." In Alex Inkeles and Kent Geiger, eds., *Soviet Society: A Book of Readings*, 558–573. Boston: Houghton Mifflin, 1961. Originally published as "Social Stratification and Mobility in the Soviet Union: 1940–1950," *American Sociological Review* 15 (1950): 465–479.

Inkeles, Alex, and Kent Geiger, eds. *Soviet Society: A Book of Readings*. Boston: Houghton Mifflin, 1961.

Jiang Changbin. "Zhi yi *gang tie shi zen yang lian cheng de* li shi bei jing" (Questioning the Historical Background of *That Is How Steel Was Tempered*). http://www.qinxiaojianqi .com/bbs/dispbbs.asp?boardID=108&ID=10489&page=5.

Jiang Nanxiang. "Yu kai de jie shou ren min zheng fu de an pai, beng fu jian she de zhan dou gang wei" (Cheerfully Accept the Assignment of the People's Government and Go to the Fighting Positions of Construction). In Propaganda Department of the Committee of the Youth League of Northwestern China, ed., *Fu cong zhu guo yao qiu, can jia zu guo jian she* (Obey the Fatherland's Demand, Participate in the Fatherland's Construction), 2–7. Lanzhou: Xibei Qingnian Publisher, 1952.

Joint editorial of *People's Daily* and *Red Flag*. "Guan yu he lu xiao fu de jia gong chan zhu yi ji qi zai shi jie lis hi shang de jiao xun: Jiu ping su gong zhong yang de gong kai xin" (On Khrushchev's Phony Communism and Its Lesson in World History: The Ninth Commentary on the Open Letter of the Central Committee of the Communist Party of the Soviet Union). *People's Daily*, August 3, 1964.

Judson, C. Fred. *Cuba and the Revolutionary Myth: The Political Education of the Cuban Rebel Army, 1953–1963*. Boulder, CO, and London: Westview Press, 1984.

Karol, K. S. *Guerrillas in Power*. New York: Hill and Wang, 1970.

Kelly, Catriona. *Comrade Pavlik: The Rise and Fall of a Soviet Boy Hero*. London: Granta Books, 2006.

Kiernan, Ben. *The Pol Pot Regime: Race, Power, and Genocide in Cambodia under the Khmer Rouge, 1975–79*. New Haven, CT: Yale University Press, 2002.

Kirillov, Vladimir. "The Iron Messiah." In James von Geldern and Richard Stites, eds., *Mass Culture in Soviet Russia*, 4. Bloomington: Indiana University Press, 1995.

Kirk, John M. *Jose Marti, Mentor of the Cuban Nation*. Tampa: University Press of Florida, 1983.

Kollontai, Alexandra. *The Autobiography of a Sexually Emancipated Communist Woman*. New York: Schocken Books, 1975.

Kong Mai. "Da kai mei guo hou yuan de tu puo kou—gu ba du li zhi chu cai fang ji shi" (The Breakthrough in America's Backyard—My Journalistic Career in the Early Years of Cuba's Independence). In Gao Qiufu, ed., *My Journalistic Career in the Countries without Official Relationships with China*, 229–237. Beijing: Xinhua Publisher, 1999.

Kosa, John. *Two Generations of Soviet Man: A Study in the Psychology of Communism*. Chapel Hill: University of North Carolina Press, 1962.

Lancaster, Roger N. *Life Is Hard: Machismo, Danger, and the Intimacy of Power in Nicaragua*. Berkeley: University of California Press, 1993.

Lei Feng. *Lei Feng ri ji* (Lei Feng's Diary). Beijing: Zhongguo Qingnian Publisher, 1965.

Levinson, Sandra, and Carol Brightman, eds. *Venceremos Brigade: Young Americans Sharing the Life and Work of Revolutionary Cuba; Diaries, Interviews, Tapes, Essays, and Poetry by the Venceremos Brigade*. New York: Monthly Review Press, 1971.

Lewis, Oscar, Ruth M. Lewis, and Susan M. Rigdon, eds. *Four Men: Living the Revolution; An Oral History of Contemporary Cuba*. Chicago: University of Chicago Press, 1977.

———. *Four Women: Living the Revolution; An Oral History of Contemporary Cuba*. Chicago: University of Chicago Press, 1977.

Li Dazhao. *Li Dazhao wen xuan* (Selected Works of Li Dazhao). Beijing: Renmin Publisher, 1984.

Li Yongtai. *Zhong xi wen hua yu mao ze dong zhao qi si xiang* (Mao's Early Ideological Development under the Influence of Chinese and Western Cultures). Chengdu: Sichuan University Press, 1989.

Liberman, E. "Notes on Incentive Systems of Socialist Enterprises." *Economics of Planning* 7, no. 3 (1967): 258–265.

———. "The Plan, Profits and Bonus." *Economics of Planning* 3, no. 1 (1963): 55–61.

Lifton, Robert Jay, *Thought Reform and the Psychology of Totalism.* New York: Norton, 1969.

Lin Biao. "Lin biao tong zhi zai qing zhu wu chan ji jie wen hua da ge min qun zhong da hui shang de jiang hua" (Comrade Lin Biao's Speech at the Mass Rally Celebrating the Great Proletarian Cultural Revolution), August 18, 1966. Reprinted in Anonymous, ed., *Ba wu chan jie ji wen hua da ge min jin xin dao di* (Carry the Great Proletarian Revolution through to the End), 29–34. Beijing, 1966.

Lin Jin. *The Red Guards' Path to Violence: Political, Educational and Psychological Factors.* New York: Praeger, 1991.

Lin Zi. *Gong chan dang zhong guo de si xiang gai zhao* (Thought Reform in Communist China). Hong Kong: Chuang Keng Publisher, 1953.

Liss, Sheldon B. *Fidel! Castro's Political and Social Thoughts.* Boulder, CO: Westview Press, 1994.

———. *Roots of Revolution: Radical Thought in Cuba.* Lincoln, NE, and London: University of Nebraska Press, 1987.

Liu Shaoqi. "Ren de jie ji xing" (The Class Nature of People). In *Si xiang zhi nan* (Ideological Guidelines), 33–45. Hong Kong: Hong Kong Sanlian Publisher, 1949.

———. *Zen yang zhuo yi ge hao de gong chan dang yuan* (How to Be a Good Communist). Hong Kong: New Democracy Press, 1950.

Lowy, Michael. *The Marxism of Che Guevara: Philosophy, Economics, and Revolutionary Warfare.* New York: Monthly Review Press, 1973.

Lynd, Staughton, and Tom Hayden. *The Other Side.* New York: New American Library, 1966.

Ma Jisen. *Wai jiao bu wen ge ji shi* (The Chinese Foreign Ministry in the Cultural Revolution). Hong Kong: Chinese University Publisher, 2003.

Macale, Shawn. "Vietnamese Marxism, Dissent, and the Politics of Postcolonial Memory: Tran Duc Thao, 1946–1993." *Journal of Asian Studies* 61 (2002): 7–32.

Macciocchi, Maria Antonietta. *Daily Life in Revolutionary China.* New York: Monthly Review Press, 1972.

MacLaine, Shirley. *You Can Get There.* New York: Bantam Books, 1976.

Mandela, Nelson. "An Unparalleled Contribution to African Freedom." In Armando Choy, Gustavo Chui, and Moises Sio Wong, *Our History Is Still Being Written,* 179–182. New York: Pathfinder Press, 2005.

Mao Zedong. *Guan yu zheng qi chu li Ren min nei bu mao dun wen ti* (On Correctly Dealing with Contradictions among the People). Beijing: Renmin Publisher, 1959.

———. *Jian guo yi lai mao ze dong wen gao* (Mao Zedong's *Manuscripts since the Foundation of the PRC*). Vols. 1–8. Beijing: Renmin Publisher, 1996.

———. *Mao Zedong xuan jie* (Selected Works of Mao Zedong). Combined edition of vols. 1–4 (1968); vol. 5 (1977); and vol. 6 (1995). Beijing: Renmin Publisher.

———. *Selected Works of Mao Tse-Tung.* Vols. 1–4. Beijing: Foreign Language Press, 1967.

———. *Talks at the Yan'an Conference on Literature and Art.* Ann Arbor: Center for Chinese Studies, University of Michigan, 1980.

———. "Xue sheng de gong zuo" (Students' Work). In Editing Group of Mao Zedong's Early Writings, Hunan Province Committee of the Chinese Communist Party, ed., *Mao ze dong zao nian wen gao* (Mao Zedong's Early Writings), 449–451. Changsha: Hunan Publisher, 1990.

Marx, Karl. *Capital.* New York: Bennett A. Cerf and Donald S. Klopfer, 1936.

———. *A Contribution to the Critique of Political Economy.* Chicago: Charles H. Kerr and Co., 1904.

———. *Poverty of History.* Edited by C. P. Dutt and V. Chattopadhyaya. New York: International Publisher, 1936.

Matthews, Herbert L. *Revolution in Cuba.* New York: Scribner, 1975.

Medin, Tzvi. *Cuba: The Shaping of Revolutionary Consciousness.* Boulder, CO, and London: Lynne Rienner, 1990.

Meerloo, Joost A. M. *The Rape of the Mind: The Psychology of Thought Control, Menticide, and Brainwashing.* New York: University Library, Grosset and Dunlap, 1955.

Meisner, Maurice. *Marxism, Maoism, and Utopianism: Eight Essays,* Madison: University of Wisconsin Press, 1982.

Mesa-Lago, Carmelo. "A Continuum Model for Global Comparison." In Mesa-Lago, ed., *Comparative Socialist Systems: Essays on Politics and Economics,* 93–120. Pittsburgh: University of Pittsburgh Press, 1975.

Meyer, Frank S. *The Molding of Communists.* New York: Harcourt, Brace and Co., 1961.

Milton, David, and Nancy Milton. *People's China: Social Experimentation; Politics, Entry onto the World Scene, 1966 through 1972.* New York: Random House, 1974.

Mujal-Leon, Eusebio. "Higher Education and the Institutionalized Regime." In Irving Louis Horowitz, ed., *Cuban Communism,* 281–303. New Brunswick, NJ: Transaction Publishers, 1989.

Munro, Donald J. *The Conception of Man in Contemporary China.* Ann Arbor: University of Michigan Press, 1977.

Nahirny, Vladimir C. *The Russian Intelligentsia: From Torment to Silence.* New Brunswick, NJ: Transaction Books, 1987.

Nelson, Lowry. *Cuba: The Measures of a Revolution.* Minneapolis: University of Minnesota Press, 1972.

Ozouf, Mona. *Festivals and French Revolution.* Cambridge, MA: Harvard University Press, 1988.

Padover, Saul K., ed. *On the First International.* New York: McGraw-Hill, 1973.

Paulston, Rolland G. "On Cuban Education." In Carmelo Mesa-Lago, ed., *Revolutionary Change in Cuba,* 380–395. Pittsburgh: University of Pittsburgh Press, 1971.

Pei Yiran. "Dang dai zhong guo gong nong gan bu yu zhi shi feng zhi mao dun de you lai yu hou guo" (The Origin and Consequences of the Contradiction between Worker-Peasant Cadres and Intellectuals in Contemporary China). *Dang dai zhong guo yan jiu* (Modern China Studies) 14, no. 2 (2007): 91–111.

Pipes, Richard. *Russian Revolution.* New York: Knopf, 1990.

Plekhanov, G. V. *Essays in the History of Materialism.* New York: Howard Fertig, 1967.

Pomper, Philip. *Sergei Nechaev.* New Brunswick, NJ. Rutgers University Press, 1979.

Porsholt, Lars. "Socialist Market Economy in Czechoslovakia?" *Economics of Planning* 5, nos. 1–2 (1965): 87–93.

Price, Jane L. *Cadres, Communists, and Commissars: The Training of the Chinese Communist Leadership, 1920–1945.* Boulder, CO: Westview Press, 1976.

Price, R. *Education in Communist China.* New York: Praeger, 1970.

Qin Hongyi. "Mao zedong he liu shao qi zai nong ye he zuo hua wen ti shang reng shi de cao yi" (The Differences between Mao Zedong and Liu Shaoqi on Agricultural Collectivization). *Gunagxi she hui ke xue* (Guangxi Social Science Journal) 7 (2004): 118–130.

Qiu Yihong. *Sheng min ru he liu: Xin, ma, tai shi liu wei nu xin de gu shi* (Life Is Like a River: Stories of 16 Women from Singapore, Malaya, and Thailand). Selangor, Malaysia: Che Lue Zi Xun Yan Jiu Zhong Xin, 2004.

Qu Changchuan. "Lun ke fu ge ren zhu yi: Wo zai yan an zheng feng zhong de jin li" (On Overcoming Individualism: My Experience in the Yan'an Rectification). In Qiang Xiaochu, ed., *Hui yi yan an zheng feng* (Memoirs of the Yan'an Rectification), 19–25. Harbin: Heilongjiang People's Publisher, 1958.

Quirk, Robert E. *Fidel Castro*. New York: Norton, 1993.

Ratliff, William. "Cuban Foreign Policy toward Far East and Southern Asia." In George Fauriol and Eva Loser, eds., *Cuba: The International Dimension*, 207–208. New Brunswick, NJ: Transaction Publishers, 1990.

Read, Gerald H. "The Revolutionary Offensive in Education." In James Nelson Goodsell, ed., *Fidel Castro's Personal Revolution in Cuba, 1959–1973*. New York: Knopf, 1975.

Reckord, Barry. *Does Fidel Eat More?* New York: Praeger, 1971.

Redl, Helen, ed. *Soviet Educators on Soviet Education*. New York: Free Press, 1964.

Renshon, Stanley Allen, ed. *Handbook of Political Socialization: Theory and Research*. New York: Free Press, 1977.

Ridley, Charles, and Dennis Doolin. *The Making of a Model Citizen in Communist China*. Stanford, CA: Hoover Institution Press, 1971.

Ripoll, Carlos. *Jose Marti, the United States, and the Marxist Interpretation of Cuban History*. New Brunswick, NJ: Transaction Books, 1984.

Robb, Peter. "Children, Emotion, Identity and Empire: Views from the Blechyndens' Calcutta Diaries (1790–1822)." *Modern Asian Studies* 40, no. 1 (2006): 175–201.

Rousseau, Jean-Jacques. *On the Social Contract*. New York: St. Martin's Press, 1978.

Russell, Bertrand. *The Practice and Theory of Bolshevism*. New York: Simon and Schuster, 1964.

Rychetnik, Ludek. "Two Models of an Enterprise in Market Socialism." *Economics of Planning* 8, no. 3 (1968): 216–231.

Santi, Enrico Mario. "Jose Marti and the Cuban Revolution." *Cuban Studies* 16 (1986): 139–150.

Sartre, Jean-Paul. *Sartre on Cuba*. New York: Vintage Press, 1961.

Schama, Simon. *Citizens: A Chronicle of the French Revolution*. New York: Alfred A. Knopf, 1989.

Schell, Orville. *In the People's Republic: An American's First-hand View of Living and Working in China*. New York: Vintage Books, 1977.

Schmid, Peter. "Letter from Havana." *Commentary* 40, no. 3 (1965).

Schneider, L. A. "Learning from Russia: Lysenkoism and the Fate of Genetics in China, 1950–1986." In Denis Fred Simon and Merle Goldman, eds., *Science and Technology in Post-Mao China*, Harvard Contemporary China Series, vol. 5, 45–68. Cambridge, MA: Harvard University Press, 1989.

Schram, Stuart, ed. *Chairman Mao Talks to the People*. New York: Pantheon Books, 1974.

Schwarcz, Vera. *Chinese Enlightenment: Intellectuals and the Legacy of the May Fourth Movement of 1919*. Berkeley: University of California Press, 1986.

Serra, Ana. "The Historical Zafra and Nation Building in Revolutionary Cuba: Miguel Cossio Woodward's *Sacchario* (1970)." *Revista de Estudios Hispánicos* 37 (2003): 614–615.

———. "The Literacy Campaign in the Cuban Revolution and the Transformation of Identity in the Liminal Space of the Sierra." *Journal of Latin American Cultural Studies* 10, no. 1 (2001): 313–332.

Seth, Sanjay. "Indian Maoism: The Significance of Naxalbari." In Arif Dirlik, Paul Michael Healy, and Nick Knight, eds., *Critical Perspectives on Mao Zedong's Thought*, 289–313. Atlantic Highlands, NJ: Humanities Press, 1997.

Shen Jian. "Wo de wai jia shen ya" (The Bygones of My Foreign Missions). In Wu Xiuquan and Liu Xiao, eds., *Wo de da si shen ya* (My Career as an Ambassador), 109–134. Nanjing: Jiangsu Renmin Publisher, 1993.

Shen Yan. *Min Suofu: An quan xin shi de yi mian qi zhi* (Min Suofu: A Model of Safe Driving). Shanghai: Shanghai Renmin Publisher, 1956.

Sheng Zhihua and Li Danhui. "Xi ha nu ke, Bo er bu te yu zhong guo" (Xihanuke, Pol Pot, and China, 1960–1970s). http://www.shenzhihua.net/ynzz/000032_2.htm.

Sheridan, Mary. "The Emulation of Heroes." *China Quarterly* (January–March 1968): 47–72.

Shils, Edward. "The Intellectuals and the Powers: Some Perspectives for Comparative Analysis." In Philip Rieff, ed., *On Intellectuals*. New York: Anchor Books, 1970.

Sidel, Ruth. *Women and Child Care in China*. New York: Penguin Books, 1982.

Sigel, R. S. "Assumptions about the Learning of Political Values." In Mary Hawkesworth and Maurice Kogan, eds., *Handbook of Political Socialization: Theory and Research*, 5–7. New York: Free Press, 1977.

Silverman, Bertram. *Man and Socialism in Cuba: The Great Debate*. New York: Atheneum, 1971.

Sinyavsky, Andrei. *Soviet Communism: A Cultural History*. New York: Arcade Publishing, Little, Brown, 1990.

Slonim, Marc. *Soviet Russian Literature: Writers and Problems, 1917–1977*. New York: Oxford University Press, 1977.

Smith, William Edgett. *We Must Run While They Walk: A Portrait of Africa's Julius Nyerere*. New York: Random House, 1971.

Snow, Edgar. *Red China Today: The Other Side of the River*. New York: Random House, 1972.

Snow, Lois Wheeler Snow. *China on Stage*. New York: Vintage Books, 1976.

Stalin, Joseph. *Lenin*. New York: International Publishers, 1939.

Starr, John. *Continuing the Revolution: The Political Thought of Mao*. Princeton, NJ: Princeton University Press, 1979.

Sun Tingzheng. "Yi bai lin liu shui de lao fu zhai diao liao wen mang de mao zi" (One-Hundred-Six-Year-Old Woman Became Literate). *Guangming Daily*, July 26, 1961.

Sutherland, Elizabeth. *The Youngest Revolution: A Personal Report on Cuba*. New York: Dial Press, 1969.

Tan Wenrui. "Gu ba ge min de wei da duo shou" (The Great Helmsman of the Cuban Revolution). In Anonymous, ed., *Yin xiong de gu ba* (Heroic Cuba), 1–2. Beijing: Shijie Zhishi Publisher, 1962.

Tavris, Carol. "Field Report: Women in China." *Psychology Today*, May 1974.

Thompson, J. M. *Leaders of the French Revolution*. New York: Barnes and Noble, 1968.

———. *Robespierre*. New York: D. Appleton–Century, 1936.

Trachtenberg, Zev M. *Making Citizens: Rousseau's Theory of Culture*. New York: St. Martin's Press, 1993.

Tretiak, Daniel. *Cuba and the Soviet Union: A Growing Accommodation*. US Air Force Project, Rand Corporation, July 1966.

Trotsky, Leon. *Leon Trotsky on Literature and Art*. New York: Pathfinder Press, 1970.

van de Ven, Hans. *From Friends to Comrades: The Founding of the Chinese Communist Party, 1920–1927*. Berkeley: University of California Press, 1991.

Volkogonov, Dmitri. *Lenin: A New Biography*. New York: Freedom Press, 1994.

Wang Jie. *Wang jie ri ji* (Wang Jie's Diary). Beijing: Renmin Publisher, 1965.

Wang Jingxi. *Du zhu xi de shu, ting mao zhu xi de hua, wei shi you shi ye er feng dou* (Read Chairman's Book, Listen to Chairman's Words, Strive for the Cause of the Proletariat). Beijing: Shiyou Huagong Publisher, 1977.

Wang Ruoshui, *Wei ren dao zhu yi bian hu* (Defending Humanism). Beijing: Sanlian Publisher, 1986.

Wang Taipin. *Zhong hua Renmin gong he guo wai jiao shi* (The Diplomatic History of the People's Republic of China). Vol. 2, *1957–1969*. Beijing: Shijie Zhishi Publisher, 1998.

Wang Youping. *Wo zai qi ge guo jia de wai jiao shen ya* (My Career as an Ambassador in Seven Countries). Nanjing: Jiangsu Renmin Publisher, 1996.

Wang Youqin. "Student Attacks against Teachers: The Revolution of 1966." *Journal of Chinese and International Affairs* (March–April 2001): 29–79.

———. *Wen ge shou nan zhe* (Victims of the Cultural Revolution). Hong Kong: Open Monthly Publisher, 2004.

Ward, Fred. *Inside Cuba*. New York: Crown, 1978.

Webb, Sidney, and Beatrice Webb. *Soviet Communism: A New Civilization?* New York: Charles Scribner's Sons, 1936.

Wei Chengsi, ed. *Zhong guo dang dai jiao yu si chao 1949–1987* (Educational Thought in Contemporary China, 1949–1987). Shanghai: Sanlian Publisher, 1988.

Wells, H. G. *Experimental Biography*. Philadelphia: Lippincott, 1967.

Wellens, John. "The Anti-Intellectual Tradition in the West." *British Journal of Educational Studies* 8, no. 1 (1959): 22–28.

Wheeler, Lois Snow. *China on Stage*. New York: Vintage Books, 1976.

Williams, Frankwood E. *Russia Youth and the Present-Day World*. New York: Farrar and Rinehart, 1934.

Winter, Ella. *Red Virtue: Human Relationships in the New Russia*. New York: Harcourt, Brace and Co., 1933.

Wood, Elizabeth A. *The Baba and the Comrade: The Bolsheviks and the Genealogy of the Woman Question*. Bloomington: University of Indiana Press, 1997.

Worsley, Peter. *Inside China*. London: Allen Lane, 1975.

Wu Si. *Chen yong gui chen fu zhong nan hai: Gai zhao zhong guo de shi yan* (The Rise and Fall of Chen Yonggui: The Experiment of Reforming China). Guangzhou: Huacheng Publisher, 1993.

Wu Yunduo. *Ba yi qie xian gei dang* (Dedicating Everything to the Party). Beijing: Gongren Publisher, 1963.

Xiao Yu. *Mao ze dong de qin nian shi dai* (Biography of Early Mao Zedong). Taipei: Libai Publisher, 1987.

Xu Youyu. *Xin xin se se de zhao fan pai: Hong wei bin jing sheng shu zhi de xing cheng ji yan bian* (Rebels of All Stripes: A Study of Red Guard Mentalities). Hong Kong: Chinese University Press, 1999.

Yang Dali. "Da yue jin yu dang dai zhong guo" (The Great Leap Forward and Contemporary China). *Twenty First Century* (August 1998): 4–13.

Yu, George T. *China and Tanzania: A Study in Cooperative Interaction.* Berkeley, CA: Center for Chinese Studies, 1970.

Zhang Xianling, "Hui yi yan an zheng feng" (Memoirs of the Yan'an Rectification). In Qiang Xiaochu, ed., *Hui yi yan an zheng feng* (Memoirs of the Yan'an Rectification), 21–28. Harbin: Heilongjiang Renmin Publisher, 1958.

Zhao Feng. *Hong se niu peng—wu qie gan xiao de zheng shi gu shi* (Red Cowsheds—the Real Stories of the May Seventh Cadre Schools). Xining: Qinghai Renmin Publisher, 1999.

Zeng Tao. *Wai jiao shen ya shi qi nian* (My Seventeen-Year Diplomatic Career). Nanjing: Jiangsu Renmin Publisher, 1997.

Zhen Zhi. *Ye ge ge min de xing chun zhe* (A Survivor of the Revolution). Guangzhou: Guangdong Renmin Publisher, 1999.

Zhong gong zhong yang dang shi yan jiu shi (Research Department of the History of the Chinese Communist Party). *Zhong guo gong chan dang li shi da shi jie* (Chronology of the History of the Chinese Communist Party). Beijing: Zhongdong Dangshi Publisher, 2006.

Zhou Boping. *Fei chang shi qi de wai jiao shen ya* (Diplomatic Career in an Unusual Time). Beijing: Shejie Zhishi Publisher, 2003.

Zhou Quanhua. *Wen hua da ge ming zhong de jiao yu ge ming* (The Education Revolution in the Cultural Revolution). Guangzhou: Gunagdong Jiaoyu Publisher, 1999.

Zhu Chengfa. *Hong chao: Xin hua zuo yi wen xue de wen ge chao* (The Red Tide: Singapore's Chinese Left Literature under the Influence of China's Cultural Revolution). Singapore: Lingzi Media, 2004.

Zielinski, Janusz G. "Centralization and Decentralization in Decision-Making." *Economic Planning* 3, no. 3 (1963): 196–203.

———. "Notes on Incentive Systems of Socialist Enterprises." *Economics of Planning* 7, no. 3 (1967): 258–265.

Zinoviev, Alexander. *Homo Sovieticus,* London: Victor Gollancz, 1985.

Index

methods applied in, 97; "the three old essays" in, 63; Wei Fengying in, 100; and Western intellectuals, 203; Zhou Enlai and "Serve the People" in, 62. *See also* Mao Zedong

Daqing, 101–103, 106, 107. *See also* Wang Jingxi
Dalton, Thomas, 135
Dazhai, 103–106, 107, 122, 193. *See also* Chen Yonggui
Deng Xiaoping, 91, 94, 105, 106
Dewey, John, 89
Ding Yizhuang, 121, 124
Dong Jiagen, 122
Dorticós Torrado, Osvaldo, 155–156
Dulles, John Foster, 91
Dumont, René, 154, 158–159

Education: abolished in the Khmer Rouge regime, 194; in Enlightenment thinking, 8–10; in French Revolution, 10–12; Marx's ideas of, 14–15; and party schools in the Soviet Union, 25–26; and party schools in Yan'an, 61; and the Red Guards, 113–114; and reforms in Cuban revolution, 165–175, 179; and reforms in the People's Commune campaign in China and the comparison with the Soviet reforms, 82–90; and revolutionary changes in China in the 1960s, 109–112; and Soviet camps for delinquent young adults, 30; and Soviet reforms in the 1920s and the setback in the 1930s, 31–33
Enlightenment, 2, 4, 6, 8–13, 45, 50; and Berlin, 217; and Castro and Guevara, 135; and Foucault, 216; and Kant, 214; and the Isle of Youth, 178; and Marx, 14; and the Russian, Chinese, and Cuban Revolutions, 219–223; and Russian intelligentsia, 15; and Western intellectuals, 196, 199
Environmental determinism, 13, 46, 133, 178, 199, 219
Exemplary Eighth Company on the Nanjing Road, 107–108

Fagen, Richard, 127, 132, 140, 142, 145, 163, 174
Foucault, Michel, 23, 216
Fourier, Charles, 81
Frank País Pedagogical Institute, 168
Fred, Judson, 138
Frunze, Mikhail, 33
Fueloep-Miller, René, 44, 196
Fukuzawa Yukichi, 51

Gao Hua, 6, 68
García, Gaspar Jorge, 165
Gastev, Aleksei, 42
Gates, Bill, 130–131
Ge Tingshui, 71
Gerovitch, Slava, 46
"Going to the People," 19, 53
Gong Yuzhi, 88
Gorky, Marxim, 20–22, 2, 87, 110. See also *Mother*
Great Leap Forward, 48; Chen Yonggui in, 106; compared with the Cuban efforts, 128, 153, 162; consequences of, 97, 105, 122, 149; and the credibility of the party and Mao, 90; and educational reforms, 88–89, 109; and peasants, 80–85; Peng Dehuai's criticism of, 93; Xiyang county in, 104
Guards under Neon Lights, The, 107
Guevara, Che, 127, 128, 131, 175; and China, 147, 149–151; and Cuban workers, 180; and the debate on incentives, 157–160; on education, 166; on French Revolution and October Revolution, 13; on human nature and the new man, 133–135; and labor mobilization, 185–186; and militarization, 185; as the model for the new man, 176–177; on revolutionary voluntarism, 137–139; on the Soviet Union, 154–156; on volunteer work, 164–165; and Western intellectuals, 205, 206, 215, 220
Guo Moruo, 116

Heller, Mikhail, 5–6, 214
Helvétius, Claude-Adrien, 8–11, 217
Hilsman, Roger, 91

individual models, 93–100; and the Khmer Rouge, 192–194; and the May Seventh Directive, 117, 125; on model emulation, 61–63, 69; and money, 163–164; on the "new village" and putting children under direct state supervision, 57, 59, 82; on peasants and the people's communes, 78–80; personal cult of, 90; and populism, 78; and the Red Guard violence, 115; and the "revolutionary successors," 90–92; on self-reform, 59, 113–115; and Sino-Cuban relations, 147, 149; and Soviet educational reforms and the setback, 87–88; on thought reform, 70

Market socialism, 42

Márquez, Gabriel García, 134

Martí, José, 128–129, 188

Marx and Marxism, 13; and Castro and Guevara, 127, 135; Castroist challenge to, 136–138, 222; on early integration of work and study, 14–15; and Mao Zedong and Liu Shaoqi's concepts of human nature, 56–57; on peasants, 78–79

Matthews, Herbert, 173, 176

Meisner, Maurice, 20,

May Fourth Movement, 52, 53, 116

May Seventh Cadre Schools, 116–120, 205

Medin, Tzvi, 139–140

Meerloo, Joost A. M., 24

Meyer, Frank S., 23

Millar, José M., 174

Min Suofu, 77

Morozov, Pavlik, 31

Mother (by Gorky), 20–21

Munro, Donald, 13

Nahirny, Vladimir C., 15

Nechaev, Serge, 18

Neo-Confucianism, 49

New Culture Movement, 51–53, 63, 74, 86, 116

New Economic Policy, 35, 40, 156

Nietzsche, Friedrich, 52, 214

Niutianyang, 124–125

Nyerere, Julius, 210–212

Ordzhonikidze, Sergo, 34

Ostrovsky, Nikolai, 34–40, 76. See also *That Is How Steel Was Tempered*

Ouyang Hai, 96, 97, 108

Ozouf, Mona, 12

País, Frank, 175

Pavlov, Ivan Petrovich, 24–25

Peng Dehuai, 93

Perovskaya, Sofia, 37

Pinares de Mayarí, 179

Prague Spring, 42, 161

Pu Yi, 59

Qian Weichang, 72

Qian Xuesen, 72, 105, 122

Red Guard, 111–115, 124, 143

Revolutionary Catechism, 18

Revolutionary Offensive, 128, 180, 181–188, 222

Ripoll, Carlos, 131

Robespierre, Maximilien, 11–12

Rodríguez, Carlos Rafael, 150, 157, 181

Rousseau, Jean-Jacques, 10–12, 217

Saccharío, 187

Schama, Simon, 12

School Goes to the Country, 170

Schools of Revolutionary Instruction, 167, 170

Serra, Ana, 143, 187

Shen Jian, 148, 150, 151

sheng ren, 50

Sheridan, Mary, 93

Shul'gin, V. N., 32, 89

Slonim, Marc, 43

Stakhanov, Alexei, 34, 40

Stalin, Joseph: and collectivization, 79; and industrialization, 32, 34, 39–40, 88; on the new man, 9, 23, 45, 134, 217; and Soviet aviators as the model of the new man, 46; and Svetlana Alliluyeva, 45. See also Stalinists and Stalinism

Stalinists and Stalinism, 37, 43, 89, 152, 156, 200

.

About the Author

YINGHONG CHENG'S major research interests are Chinese communism and world communism. His research articles have appeared in *The China Quarterly, Modern Asian Studies, Journal of World History, Journal of Cold War Studies, Journal of Contemporary China, History Compass,* and *Modern Chinese Literature and Culture Since 2003.* He has also authored three books and numerous articles in Chinese. He is currently associate professor of history at Delaware State University.

Production Notes for Cheng CREATING THE "NEW MAN"

Cover designed by Julie Matsuo-Chun
Interior designed by Elsa Carl in Adobe Caslon, with
display type in Tiepolo

Composition by Lucille C. Aono

Printing and binding by The Maple-Vail Book
Manufacturing Group